CORTINA METHOD

CONVERSATIONAL
SPANISH
IN 20 LESSONS

Cortina Method Books

FRENCH IN 20 LESSONS
SPANISH IN 20 LESSONS
GERMAN IN 20 LESSONS
ITALIAN IN 20 LESSONS
AMERICAN ENGLISH IN 20 LESSONS
MODERN GREEK IN 20 LESSONS
RUSSIAN IN 20 LESSONS
INGLÉS EN 20 LECCIONES
FRANCÉS EN 20 LECCIONES
INGLÊS EM 20 LIÇÕES
CONVERSATIONAL BRAZILIAN PORTUGUESE
CONVERSATIONAL JAPANESE
SPANISH CONVERSATIONAL GUIDE
SPANISH IN SPANISH
FRANÇAIS EN FRANÇAIS
ENGLISH IN ENGLISH
DEUTSCH AUF DEUTSCH
ITALIANO IN ITALIANO

CORTINA METHOD

CONVERSATIONAL
SPANISH
IN 20 LESSONS

Hard Cover Edition: SPANISH IN 20 LESSONS

ILLUSTRATED

Intended for self-study and for use in schools

With a Simplified System of Phonetic Pronunciation

By
R. DIEZ DE LA CORTINA

UNIVERSITY OF MADRID
THE WAR COLLEGE OF VALLADOLID
EX-INSPECTOR OF PUBLIC INSTRUCTION, ARGENTINA
EX-TECHNICAL ADVISOR TO
THE SECRETARY OF INSTRUCTION, BOLIVIA
AUTHOR OF THE CORTINA METHOD
ORIGINATOR OF THE PHONOGRAPHIC METHOD OF
TEACHING LANGUAGES.

154TH EDITION
Completely Revised

CORTINA LEARNING INTERNATIONAL, INC.
Publishers • WESTPORT, CT 06880

Library of Congress Cataloging in Publication Data

Cortina, Rafael Diez de la, 1859–
    Spanish in 20 Lessons, illustrated.
    (Cortina method)
        1. Spanish language—Grammar—1950–
2. Spanish language—Self-instruction. I. Title.
PC4112.C63 1976   468'.2'421   76-52471
ISBN 0-8327-0002-9 (hardbound)
ISBN 0-8327-0010-X (paperback)

INTRODUCTION

How a Knowledge of Spanish Can Help You

No other language today offers Americans so many advantages as does Spanish. The Spanish-speaking American can choose from dozens of interesting and well-paid jobs with the government and private industry. These jobs are now open both here in the States and in all the Spanish-speaking countries of South and Central America.

This is not a temporary situation. The future of the United States is definitely linked up with our Latin American neighbors. Our trade with these countries is at an all-time high and it is bound to increase. Our foreign policies are also a basis of mutual understanding and aid. The Spanish-speaking American will always be able to use his knowledge of Spanish to get a better-paying and more interesting job.

The pleasures of travel also are enhanced when you know how to speak and understand Spanish. Both Spain and the countries of Latin America offer a tremendous variety of exotic and scenic beauties for a most memorable visit. From the art and culture of Spain, to the historical monuments of Mexico and Peru, from the dramatic scenery of Argentina and Chile to the sunny beaches of Venezuela and Central America—the Spanish-speaking world holds myriad treasures. And since travel is becoming faster and easier all the time, these treasures are available to more and more Americans.

When you arrive in Latin America, your knowledge of Spanish will be a great help. You will be welcomed as a cultured neighbor instead of "just a tourist". You will feel confident to travel off the "beaten path" to see the unusual sights that are closed to the traveler who does not speak Spanish. You will be invited into people's homes and get the real foreign flavor. And, incidentally, you'll find that your knowledge of the language saves you money in dealing with tradespeople, hotel clerks, ticket agents and so on.

Finally, your knowledge of Spanish will offer you many cultural pleasures through a fuller understanding of the literature and art of both Spain and Spanish America. The works of Lope de Vega, Cervantes, Calderon and others are but imperfectly known to most English-speaking people, because the true meaning, richness and humor of these immortal authors are lost when they are not read *in the original Spanish*. Discover these literary treasures for yourself and have the real fun of learning Spanish at the same time.

PREFACE

In 1882, Count Cortina arrived in the United States and established his Academy of Languages. He specialized, at that time, in teaching *his native Spanish language to Americans.*

From this actual teaching experience, Professor Cortina developed a new simplified method that became an instant success. It has never been surpassed since. For the past 95 years the method has been constantly refined and improved from the Academy's long experience in teaching languages, and in terms of the changing needs of the present-day language student. It is now known all over the world as THE CORTINA METHOD.

Because of this success, Count Cortina very soon had to enlarge his faculty and engage teachers in French, German, Italian and English, using his *basic method* for the teaching of these languages. Because of the demand for Cortina instruction from students who could not attend classes, the Academy was forced to publish the Cortina lessons in book form. Well over two million Cortina books have been sold and they are a clear testimonial to the ease with which students have learned a new language through THE CORTINA METHOD.

Many thousands of students have learned a new language by this method at home, in their spare time. Many others have used THE CORTINA METHOD in schools and colleges throughout the United States and South America.

You may ask: "What is the secret of THE CORTINA METHOD's success? How is it different from other ways to learn a language?" One of the main reasons is that the lessons are devoted to intensely interesting and every-day topics which encourage the student to learn. The lessons begin with subjects that we all used as children when we learned our native tongue. For instance, right from the start, the first lessons teach you the same words that a child first speaks: *Mother, father, brother, sister,* as well as every-day words relating to meals, drinks, clothing, footwear and so on. Not only are these words easily put to use at once; not only are they much more interesting than the usual abstract and academic words a student is asked to learn—but they also strike a deeply primeval chord in all of us. This adds color and excitement and arouses in the student a desire to learn the language.

Features of this New Edition

The Editors have included two new features in this edition which will also be found of great help to the student:

First, the format of the lessons has been changed to allow for carefully chosen illustrations which have been drawn by an excellent artist. The drawings have been arranged to highlight the subject matter of the lessons and thus will greatly aid the student in memorizing the foreign words through the graphic representation.

Second, a complete REFERENCE GRAMMAR has been appended at the back of the book so that the student may refer to any part of speech he wishes as he advances in his studies. The necessary grammar for the lessons is included in the footnotes, lesson by lesson, for the student's convenience.

HOW TO STUDY

Language is habit. We are constantly expressing thoughts and ideas in speech, from habit, without paying any particular attention to the words, phrases or idioms we use. When we say *"How do you do," "I've had a wonderful trip," "All right, let's go,"* we do so spontaneously. We are merely repeating a speech pattern that we have used so many times before it has become automatic, or, a habit. Repetition, therefore, is the basis of language learning, and so it is extremely important that the student acquire a correct pronunciation at the very beginning so that he learns *the right speech habits.*

For this purpose the CORTINA METHOD provides *The Spanish Alphabet* on page 15 and *Pronunciation Guide* on page 17. They explain how to pronounce Spanish sounds, words and phrases through simplified English spelling (phonetic symbols). In Lesson 1 the entire Spanish vocabulary and conversations are transcribed in these symbols. Using them as a guide the student will be able to read the entire lesson aloud, and he should do so as many times as necessary to read the Spanish text aloud *easily and correctly.* Through this practice, not only will the student attain fluency, but he will eventually express his *ideas* in Spanish just as easily and effortlessly as he does in English. Should any student wish to accelerate his progress and master spoken Spanish in the easiest possible manner, the Cortina Company has recorded the Spanish text of this book. The vocabularies and conversations are spoken by native Spanish speaking instructors whose voices have been chosen for their excellence of accent, clarity of speech and pleasing tonal quality. In classroom study too, *the phonograph method of learning languages* (originated by Cortina) has been found an invaluable aid to both student and teacher for oral practice and ear training.

LESSON ARRANGEMENT. The lessons are arranged so that the student can follow them easily. For each lesson there is (a) a vocabulary of important words of a general character, (b) a specific vocabulary covering the topic of the lesson and (c) conversations showing how these vocabularies are used in everyday conversations. To the right of each word or sentence is given the phonetic spelling so that the student can pronounce them correctly, and in the next column is given the English translation of the Spanish text.

The student should start each lesson by memorizing as much of the general (active) vocabulary as possible. Then, in turning to the conversation that follows, he will complete his mastery of these words by actually using them *to express thoughts*. The CONVERSATION sentences should be read *aloud* and at the same time general reference should be made to the translation of each sentence. *Learn the thoughts* that the Spanish sentence conveys rather than a word for word translation. The lesson has been mastered when the student can read the text aloud and understand it without reference to either the PRONUNCIATION or TRANSLATION columns.

The special arrangement of columnizing the TEXT, PRONUNCIATION and TRANSLATION is for the student's convenience in checking his own progress. This is done by merely covering the TRANSLATION with a piece of paper to test if he knows what the Spanish words and sentences mean, and in reverse, by covering the Spanish text and translating aloud the English words into Spanish. It cannot be emphasized too strongly that the student should read the Spanish *aloud. Speak out clearly* and don't be embarrassed by the sound of your own voice. Let a friend take part in the conversation with you. *Go to a Spanish restaurant*—or pretend you do—*do anything* just as long as it helps you to keep *speaking Spanish.*

The grammatical explanations in the FOOTNOTES are of great importance to the student and close attention should be paid to them. They also clear up many of the idiomatic difficulties and are very helpful because they give other illustrations of the language in actual use. For more elaborate grammatical explanation the student can refer to the *Complete Reference Grammar* on page 191.

In conclusion there is no better way to learn a language than the way children learn *by speaking it*. THE CORTINA METHOD is based upon this principle with a few modifications to adjust *this natural method* to the adult mind. The first words a child learns are those necessary to satisfy his instinctive interests and desires. What are these first words? *Mother, father*, something to eat and drink, and after that something to wear and protect the body. After these wants are satisfied he grows in stature until he gradually builds up a vocabulary and speech patterns covering every conceivable subject, but his primary wants must be satisfied first. The Cortina lessons begin exactly this way, *mother, father*, eatables, clothing, footwear, etc. With a little application you will have a lot of fun learning Spanish this way and what a satisfaction it will be to have *this important language* at your command.

TABLE OF CONTENTS

	PAGE
Introduction	1
Preface	3
How to Study	5
The Spanish Alphabet	15
Guide to Spanish Pronunciation	17
Guide to Writing Spanish	23

VOCABULARIES AND CONVERSATIONS

FIRST LESSON **The Family • Nationalities • Languages**

Vocabularies	26
Conversation	28

SECOND LESSON **Meals and Beverages**

Vocabularies	34
Conversation	36

THIRD LESSON **Clothing and Footwear**

Vocabularies	42
Conversation	44

7

Fourth Lesson **Traveling: By Ship, Train and Airplane**

Vocabularies	*50*
Conversation	*52*

Fifth Lesson **Numbers • Fractions • Counting**

Vocabularies	*58*
Conversation	*60*

Sixth Lesson **Days • Months • Seasons**

Vocabularies	*64*
Conversation	*66*

Seventh Lesson **Telling Time:**
The Watch • The Watchmaker

Vocabularies	*70*
Conversation	*72*

Eighth Lesson **About Business**

Vocabularies	*78*
Conversation	*80*

Ninth Lesson **At the Restaurant**

Vocabularies	*86*
Conversation	*88*

Tenth Lesson **The House and Furniture**

Vocabularies	*92*
Conversation	*94*

Eleventh Lesson **About the Weather**

Vocabularies	*100*
Conversation	*102*

TWELFTH LESSON   *The Tailor • The Dressmaker • Styles*

Vocabularies   *108*
Conversation   *110*

THIRTEENTH LESSON   *Visiting the City*

Vocabularies   *116*
Conversation   *118*

FOURTEENTH LESSON   *A Visit to the Doctor*

Vocabularies   *124*
Conversation   *126*

FIFTEENTH LESSON   *Renting a Room • Toilet Articles*

Vocabularies   *132*
Conversation   *134*

SIXTEENTH LESSON   *Commercial Relations*

Vocabularies   *140*
Conversation   *142*

SEVENTEENTH LESSON   *A Trip Through Spanish America*

Reading Text   *148*

EIGHTEENTH LESSON   *A Trip Through Spain*

Reading Text   *160*

NINETEENTH LESSON   *Classical Spanish Literature*

Dialogue   *172*

TWENTIETH LESSON *Modern Spanish Literature*

Dialogue *180*

REFERENCE GRAMMAR

	PAGE
Plan for Study	193

The Article
*§1 The Definite Article	199
§2 Uses of the Definite Article	199
§3 The Indefinite Article	201
§4 Omission of the Indefinite Article	201
§5 The Neuter Article *lo*	202

The Noun
§6 Gender of the Noun	204
§7 Plural of Nouns	206
§8 The Use of Prepositions	207
§9 Diminutives and Augmentatives	207
§10 Cognate Suffixes	209

The Adjective
§11 Classes and Forms of the Adjective	210
§12 Position of Adjective	211
§13 Substantivised Adjectives	213
§14 Comparison of Adjectives	213

*§ *is the symbol for paragraph*

§15 The Absolute Superlative   213
§16 Pronominal Adjectives   214
§17 Demonstrative Adjectives   215
§18 Indefinite Adjectives   215
§19 Interrogative Adjectives   216
§20 Possessive Adjectives   216
§21 The Numerals   217

The Pronoun

§22 Subject Pronouns   218
§23 Object Pronouns   219
§24 Two-object Pronouns   220
§25 Reflexive Pronouns   221
§26 Additional Uses of *Se*   221
§27 Interrogative Pronouns   222
§28 Demonstrative Pronouns   222
§29 Relative Pronouns   223
§30 Possessive Pronouns   224
§31 Indefinite Pronouns   225

The Preposition

§32 Uses of Prepositions   227
§33 Common Simple Prepositions   227
§34 The Preposition *a*   227
§35 The Preposition *de*   228
§36 The Preposition *para*   229
§37 The Preposition *por*   230
§38 Compound Prepositions   231

The Adverb

§39 Formation of Adverbs   232
§40 Comparison of Adverbs   232
§41 Classes of Adverbs   233

The Conjunction

§42 Co-ordinating Conjunctions   235
§43 Subordinating Conjunctions   235

The Interjection

§44 Interjections   237

The Verb

§45 Nature of the Spanish Verb 238
§46 General Remarks about the Conjugations 238
§47 The Present Indicative 238
§48 The Imperfect Indicative 240
§49 The Future Indicative 242
§50 The Preterite Indicative 243
§51 The Conditional 244
§52 The Perfect Indicative 245
§53 The Pluperfect Indicative 246
§54 The Future and Conditional Perfect 247
§55 The Present Subjunctive 248
§56 The Imperfect Subjunctive 249
§57 Uses of the Subjunctive 250
§58 The Subjunctive—Sequence of Tenses 252
§59 The Imperative Mood 254
§60 The Infinitive 254
§61 The Present Participle or Gerund 258
§62 The Past Participle 258
§63 Government of Verbs 259
§64 Orthographic Changes 262
§65 Conjugation of Auxiliary Verb *haber* 264
§66 Uses of Auxiliary Verb *haber* 265
§67 Conjugation of Impersonal Verb *haber* 266
§68 Conjugation of the Verb *tener* 268
§69 Uses of the Verb *tener* 270
§70 Conjugation of the Verb *ser* 272
§71 Uses of the Verb *ser* 274
§72 Conjugation of the Verb *estar* 276
§73 Uses of the Verb *estar* 278
§74 Comparison of the Verbs *ser* and *estar* 280
§75 Reflexive Verbs 281
§76 Conjugation of the Reflexive Verbs 281
§77 Types of Reflexive Verbs 285
§78 The Possessive Voice 289
§79 Uses of the Passive Forms 289
§80 Impersonal Verbs 291
§81 Verbs Functioning as Impersonal Verbs 292
§82 Nature of Irregular Verbs 295
§83 Classes of Irregular Verbs 295
Irregular Verb list 297
Spanish Letter Form 300

APPENDIX

Vocabularies

The Family (continuation from page 27)	303
Holidays of the Year	303
Countries of the World	304
Colors	305
The Fireplace and its Appurtenances	305
The Country and the Sea	306
The Human Body	306
The Senses and Bodily Sensations	307
Agriculture	308
The Farm	308
The Trees	308
The Fruits	308
The Vegetables	309
The Flowers	309
Quadrupeds and Birds	309
Numeral Adjectives	
Cardinal Numbers	310
Ordinal Numbers	311
Fractional Numbers	312
Collective Numbers	312
Multiple Adjectives	313
Adverbs of Time	313
of Doubt	314
of Order	314
of Comparison	314
of Place	314
of Quantity	315
of Manner	315
of Affirmation	315
of Negation	315
Conjunctions	315
Interjections	316
Prepositions	316
Indefinite Pronouns	317
Usual Phrases	318
Spanish Idioms and Proverbs	320

DICTIONARIES

English-Spanish	329
Spanish-English	349

THE SPANISH ALPHABET

The Spanish alphabet contains four letters that differ from the English: the **ñ, ch, ll** and **rr,** each being considered *one consonant.*

The following are the letters with their names in Spanish, and the English pronunciation:

Letter	Name	Pronunciation	Letter	Name	Pronunciation
A·a	*a*	ah	**N·n**	*ene*	ay′-nay
B·b	*be*	bay	**Ñ·ñ**	*eñe*	ay′-niay
C·c	*ce*	thay[1]	**O·o**	*o*	o
Ch·ch	*che*	chay	**P·p**	*pe*	pay
D·d	*de*	day	**Q·q**	*cu*	koo
E·e	*e*	ay (*short*)	**R·r**[2]	*ere*	ay′-ray
F·f	*efe*	ay′-fay	**rr**[3]	*erre*	ay′-rray
G·g	*ge*	hay	**S·s**	*ese*	ay′-ssay
H·h	*ache*	ah′-chay	**T·t**	*te*	tay
I·i	*i*	ee	**U·u**	*u*	oo
J·j	*jota*	ho′-ta	**V·v**	*ve*	vay
K·k	*ka*	kah	**X·x**	*equis*	ay′-kees
L·l	*ele*	ay′-lay	**Y·y**	*ye*	yay
LL·ll	*elle*	ay′-lliay	**Z·z**	*zeta*	thay′-tah
M·m	*eme*	ay′-may			

[1]*Th* to be pronounced as in the word *think*.
[2]The letter *r* has the rolling sound of the *rr*, at the beginning and at the end of words as well as at the end of syllables, or after letters *n* and *l*, where it is never written as *rr*.
[3]*rr* is never written at the beginning of words.

GUIDE TO SPANISH PRONUNCIATION

The pronunciation of Spanish is easy because nearly all the Spanish sounds are also used in English. The spelling of Spanish is also easy to learn because it is highly phonetic, that is, every word is usually spelled as it is pronounced.

There are no mute letters in Spanish, with two exceptions: the *h* is always silent, e.g. *hombre* (ohm'bray), man; and the *u* is not pronounced after *g* or *q* when followed by *e* or *i*, e.g. *guerra* (gay'rrah), war.

The pronunciation of Spanish words in this book is indicated by phonetic symbols based on the spelling of common English words wherever possible. Syllable divisions are indicated by a hyphen(-) and accented syllables are indicated by accent marks (').

The following list of sounds should be studied before proceeding to the lessons. It is especially important to acquire a correct pronunciation of the five Spanish vowels.

The Vowels

Each of the five vowels in Spanish has one sound. They are pronounced fully and distinctly and they are never slurred.

Spanish Spelling	Sound	Spanish Example	Phonetic Symbol
a	As in *father* or *far*	muchacha *(moo-chah'chah)*, girl	ah
e	As *e* in *let* or *ay* in *may*, but without the glide sound *y*[1]	inglés *(een-glays')*, English	ay
i	As *i* in *machine* or *ee* in *need*	dinero *(dee-nay'roh)*, money	ee
o	As *o* in *port*[1]	ropa *(roh'pah)*, clothing	oh
u	As *oo* in *moon*	blusa *(bloo'sah)*, blouse	oo

[1] Each of the vowels *e* and *o* has two slightly different pronunciations, depending on their position in the word. At the end of a syllable they are generally pronounced as in *pray* and *go*, respectively, but without any diphthongal glide. When followed by a consonant belonging to the same syllable or by *rr*, they are pronounced as in *met* and *port* respectively. However, this difference in pronunciation is unimportant because the meaning of the words is not affected by it.

17

The Consonants

Spanish Spelling	Sound	Spanish Example	Phonetic Symbol
b	As *b* in English at the beginning of a breath group and after *m*, *n*, or *l*, but as bilabial *v* in all other positions.	**boca** *(boh'kah)*, mouth	b
c	As *th* in *thick* in Castilian Spanish, as *s* in *see* before *e* and *i* in Latin American Spanish.	**cena** *(thay'nah)*, supper	th
	As *c* in *colour* before *a*, *o*, *u*, and before a consonant and at the end of a word in both Castilian and Latin American Spanish.	**casa** *(kah'sah)*, house	k
ch	As *ch* in English.	**muchacho** *(moo-chah'choh)*, boy	ch
d	Similar to *d* in English at the beginning of a word and after *l* and *n* but as *th* in *this* in all other positions.	**deseo** *(day-say'oh)*, I wish	d
f	Similar to *f* in English.	**fé** *(fay)*, faith	f
g	A strongly aspirated *h* (as *ch* in Scottish *loch* or in German *Bach*) before *e* and *i*.	**gente** *(hayn'tay)*, people	h
	As *g* in English before *a*, *o*, and *u* or a consonant, at the beginning of a word, and before *n* and *l*. In all other positions similar to *g* in *big*, but prolonged.	**gota** *(goh'tah)*, drop	g
	(In order to retain the *g*-sound of *give* before *e* and *i*, it is necessary to insert *u* after the *g*. If it is desired to retain the *u*-sound of the letter *u* which is silent after *g*, the dieresis (two dots) is placed over the *u*).		
h	Never pronounced.	**ahora** *(ah-oh'rah)*, now	

Spanish Spelling	Sound	Spanish Example	Phonetic Symbol
j	As a strongly aspirated *h* (exactly as *g* in Spanish before *e* and *i*).	**jugo** *(hoo'goh)*, juice	h
k	Used only in foreign words, and pronounced as in English.	**kilo** *(kee'loh)*, kilogram	k
l	Similar to English.	**lana** *(lah'nah)*, wool	l
ll	As *lli* in *million* in Castilian Spanish, but as *y* in *yes* in Latin American Spanish.	**llave** *(llyah'vay)*, key	lly
m	As in English.	**llama** *(llyah'mah)*, flame	m
n	As in English.	**negocios** *(nay-goh'thee-ohs)*, business	n
ñ	As *ni* in *onion*.	**leña** *(lay'niah)*, wood	ni
p	As in English.	**vapor** *(vah-pohr')*, ship	p
q	Always followed by a silent *u;* pronounced as *k.* (The combination *qu* occurs only before *e* and *i*).	**aqui** *(ah-kee')*, here	k
r	Slightly trilled by vibrating the tongue slightly against the hard palate. Like *r* in the English *very.* It is more trilled in the beginning of words, at the end of syllables, or after *n* and *l*.	**rosa** *(roh'sah)*, rose	r
rr	As Spanish *r* but very strongly trilled. This letter does not occur at the beginning of words.	**carro** *(kah'rroh)*, cart	rr
s	Similar to English but before *m* and other voiced consonants as *z*, as in the English word *cosmos.*	**soldado** *(sohl-dah'doh)*, soldier	s
t	As in English but with the tip of the tongue touching the upper teeth instead of the gum-ridge.	**tia** *(tee'ah)*, aunt	t
v	Exactly as Spanish *b* in its respective positions.	**evidencia** *(ay-vee-dayn'thee-ah)*, evidence	v

Spanish Spelling	Sound	Spanish Example	Phonetic Symbol
x	As in English, but as *gz* between vowels, before consonants it is pronounced *x* or *s* depending on the speaker, as in English.	**sexto** *(sayks'toh)*, sixth	x
y	As in English before a vowel, but as the Spanish vowel *i* at the end of a word or when standing alone.	**yerno** *(yayr'noh)*, son-in-law	y
		ley *(lay'ee)*, law	ee
z	In Castilian Spanish as *th* in *thin*, but in Latin American Spanish as *s* in *see*.	**zumo** *(thoo'moh)*, juice	th

The Diphthongs

A diphthong is a combination of two vowels pronounced as one sound.

Spanish Spelling	Sound	Spanish Example	Phonetic Symbol
ai or ay	Similar to the *i* of *high*.	**baile** *(bahee'lay)*, dance	ahee
ei or ey	Similar to the *ay* of *day*.	**reino** *(rayee'noh)*, kingdom	ayee
oi or oy	Similar to the *oy* of *boy*.	**oigo** *(ohee'goh)*, I hear	ohee
ui or uy	Similar to *we*, but toward the sound of *wooi* in *wooing*.	**cuidado** *(kwee-dah'do)*, care	wee
		muy *(mwee)*, very	
au	Similar to the *ou* of *house* and the *ow* of *cow*.	**causa** *(kahw'sah)*, cause	ahw
eu	No English equivalent. A combination of *eh* and *oo*.	**deuda** *(dayoo'dah)*, debt	ayoo
ia	Similar to the *ya* of *yacht*, but toward the sound of *ia* in fiancé.	**diablo** *(dyah'bloh)*, devil	yah
ie	No exact equivalent in English. The *ye* of *yes* and *yet* is the closest approximation.	**cielo** *(thyay'loh)*, sky	yay

io (yo at the beginning of a syllable)	Similar to the *io* of *tapioca*.	precio *(pray'thyoh)*, price mayo *(mah'yoh)*, May	yoh yoh
iu	Similar to the *u* of *cute*.	ciudad *(thyoo-dahd')*, city	yoo
ua	Similar to the *wa* of *was*, but without the consonant sound of *w*.	cuando *(kwahn'doh)*, when	wah
ue	No exact equivalent in English. The *we* of *wet* is the closest approximation.	huevos *(way'vohs)*, eggs	way
uo	Similar to the *uo* of *quota*.	arduo *(ahr'dwoh)*, arduous	woh

Usually, when two different vowels are together and do not form a diphthong, an accent is placed over the vowel of the syllable on which the stress is laid. Examples: *raíz* (rah-eeth'), root; *caí* (kah-ee'), I fell; *oí* (oh-ee'), I heard; *varía* (vah-ree'ah), it varies; *Sebastián* (say-bah-stee-ahn'), Sebastian, etc.

Triphthongs

A triphthong is a combination of three vowels that are blended into one sound.

Spanish Spelling   *Spanish Example*

iai	apreciáis *(ah-pray-thyahees')*, you value	yahee
iei	vaciéis *(vah-thyayees')*, you empty (subj.)	yayee
uai (or uay)	santiguáis *(sahn-tee-gwahees)*, you bless Paraguay *(pah-rah-gwahee)*, Paraguay	wahee
uei (or uey)	averigüéis *(ah-vay-ree-gwayees)*, you find out (subj.) buey *(bwayee)*, ox	wayee

GUIDE TO WRITING SPANISH

Accents

The general rule of accentuation in Spanish is that in words ending with a vowel the stress should be placed on the next to the last syllable, and in those ending with a consonant on the last. Examples:

butaca *(boo-tah'kah)*, armchair   **general** *(hay-nay-rahl')*, general

In words not following this rule, the accented vowel must be marked with the acute accent ('). This is the only written accent in Spanish. Examples:

papá *(pah-pah')*, daddy (distinguished from **papa** [*pah'pah*], potato)

está *(ays-tah')*, it is (distinguished from **esta** [*ays'tah*], this *fem.*)

próximo *(prohk'see-moh)*, next

azúcar *(ah-thoo'kar)*, sugar

If no written accent is placed on words ending in *n* or *s*, they must be stressed on the next to the last syllable; in all other cases an accent must be placed on the stressed syllable. Examples:

joven *(hoh'vayn)*, youth   **lección** *(layk-thee-ohn')*, lesson

lunes *(loo'nays)*, Monday   **compás** *(kohm-pahs')*, compass

Note that, according to the general rule of accentuation, the accent is needed for the plural although the singular may not take it, and vice-versa. Examples:

joven—jóvenes   **compás—compases**

The change of a word from singular to plural does not affect the stress, with one single exception:

carácter *(kah-rahk'tayr)*, character   **caracteres** *(kah-rahk-tay'rays)*, characters

Family names ending with *z*, contrary to the rule of accents, have a written accent on the last syllable but one. Examples:

Jiménez *(hee-may'nayth)*; **Pérez** *(pay'rayth)*; **Ramírez** *(rah-mee'rayth)*

Division of Words Into Syllables

Words are divided into syllables according to the following rules:

1. A single consonant between two vowels is made to begin a syllable; for instance, *mesa, silla, perro, muchacho,* etc., are divided thus: me-sa, si-lla, pe-rro, mu-cha-cho, etc.

2. Two consonants standing between vowels are separated; as, *consonante, gente, gasto, parte,* etc., thus: con-so-nan-te, gen-te, gas-to, par-te.

The combinations *bl, br, cl, cr, dr, gl, gr, fl, fr, pl, pr,* and *tr* are exceptions to this rule, viz.: *hablo,* ha-blo; *abre,* a-bre; *tecla,* te-cla; *sangre,* san-gre; *zafra,* za-fra; *extra,* ex-tra, etc.

3. Diphthongs and triphthongs must not be divided, viz.: *guapo,* gua-po; *gracias,* gra-cias; *buey* (one syllable), etc.

Punctuation

In Spanish the marks of punctuation are the same as in English with the difference that the interrogation and exclamation marks must *both precede and follow* the sentence.

The marks used in Spanish are these:

(,)	coma *(koh'mah)*
(;)	punto y coma *(poon'toh ee koh'mah)*
(:)	dos puntos *(dohs poon'tohs)*
(.)	punto final *(poon'toh fee-nahl')*
(...)	puntos suspensivos *(-soos'payn-see'vohs)*
(¿)	principio de interrogación *(preen-thee'peeoh-)*
(?)	fin de interrogación *(-een-tay-rroh-gah-theeohn')*
(¡)	principio de admiración *(-ahd-mee-rah-theeohn')*
(!)	fin de admiración *(feen day-)*
( )	paréntesis *(pah-rayn'tay-sees)*
(-)	guión *(gee-ohn')*
(" ")	comillas *(coh-mee'lyahs)*
(—)	raya *(rah'yah)*

Dialogues are marked with an initial dash (—) for each person speaking.

Vocabularies
and
Conversations

1 LECCION PRIMERA

First Lesson   (*layk-thee-ohn′ pree-may′rah*)

Vocabulario usado en esta lección · VOCABULARY USED IN THIS LESSON

(*voh-kah-boo-lah′ree-oh oo-sah′doh ayn ays′tah layk-thee-ohn′*)

hablarme (*ah-blahrr′may*)	to speak to me
hablarle (*ah-blahrr′lay*)	to speak to you
para ir (*pah′rah eer*)	in order to go
¿a qué hora? (*ah kay oh′rah*)	at what time?
automóvil (*ahw-to-moh′veel*)	automobile
negocios (*nay-goh′thee-ohs*)	business

viaje (*vee-ah′hay*)	the trip
vapor (*vah-pohrr′*)	steamship, steam
aeroplano (*ah-ay-roh-plah′noh*)	airplane

yo, (*yoh*)	I	también (*tahm-bee-ayn′*)	also
usted (*oos-tayd′*)	you	¿por qué? (*pohrr kay′*)	why?
él (*ell*)	he	porque (*pohrr kay*)	because
ella (*ay′lliah*)	she	donde (*dohn′day*)	where
deseo (*day-say′oh*)	I wish	ir (*eer*)	to go
hablar (*ah-blahrr′*)	to speak	¿quién? (*kee-ayn′*)	who?
hablarlo (*ah-blahrr′loh*)	to speak it	¿qué? (*kay*)	what?

mucho (*moo′choh*)	much
poco (*poh′koh*)	little

---

solo, con (*soh′loh, kohn*)	alone, with	cuando (*kwan′doh*)	when
sale (*sah′lay*)	leaves	bien (*bee-ayn′*)	well
largo (*lahrr′goh*)	long	pronto (*prohn′toh*)	soon
tren (*trayn*)	train	mañana (*mah-niah′nah*)	to-morrow
atender (*ah-tayn-dairr′*)	to attend	pero (*pay′roh*)	but

LA FAMILIA

THE FAMILY		*(lah fah-mee'leeah)*
el padre *(pah'dray)*	the father	**el** primo *(pree'moh)* the cousin, (male)
la madre *(mah'dray)*	mother	**la** prima *(pree'mah)* cousin, (female)
el hijo *(ee'hoh)*	son	**el** cuñado *(koo-niah'doh)* brother-in-law
la hija *(ee'hah)*	daughter	**la** cuñada *(koo-niah'dah)* sister-in-law
el niño *(nee'nioh)*	child (mas.)	**el** tío *(tee'oh)* uncle
la niña *(nee'niah)*	child (fem.)	**la** tía *(tee'ah)* aunt
la esposa *(ays-poh'sah)*	wife	**el** esposo *(ays-poh'soh)* husband

el² hombre *(ell ohm'bray)*	the man
la² mujer *(lah moo-hairr')*	woman
el muchacho *(moo-chah'choh)*	boy
la muchacha *(moo-chah'chah)*	girl
el hermano *(airr-mah'noh)*	brother
la hermana *(airr-mah'nah)*	sister

Las Nacionalidades

THE NATIONALITIES	*(lahs nah-thee-oh-nah-lee-dah'days)*
un³ español⁴ *(oon ays-pah-niohl')*	a Spaniard
un sudamericano *(-sood-ah-may-ree-kah'noh)*	South American
un norteamericano *(-nohrr-tay-ah-may-ree-kah'no)*	North American
un francés *(frahn-thays')*	Frenchman
un mejicano *(may-hee-kah'noh)*	Mexican
un colombiano *(koh-lohm-bee-ah'noh)*	Colombian
un venezolano *(vay-nay-thoh-lah'noh)*	Venezuelan
un inglés *(een-glays')*	an Englishman
un argentino *(ahrr-hayn-tee'noh)*	Argentinian

Los Idiomas

THE LANGUAGES		*(lohs ee-deeoh'-mahs)*
español Spanish	**inglés** English	**francés** French
alemán German	**italiano** Italian	**ruso** Russian

CONVERSATION

1 Yo[5] deseo.

2 ¿Qué desea usted?

3 Yo deseo hablar[6] español.

4 ¿Quién desea hablar español?

5 El desea hablar español.

6 ¿Desea[7] usted[8] hablar inglés?

7 Sí, señor; deseo hablarlo.

8 ¿Habla usted francés?

9 Yo hablo[9] francés y también inglés.

10 ¿Desea usted hablarme en español?

11 Deseo mucho hablarle, pero no[10] hablo español bien.

12 ¿Habla[11] usted el inglés perfectamente?

13 No, señor; lo hablo un poco.

14 ¿Por qué desea usted aprender[12] español?

15 Porque deseo vivir[13] en Sur América.

FOOTNOTES: *1. Primero*, first, masc. form; *primera*, fem. The masculine form loses the final *o* before a noun: *primer tren*, or *tren primero*, first train.   *2. El* (ell) *the*, DEFINITE ARTICLE, masc. sing. *La* (lah) *the*, definite article, fem. sing.   *3. Un* (oon) *a*, INDEFINITE ARTICLE, masc. sing. *Una* (oo'nah) *a*, indefinite article, fem. singular.   *4.* The nationalities are not capitalized in Spanish.   *5. Yo*, PRONOUN, first person sing.   *6. Hablar*, to speak; *desear* (day-say-ahrr') to wish; *viajar* (vee-ah-harr') to travel; *procurar* (proh-koo-rarr') to procure, to try; *practicar* (prahk-tee-carr') to practise; *necesitar* (nay-thay-see-tarr') to need, etc., belong to the 1st conjugation, the INFINITIVE of which always ends in *-ar*.   *7. To do*, when

PRONUNCIATION	TRANSLATION
1 *yoh day-say'oh.*	I wish.
2 *¿kay day-say'ah oos-tayd?*	What do you wish?
3 *yoh day-say'oh ah-blahrr' ays-pah'niol'.*	I wish to speak Spanish.
4 *¿kee-ayn' day-say'ah ah-blahrr' ays-pah-niohl'?*	Who wishes to speak Spanish?
5 *ell day-say'ah ah-blahrr' ays-pah-niohl'.*	He wishes to speak Spanish.
6 *¿day-say'ah oos-tayd' ah-blahrr' een-glays'?*	Do you wish to speak English?
7 *see, say-niohrr' day-say'oh ah-blahrr'loh.*	Yes, sir, I wish to speak it.
8 *¿ah-blah, oos-tayd' frahn-thays'?*	Do you speak French?
9 *yoh ah'bloh frahn-thays' ee tahm-bee-ayn' een-glays'.*	I speak French and also English.
10 *¿day-say'ah oos-tayd' ah-blahrr'may ayn ays-pah-niohl'?*	Do you wish to speak to me in Spanish?
11 *day-say'oh moo'choh ah-blahrr'lay, pay'roh noh ah' bloh ays-pah-niohl'.*	I wish to speak to you very much, but I do not speak Spanish well.
12 *¿ah'blah oos-tayd' ell een-glays' payrr-fayk-tah-mayn' tay?*	Do you speak English perfectly?
13 *noh, say-niohrr', loh ah' bloh oon poh'koh.*	No, sir, I speak it a little.
14 *¿pohrr kay' day-say'ah . . . ah-prayn-dayrr' ays-pah-niohl'?*	Why do you wish to learn Spanish?
15 *porr'kay day-say'oh vee-veerr' ayn Soorr Ahmay'ree-kah.*	Because I wish to live in South America.

---

used as an AUXILIARY VERB in English sentences, is never translated in Spanish. *Do you wish to speak?* is simply rendered in Spanish, *wish you to speak?*   8. In the usual style of conversation the word *you* is translated by usted (oos-tayd') when speaking to one person, and by *ustedes* (oos-tay'days) when speaking to more than one. With *usted* the VERB must be in the 3rd pers. sing., and with *ustedes* in

16 ¿Vive su[14] familia en los Estados Unidos?

17 No, señor; mi[15] familia vive en la Argentina.

18 ¿Dónde vive su hermana?

19 Mi hermana y mi hermano viven[16] en Colombia.

20 ¿Es su esposa española?

21 No, señor; mi esposa es americana.

22 ¿Es su hijo francés?

23 Sí, señor; mi hijo es francés.

24 ¿Quién es colombiano?

25 Mi primo es colombiano.

26 ¿Desea él[17] ir a Venezuela?

27 No; él desea ir a Colombia.

28 ¿Toma usted el tren para ir a Méjico?

29 No; para ir a Méjico tomo el vapor o el aeroplano.

30 ¿Desea su padre hacer el viaje en automóvil?

31 Sí, señor; el viaje en automóvil es muy interesante.

32 ¿A qué hora sale el tren?

---

the 3rd pers. pl. There are four abbreviations for the word *"usted"*: **V., Vd., U** and **Ud.**, but it is always pronounced *"Usted."*   *9.* -o is the termination of the 1st pers. sing. of the indicative mood of all regular verbs.   *10. No* always precedes the verb, as *no hablo, no deseo;* but is omitted when other negatives are placed before it, as *nada deseo,* I wish nothing; *nada hablo,* I speak nothing.   *11.* -a is the termination of the 3rd pers. sing. and also the termination for the form *usted,* you, in the indicative mood of all regular verbs of the 1st conjugation.   *12. Aprender* (ah-

16 *¿vee'vay soo fah-mee'lee-ah ayn lohs Ays-tah' dohs Oo-nee' dohs?* Does your family live in the United States?

17 *noh, say-niohrr', mee . . . vee'vay ayn lah Ahrr-hayn-tee'nah.* No, sir, my family lives in Argentina.

18 *¿dohn'day . . . soo ayrr-mah'nah?* Where does your sister live?

19 *mee ayrr-mah'nah ee mee ayrr-mah'noh vee'vayn ayn Coh-lom'bee-ah.* My sister and my brother live in Colombia.

20 *¿ays soo ays-poh'sah ays-pah-nioh'la?* Is your wife Spanish?

21 *noh, . . . mee ays-poh'sah ays ah-may-ree-kah'nah.* No, sir, my wife is American.

22 *¿ays . . . ee'hoh frahn-thays'?* Is your son French?

23 *see, . . . mee ee'hoh ays . . .* Yes, sir, my son is French.

24 *¿kee-ayn' ays coh-lohm-bee-ah'noh?* Who is a Colombian?

25 *mee pree'moh ays . . .* My cousin is a Colombian.

26 *¿day-say'ah ell eerr ah Vay-nay-thway'lah?* Does he wish to go to Venezuela?

27 *noh, ell day-say'ah eerr ah Coh-lohm'bee-ah.* No, he wishes to go to Colombia.

28 *¿toh'mah . . . ell train pah' rah eerr ah May'hee-koh?* Do you take the train to go to Mexico?

29 *noh, pah'rah eerr ah May'hee-koh toh'moh ell vah-pohrr' oh ell ah- ay-roh-plah'noh.* No, to go to Mexico I take the boat or the airplane.

30 *¿day-say'ah soo pah'dray ah-thayrr' ell vee-ah'hay ayn ahw-toh-moh'veel?* Does your father wish to make the trip by automobile?

31 *see, . . . ell . . . ayn ahw-toh-moh'veel ays mwee' een-tay-ray-sahn'tay.* Yes, sir, the trip by automobile is very interesting.

32 *¿ah kay' oh'rah sah'lay ell trayn?* At what time does the train leave?

---

prayn-dayrr') to learn; *atender* (ah-tayn-dayrr') to attend; *vender* (vayn-dayrr') to sell; *comprender* (cohm-prayn-dayrr') to understand; etc., belong to the 2nd

33 El tren sale por la mañana.

34 ¿Por qué desea usted ir a Chile?

35 Deseo ir para atender a mis negocios.

36 ¿Cuándo desea salir su madre?

37 Mi madre desea salir pronto.

38 ¿Desea usted ir solo?

39 No, señor; deseo ir con mi familia.

conjugation, all verbs of which end in *-er.* *13.* Vivir (vee-veerr′) to live; *ir* (eerr′)
to go; and *salir* (sah-leerr′) to leave, etc. belong to the 3rd conjugation, all verbs
of which end in *-ir.* *14.* To the POSSESSIVE ADJECTIVE *su*, meaning *his, her, its,*
their and *your*, it is necessary sometimes to add the complements *de él, de ella, de*
usted, etc., when the context does not clearly point out the person referred to. *Su*
familia de usted, your family (of you); *su familia de él*, his family (of he); *su*

33 *ell trayn . . . pohrr lah mah-niah'nah.*   The train leaves in the morning.

34 *¿pohrr kay' day-say'ah . . . eerr ah-Chee'lay?*   Why do you wish to go to Chile?

35 *day-say'oh . . . pah'rah ah-tayn-dayrr' ah mees nay-goh' thee-ohs.*   I wish to go in order to attend to my business.

36 *¿kwahn'doh day-say'ah sah-leerr' . . . mah'dray?*   When does your mother wish to leave?

37 *mee . . . day-say'ah . . . prohn' toh.*   My mother wishes to leave soon.

38 *¿day-say'ah . . . eerr soh'loh?*   Do you wish to go alone?

39 *noh, . . . day-say'oh eerr cohn mee fah-mee'lee-ah.*   No, sir, I wish to go with my family.

familia de ella, her family (of she), etc.
my, pl., agree with the noun in number.
pers. pl., present of the indicative mood of all regular verbs of the 2nd and 3rd
conjugations.   *17.* The accent of the pronoun *él* (ell) *he,* serves to distinguish it
from the article *el* (ell) *the,* which is pronounced the same.   *15. Mi* (mee) my, sing.; *mis* (mees)
16. -en is the termination of the 3rd

2 LECCION SEGUNDA

Second Lesson   (*layk-thee-ohn' say-goon'dah*)

Vocabulario usado en esta lección

temprano (*taym-prah'noh*)   early
permítame (*pairr-mee'tah-may*)   allow me
ofrecerle (*oh-fray-thairr'lay*)   to offer you
pasemos (*pah-say'mohs*)   let us go into, (**pass**)
las tostadas (*tohs-tah'dahs*)   the toast
generalmente (*hay-nay-rahl'mayn'tay*)   ordinarily, generally
la taza (*lah-tah'thah*)   the cup

tarde (*tahrr'day*)   late
teatro (*tay-ah'troh*)   theatre
calle (*kah'lliay*)   street

antes (*ahn'tays*)   before
después (*days-pways'*)   after
un par (*oon pahrr*)   a pair
ahora (*ah-oh'rah*)   now,
luego (*lway'goh*)   later
servir (*sairr-veerr'*)   to serve

dura (*doo'rah*)   tough,
tierna (*tee-airr'nah*)   tender
frito (*free'toh*)   fried
me gusta (*may goos'tah*)   I like
prefiero (*pray-fee-ay'-roh*)   I prefer

el comedor (*koh-may-dohrr'*)   the dining room
bebo (*bay'boh*)   I drink
Ud. come (*oos-tayd' koh'may*)   you eat

asadas (*ah-sah'dahs*)   roast, broiled
dulce (*dool'thay*)   sweet,
tomo (*toh'moh*)   I take
gusto (*goos'toh*)   taste
hay (*I*)   there is
esta (*ays'tah*)   this

buena (*bway'nah*)   good
bastante (*bahs-tahn'tay*)   enough
amargo (*ah-mahrr'goh*)   bitter
consiste (*kohn-sees'tay*)   consists
¿le gusta? (*lay goos'tah*)   do you like
lo siento (*loh see-ayn'toh*)   I am sorry

el vaso (*ell vah'soh*)   the drinking glass
acompañarme (*ah-kohm-pah-niahrr'may*)   to accompany me
comprarme (*kohm-prahrr'may*)   to buy for myself
sombrerería (*sohm-bray-ray-ree'ah*)   hat store

COMIDAS Y BEBIDAS

MEALS AND DRINKS   (*koh-mee'dahs ee bay-bee'dahs*)

la sopa (*soh'pah*)	the soup	**la comida** (*koh-mee'dah*)	the dinner
el pan (*pahn*)	bread	**la cena** (*thay'nah*)	supper
el agua (*ah'gwah*)	water	**la carne** (*kahrr'nay*)	meat
el café (*kah-fay'*)	coffee	**el jamón** (*hah mohn'*)	ham
el té (*tay*)	tea	**el tocíno** (*toh-thee'noh*)	bacon
el vino (*vee'noh*)	wine	**los huevos** (*way'vohs*)	eggs
la leche (*lay'chay*)	milk	**el pollo** (*poh'llioh*)	chicken

el postre (*pohs'tray*)	the dessert
el queso (*kay'soh*)	cheese
las frutas (*froo'tahs*)	fruit
el pastel (*pahs-tayl'*)	pie

el desayuno (*day-sa -yoo'noh*)	the breakfast
el almuerzo (*ahl-mwairr'thoh*)	lunch
el cordero (*kohrr-day'roh*)	lamb
el carnero[1] (*kahrr-nay'roh*)	sheep, mutton
la carne de vaca (*vah'kah*)	beef
la ternera[2] (*tairr-nay'rah*)	veal
las costillas (*kohs-tee'lliahs*)	ribs
las chuletas (*choo-lay'tahs*)	chops
la mantequilla (*mahn-tay-kee'lliah*)	butter
el pescado (*pays-kah'doh*)	fish
el chocolate (*choh-koh-lah'tay*)	chocolate
la ensalada (*ayn-sah-lah'dah*)	salad

CONVERSATION

1 Yo tomo el desayuno.

2 ¿A qué hora toma usted el desayuno?

3 Yo tomo el desayuno temprano.

4 ¿En qué consiste generalmente su desayuno?

5 Mi desayuno consiste en un par de huevos, tostadas y una taza de café con leche.

6 Pasemos al comedor.

7 ¿Desearía[3] usted comer ahora, o antes de[4] salir?

8 Prefiero comer después.

9 ¿Qué come usted en la cena?

10 Generalmente,[5] los martes, un par de chuletas de cordero bien asadas.

11 Yo prefiero en la comida huevos y jamón, o tocino bien frito.

12 ¿No le gusta la carne de cerdo?

13 Sí,[6] señor; pero prefiero la de ternera.

FOOTNOTES: *1. Carnero* means both sheep and mutton. *2. La ternera* also means *the calf*. *3.* -ia, -ías, -ía, -íamos, -íais, -ían, added to the infinitive of any regular verb, form the CONDITIONAL TENSE. *4.* Some ADVERBS of time or place require *de* before a noun or a verb, as: *antes de, después de, dentro de, fuera de,* etc. When a verb follows the PREPOSITION *de* it must be in the INFINITIVE, instead *of the* PRESENT PARTICIPLE as in English; so we must say: *antes de entrar* (literally, before to enter) before entering. *5.* The suffix *mente* is equivalent to the English *ly,* and is added to the feminine forms of adjectives to form the adverb, thus: *malo* (bad) *malamente* (badly); *perfecto* (perfect) *perfectamente* (perfectly). *6. Sí* (see) yes, is the AFFIRMATIVE ADVERB and is accented to distinguish it from *si* (see) if, which is a CONJUNCTION. *7. Le* (lay) to him, to her,

PRONUNCIATION	TRANSLATION
1 *yoh toh'moh ell day-sah-yoo' noh.*	I take (have) breakfast.
2 *¿ah kay' oh'rah toh'mah oostayd' ell . . . ?*	At what time do you take (the) breakfast?
3 *yoh . . . ell day-sah-yoo'noh taym-prah'noh.*	I take (the) breakfast early.
4 *¿ayn kay' cohn-sees'tay haynay-rahl-mayn'tay soo . . . ?*	Of what does your breakfast usually consist?
5 *mee . . . cohn-sees'tay ayn oon pahrr day way'vohs, tohs-tah' dahs ee oo'nah tah'thah day kah-fay' kohn lay'chay.*	My breakfast consists of two eggs, toast and a cup of coffee with milk.
6 *pah - say'mohs ahl koh-maydohrr'.*	Let us go to the dining room.
7 *¿day-say-ah-ree'ah . . . kohmayrr' ah-oh'rah oh ahn'tays day sah-leerr'?*	Would you like to eat now, or before leaving?
8 *pray-fee-ay'roh . . . dayspways'.*	I prefer to eat later.
9 *¿kay coh-may . . . ayn lah thay'nah?*	What do you eat for supper?
10 *hay - nay-rahl-mayn'tay lohs mahrr'tays oon pahrr day choo-lay'tahs . . . bee-ayn' ahsah'dahs.*	Generally, on Tuesdays, two broiled lamb chops well done.
11 *yoh pray-fee-ay'roh ayn lah koh-mee'dah way'vohs ee hahmohn' oh toh-thee'noh bee-ayn'free'toh.*	For my dinner I prefer ham and eggs, or bacon fried crisp.
12 *¿noh lay goostah lah kahrr' nay . . . thayrr'doh?*	Do you not like pork?
13 *see, . . . pay'roh pray-fee-ay' roh . . . day tayrr-nay'rah.*	Yes, sir, but I prefer veal.

to you (sing.) ; *me* (may) to me; *te* (tay) to thee; *nos* (nohs) to us; *os* (ohs) to ye; and *les* (lays) to them, to you (pl.) are object pronouns and must be placed before the verb, except with the IMPERATIVE, the infinitive or the GERUND. 8. *-aré* is the termination of the 1st pers. sing. of the future of all verbs ending in *-ar.* In Spanish it is not necessary to express the PERSONAL PRONOUN before the

14 Permítame ofrecerle[7] un poco de arroz con pollo. Este pollo está muy tierno.

15 Gracias, pero antes tomaré[8] la sopa.

16 Este asado de vaca está duro.

17 En cambio el pescado está delicioso.

18 ¿Qué desea usted para la cena?

19 Unas costillas de cordero, un poco de ensalada, pan y mantequilla.

20 ¿Y después?

21 Después tomaré los postres.

22 ¿Qué prefiere[9] usted de postre?

23 Deseo queso, frutas y un pastel.

24 ¿Tomará usted té?

25 No, señor; prefiero chocolate o un vaso de leche.

26 ¿Bebe usted vino en las comidas?

27 Generalmente bebo un vaso de vino y un vaso de agua.

verb, as the person and number are always designated by the verb ending or sufficiently pointed out by the context. *Hablo* (I speak), *come* (he eats), *tomaremos* (we shall take) are generally used instead of: *yo hablo, él come* and *nosotros tomaremos*. However, *usted, ustedes* (you), must never be omitted, unless one wants to avoid repetition. The personal pronouns, besides *usted* and *ustedes*, are: *yo, I;*

14 *Payrr-mee'tah-may oh - fray-*
   thayrr'lay oon poh'koh . . .
   ah-rrohth' kohn poh - llioh.
   Ays'tay . . . ays-tah' mwee tee-
   ayrr'noh.

Let me offer you some chicken with rice. This chicken is very tender.

15 *grah'thee-ahs, pay'roh ahn'*
   tays toh-mah-ray' lah soh'pah.

Thank you, but first I will take (the) soup.

16 *ays'tay ah-sah'doh . . . vah'*
   kah ays-tah' doo'roh.

This roastbeef is tough.

17 *ayn kahm'bee-oh ell pays-kah'*
   doh . . . day-lee-thee-oh'soh.

On the other hand the fish is delicious.

18 *¿kay day-say'ah . . . pah'rah*
   . . . thay'nah?

What do you want for supper?

19 *oo'nahs kohs-tee'lliahs . . .*
   kohrr-day'roh oon . . . day
   ayn - sah - lah'dah pahn ee
   mahn-tay-kee'lliah.

Some lamb chops (ribs), a little salad, bread and butter.

20 *¿ee days-pways'?*

And then?

21 *days-pways' toh-mah-ray' lohs*
   pohs'trays.

Then I shall take (the) dessert.

22 *¿ . . . pray-fee-ay'ray . . . day*
   pohs'tray?

What do you prefer for dessert?

23 *day-say'oh kay'soh froo'tahs*
   ee oon pahs-tayl'.

I want cheese, fruit and pie.

24 *¿toh-mah-rah' . . . tay?*

Will you take tea?

25 *noh, . . . pray-fee-ay'roh choh-*
   koh-lah'tay oh oon vah'soh
   . . . lay'chay.

No, I prefer chocolate, or a glass of milk.

26 *¿bay'bay . . . vee'noh ayn*
   lahs koh-mee'dahs?

Do you drink wine with your meals?

27 *hay - nay-rahl-mayn'tay bay'*
   boh . . . vah'soh day . . .
   day ah'gwah.

Generally I drink a glass of wine and a glass of water.

---

tú, you; *él*, he; *ella*, she; *nosotros* (masc.) *nosotras* (fem.) *we*; *vosotros* (masc.); *vosotras* (fem.) *you*; *ellos* (masc.) *ellas* (fem.) *they*.   9. **Prefiere**, from *preferir* (to prefer), is the 3rd pers. sing. of the present indicative.   10. **Lo siento**, from *sentir*, to feel, is translated in this case as *I am sorry*. The opposite is *me alegro*.

28 ¿Está el café a su gusto, o está amargo?

29 No, señor; está bastante dulce.

30 ¿Desea usted acompañarme al teatro después de la comida?

31 Lo siento,[10] pero tengo[11] que ir a comprarme un sombrero.

32 En esta calle hay una buena sombrerería.

33 ¿Venden allí buenos sombreros?

34 Sí, señor; los sombreros son de excelente calidad y se venden a precios razonables.

I am glad.   *11. Tengo que,* from *tener que,* to have to, to be obliged to. When *tener* is followed by *que* it must precede the infinitive of the principal verb, and, like *haber de,* implies the necessity or obligation to do something in particular. The

28 *¿ays-tah' ell kah-fay' ah . . . goos-toh oh . . . ah-mahrr' goh?*

Is the coffee to your taste, or is it bitter?

29 *noh . . . ays-tah' bahs-tahn'tay dool'thay.*

No, sir, it is sweet enough.

30 *¿day-say'ah . . . ah-kohm-pah-niahrr'may ahl tay-ah'troh days-pways' day . . . koh-mee' dah?*

Do you wish to accompany me to the theatre after dinner?

31 *loh see-ayn'toh, pay'roh tayn' goh kay eerr ah kohm-prahrr' may . . . sohm-bray'roh.*

I am sorry, but I have to go to buy a hat for myself.

32 *ayn ays'tah kah'lliay ah' ee oo'nah bway'nah sohm-bray-ray-ree'ah.*

On this street there is a good hat store.

33 *¿vayn'dayn ah - lliee' bway' nohs sohm-bray'rohs?*

Do they sell good hats there?

34 *see, . . . lohs . . . sohn day ayks-thay-layn'tay kah - lee - dahd' ee say vayn'dayn ah pray'thee - ohs rra-thoh-nah' blays.*

Yes, sir, the hats are of excellent quality and they sell them at reasonable prices.

present indicative is conjugated thus: *tengo que,* I have to; *tiene que,* he, she or you have to; *tenemos que,* we have to; *tienen que,* they (masc. or fem.) you (pl.) have to.

3 LECCION TERCERA

Third Lesson   (*layk-thee-ohn' tayrr-thay'rah*)

Vocabulario usado en esta lección

¿ es verdad? (*ays vairr-dahd'*)	is it so?
¿ no es verdad? (*noh ays vairr-dahd'*)	is it not so?
le sientan (*lay seè-ayn'tahn*)	they fit you
lo que necesite (*loh kay nay-thay-see'tay*)	anything you need
hacer juego (*ah-thairr' hway'goh*)	to match
elegantes (*ay-lay-gahn'tays*)	elegant
apretados (*ah-pray-tah'dohs*)	tight

el dinero (*dee-nay'roh*)	the money
cuesta (*kways'tah*)	it costs
barato (*bah-rah toh*)	cheap
caro (*kah'roh*)	expensive

la tienda (*tee-ayn'dah*)	the store	mismo (*mees'moh*)	same
la seda (*say'dah*)	silk	diferente (*dee-fay-rain'tay*)	different
el fieltro (*fee-ayl'troh*)	felt	cuanto (*kwan'toh*)	how much
la suela (*sway'lah*)	sole	clase (*klah'say*)	kind, class
el tacón (*tah-kohn'*)	heel	dentro (*dayn'troh*)	inside
color (*koh-lohrr'*)	color	comprar (*kohm-prahrr'*)	to buy

largo (*lahrr'go*)	long
corto (*kohrr'toh*)	short
alto (*ahl'toh*)	high
bajo (*bah'hoh*)	low

puede (*pway'day*)	he can, he may
naturalmente (*nah-too-rahl'mayn'tay*)	of course, naturally
unos (*oo'nohs*)	some (mas.)
unas (*oo'nahs*)	some (fem.)
demasiado (*day-mah-see-ah'doh*)	too much
la tela (*tay'lah*)	the light fabric
los pantalones (*pahn-tah-loh'nays*)	trousers
el sombrero[1] (*sohm-bray'roh*)	hat
la corbata (*kohrr-bah'tah*)	necktie
los puños[2] (*poo'niohs*)	cuffs
la cartera[3] (*kahrr-tay'rah*)	handbag, wallet
los botones (*boh-toh'nays*)	buttons

LA ROPA y EL CALZADO

CLOTHING AND FOOTWEAR   (*lah rroh'pah ee ell kahl-thah'doh*)

el traje (*trah'hay*)	the suit	el saco (*sah'koh*)	the coat
el abrigo (*ah-bree'goh*)	overcoat	la chaqueta (*chah-kay-tah*)	coat
la gorra (*goh'rrah*)	cap	el chaleco (*chah-lay'koh*)	vest
la camisa (*kah-mee'sah*)	shirt	el bolsillo (*bohl-see'llioh*)	pocket
el cuello (*kway'llioh*)	collar	el bolso (*bohl-soh*)	purse
la manga (*mahn'gah*)	sleeve	los guantes (*gwahn'tays*)	gloves
la falda (*fahl'dah*)	skirt	el vestido (*vays-tee'doh*)	dress
la blusa (*bloo'sah*)	blouse	el refajo (*rray-fah'hoh*)	slip
la faja (*fah'hah*)	girdle	las medias (*may'deeahs*)	stockings
la piel (*pee-ayl'*)	leather	las botas (*boh-tahs*)	high shoes

el paño (*pah'nioh*)	cloth	
la lana (*lah'nah*)	wool	

el pañuelo (*pah-niway'loh*)	the handkerchief
la ropa interior[4] (*rroh'pah . . .*)	underwear
la camiseta (*kah-mee-say'tah*)	undershirt
los calzoncillos (*kahl-thohn-thee'lliohs*)	drawers
los calcetines (*kahl-thay-tee'nays*)	socks
el justillo (*hoos-tee'llioh*)	brassiere
los zapatos (*thah-pah'tohs*)	shoes
las zapatillas (*tha-pah-tee'lliahs*)	slippers
la zapatería (*thah-pah-tay-ree'ah*)	shoe store

CONVERSATION

1 Buenos días.—Buenas tardes.— Buenas noches.[5]

2 ¿De qué hablaban[6] ustedes cuando yo entré?[7]

3 Hablábamos de la ropa y del calzado.

4 Usted tiene un traje que le sienta muy bien.

5 Sí; es un traje de buen paño; pero el saco me está largo y el chaleco corto.

6 ¿Le sientan bien los pantalones?

7 Sí, los pantalones me sientan muy bien.

8 Yo necesito un abrigo, un sombrero y un par de guantes.

9 En esta[8] tienda puede comprar lo que necesite: corbatas, pañuelos, camisas y calcetines.[9]

10 ¿Necesita también ropa interior?

11 Sí, señor; necesito camisetas y calzoncillos de lana.

12 Esta camisa de seda tiene los puños demasiado largos.[10]

FOOTNOTES: *1.* Nouns ending in *-o* are masculine with a few exceptions, such as *la mano,* the hand, which are feminine. *2. Puños* (cuffs), pl. of *puño.* In order to form the plural of words ending in unaccented vowels, add one *-s.* *3.* Nouns ending in *-a* are feminine, with the exception of *el día,* the day, *el sofá,* the sofa, and a few more. Other exceptions are words derived from the Greek and ending in *-a* or *-ma,* as: *el déspota,* the despot; *el monarca,* the monarch; *el clima,* the climate; *el idioma,* the language, etc. *El cólera,* the cholera morbus, is masculine, but *la cólera,* anger, rage, is feminine. *4. Ropa interior,* lit. *clothes interior,* (underwear). *5.* These forms of greeting are used in the plural only. *6. -aban* is the ending of the 3rd pers. pl. of the imperfect of verbs of the first conjugation (*-ar*). The imperfect tense implies that the past action or event spoken of, was

PRONUNCIATION	TRANSLATION

1 *bway'nohs dee'ahs. Bway' nahs tahrr'days. Bway'nahs noh'chays.*

Good morning.—Good afternoon. —Good evening or good night.

2 *¿day . . . ah-blah'ban oostay' days kwan'doh yoh ayn-tray'?*

About what were you talking when I came in?

3 *ah-blah'bah mohs day . . . lah roh' pah ee . . . kahl-thah'doh.*

We were speaking about clothes and shoes.

4 *. . . tee-ay'nay . . . trah'hay . . . lay see-ayn'tah mwee bee-ayn'.*

You have a suit on that fits you very well.

5 *see, ays oon . . .day bwayn pah'nioh; pay'roh ell sah'koh may ays-tah' lahrr'goh ee ell chah-lay'koh kohrr'toh.*

Yes, it is a suit of good cloth, but the coat is long and the vest short.

6 *¿lay see-ayn'tahn bee-ayn' lohs pahn-tah-loh'nays?*

Do the trousers fit you well?

7 *see, lohs pahn-tah-loh' nays may . . . bee-ayn'.*

Yes, the trousers fit me very well.

8 *yoh nay-thay-see'toh . . . ee oon . . . day gwahn'tays.*

I need an overcoat, a hat and a pair of gloves.

9 *ayn . . . tee-ayn'dah pwa day kohm-prahrr' loh . . . nay-thay-see'tay: kohrr-bah'tahs pah-ni-way'lohs kah-mee'sahs ee kahl-thay-tee'nays.*

In this store you can buy anything you need: neckties, handkerchiefs, shirts and socks.

10 *¿nay-thay-see'tah tahm - bee - ayn' rroh'pah een - tay - ree - ohrr'?*

Do you need underwear also?

11 *see, . . . na -thay-see'toh kah-mee-say'tahs ee kahl-thohn-thee'lliohs day lah'nah.*

Yes, I need woolen undershirts and drawers.

12 *ays'tah kah-mee'sah day say' dah tee-ay'nay lohs poo-niohs day - mah - see - ah'doh lahrr' gohs.*

The cuffs on this silk shirt are too long.

---

continuous or going on at the time that some other action or event took place. *Hablaban* translates into English as *you, they were speaking, used to speak*. It may also be rendered in Spanish as *estaban hablando*.   7. *Entré*, 1st pers. past of *entrar* (ayn-trahhrr'), to enter. This tense, called also absolute, marks a past action or event completed at a specified past time. It corresponds to the English

13 Deseo comprar un vestido de dos piezas para mi señora.

14 ¿Qué tela prefiere usted?

15 Una tela fina y no muy cara.

16 ¿Desea usted que la falda y la blusa hagan juego?

17 Naturalmente. Y prefiero las dos piezas del mismo color.

18 Tenemos unos vestidos de manga corta y cuello bajo que son muy elegantes.

19 ¿Cuánto cuesta este sombrero de fieltro?

20 El sombrero es caro,[11] pero la gorra es muy barata.

21 La señorita Martínez desea comprar un refajo y unas medias, ¿no es verdad?

22 Sí, señor; y también necesito una faja y un justillo.

---

did, took, etc. *Ayer hablé español* (ah-yayrr′ ah-blay′ ays-pah-niohl′) I spoke Spanish yesterday; *compré un caballo* (kah-bah′llioh) I bought (did buy) a horse.   8. The DEMONSTRATIVE ADJECTIVES AND PRONOUNS are *Este* (ays′tay) masc., *esta* (ays′tah) fem. this one; *estos* (ays′tohs) masc., *estas* (ays′tahs) fem., these. *Ese, esa* (ay′say, ay′sah) that one; *esos, esas* (ay′sohs, ay′sahs) those. *Aquel, aquella* (ah′kayl, ah-kay′lliah) that one (yonder); *aquellos, aquellas* (ah-kay′lliohs, ah-kay′lliahs) those (yonder). *Este* points out the person or object nearest to the speaker; *ese,* the person or object nearest to the person spoken to; *aquel,* the person or object remote from both speaker and person spoken to. They always agree in gender and number with the nouns. *Esto, eso, aquello* are neuter forms expressing something indefinite, as *¿Qué es esto?* (kay ays ays′toh) what is this? *eso es,* that is.   9. Words ending in a consonant take *-es* for the formation of the plural. Examples: *El calcetín* (kahl-thay-teen′) the sock; pl.: *los calcetines* (kahl-thay-tee′nays). *El ojal* (oh-hahl′) the button-hole; pl.: *los ojales*

13 *day-say'oh kohm-prahrr'* . . .   I wish to buy a two piece dress
    vays-tee'doh . . . dohs pee-ay'   for my wife.
    thahs . . . mee say-nioh'rah.
14 *¿. . . tay'lah pray-fee-ay'*   What kind of fabric do you pre-
    ray . . . ?   fer?
15 *oo'nah . . . fee'nah ee noh . . .*   A fine material and not very ex-
    kah'rah.   pensive.

16 *¿day-say'ah . . . lah fahl'*   Do you want the skirt and the
    dah ee . . . bloo'sah ah' gahn   blouse to match?
    hoo-ay'goh?
17 *nah-too-rahl-mayn'tay. E pray-*   Of course. And I prefer the two
    fee-ay'roh . . . dohs pee-ay'   pieces of the same color.
    thahs dayl mees'moh koh-
    lohrr'
18 *tay-nay'mohs oo'nohs . . . day*   We have some dresses with short
    mahn'gah kohrr' tah ee kway'   sleeves and low neck which are
    llioh bah' hoh . . . sohn . . .   very elegant.
    ay-lay-gahn'tays.
19 *¿kwahn'toh kways'tah ays'*   How much does this felt hat cost?
    tay . . . day fee-ayl' troh?
20 *ell . . . ays kah'roh pay'roh*   The hat is expensive but the cap
    lah goh'rrah ays mwee bah-   is very cheap.
    rah'tah.

21 *lah say-nioh-ree'tah Mahrr-*   Miss Martinez wishes to buy a
    tee'nayth day-say-ah kohm-   slip and some stockings, doesn't
    prahrr' oon rray-fah'hoh ee   she? (is it not so?)
    oo' nahs may'dee-ahs ¿noh
    ays vayrr'dahd'?
22 *see, . . . ee tahm-bee-ayn'nay-*   Yes, and I also need a girdle and
    thay-see'toh . . . fah'hah ee   a brassiere.
    oon hoos-tee'llioh.

(oh-hah'lays). *El país* (pah-ees') the country; pl.: *los países* (pah-ee'says). The
plural of words ending in accented vowel is formed in the same manner. Examples:
El jabalí (hab-bah-lee') the boar; pl.: *los jabalíes* (hah-bah-lee'ays). *El tisú*
(tee-soo) the tissue; pl.: *los tisúes* (tee-soo'ays). Exceptions to this rule are:
papá, papa and *mamá,* mama, the plural of which are respectively *papás* and
mamás, and words ending in *-e,* which take only *-s,* as: *pie* (pee-ay'); pl.: *pies*
(pee-ays') *canapé* (kah-nah-pay') lounge; pl.: *canapés* (kah-nah-pays'). *10.* AD-
JECTIVES ending in *-o* are of the masculine gender, and those in *-a* of the feminine.

23 ¿Sabe usted dónde puedo comprar calzado?

24 En la zapatería[12] se vende toda clase de calzado.

25 La señora López desea comprar un par de zapatos de tacón alto y suela fina.

26 Y nosotros deseamos comprar un par de zapatos de baile y unas zapatillas.

27 Estos zapatos me están un poco apretados.

28 ¿Desearía usted una cartera de piel?[13]

29 Sí, desearía una cartera con un bolsillo dentro para el dinero.

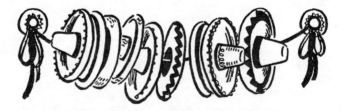

They must agree with the nouns they qualify. *11. Caro* means *dear* referring to price, while *querido* (kay-ree′doh), the past participle of *querer* (kay-rairr′, to want), means *dear* with reference to the affections, as: *mi querido amigo,* my dear friend. *12.* This termination *-ría* is synonymous with the English *-ry,* as in baker, bakery, *panadero, panadería.* This construction is formed by striking off the endings and replacing them by ría. *Guantero* (from *guante,* glove), one who sells gloves, will make *guantería* or *tienda de guantes; librero,* book-seller (from *libro,*

23 *¿sah'bay ... dohn'day pway'*
   doh ... kahl-tha'doh?

Do you know where I can buy
shoes?

24 *ayn lah thah-pah-tay-ree' ah*
   say vayn'day toh' dah klah'
   say day ...

In the shoe store all kinds of footwear are sold.

25 *lah ... loh'pawth day say'ah*
   ... pahrr day tha-pah'tohs
   ... tah-kohn' ahl'toh ee
   sway'lah fee'nah.

Mrs. López wants to buy a pair of
shoes with high heels and a thin
sole.

26 *ee noh-soh'trohs day-say-ah'*
   mohs ... oon ... day ... day
   bah-ee'lay ee oo'nahs thah-
   pah-tee'lliahs.

And we wish to buy a pair of
evening shoes and slippers.

27 *ays'tohs ... may ays-tahn' ...*
   poh'koh ah-pray-tah'dohs.

These shoes are a little tight for
me.

28 *¿day-say-ah-ree'ah ... oo'nah*
   kahrr-tay'rah ... pee-ayl'?

Would you like a leather handbag?

29 *see, ... oo'nah ... kohn oon*
   bohl-see'llioh dayn'troh ...
   ell dee-nay' roh.

Yes, I would like a handbag with
a change purse for my money.

book), *librería* or *tienda de libros*, etc. Notice that all these words implying
tiendas, (stores) fem., are also feminine, and the feminine article must therefore
be used.   *13.* The POSSESSIVE CASE is expressed in Spanish by means of *de*, of;
thus, *el sombrero de Pedro* (pay'droh) *Peter's hat* (lit. *the hat of Peter*). The
material of a thing, its nature, uses, qualities, species, etc., are expressed also by
means of *de*, the order of the words becoming inverted, as in the present instance.

4 LECCION CUARTA

Fourth Lesson   (*layk-thee-ohn' kwarr'tah*)

Vocabulario usado en esta lección

la velocidad (*vay-loh-thee-dahd'*)	speed
Sur América (*soor ah-may'ree-kah*)	South America
hay (*I*)	there is, there are
¿de veras? (*day vay'rahs*)	really?
en verdad (*ayn vairr-dahd'*)	indeed
ida y vuelta (*ee'dah ee vwayl'tah*)	round trip
tengo que (*tayn'goh kay*)	I have to, ought to
preparado (*pray-pah-rah'doh*)	prepared
ruego (*rrway'goh*)	I beg you, (please)
mañana por la mañana	tomorrow morning
la llegada (*lliay-gah'dah*)	the arrival

embarcar (*aym-bahrr-kahrr'*)	to sail, embark
visitar (*vee-see-tahrr'*)	to visit
extranjero (*ayks-trahn-hay'roh*)	foreign, abroad

calle (*kah'lliay*)	street
avenida (*ah-vay-nee'dah*)	avenue

pesa (*pay'sah*)	it weighs
facturar	to check the baggage
(*fahk-too-rahrr'*)	

donde (*dohn'day*)	where	la salida·(*sah-lee'dah*)	the departure
países (*pah-ee'says*)	countries	entonces (*ayn-tohn'thays*)	then
de prisa (*day pree'sah*)	quickly, fast	cómodos (*koh'moh-dohs*)	comfortable
aquí (*ah-kee'*)	here	seguros (*say-goo'rohs*)	safe
ya (*yah*)	already	al llegar (*ahl lliay-gahrr'*)	upon arriving
aun no (*ah-oon' noh*)	not yet	a tiempo (*ah tee-aym'poh*)	in time
darme (*dahrr'may*)	to give to me	en marcha (*mahrr'chah*)	it is starting
sé (*say*)	I know	subamos (*soo-bah'mohs*)	let us get in

De Viaje por Ferrocarril, Vapor y Aeroplano

TRAVELING BY RAILROAD, STEAMER AND AIRPLANE   (*day veeah'hay
pohrr fay-rroh-kah-rreel', vah-pohrr ee ah-ay-roh plah'noh*)

el tren (*train*)	the train	**el avión** (*ah-vee-ohn'*)	the airliner
el coche (*koh'chay*)	railroad car	**la ruta** (*rroo'tah*)	route
el vapor (*vah-pohrr'*)	steamship	**el piloto** (*pee-loh'toh*)	pilot
el puerto (*pwairr'toh*)	port	**las hélices** (*ay'lee-thays*)	propellers
el muelle (*mway'lliay*)	pier	**giran** (*hee'rahn*)	they spin

el equipaje (*ay-kee-pah'hay*)	the baggage
las maletas (*mah-lay'tahs*)	suit cases
los baúles (*bah-oo'lays*)	trunks
la estación[1] (*ays-tah-thee-ohn'*)	station
el billete (*bee-lliay'tay*)	
el boleto (*boh-lay'toh*)	ticket
el despacho de billetes (*days-pah'choh*)	ticket office
el talón (*tah-lohn'*)	baggage check
la guía-itinerario (*ghee'ah ee-tee-nay-rah'ree-oh*)	time table
el camarote (*kah-mah-roh'tay*)	cabin
la cabina (*kah-bee'nah*)	cabin (aeroplane)
el pasaje (*pah-sah'hay*)	steamship ticket
el despacho de equipajes (*-ay-kee-pah'hays*)	baggage office
el aeroplano (*ah-ay-roh-plah'noh*)	airplane
el aeródromo[2] (*ah-ay-roh'droh-moh*)	airport
el asiento (*ah-see-ayn'toh*)	seat
los motores (*moh-toh'rays*)	motors
la agencia de pasajes (*ah-hayn'thee-ah-*)	ticket agency

FOOTNOTES: *1. Estación*, station. All nouns ending in *-ción* are feminine.
2. Aeropuerto also means: airport.   *3.* When *el* (the) comes after *de* (of, from)

CONVERSATION

1 ¿Dónde está la estación del[3] ferrocarril?

2 Hay una en la calle Madero y Avenida del Sol, y otra en la calle Bolívar.

3 ¿A qué estación necesita usted ir?

4 Para[4] ir a Santiago necesitamos salir por[4] la estación del Norte.

5 ¿A qué hora es la salida del primer tren?

6 El primer tren sale por la mañana muy temprano.

7 Entonces será necesario tomar un automóvil para ir de prisa.

8 ¿Está listo su equipaje?

9 Sí, señor; las maletas y los baúles están ya en la estación.

10 Le ruego me diga dónde está el despacho de billetes.

11 ¿Cuánto cuesta[5] un billete[6] de ida y vuelta a Méjico?

12 ¿Por cuánto tiempo es válido este billete?

---

or *a* (to, at) both words contract into one, respectively, thus: *del*, of the, from the; *al*, to the, at the.   *4.* These two prepositions, *por* and *para*, will be explained more fully further on. For the present it will be sufficient to remark that *para* means *for*, *to*, *in order to*, and *por* means *by*, *through*, *for*. *Para* means *for* when expressing direction: *sale para Madrid*, he leaves for Madrid; and *por* means *by* when referring to manner or way of doing something: *él viaja por ferrocarril*, he travels by railroad.   *5. Cuesta* is the 3rd pers. sing., indicative present, of the irregular verb *costar*, to cost. Irregular verbs ending in *-ar* or *-er*, and having the vowel *o* in the syllable before last, as in this case, change the *o* into *ue* in the sing. and the third

PRONUNCIATION	TRANSLATION
1 *¿dohn-day ays-tah' . . . ays-tah-thee-ohn' . . . fay-rroh-kah-rreel'?*	Where is the railroad station?
2 *I . . . ayn . . . kah'llay Mah-day'roh ee Ah-vay-nee'dah . . . Sohl ee oh-trah . . . lah . . . Boh-lee'vahrr.*	There is one on Madero Street and Sun Avenue and another on Bolivar Street.
3 *¿ah . . . nay-thay-see'tah . . . eerr?*	To which station do you have to go?
4 *pah'rah . . . ah Sahn-tee-ah' goh . . . sah-leerr'pohrr lah . . . dayl Nohrr'tay.*	In order to go to Santiago we need (have) to leave from the Northern Station.
5 *¿ah . . . oh'rah ays . . . sah-lee'dah dayl pree-mayrr' . . .?*	At what time does the first train leave?
6 *ell pree-mayrr' train sah'lay . . . lah . . . mwee taym-prah' noh.*	The first train leaves very early in the morning.
7 *ayn - tohn'thays say-rah'nay-thay-sah'ree-oh-toh-mahrr' oon ahw-toh-moh'veel pah'rah . . . day pree'sah.*	Then it will be necessary to take an automobile in order to go quickly (to the station).
8 *¿ays-tah' lees'toh soo ay-kee-pah'hay?*	Is your baggage ready?
9 *see, . . . lahs mah-lay'tahs ee lohs bah-oo'lays ays-tahn' yah*	Yes, the bags and trunks are already at the station.
10 *lay rrway'goh may dee' gah . . . ays-tah' days-pah'choh day bee-llidy'tays.*	Please tell me where the ticket office is.
11 *¿kwan'toh kways'tah oon . . . day ee'dah ee voo-ayl'tah ah May'hee-koh?*	How much is a round trip ticket to Mexico?
12 *¿pohrr . . . tee-aym'poh ays vah'lee-doh ays'tay . . .?*	For how long is this ticket good?

---

pers. pl. of the ind. present subj. and imp. *Almorzar*, to have lunch: *almuerzo*, I have lunch; *almuerza*, he has lunch; *almorzamos*, we have lunch; *almuerzan*, they have lunch.   6. *Billete*, ticket, is called in Mexico, Central and South America *boleto* (boh-lay'toh). Both words mean the same thing.   7. The adjectives *bueno*, good, *malo*, bad, *ninguno*, no one, *primero*, first, and *postrero*, last, drop the *o*

13 Un billete de ida y vuelta es bueno[7] por diez (10) días.

14 ¿Dónde está el despacho de equipajes? Deseo facturar mis baúles.

15 Haga el favor de darme[8] el talón de mi equipaje.

16 Aquí tiene[9] su talón, Sra.[10] García.

17 ¿Cuánto pesa mi baúl?

18 Su baúl pesa cincuenta (50) kilos.[11]

19 Subamos al coche. El tren se pone en marcha.

20 Aquí tiene un buen asiento. ¿Tiene usted una **guía-itinerario**?

21 No, pero sé que la llegada será mañana por la mañana.[12]

22 Entonces llegaremos al muelle a tiempo para tomar el vapor.

23 ¿Tiene usted el pasaje para su camarote?

24 Aun no; pero lo[13] compraré al llegar al puerto en la agencia de pasajes.

---

before a masculine noun in the singular, but keep it when they are placed after the noun: *un buen caballo* (kah-bah'llioh), a good horse, or *un caballo bueno*, etc. **8.** The INDIRECT OBJECT PERSONAL PRONOUNS are always placed before the verb except when used with an infinitive, (as in this case) or with the imperative or the gerund. In these cases they are joined to the verb as suffixes, thus forming one word. **9.** *Tiene*, has, is the 3rd pers. sing., present indicative, of the irregular verb *tener* (tay-nairr'), to have; the 1st person is *tengo* (tayn'goh), I have. **10.** *Sra.* is the abbreviation for *señora*, madam, and is written with a capital letter, as is also *Sr.*, the abbreviation for *señor*, sir. **11.** A kilo is 2.2 lbs. **12.** *Mañana*

13 . . . *day ee'dah ee . . . ays bway'noh . . . dee-ayth' dee' ahs.*

A round trip ticket is good for ten (10) days.

14 *¿. . . ays-tah' ell days-pah' choh day ay-kee-pah'hays? Day-say'oh fahk - too - rahrr' mees bah-oo'lays.*

Where is the baggage office? I wish to check my trunks.

15 *hah gah . . . fah-vorr' day dahrr'may ell tah-lohn' day mee . . .*

Please give me the check for my baggage.

16 *ah-kee' tee-ay'nay soo . . . say-nioh'rah Gahrr'thee' ah.*

Here is your check, Mrs. Garcia.

17 *¿. . . pay'sah mee bah-ool'?*

How much does my trunk weigh?

18 *soo . . . pay'sah theen-kwayn' tah kee'lohs.*

Your trunk weighs fifty (50) kilograms.

19 *soo-bah'mohs ahl coh'chay. Ell train say poh'nay . . . mahrr'chah.*

Let us get in the car. The train is starting.

20 *ah-kee' tee-ay'nay . . . bwayn ah-see-ayn'toh. ¿. . . oo'nah ghee'ah ee-tee-nay-rah'ree-oh?*

Here you have a good seat. Have you a time table?

21 *noh, pay'roh say . . . lliay-gah-dah say-rah' . . . pohrr lah . . .*

No, but I know that the train arrives tomorrow morning.

22 *ayn-tohn'thays lliay-gah-ray' mohs ahl mway' lliay ah tee-aym'poh pah'rah toh-mahrr' ell . . .*

Then we shall arrive at the pier in time to take the boat.

23 *¿tee-ay'nay . . . ell pah-sah' hay pah'rah soo kah-mah-roh' tay?*

Have you the ticket for your cabin?

24 *ah-oon' noh; pay'roh . . . kohm-prah-ray' ahl lliay - gahrr' . . . pwayrr'toh . . . ah-hayn'thee-ah day pah-sah'hays.*

Not yet, but I shall buy it at the ticket office upon arriving at the port.

---

means *tomorrow*, but when *la* precedes the word (*la mañana*) it means *the morning*. 13. *Lo* (it) and *los*, *las* (them) as in the case of *me*, *te*, *le*, etc., are always placed before the verb, except with the imperative, the infinitive and the gerund, in which cases these pronouns are placed after the verb, thus forming only one word.

25 El Sr. Sánchez va a Buenos Aires en aeroplano.

26 ¿De veras? Me gustaría hacer un viaje por avión.

27 Desearía visitar un aeródromo antes de embarcar.

28 Muy bien, visitaremos el aeródromo del cual salen aviones para todos los países de Sur América.

25 *ell . . . Sahn'chayth vah ah Bway'nohs I-rays . . . ah-ay-roh-plah'noh.*

Mr. Sánchez is going to Buenos Aires by airplane.

26 *¿day vay'rahs? May goos-tah-ree'ah ah-thayrr' . . . vee-ah' hay . . . ah-vee-on'.*

Really? I should like to take a trip by airliner.

27 *day - say - ah - ree'ah vee-see-tahrr' . . . ah-ay-roh'droh-moh ahn'tays day aym - bahrr - kahrr'.*

I should like to visit an airport before sailing.

28 *mwee bee-ayn' vee-see-tah-ray' mohs ell . . . dayl kwahl sah' laygn ah-vee-oh'nays pah'rah toh'dohs lohs pah-ee'says . . . Soor . . .*

Very well, we shall visit the airport from which airliners leave for all the South American countries.

5 LECCION QUINTA

Nuevo Vocabulario

a (*ah*)	to		¿cuántos? (*kwahn'tohs*)	how many?
de (*day*)	from (of)		una vez (*oo'nah vaith*)	once
¿sabe? (*sah'bay*)	do you know?		quincena (*keen-thay'nah*)	a fortnight
hasta (*ahs'tah*)	up to, until		doble (*doh'blay*)	double
allí (*ah-lliee'*)	there		¿cuáles? (*kwah'lays*)	which?
en (*ayn*)	in, on, at		gruesa (*grway'sah*)	gross

contar (*kohn-tahrr'*)	to count	
más . . . que (*mahs . . . kay*)	more . . . than	
menos . . . que (*may'nohs . . . kay*)	less . . . than	

lo mismo (*loh mees'moh*)	the same
frecuentemente (*fray-kwayn'tay-mayn'tay*)	frequently
comúnmente (*koh-moon' mayn'tay*)	commonly
tantos . . . como (*tahn'tohs . . . koh'moh*)	as many . . . as
cuadernos (*kwah-dairr'nohs*)	notebooks
la próxima vez (*prohk'see-mah vaith*)	next time
la última vez (*ool'tee-mah vaith*)	last time
más o menos (*mahs oh may'nohs*)	more or less

Los Números Ordinales

THE ORDINAL NUMBERS   (*lohs noo-may-rohs or-dee-nah-lays*)

PRIMERA CLASE   SEGUNDA CLASE   TERCERA CLASE

1o.9	1a.9	primero, -ra	(*pree-may'roh, -rah*)		1st
2o.	2a.	segundo, -da	(*say-goon'doh, -dah*)		2nd
3o.	3a.	tercero, -ra	(*tairr-thay'roh, -rah*)		3rd
4o.	4a.	cuarto,	-ta	(*kwahrr'toh, -tah*)	4th
5o.	5a.	quinto,	-ta	(*keen'toh, -tah*)	5th
6o.	6a.	sexto,	-ta	(*sayks'toh, -tah*)	6th
7o.	7a.	séptimo,	-ma	(*sayp'tee-moh, -mah*)	7th
8o.	8a.	octavo,	-va	(*ohk-tah'voh, -vah*)	8th
9o.	9a.	noveno,	-na	(*noh-vay'noh, -nah*)	9th
10o.	10a.	décimo,	-ma	(*day'thee-moh, -mah*)	10th
11o.	11a.	undécimo,	-ma	(*oon-day'thee-moh, -mah*)	11th
12o.	12a.	duodécimo,	-ma	(*doo-oh-day'thee-moh, -mah*)	12th

LOS NÚMEROS CARDINALES

The Cardinal Numbers   (*lohs noo'may-rohs car-dee-nah-lays*)

0. cero (*thay'roh*)	**6.** seis (*say'ees*)	**13.** trece (*tray'thay*)
1. uno,[1] *masc.* (*oo'noh*).	**7.** siete (*see-ay'tay*)	**14.** catorce
una, *fem.* (*oo'nah*)	**8.** ocho (*oh'choh*)	(*kah-tohrr'thay*)
2. dos[2] (*dohs*)	**9.** nueve (*nway'vay*)	**15.** quince (*keen'thay*)
3. tres (*trays*)	**10.** diez (*dee-ayth'*)	**16.** diez y seis[3]
4. cuatro (*kwah'troh*)	**11.** once (*ohn'thay*)	**17.** diez y siete
5. cinco (*theen'koh*)	**12.** doce (*doh'thay*)	**18.** diez y ocho

19. diez y nueve	**100.** ciento[5] (*thee-ayn'toh*)
20. veinte (*vayin'tay*)	**200.** doscientos[6] (*dohs-thee-ayn'tohs*)
21. veintiuno (*vayin-tee-oo'noh*)	**300.** trescientos (*trays . . .*)
22. veintidós (*vayin-tee-dohs'*)	**400.** cuatrocientos (*kwah-troh . . .*)
23. veintitrés, etc. (*vayin-tee-trays'*)	**500.** quinientos (*kee-nee-ayn'tohs*)
30. treinta (*trayin'tah*)	**600.** seiscientos (*say-ees-thee-ayn'*
31. treinta y uno (*trayin'tah ee oo'*	*tohs*)
noh)	**700.** setecientos (*say-tay . . .*)
40. cuarenta (*kwah-rayn'tah*)	**800.** ochocientos (*oh-choh . . .*)
50. cincuenta[4] (*theen-kwayn'tah*)	**900.** novecientos (*noh-vay . . .*)
60. sesenta (*say-sayn'tah*)	**1000.** mil[7] (*meel*)
70. setenta (*say-tayn'tah*)	**2000.** dos mil[8] (*dohs meel*)
80. ochenta (*oh-chayn'tah*)	**1,000,000.** un millón (*oon mee*
90. noventa (*noh-vayn'tah*)	*lliohn'*)

Las Fracciones

Fractions   (*frak-thee-oh-nays*)

la mitad,[10] **medio, -a**	(*may'dee-oh, -ah*)	one-half
un tercio	(*oon tairr'thee-oh*)	one-third
tres cuartos	(*trays kwahrr'tohs*)	three-quarters
un doceavo[11]	(*oon doh-thay-ah'voh*)	one-twelfth

CONVERSATION

1 ¿Sabe¹² usted contar?

2 Sí, señor; yo sé contar.

3 Cuente¹³ usted.

4 Uno, dos, tres, cuatro y cinco.

5 Usted contó de uno a cinco.

6 ¿Sabe la señorita Morales contar hasta ciento?

7 Sí, señor; yo sé contar hasta ciento.

8 ¿Cuáles son los números ordinales, Sr. Gómez?

9 Los números ordinales son: Primero, segundo, tercero, cuarto, quinto, etc.

10 Yo tengo diez libros. ¿Cuántos libros tiene¹⁴ usted?

11 Yo tengo la mitad; yo tengo cinco.

12 Entonces usted tiene tantos¹⁵ libros como yo, ¿no es verdad?

13 No, señor; yo tengo menos libros que usted.

14 La señorita Martínez tiene tres sombreros y yo sólo tengo uno.

FOOTNOTES: *1. Uno,* one, loses the final *-o* before a masculine noun, *un libro. Una is the feminine.* *2. Dos, tres,* etc., up to *novento y nueve,* are unalterable, as: *dos hombres,* two men; *dos mujeres,* two women. *3.* It is correct to use either *diez y seis, diez y siete,* etc., or simply *dieciséis, diecisiete,* etc. From 20 to 29 one word is used, thus: *veintiuno veintidós, veintitrés,* etc. From 30 up to 99, three words are used, viz.: *treinta y uno, treinta y dos,* etc. *4. Cincuenta y uno, cincuenta y dos, cincuenta y tres,* etc. *5. Ciento* loses its final syllable *-to* when placed immediately before a noun or adjective, as: *cien libros,* one hundred books; *cien buenos libros,* one hundred good books. It must be noticed that the *y* (and) is omitted where zero is the figure before the last, thus: *ciento uno,* instead

PRONUNCIATION	TRANSLATION
1 *¿sah'bay . . . kohn-tahrr'?*	Do you know how to count?
2 *see, say-niohrr', yoh say . . .*	Yes, sir, I know how to count.
3 *kwayn'tay . . .*	You count.
4 *oo'noh, dohs, trays, kwah' troh ee theen'koh.*	One, two, three, four and five.
5 *. . . kohntoh' day oo'noh ah theen'koh.*	You counted from one to five.
6 *¿ . . . ahs'tah theeayn'toh?*	Does Miss Morales know how to count up to one hundred?
7 *. . .*	Yes, sir, I know how to count up to one hundred.
8 *¿kwah'lays sohn lohs noo' may-rohs ohrr-dee-nah' lays, say-niohrr Goh' mayth?*	Which are the ordinal numbers, Mr. Gómez?
9 *. . . : pree-may'roh, say-goon' doh, tairr-thay'roh, kwahr'toh, keen'toh, ayt-thay'tay-rah.*	The ordinal numbers are: First, second, third, fourth, fifth, etc.
10 *yo tayn'goh . . . leebrohs. ¿kwahn'tohs . . . teeay'nay oos-tayd'?*	I have ten books. How many books have you?
11 *. . . lah mee-tahd';. . .*	I have half that number; I have five.
12 *ayn-tohn'thays . . tahn'tohs koh'moh yoh . . .*	Then you have as many books as I. Is it not so?
13 *. . . may'nohs . . . kay . . .*	No, sir, I have fewer books than you.
14 *lah say-nioh-ree'tah Mahrr-tee'nayth . . . sohm-bray'rohs.*	Miss Martinez has three hats and I have only one.

of *ciento y uno; cientos dos, ciento tres,* instead of *ciento y dos, ciento y tres,* etc.
6. *Doscientos,* etc., up to *novecientos,* also have feminine forms; viz., *doscientas casas,* two hundred houses; *quinientas personas,* five hundred persons.   7. *Mil* is invariable as a numeral, thus: *cien mil, doscientos mil.* When used as a noun it has a plural, as: *muchos miles de pesos,* many thousands of dollars.   8. Such English expressions as, eleven hundred, eighteen hundred, etc., are rendered in Spanish by *mil ciento,* one thousand one hundred; *mil ochocientos,* one thousand eight hundred.   9. ¹º· is the abbreviation for *primero,* (masc.) first, and ¹ª· for *primera,* (fem.) first.   10. *Mitad* is synonymous with *medio,* but the former is a noun, while the latter is an adjective. *Medio* therefore also takes the feminine gender, as *media libra de azúcar,* half a pound of sugar; *media vara de paño,* half a yard of

15 Ella tiene más[16] sombreros que yo.

16 Una vez yo compré una gruesa de cuadernos.

17 La próxima vez no necesitará usted comprar tantos.

18 La última vez que estuve en La Habana fué mi quinto viaje a esa ciudad.

19 Yo he estado allí veinte veces.

20 Esta vez voy a ir a Lima, Perú.

21 Un pasaje a la Argentina vale el doble que a Colombia, ¿no es verdad?

22 Sí, señor; aproximadamente. Y un pasaje a Montevideo cuesta más[16] o menos lo mismo que a Buenos Aires.

---

cloth. *11.* In the fractional numbers the particle *-avo* corresponds to the English *-th,* and is variable: *avo, avos* (masc. sing. and pl.); *ava, avas* (fem. sing. and pl.). *12. Sabe,* from *saber,* to know, an irregular verb, is the 3rd pers. sing. of the present indicative. The 1st pers. is *sé,* I know. *13. Cuente,* from *contar,* to count, is the 3rd pers. sing. of the imperative. *14. Tiene,* has, is the 3rd pers. sing. present indicative of *tener,* to have. *Tengo,* I have; *tenemos,* we have; *tienen,* they have. *15. Tanto, tanta,* so much, as much, and *tantos, tantas,* so many, as many (pl.), are adverbs of quantity and are used before nouns; *tan* meaning *so, as,* is used with adjectives and adverbs. The comparative expressions, *as*

15 ...

She has more hats than I.

16 *oo'nah vayth yoh kohm-pray' ... grway'sah day kwah-dairr' nohs.*

Once I bought a gross of note-books.

17 *lah prohk'see-mah . . . nay-thay-see-tah-rah' tahn'tohs.*

Next time you will not have to buy so many.

18 *. . . ool'tee-mah . . . ays-too' vay . . . Ah-bah'nah fway' me keen'toh vee-ah'hay ah ay'sah theew-dahd'.*

The last time I was in Havana it was my fifth trip to that city.

19 *yoh ayh ays-tah'doh ah-lliee' vayin'tay vay' thays.*

I have been there twenty times.

20 *ays'tah vayth voh'ee ah eerr ah Lee'mah, Pay-roo'.*

This time I am going to Lima, Peru.

21 *. . . pah-sah'hay . . . Ahrr-hayn-tee'nah vah'lay ell doh' blay kay ah Koh-lohm'bee-ah.*

A steamship ticket to Argentina costs twice as much as to Co-lombia, is it not so?

22 *. . . ah-prohk-see-mah' dah-mayn'tay . . . Mohn-tay-vee-day'oh kways'tah mahs oh may'nohs loh mees'moh . . . Bway'nohs I'rays.*

Yes, approximately. And a pas-sage to Montevideo costs more or less the same as to Buenos Aires.

much as, or so much as, are rendered in Spanish by, *tanto como* and *tanta como* (sing.) ; as many as and so many as become *tantos como* and *tantas como* (pl.). 16. The comparatives of *superiority* and *inferiority* are formed by placing the comparative particles *más* and *menos*, respectively, before the adjective or adverb, and *que* after, viz.: Mi hermano es *más* rico *que* yo; my brother is *richer* than I. Yo tengo *menos* dinero *que* él; I have *less* money *than* he. *Que*, than, changes to *de* in numeral comparatives, viz.: El tiene *más* (menos) *de* mil pesos; He has *more* (less) *than* a thousand dollars.

6 LECCION SEXTA

Nuevo Vocabulario

el frío (*ell free'oh*)	the cold	**consta** (*cohns'tah*)	it consists of	
el calor (*kah-lohrr'*)	heat	**descanso** (*days-kahn'soh*)	rest	
¿cómo? (*coh'moh*)	how?	**ni ... ni** (*nee ... nee*)	neither ... nor	
dura (*doo'rah*)	it lasts	**pasado** (*pah-sah'doh*)	last, past	

el sol se pone (*... say poh'nay*) the sun sets
pasado mañana (*pah-sah'doh mah-niah'nah*) day after to-morrow
anteayer (*ahn-tay-ah-yairr'*) day before yesterday
se divide (*say dee-vee'day*) it is divided
se compone (*say cohm-poh'nay*) it is composed of

hace buen tiempo it is good weather
(*... bwayn ...*)
hace calor (*...kah-lohrr'*) it is warm weather
hace frío (*...free'oh*) it is cold

comienza (*coh-mee-ayn'thah*) it begins
día de fiesta (*dee'ah day fee-ays'tah*) holiday
hace mal tiempo (*ah'thay mahl tee-aym'poh*) it is bad weather
exactamente (*ayk-sahk-tah-mayn'tay*) exactly
llamamos (*lliah-mah'mohs*) we call
anochece (*ah-noh-chay'thay*) it gets dark

Meses Del Año

(*may-says del ahnioh*)

enero (*ay-nay'roh*)	January	
febrero (*fay-bray'roh*)	February	
marzo (*mahrr'thoh*)	March	
abril (*ah-breel'*)	April	
mayo (*mah'yoh*)	May	
junio (*hoo'neeoh*)	June	
julio (*hoo'leeoh*)	July	

agosto (*ah-gohs'toh*) August
septiembre (*sayp-tee-aym'bray*) September
octubre (*ohk-too'bray*) October
noviembre (*noh-veeaym'bray*) November
diciembre (*dee-theeaym'bray*) December

64

EL DÍA • EL AÑO • LAS ESTACIONES

(ell dee'ah, ell ah'nioh, lahs aystah-thee-oh'nays)

THE DAY, THE YEAR, THE SEASONS

la mañana (*mah-niah'nah*)	the morning	**el día** (*dee'ah*)	the day
la tarde (*tahrr'day*)	afternoon	**el mes** (*mays*)	month
el verano (*vay-rah'noh*)	Summer	**el año** (*ah'nioh*)	year
el otoño (*oh-toh'nioh*)	Autumn	**el siglo** (*see'gloh*)	century
la aurora (*ahw-roh'rah*)	dawn	**la fecha** (*fay'chah*)	date

la noche (*noh'chay*)	the evening, night
la semana[1] (*say-mah'nah*)	week
la primavera (*pree-mah-vay'rah*)	Spring
el invierno (*een-vee-ayrr'noh*)	Winter

hoy (*oh'ee*)	today
ayer (*ah-yairr'*)	yesterday
mañana (*mah-niah'nah*)	to-morrow

el amanecer (*ah-mah-nay-thayrr'*)	the daybreak
la puesta del sol (*pways'tah dayll sohl*)	sunset
la madrugada (*mah-droo-gah'dah*)	sunrise
el mediodía (*may-déeoh-dee'ah*)	midday, noon
la media noche (*may'dee-ah noh'chay*)	midnight

Días De La Semana

DAYS OF THE WEEK
(dee-ahs day la se-mah-nah)

lunes (*loo'nays*)	Monday	**jueves** (*hoo-ay'vays*)	Thursday
martes (*mahrr'tays*)	Tuesday	**viernes** (*vee-ayrr'nays*)	Friday
miércoles (*mee-ayrr'coh-lays*)	Wednesday	**sábado** (*sah'bah-doh*)	Saturday
		domingo (*doh-meen'goh*)	Sunday

CONVERSATION

1 ¿Cómo se divide el día?

2 El día se divide en mañana, tarde y noche.

3 La mañana dura[2] hasta las doce del día, mediodía. La tarde dura hasta el anochecer.

4 ¿Cuándo comienza la noche?

5 La noche comienza exactamente cuando el sol se pone.

6 ¿A qué llamamos la madrugada?[3]

7 La madrugada es muy temprano en la mañana, poco después del amanecer (la aurora).

8 ¿De cuántos días se compone una semana?

9 Una semana se compone de siete días.

10 ¿Qué día de la semana es hoy?

11 Hoy es lunes, el primer día de la semana. El último día es el domingo, que es un día de fiesta o de descanso.

12 ¿Qué día será[4] mañana?

13 Mañana será martes y pasado mañana[5] será miércoles.

14 ¿Fué ayer miércoles?

15 No, señor; ayer fué domingo, y anteayer[6] fué sábado.

FOOTNOTES: *1.* From the Latin *septemana*, siete mañanas (seven morns), the space of seven days. *2. Dura*, from *durar*, to last, implies duration of time: *¿Cuánto tiempo dura la travesía de Nueva York a Europa?* How long does it take

PRONUNCIATION	TRANSLATION

PRONUNCIATION

1 *¿koh'moh say dee-vee'day ell dee'ah?*

2 . . . *mah-niah'nah, tahrr' day ee noh'chay.*

3 . . . *doo'rah ahs'tah lahs doh' thay . . . may'deeoh-dee'ah . . . ah-noh-chay-thairr'.*

4 *¿kwahn'doh koh - meeayn' thah . . . ?*

5 . . . *ayk-sahk'tah-mayn'tay . . .*

6 *¿ah . . . lliah-mah'mohs mah-droo-gah'dah?*

7 . . . *mwee' taym-prah'noh . . . days-pways' dell ah-mah-nay-thairr' (aw-roh'rah).*

8 *¿day kwahn'tohs . . . say kohm-poh'nay oo'nah say-mah'nah?*

9 . . . *seeay'tay dee'ahs.*

10 *¿ . . . oh'ee?*

11 . . . *ell pree-mairr' . . .*

12 *¿ . . . say-rah' . . . ?*

13 . . . *mahrr'tays . . . mee-airr' koh-lays.*

14 *¿fway' ah-yairr' . . . ?*

15 . . . *doh-meen'goh . . . ahn-tay-ah-yairr' . . . sah'bah-doh.*

TRANSLATION

How is the day divided?

The day is divided into morning, afternoon, and evening (or night).

The morning lasts until twelve o'clock noon, midday. The afternoon lasts until dark.

When does the evening begin?

The evening begins exactly when the sun sets.

What do we call sunrise?

Sunrise is very early in the morning, a little after daybreak, (dawn).

How many days are there in a week?

A week consists of seven days.

What day of the week is it today?

Today is Monday, the first day of the week. The last day is Sunday, which is a holiday, or a day of rest.

What day will it be tomorrow?

Tomorrow it will be Tuesday and the day after tomorrow will be Wednesday.

Was yesterday Wednesday?

No, sir, yesterday was Sunday, and the day before yesterday was Saturday.

---

to cross from New York to Europe?   3. *Madrugada*, from *madrugar*, meaning *to rise with the dawn*.   4. The English neuter pronoun *-it*, when accompanying the verb to be, *ser*, or any other verb is never translated in Spanish. *It is*, or *is it*,

16 ¿Puede usted decirme cómo se divide el año?

    17 El año se divide en doce meses.

    18 ¿En qué mes estamos?

    19 Estamos en septiembre, el mes pró-
ximo será octubre y el mes pasado
fué agosto.

    20 ¿Cuál es el primer mes del año?

    21 El primer mes del año es enero y
el último es diciembre.

    22 ¿Cuántas estaciones hay en el año?

23 El año tiene cuatro estaciones, que son: la primavera, el
verano, el otoño y el invierno.

24 ¿Cuáles son los meses de la primavera?

25 Los meses de la primavera son:
marzo, abril y mayo.

26 ¿Hace mal o buen tiempo en esta
estación?[7]

27 En la primavera hace generalmente buen tiempo, ni[8] mucho frío, ni[8]
mucho calor.

28 ¿Cuáles son los meses del verano?

29 Los meses del verano son: junio, julio y agosto.

30 ¿Hace frío en esta estación?

31 No, señor; en el verano hace siempre calor.

32 ¿Cuántos años tiene un siglo?

33 Un siglo tiene cien años.

---

for instance, is always *es* (is). *Será*, as in this case, is translated *will be.*   5. *Pasado mañana*, lit. passed tomorrow.   6. *Anteayer*, lit. before yesterday.   7. *Estación* in this case means season.   8. *Ni-ni* means neither-nor: *no hace ni frío ni calor,*

16 *¿pway'day . . . day-theer'may . . . ah'nioh?*	Can you tell me how the year is divided?
17 *. . . doh'thay may'says.*	The year is divided into twelve months.
18 *¿ . . . mays ays-tah'mohs?*	In what month are we now?
19 *. . . sayp-teeaym'bray . . . prohk'see-moh . . . ohk-too' bray . . . ah-gohs'toh.*	We are in September, next month will be October and last month was August.
20 *¿kwahl' . . . ?*	Which is the first month of the year?
21 *. . . ay-nay'roh . . . ool'tee-moh ays dee-thee-aym'bray.*	The first month of the year is January, and the last is December.
22 *¿ . . . ays-tah-theeoh'nays Í . . . ?*	How many seasons are there in the year?
23 *. . . pree-mah-vay'rah, vay-rah'noh, oh-toh'nioh . . . een-veeairr'noh.*	The year has four seasons, which are: Spring, Summer, Autumn and Winter.
24 *¿kwah'lays sohn . . . ?*	Which are the months of the Spring?
25 *. . . mahrr'thoh, ah-breel' ee mah'yoh.*	The Spring months are: March, April and May.
26 *¿ah'thay mahl oh bwayn teeaym'poh . . . ays'tah . . . ?*	Is the weather bad or good in this season?
27 *. . . nee moo'choh free'oh nee . . . kah-lohrr'.*	In the Spring the weather is generally good, neither too cold nor too warm.
28 *¿ . . . ?*	Which are the Summer months?
29 *. . . hoo'neeoh, hoo'leeoh, ah-gohs'toh.*	The Summer months are: June, July and August.
30 *¿ . . . ?*	Is the weather cold in this season?
31 *. . . seeaym'pray kah-lohrr'.*	No, sir; in the Summer it is always warm.
32 *¿kwahn'tohs ah'niohs tee-ay' nay oon see'gloh?*	How many years are there in a century?
33 *. . . theeyan' . . .*	A century has one hundred years.

---

it is neither cold nor warm. The use of two negatives makes the phrase more emphatic in Spanish as in the above sentence.

7 LECCION SEPTIMA

Nuevo Vocabulario

componer (*kohm-poh-nairr'*)	to repair, fix
compuesto (*kohm-pways'toh*)	repaired, fixed
la compostura (*kohm-pohs-too'rah*)	the repair
descompuesto (*days-kohm-pways'toh*)	out of order
señalar (*say-niah-lahrr'*)	to show, point
dispénseme (*dees-payn'say-may*)	excuse me
hay que (*I kay*)	it is necessary

¿qué hora es?	what time is it?
(*kay oh'rah ays*)	
es la una (*ays la oo'nah*)	it is one o'clock
son las dos (*sohn lahs dohs*)	it is two o'clock

sucio (*soo'thee-oh*)	dirty	se llama (*say lliah'mah*)	it is called, named
nuevo (*nway'voh*)	new	cerca (*thairr'kah*)	near
el resto (*rays'toh*)	the rest	servirle (*sairr-veer'lay*)	to serve you
aun (*ah-oon'*)	yet, still	en casa (*ayn kah'sah*)	at home
sino (*see'noh*)	but	más que (*mahs kay*)	more than

dentro de (*dayn'troh day*)	within
por menos (*porr may'nohs*)	for less

lo examine (*loh ayk-sah-mee'nay*)	examine it
limpiarlo (*leem-pee-ahrr'loh*)	to clean it

un reloj de oro (*-oh'roh*)	a gold watch
un minuto (*-mee-noo'toh*)	minute
un segundo (*say-goon'doh*)	second
un reloj de diamantes (*-dee-ah-mahn'tays*)	diamond watch
dar la hora (*dahrr-*)	to strike the hour
adelantado (*ah-day-lahn-tah'doh*)	fast
atrasado (*ah-trah-sah'doh*)	slow
parado (*pah-rah'doh*)	stopped

LA HORA • EL RELOJ • EL RELOJERO
(lah oh'rah, ell rray-loh', ell rray-loh-hay'roh)

THE HOUR (TIME), THE WATCH, THE WATCHMAKER

el reloj (*rray-loh'*)	the watch
el reloj de bolsillo (*-bohl-see'llio*)	pocket watch
el reloj de pared (*-pah-raid'*)	wall clock
el reloj de pulsera (*pool-say'rah*)	wrist watch
el horario (*oh-rah'ree-oh*)	hour hand
el minutero (*mee-noo-tay'roh*)	minute hand
las manecillas (*mah-nay-thee'lliahs*)	hands (of a watch)
la relojería (*rray-loh-hay-ree'ah*)	watch shop
las campanadas (*kahm-pah-nah'dahs*)	strokes of a bell
el relojero (*rray-loh-hay'roh*)	watchmaker
el cristal (*krees-tahl'*)	crystal
una hora (*-oh'rah*)	one hour

el muelle (*mway'lliay*)   the spring
la maquinaria   works, movement
(*mah-kee-nah'ree-ah*)
las piedras (*pee-ay'drahs*)   jewels, stones

FOOTNOTES: *1.* Synonyms in common use, such as *dispénseme, excuseme* and *perdóneme*, are given in different sentences, so that the student may become acquainted with all of them. *Dispénseme*, from *dispensar*, to excuse, is the 3rd pers. of the imperative mood. *To excuse* may also be translated by *excusar* and *perdonar*, to pardon, but *dispensar* is more frequently used. *2.* Son is the 3rd pers. pl., present indicative of *ser*, to be. *It*, as stated before, is not translated. All the hours

CONVERSATION

1 Dispénseme[1] usted, señor; ¿puede usted decirme qué hora es?

2 Sí, señor; son[2] las dos[3] y veinte.

3 ¿Ha dado la una?

4 Sí, señor; es la una en punto.

5 ¿No son más que[4] las tres menos cuarto todavía?[5]

6 Efectivamente, aun no son las tres.

7 ¿No acaban de dar[6] las cuatro?

8 No, Pedro; su reloj[7] no anda[8] bien. Creo que está adelantado[9] cinco minutos.

9 Por el contrario, mi reloj está atrasado[9] un cuarto de hora.

10 ¿Está su reloj atrasado?

11 Creo que está parado; está descompuesto[10] y es necesario llevarlo a casa del relojero.[11]

12 ¿Le ha dado usted cuerda?[12]

13 Sí, pero está[13] sucio y hay que[14] limpiarlo.

14 ¿Dónde hay una relojería buena y barata?

15 En la calle[15] Catorce, número 45, al oeste.

---

except *una*, one, are plural, and the verb must therefore also be in the plural form to agree with them: *Son las dos, las tres*, etc. When inquiring about the time, however, the verb must always be used in the singular, viz.: *¿Qué hora es?* What time is it? 3. *Y*, and, is used in this case to denote the minutes passed after the hour; similarly, *menos*, less, is used to denote the minutes before the hour. The number of hours is always mentioned first, and *hora*, hour, is understood. 4. *Más que*, more than, is synonymous with *sino*, meaning but, viz.: *No tengo más que un libro*,

PRONUNCIATION	TRANSLATION
1 *dees-payn'saymay . . . ¿pway' day . . . day-theerr'may . . . ?*	Excuse me, sir, can you tell me what time it is?
2 *. . .*	Yes, sir, it is twenty (minutes) past two.
3 *¿ah dah'doh lah oo'nah?*	Is it one o'clock (yet)?
4 *. . . ayn poon'toh.*	Yes, it is one o'clock exactly.
5 *¿ . . . may'nohs kwahrr' toh toh-dah-vee'ah?*	Is it not yet more than a quarter to three?
6 *ay-fayk-tee'vah-mayn'tay ah-oon' . . .*	That is right; it is not three o'clock yet.
7 *¿ . . . ah-kah'bahn . . . ?*	Hasn't the clock just struck four?
8 *. . . soo rray-loh' noh ahn' dah beeayn'. Kray'oh . . . ah-day-lahn-tah'doh . . . mee-noo'tohs.*	No, Pedro, your watch does not keep good time. I believe it is five minutes fast.
9 *. . . kohn-trah'reeoh . . . ah-trah-sah'doh.*	On the contrary, my watch is a quarter of an hour slow.
10 *¿ . . . ?*	Is your watch slow?
11 *. . . pah-rah'doh . . . days-kohm-pways'toh . . . nay-thay-sah'reeoh lliay-vahrr'loh . . . rray-loh-hay'roh.*	I think it has stopped; it is out of order and must be taken to the watchmaker.
12 *¿lay ah dah'doh . . . kwairr' dah?*	Have you wound it?
13 *. . . pay'roh . . . soo'theeoh ee l kay leem-peeahrr'loh.*	Yes, but it is dirty and must be cleaned.
14 *¿dohn'day l oo'nah rray-loh-hay-ree'ah . . . bah-rah'tah?*	Where is there a good and inexpensive watch repair shop?
15 *. . . kah'lliay cah-tohrr'thay noo'may-roh kwah-rayn'tah ee theen'koh.*	At (No.) 45 West Fourteenth Street.

I have but one book.   5. *Todavía,* yet, is used mostly in negative sentences, while *ya,* already, is used in affirmative or interrogative—affirmative sentences, viz.: *No ha venido todavía,* he has not come yet; *Ha venido ya,* he has come already; *¿No ha venido todavía?* Has he not come yet?   6. *Acaban de dar,* idiomatic expression for the clock has just struck. *Acabar de,* to have just, must be always followed by the infinitive of the verb used, as: *Acabo de escribir,* I have just written, or finished writing.   7. *Reloj* means both watch and clock, and each is distinguished by expressing its kind, as: *reloj de bolsillo,* pocket-watch, *reloj de pared,* wall-

16 ¿Cómo se llama[16] (cuál es el nombre de) el relojero?

17 Se llama (su nombre es) Ceballos.

18 El número 45 está cerca de la Sexta Avenida, ¿no es verdad?

19 Sí, señor; está entre las avenidas Quinta y Sexta.

20 ¿Está el Sr. Ceballos en casa?

21 Servidor de usted;[17] ¿en qué puedo servirle?

22 Un amigo mío me ha dado su dirección. ¿Me haría[18] usted el favor de componerme[19] este reloj?

23 Sí, señor; pero debo examinarlo primero.

24 ¿Cuándo lo tendrá usted compuesto? ¿Cuánto me llevará[20] por la compostura?

25 Lo tendré compuesto dentro de[21] cinco días y le costará cinco pesos.

26 Me parece algo caro. ¿ No puede usted hacerlo por menos?

27 No, señor; no puedo; tiene roto[22] el muelle[23] que[24] es necesario poner nuevo.

---

clock, etc. The *-h* of the figured pronunciation must in this instance and in similar cases in which the Spanish word ends in *-j* be pronounced strongly aspirated to give the sound of the Spanish *-j*. All words ending in *-j* are masculine. *8. Anda* from *andar*, to walk, to go, is the 3rd pers. sing., present indicative, and is used when referring to the movement of a watch or clock. *9. Adelantado*, from *adelantar*, to advance, when used in connection with clocks and watches, is synonymous with the English *to gain. Atrasado*, from *atrasar*, to go back, to retard, means *to be slow*. *10. Descompuesto* is the past participle of the irregular verb *descomponer to get out of order*. This is a compound word made up of the prefix *des* and the verb *componer* (to mend, to repair). *11.* Either *a la relojería* or *casa del*

16 ¿ ... *say lliah'mah ... nohm' bray ...?*   What is the name of the watchmaker?

17 ... *Thay-bah'lliohs.*   His name is Ceballos.

18 ... *thairr'kah ... Sayks'tah Ah-vay-nee'dah ... ¿vairr-dahd'?*   Number 45 is near Sixth Avenue, is it not?

19 ... *ayn'tray Keen'tah ...*   Yes sir, it is between Fifth and Sixth Avenues.

20 ¿ ... *ayn cah'sah?*   Is Mr. Ceballos at home?

21 *sairr-vee-dohrr' day ...*   At your service, sir; what can I do for you?

22 ... *ah-mee'goh ... ah dah' doh soo dee-rayk-theeohn'. ¿ ... fah-vohrr' ... kohm-poh-nairr' may ays'tay ...?*   A friend of mine has given me your address; would you please repair this watch for me?

23 ... *day'boh ayk-sah-mee-nahrr'loh pree-may'roh.*   Yes, sir, but I must examine it first.

24 ¿ ... *tayn-drah' ... kohm-pways'toh ... lliay-vah-rah' ... kohm-pohs-too'rah?*   When will you have it repaired? How much will you charge me for it?

25 *loh tayn-dray' ... dayn-troh ... kohs-tah-rah' theen'koh pay'sohs.*   It will be repaired within five days and it will cost you five dollars.

26 *may pah-ray'thay ahl'goh kah' roh ... ¿ah-thairr'loh ... may'nohs?*   It seems to me a little high. Can't you do it for less?

27 ... *rroh'toh ell mway'lliay ... poh-nairr' nway'voh.*   No, sir, I cannot; it has a broken spring and a new one must be put in.

---

relojero may be correctly used.   12. *Dar cuerda a un reloj* means to wind a watch or clock.   13. *Está* is the 3rd pers. sing., present indicative, of the verb *estar*, to be. There are two verbs in Spanish for the English to be, *ser* and *estar*, but they do not have the same meaning. *Ser* is used when the attribute is inherent or essential to the subject and implies a permanent quality of things or persons, rank, condition, position, profession and possession. It answers to the questions *what? what of? what for? whom for?* and *whose?* Examples: *él es alto*, he is tall; *mi reloj es de oro*, my watch is of gold; *los pies son para andar*, the feet are for walking; *este sombrero es para usted*, this hat is for you; *el libro es mío*, the book is mine, etc. *Estar* is used when the state or condition, quality or position of the sub-

28 Y el resto de la maquinaria ¿está buena?

29 Sí, señor; pero tendré que ponerle un cristal nuevo.

30 Bueno,[25] pues; buenas tardes y hasta el jueves.

31 ¿Tiene usted un reloj de bolsillo?

32 Sí, señor; y mi señora tiene un reloj de pulsera de oro.

33 ¿Son caros los relojes de diaman-tes?

34 Naturalmente. Un reloj de dia-mantes, y que tenga de quince a veinte piedras, es siempre caro.

35 ¿Puede usted decirme cuántos mi-nutos tiene una hora?

36 Una hora tiene sesenta minutos, y un minuto, sesenta segundos.

37 ¿Cómo señala el reloj la hora?

38 El reloj señala la hora con dos manecillas: una larga, que se llama minutero, y otra corta que se llama horario.

---

ject is accidental, temporary or transitory. It answers to the questions *where? how?* and *who?* as: *estoy bien,* I am well; *el libro está sobre la mesa,* the book is on the table; *Juan está escribiendo,* John is writing, etc. *Estar* is also used as an auxiliary to the present participle: *él está leyendo,* he is reading, etc. See Grammar, Book II, Auxiliary Verbs.   14. *Hay que* is synonymous with *es necesario,* it is necessary. 15. *Calle* is feminine. In naming numbers of streets, cardinal numbers are used in Spanish instead of ordinal. *Calle Catorce,* street fourteen, instead of, *Calle Decimocuarta,* fourteenth street.   16. *Se llama,* from *llamarse,* to call it or him-self, is a reflexive verb.   17. People wishing to be polite, either in social or busi-ness life, will answer by, *servidor de usted,* your servant, instead of the English, *that is my name.*   18. *Haría,* would do, from *hacer,* to do.   19. *Componer,* to

28 . . . *rrays'toh . . . mah-kee-nah'reeah ¿ays-tah' bway' nah?*

And is the rest of the movement in good condition?

29 . . . *krees-tahl'* . . .

Yes, sir, but I will have to put in a new crystal.

30 . . . *pways . . . tahrr'days ee ahs'tah ell hway'vays.*

Very well then; good afternoon and until Thursday.

31 ¿ . . . *bohl-see'llioh?*

Have you a (pocket) watch?

32 . . . *say-nioh'rah . . . pool-say'rah day oh'roh.*

Yes, and my wife has a gold wrist watch.

33 ¿ . . . *kah'rohs . . .rray-loh' hays day dee-ah-mahn'tays?*

Are diamond watches expensive?

34 . . . *tayn'gah day keen'thay a vain'tay peeay'drahs . . . seeaym'pray . . .*

Naturally. A diamond watch with from 15 to 20 jewels is always expensive.

35 ¿ . . . ?

Can you tell me how many minutes are there in an hour?

36 . . . *say-sayn'tah . . . ee . . . say-goon'dohs.*

One hour has sixty minutes and one minute has sixty seconds.

37 ¿*koh'moh say-niah'lah . . . ?*

How does the clock show the time?

38 . . . *mah-nay-thee'lliahs: . . . lahrr'gah . . . say lliah'mah mee-noo-tay'roh . . . oh'trah kohrr'tah . . . oh-rah'reeoh.*

The clock shows the time with two hands; one long, which is called the minute hand, and a short one which is called the hour hand.

---

mend, to fix, to repair, is synonymous with *arreglar*, to arrange.   20. *Llevará*, from *llevar*, to carry, is in this case used idiomatically for *to charge*.   21. *Dentro de* (lit. inside of) within.   22. *Roto*, broken, is the past participle of *romper*, to break.   23. *Muelle* means *a spring of metal*. *Muelle* means also in Spanish *pier*. 24. *Que* is a RELATIVE PRONOUN, invariable in gender and number. It refers to persons or things only when placed *immediately after the noun* to which it refers, and is used instead of the English *who, whom, which, what* and *that*. The relative pronouns can never be omitted in Spanish. *Que* alone or with a preposition means *what* or *which*, but when referring to persons is replaced by *quien* or *quienes*. 25. *Bueno*, good, as well as *bien*, well, are both exclamations in Spanish. Well then! is rendered by ¡*bueno pues!* or ¡*bien pues!*

8 LECCION OCTAVA

Nuevo Vocabulario

a crédito (*ah kray'dee-toh*)	on credit	
importar (*eem-pohrr-tahrr'*)	to import	
exportar (*ayks-pohrr-tahrr'*)	export	
establecer (*ays-tah-blay-thairr'*)	establish	
sucursal (*soo-koor-sahl'*)	branch (store, office)	
cualquier (*kwahl-kee-airr'*)	any	

comprar (*kohm-prahrr'*)	to buy
al contado (*kohn-tah'doh*)	in cash
vender (*vayn-dairr'*)	to sell

los giros (*hee'rohs*)	the drafts	firma (*feerr'mah*)	firm, concern
el envío (*ayn-vee'oh*)	shipment	contra (*kohn'trah*)	against
el testigo (*tays-tee'goh*)	witness	ambos (*ahm'bohs*)	both
el poder (*poh-dairr'*)	power of attorney	firmado (*feerr-mah'doh*)	signed
los asuntos (*ah-soon'tohs*)	affairs	¿qué hay? (*kay I*)	what is there? (how are things?)

PAGADOR

el banco (*bahn'koh*)	the bank
la ganancia (*gah-nahn'thee-ah*)	profit
la moneda (*moh-nay'dah*)	money, currency

sin duda (*seen doo'dah*)	without doubt
realizaría (*rray-ah-lee-thah-ree'ah*)	would make
para servirle (*pah'rah sairr-veerr'lay*)	at your service
el notario público (*noh-tah'ree-oh*)	the notary public
las restricciones (*rrays-treek-thee-oh'nays*)	restrictions
las transacciones (*trahn-sahk-thee-oh'nays*)	transactions
la cotización (*koh-tee-thah-thee-ohn'*)	quotation
los fertilizantes (*fairr-tee-lee-thahn'tays*)	fertilizers
los artículos (*ahrr-tee'koo-lohs*)	goods
los productos (*proh-dook'tohs*)	products
el comerciante (*koh-mayrr-thee-ahn'tay*)	merchant

78

LOS NEGOCIOS

BUSINESS   (*lohs nay-goh'thee-ohs*)

el **tabaco** (*tah-bah'koh*)	the tobacco
el **coco** (*koh'koh*)	coconut
el **petróleo** (*pay-troh'lay-oh*)	petroleum (crude oil)
el **estaño** (*ays-tah'nioh*)	tin
el **cobre** (*koh'bray*)	copper
el **plátano** (*plah'tah-noh*)	banana
el **cacao** (*kah-kah'oh*)	cocoa
la **lana** (*lah'nah*)	wool
la **piña** (*pee'niah*)	pineapple
las **pieles** (*pee-ay'lays*)	hides
la **carne congelada** (*kahrr'nay kohn-hay-lah'dah*)	frozen meat
la **casa** (*kah'sah*)	house, firm
el **cambio** (*kahm'bee-oh*)	change

los sombreros de paja   straw hats
  (*sohm-bray'rohs -pah'hah*)
las mercancías   merchandise
  (*mairr-kahn-thee'ahs*)

FOOTNOTES: *1. Está,* is. When *to be* refers to the state of one's health, *estar* is always used. *Estoy,* I am; *está,* he, she is, or you are; *estamos,* we are; *están,* they (masc. and fem.) and you (pl.) are. *2. En,* in or on, (prep.). In Spanish, prepositions must be followed by the infinitive instead of the present participle, as in English. *3. Para servir a usted,* to serve you or at your service, is an idiomatic expression in this case. *4. Viene,* 3rd pers. sing., present indicative of the irregular verb *venir,* to come. *Vengo,* I come; *venimos,* we come; *vienen,* they (masc. and fem.) and you (pl.) come. *5. Sólo,* alone or only, as in this case. When thus used as an adverb. instead of *solamente,* the *-o* in the first syllable is accented.

CONVERSATION

1 ¿Cómo está[1] usted? Tengo mucho gusto en[2] verle.

2 Estoy muy bien, gracias; ¿y usted?

3 Para servir[3] a usted, gracias.

4 ¿Viene[4] usted a pasar mucho tiempo en Nueva York?

5 No, señor; vengo sólo[5] (solamente) por unos (algunos) meses para asuntos comerciales (negocios).

6 ¿Y qué hay[6] en Colombia? Sin duda usted estará allí para la próxima primavera.

7 Sí, señor; espero[7] haber arreglado mis asuntos[8] aquí antes de esa fecha.

8 ¿Piensa usted importar algo?[9]

9 Desearía importar café, tabaco, azúcar, lana y algunas frutas.

10 ¿Piensa usted importar esos productos de Cuba y Sur América?

11 De ambas[10] partes; de Cuba recibiré tabaco, azúcar, cocos, plátanos[11] (bananas) y piñas.

12 ¿Y qué recibirá de Sur América?

---

6. *¿Qué hay?* lit. what is there?, is an idiomatic expression commonly used in Spanish, which may be translated by *what is new?* Two Spanish speaking persons, on meeting, will address each other with this question. The answer may be, *nada,* nothing; *nada de nuevo,* nothing new; *que los negocios están muy malos,* that business is very poor; *que todo anda bien,* that everything is all right. There may be many other answers, all referring to different subjects, and all of them being proper replies to the question *¿qué hay?*   7. *Espero,* I expect or hope, 1st pers. sing., present indicative, from the verb *esperar,* synonymous with *aguardar,* to expect or to wait. *Esperar* requires the use of the subjunctive mood when referring to a third

PRONUNCIATION	TRANSLATION
1 ¿ . . . *tayn'goh moo'choh goos'toh . . . vairr'lay.*	How are you? I am very glad to see you.
2 *ays-toh'ee mwee' beeayn' grah' theeahs . . .*	I am very well, thank (you); how are you?
3 *pah'rah sairr-veerr' . . .*	At your service, thank (you).
4 ¿*veeay'nay ah pah-sahrr' . . . Nway'vah Yohrk'?*	Do (have) you come to spend a long time in New York?
5 *. . . vayn'goh . . . pohrr . . . (ahl-goo'nohs) . . .*	No, sir; I (have) come only for a few months on business matters.
6 ¿ *. . . Koh-lohm'bee-ah? Seen doo'dah . . . ah-lliee' . . . pree-mah-vay'rah.*	And how is everything in Colombia? No doubt you will be there by next Spring.
7 *. . . ays-pay'roh ah-bairr' ah-rray-glah'doh mees ah-soon' tohs ah-kee' . . . fay'chah.*	Yes, sir, I expect to have my affairs arranged here before then.
8 ¿*peeayn'sah . . . eem-pohrr-tahrr' ahl'goh?*	Do you intend to import something?
9 *. . . kah-fay', tah-bah'koh, ah-thoo'kahrr, lah'nah . . . froo' tahs.*	I should like to import coffee, tobacco, sugar, wool and some fruits.
10 ¿ *. . . proh-dook'tohs day Koo'bah ee Soorr Ah-may'ree-kah?*	Are you thinking of importing those products from Cuba and South America?
11 *day ahmbahs pahrr'tays; . . . rray-thee-bee-ray' . . . koh' kohs, plah'tah-nohs . . . pee' niahs.*	From both places; from Cuba I shall receive tobacco, sugar, coconuts, bananas and pineapples.
12 ¿ *. . . rray-thee-bee-rah' . . . ?*	And what will you receive from South America?

person, as: *espero que hable* (lit. I expect, or I hope that he may speak); *espero que llegue*, I hope he arrives (lit. I hope that he may arrive). 8. *Asuntos*, is generally used for *affairs*, while *negocios* is translated for *business*. 9. *Algo* means *something* or *anything*; *nada*, the opposite, means *nothing* or *not anything*. 10. *Ambas*, both (fem. pl.), *ambos*, both (masc. pl.). *Partes* is fem. pl. 11. *Plátano* is synonymous with *banana*. 12. *Plazo* is the commercial Spanish word for the English *terms: a plazos*, on credit; *a largo plazo*, on a long credit; *a corto plazo*, on a short credit. 13. *Cuyo*, whose, agrees in gender and number with the noun: *cuyo, cuyos* (masc., sing. and pl.); *cuya, cuyas* (fem., sing. and pl.). *Frente*, front, is in this case masculine; *la frente*, the forehead, is feminine. *Estar al frente*

13 De Sur América recibiré: café, de Colombia; petróleo, de Venezuela; carnes congeladas, de la Argentina; pieles, del Uruguay; estaño, de Bolivia; fertilizantes, del Perú; cobre, de Chile, y cacao y sombreros de paja, del Ecuador.

14 ¿Desea usted vender al contado o a crédito?

15 A algunos comerciantes les venderé a un corto plazo[12] o cambiaré mis productos por artículos norteamericanos.

16 ¿Cómo piensa usted hacer esas transacciones?

17 Mi idea es establecer aquí una sucursal de mi casa de Buenos Aires, a cuyo[13] frente estará un hermano mío.[14]

18 ¿Necesitará él un poder[15] de la casa para hacer legales sus transacciones?

19 Naturalmente; para comprar y vender en nombre de la casa necesitará un poder legalizado.

20 ¿Quién tiene que firmar el poder para que sea válido?

21 Tiene que ser firmado ante[16] un notario público y por dos testigos.

22 ¿A cómo está hoy el cambio con el extranjero?

23 La cotización de la moneda extranjera está muy baja.

24 ¿Podría yo girar dólares a Chile?

---

de, means *to be at the head of.* *14. Mí*, mine, is a possessive adjective and, as such, agrees with the noun in gender and number. The English expressions *of mine, of thine, of his, of hers, of theirs, of ours*, after a noun, are rendered in Spanish without the *of*, as: *un hermano mío*, instead of *un hermano de mío*. The possessive adjectives are: *mío; tuyo*, thine; *suyo*, his, hers and yours; *nuestro*, ours; *vuestro*, yours. *Mío, tuyo, suyo* drop the final syllable before a noun, thus: *mi libro, tu libro, su libro.* But whether they are possessive pronouns or possessive adjectives, they always agree with the *noun*, and not with the *person*, as in English.

13 ... *pay-tro'lay-oh ... kahrr'* *nays kohn-hay-lah'dahs ...* *peeay'lays day Oo-roo-gwah' ee; ays-tah'nioh day Boh-lee' veeah; fairr-tee-lee-than'tays del Pay-roo'; koh'bray day Chee'lay ee kah-kah'oh ee sohm-bray'rohs day pah'hah dell Ay-kwah-dohrr'.*

From South America I shall receive: coffee from Colombia; petroleum from Venezuela; frozen meats from Argentina; hides from Uruguay; tin from Bolivia; fertilizers from Peru; copper from Chile, and cocoa and straw hats from Ecuador.

14 ¿ ... *vayn-dairr' ... kohn-tah'doh ... kray'dee-toh?*

Do you intend to sell for cash or credit?

15 ... *koh-mairr-thee-ahn'tays lays vayn-day-ray' ... plah' thoh oh kahm-bee-ah-ray' mees proh-dook'tohs pohrr arr-tee'koo-lohs norr-tay ah-may-ree-kah'nohs.*

To some merchants I shall sell on short credit; or I shall exchange my products for American goods.

16 ¿*koh'moh ... trahn-sahk-theeoh'nays?*

How do you propose to do this business?

17 *mee ee-day-ah ays ays-tah-blay-tairr ah-kee' ... soo-koor-sahl' ... koo'yoh frayn' tay ... airr-mah'noh mee'oh.*

My idea is to establish here a branch of my Buenos Aires house, at the head of which will be one of my brothers.

18 ¿*nay-thay-see-tah-rah' ell ... ah-thairr' lay-gah'lays ...?*

Will he need a power of attorney from the firm in order to legalize his transactions?

19 *nah-too-rahl'mayn'tay; ... lay-gah-lee-thah'doh.*

Naturally; in order to buy and sell in the firm's name he will need a power of attorney.

20 ¿*keeayn' ... feerr-marr' ... vah'lee-doh?*

Who has to sign a power of attorney to make it valid?

21 *tee-ay'nay ... noh-tah'reeoh poo'blee-koh ... tays-tee'gohs.*

It has to be signed before a notary public and by two witnesses.

22 ¿*ah koh'moh ... ayks-trahn-hay'roh?*

How is the rate for foreign exchange today?

23 *lah koh-tee-tha-theeohn' moh-nay'dah ... mwee'bah'hah.*

The rate of foreign money is very low.

24 ¿*poh-dree'ah ... hee-rarr' doh'lah-rays ah Chee'lay?*

Could I draw dollar drafts for Chile?

For this reason, in the case of *su* or *suyo,* which can refer to: his, her, its, your and their, the following phraseology is used to avoid ambiguity: *su libro de él; su libro*

25 Ahora hay ciertas restricciones para los giros al extranjero; pero creo que le será fácil girar 1,000 dólares contra cualquier banco de Santiago de Chile.

26 También desearía exportar algunas mercancías a Centro América.

27 Si ustedes exportan[17] artículos manufacturados realizaran una buena ganancia.

25 *ah-oh'rah I thee-airr'tahs . . . hee'rohs . . . meel . . . kwahl-kee-airr' . . .*

Right now there are certain restrictions on foreign drafts; but I think you could easily draw a $1,000.00 draft against any bank in Santiago de Chile.

26 *tahm-bee-ayn' . . . mairr-kahn-thee'ahs ah Thayn'troh Ah-may'ree-kah.*

I should also like to export some merchandise to Central America.

27 *see . . . ayks-porr'tahn arr-tee' koo - lohs mah-noo-fahk-too-rah'dohs rray - ah - lee - thah-rahn' . . . gah-nahn'theeah.*

If you (pl.) export manufactured goods you (pl.) will make a good profit.

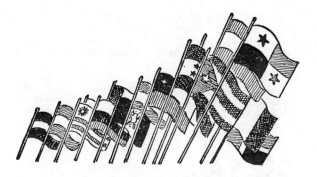

preposition and *delante*, an adverb of place.   17. *Exportan*, from *exportar*, to export; *-an* is the termination of the 3rd pers. pl., present indicative, of all verbs ending in *-ar*.

9 LECCION NOVENA

Nuevo Vocabulario

la lista de platos (*lees'tah plah'tohs*)   the bill of fare
la cafetera (*kah-fay-tay'rah*)   coffee pot
la ensalada (*ayn-sah-lah'dah*)   salad
la salsa (*sahl'sah*)   sauce, dressing
la pimienta (*pee-mee-ayn'tah*)   pepper
la mostaza (*mohs-tah'thah*)   mustard

el **vaso** (*vah'soh*) the drinking glass

la **taza** (*tah'thah*)   cup

el menú (*may-noo'*)   the menu
el filete (*fee-lay'tay*)   cutlet
la jarra (*hah'rrah*)   pitcher
el cajero (*kah-hay'roh*)   cashier

cruda (*kroo'dah*)   raw
salada (*sah-lah'dah*)   salty
sosa (*soh'sah*)   lacking salt
picante (*pee-kahn'tay*)   spicy

el agua de hielo (*ah'gwah day yay'loh*)   ice water
el sacacorchos (*sah-kah-kohrr'chohs*)   corkscrew
desabrida (*day-sah-bree'dah*)   tasteless

el vino tinto (*vee'noh teen'toh*)   red wine
la botella (*boh-tay'lliah*)   bottle

poner la mesa (*poh-nairr' lah may'sah*)   to set the table
al contrario (*ahl kohn-trah'ree-oh*)   on the contrary
a mí me parece (*ah mee may pah-ray'thay*)   it seems to me
bien asada (*beeayn' ah-sah'dah*)   well done
la tortilla (*tohrr-tee'lliah*)   the omelet
el apetito (*ah-pay-tee'toh*)   appetite
el alimento (*ah-lee-mayn'toh*)   food
el azucarero (*ah-thoo-kah-ray'roh*)   sugar bowl

El Restaurante • La Mesa • Los Alimentos
(ell res-tah-ooran'-tay, la may' sah, los ah-lee-men-tohs)

THE RESTAURANT, THE TABLE, THE FOOD

la mesa *(may'sah)*	the table	el mantel *(mahn-tayl')*	the tablecloth
la sal *(sahl)*	salt	el vinagre *(vee-nah'gray)*	vinegar
el pollo *(poh'llioh)*	chicken	el tomate *(toh-mah'tay)*	tomato
el arroz[1] *(ah-rroth')*	rice	el azúcar *(ah-thoo'kahrr)*	sugar

el tenedor *(tay-nay-dohrr')*   the fork
el cuchillo *(koo-chee'llioh)*   knife
la cucharita *(koo-chah-ree'tah)*   teaspoon
el plato *(plah'toh)*   dish, plate

el cubierto *(koo-bee-airr'toh)*   the silverware
la cuchara *(koo-chah'rah)*   spoon
la fuente *(fwayn'tay)*   platter, tray
la servilleta *(sairr-vee-lliay'tah)*   napkin
el camarero *(kah-mah-ray'roh)*   waiter
el aceite *(ah-thay'ee-tay)*   oil, (vegetable)
la lechuga *(lay-choo'gah)*   lettuce
las legumbres *(lay-goom'brays)*   vegetables
las patatas *(pah-tah'tahs)*   potatoes

FOOTNOTES: Nouns ending in -z are for the most part feminine, with the exceptions of *el pez*, the fish; *el matiz*, the hue; *el cáliz*, the chalice; *el capuz*, the hood,
etc. All abstract nouns ending in -ez are also feminine: *la niñez*, childhood: *la
vejez*, old age; *la embriaguez*, intoxication, etc. 2. *Haga* is the 2nd pers. sing.,

CONVERSATION

1 Haga[2] el favor de decirme dónde puedo encontrar un restaurante.

2 En la calle Mayor hay varios restaurantes en los cuales se come muy bien.

3 ¿Desearía usted acompañarme allí?

4 Con mucho gusto.

5 Sentémonos a la mesa. El camarero acaba de ponerla.

6 Esta mesa está cubierta con un mantel[3] blanco.

7 ¿Y qué hay sobre la mesa?

8 Sobre la mesa están los cubiertos: tenedores, cuchillos, cucharas y cucharitas. También hay servilletas, platos, una jarra de agua con hielo y varios vasos.

9 Llamemos al camarero.

10 Camarero (mozo), sírvase[4] traerme el menú (la lista de platos).

11 Yo deseo un plato de sopa, un filete de ternera con legumbres y patatas fritas, un plato de pescado y ensalada de lechuga y tomate.

12 A mí me gusta[5] la carne bien asada.

13 Se dice, sin embargo, que la carne algo[6] cruda es de muchísimo[7] más alimento.

---

polite form, of the imperative of the irregular verb *hacer*. It is also the 3rd pers. sing. of the subjunctive mood. *Haga el favor* is the usual expression for *please.* **3.** Nouns ending in *-l* are masculine, with few exceptions, such as: *la capital*, meaning the capital city of a country; *la cárcel*, the jail; *la col*, the cabbage; *la sal*, the salt; *la vocal*, the vowel; *la señal*, the sign, etc. **4.** *Sírvase*, imperative of

PRONUNCIATION	TRANSLATION
1 *ah'gah . . . fah-vohrr' . . . day-theerr'may . . . pway'doh . . . ayn-kohn-trahrr' . . .*	Please tell me where I can find a restaurant.
2 *. . . kah'lliay Mah-yohrr' . . . kwah'lays . . .*	On Main Street there are several restaurants which serve very good meals.
3 *¿day-say-ah-ree'ah . . . ah-kohm-pah-niahrr'may . . . ?*	Would you like to accompany me there?
4 *. . . goos'toh.*	With great pleasure.
5 *sayntay'moh-nohs . . .*	Let us sit at the table. The waiter has just set it.
6 *ays'tah . . . koo-bee-ayrr'tah . . . mahn-tail' . . .*	This table is covered with a white table cloth.
7 *¿ . . .soh'bray . . . ?*	And what is there on the table?
8 *. . . koo-bee-ayrr'tohs . . . hah' rrah . . . kohn ee-ay'loh . . .*	On the table is the silverware: forks, knives, spoons and teaspoons. There are also napkins, dishes, a pitcher for ice water and several glasses.
9 *lliah-may'mohs . . . kah-mah-ray'oh.*	Let us call the waiter.
10 *. . . (moh'thoh) seerr'vah-say . . . may-noo' . . .*	Waiter, please bring me the menu (the bill of fare).
11 *. . . soh'pah . . . lay-goom' brays . . . lay-choo'gah . . .*	I want a bowl of soup, a veal cutlet with vegetables and fried potatoes, a dish of fish and a lettuce and tomato salad.
12 *. . . kahrr'nay . . .*	I like the meat well done.
13 *. . . dee'thay, seen aym-bahrr' goh . . . moo-chee'see-moh . . .*	They say, however, that meat a little rare is much more nourishing.

servirse, is equivalent in this sense to *please,* and is synonymous with *haga el favor* and *tenga la bondad.* 5. Some verbs, like *gustar, agradar,* to please, to like, when used in a reflexive way, take two object pronouns for emphasis, thus: *a mí me, a ti te, a él le, a nosotros nos, a vosotros os, a ellos les. Gustar,* derived from the noun *gusto,* is generally used in a reflexive way, as: *a usted le gusta,* it pleases you; *a mí me gusta,* it pleases me. *Gustar de* means to be fond of and is used only when referring to activities. 6. *Algo* something, is synonymous with *alguna cosa,* and may be used in Spanish to imply either a question or a statement: *¿Hay algo de nuevo?* Is there anything new? (lit. is there something of new?); *Tengo algo que*

14 A mí, tráigame un poco de arroz con pollo y una botella de vino tinto.

15 ¿Desea ponerle sal, aceite y vinagre a su ensalada?

16 Sí, señor; a menos que ya esté preparada con alguna otra salsa.

17 Yo no tengo apetito porque almorcé tarde, a las once de la mañana, y desearía sólo una tortilla de jamón y huevos.

18 Esta comida está algo salada y picante.

19 Al contrario, a mí me parece un poco sosa (desabrida).

20 Tenga la bondad de pasarme la cafetera; deseo servirme café en esta taza.

21 Aquí tiene el azúcar,[8] en el azucarero.

22 Mozo, sírvase traerme la cuenta. ¿Cuánto es?

23 La comida importa tres pesos y cincuenta centavos. ($3.50) Tenga la bondad de pagar al cajero.

24 Muy bien. Dejemos la propina para el camarero sobre la mesa.

25 Y después de esta suculenta cena, ¿no le parece que debemos dar un paseo?

26 Me agradaría mucho.

---

decir a usted, I have something to tell you. It also means *some, somewhat*, as: *Está algo salada*, it is somewhat salty, etc. The contrary of *algo* is *nada. Aquí no hay nada*, there is nothing here; *¿No hay nada de nuevo?* is there nothing new? *No tengo nada que decirle*, I have nothing to tell you; *¿No tiene usted nada que hacer?* Haven't you anything to do? 7. Although the superlative is formed with *muy, very*, as in English, in Spanish there is another form, stronger in meaning. This

14 ... *trah-ee'gah-may* ... *ah-rrohth'* ... *poh'llioh* ... *boh-tay'lliah* ...

Bring me some chicken with rice and a bottle of red wine.

15 ¿ ... *poh-nayrr'lay* ... *ah-thay'ee-tay* ...?

Do you wish to put salt, oil and vinegar on your salad?

16 ... *may'nohs* ... *ahl-goo'nah* ... *sahl'sah.*

Yes, unless it is already seasoned with some other dressing.

17 ... *ah-pay-tee'toh* ... *ahl-mohrr-thay'* ... *hah-mohn' ee way'vohs.*

I have no appetite, because I had breakfast late, at eleven o'clock, and I should like only a ham and egg omelet.

18 ... *pee-kahn'tay.*

This meal is a bit salty and spicy.

19 ... *kohn-trah'ree-oh* ... *pah-ray'thay* ...

On the contrary, I find it lacking salt a little.

20 ... *bohn-dahd'* ... *pah-sahrr' may* ... *sayrr-veerr'may* ...

Please pass me the coffee pot; I want to serve myself some coffee in this cup.

21 ... *ah-thoo'kahrr* ... *ah-thoo-kah-ray'roh.*

Here is the sugar, in the sugar bowl.

22 *moh-thoh* ... *kwayn'tah.* ¿*kwahn'toh* ...?

Waiter, please bring me the check. How much is it?

23 ... *eem-pohrr'tah* ... *pah-gahrr' ahl kah-hay'roh.*

The meal amounts to three dollars and fifty cents ($3.50). Please pay the cashier.

24 ... *day-hay'mohs* ... *proh-pee'nah* ...

Very well. Let us leave the tip for the waiter on the table.

25 ... *days-pways'* ... *thay' nah* ...

And after this succulent (delicious) supper do you not think that we ought to go for a walk?

26 *may ah-grah-dah-ree'ah moo' choh.*

I should like to very much.

---

form consists of the suffix *-ísimo, -ísima, -ísimos, -ísimas* for the masc. and fem., sing. and pl. respectively, added to the adjective. The adjective sometimes drops the last vowel, as: from *mucho*, much, *muchísimo*, very, very much; from *grande*, large, *grandísimo*, very, very large. When the adjective ends in a consonant there is no change in the word, as: from *fácil*, easy, *facilísmo*, very, very easy. The exceptions to this rule: adjectives ending in *-co, -go, -ca* or *-ga* change these syllables into *-quísimo, -guísimo, -quísima, -guísima*, respectively, as: from *poco*, little, *poquísimo; largo, larguísimo; rica, riquísima*, etc. Those ending in *-ble* change to *bilísimo*, as: from *amable, amabilísimo; admirable, admirabilísimo*, etc.   8. *Azúcar* is masculine, as are almost all nouns ending in *-r*, with the exception of *la flor*, the flower; *la labor*, the labor; *la pleamar*, the high tide; *la bajamar*, the ebb tide.

10 LECCION DECIMA

Nuevo Vocabulario

la **refrigeradora** (*rray-free-hay-rah-dho'rah*)	the **refrigerator**
la **lámpara** (*lahm'pah-rah*)	lamp
los **cuadros** (*kwah'drohs*)	pictures
la **jabonera** (*hah-boh-nay'rah*)	soap dish
la **biblioteca** (*bee-blee-oh tay'kah*)	library
la **electricidad** (*ay-layk-tree-thee-dahd'*)	electricity

el **espejo** (*ays-pay'hoh*) the mirror

el **tocador** (*toh-kah-dohrr'*) boudoir, dresser

estilo moderno modern style
(*ays-tee'loh moh-dairr'noh*)
el **sofá** (*soh-fah'*) sofa
los **sillones** (*see-llioh'nays*) armchairs

el **jardín** (*hahrr-deen'*) the garden

el **patio** (*pah'tee-oh*) inner court

la **toalla** (*toh-ah'lliah*) the towel		**si gusta** (*see goos'tah*)	if you please
la **vajilla** (*vah-hee'lliah*)	table service	**a veces** (*ah vay'thays*)	some times
el **colchón** (*kohl-chohn'*)	mattress	**blando** (*blahn'doh*)	soft
la **madera** (*mah-day'rah*)	wood	la **cocina** (*koh-thee'nah*)	kitchen

amueblados (*ah-mway-blah'dohs*)	furnished
encender (la luz) (*ayn-thayn-dairr'lah looth*)	to put on (the light)
seleccionar (*say-layk-thee-oh-nahrr'*)	to select, choose
duradero (*doo-rah-day'roh*)	durable, lasting
invitados (*een-vee-tah'dohs*)	guests, visitors
apagar (la luz) (*ah-pah-gahrr'*)	to turn off (light)

92

LA CASA • LOS MUEBLES

<small>THE HOUSE, THE FURNITURE</small>   *(lah kah'sah, lohs mway'blays)*

el piso (*pee'soh*) the floor, apartment
la silla (*see'lliah*) chair
la cama (*kah'mah*) bed
la colcha (*kohl'chah*) bedspread
la llave (*lliah'vay*) key
el gas (*gahs*) gas

el piso bajo (*-bah'hoh*) the ground floor
el cuarto (*kwahrr'toh*) room
la alcoba (*ahl-koh'bah*) bedroom
la bañera (*bah-niay'rah*) bathtub
la sábana (*sah'bah-nah*) sheet
la puerta (*pwairr'tah*) door

la escalera (*ays-kah-lay'rah*)   the staircase
los escalones (*ays-kah-loh'nays*)   stairs, steps
el ascensor (*ahs-thayn-sohrr'*)   elevator
la habitación (*ah-bee-tah-thee-ohn'*)   room (to live in)
el dormitorio (*dohrr-mee-toh'ree-oh*)   dormitory
el cuarto de baño (*-bah'nioh*)   bath room
el recibidor (*rray-thee-bee-dohrr'*)[1]   living room
el fregadero (*fray-gah-day'roh*)   kitchen sink
los muebles (*mway'blays*)   furniture
el armario (*arr-mah'ree-oh*)   closet
la cómoda (*koh'moh-dah*)   chest of drawers
las almohadas (*ahl-moh-ah'dahs*)   pillows
la alfombra (*ahl-fohm'brah*)   rug
la ventana (*vayn-tah'nah*)   window
la cortina (*kohrr-tee'nah*)   curtain

FOOTNOTES: *1. La sala,* is another commonly used word meaning *living room.*
2. In some countries *apartamiento* is used.   *3. Para* conveys the general idea of

CONVERSATION

1 Yo vivo en la ciudad. ¿Dónde viven ustedes?

2 Nosotros vivimos en las afueras (en los suburbios).

3 ¿Tiene su casa muchos pisos?

4 No, solamente cuatro, contando el piso bajo.

5 ¿De cuántos cuartos consta su apartamento² (piso)?

6 Mi piso consta de siete habitaciones (piezas): el recibidor, el comedor, dos alcobas o dormitorios, la cocina, el cuarto de baño y la biblioteca.

7 ¿Suben ustedes a su piso por la escalera?

8 No; para³ subir usamos el ascensor.

9 ¿Han sido los cuartos amueblados por usted, señor López?

10 Sí, pero, naturalmente, mi esposa me ayudó⁴ a seleccionar los muebles, que son de estilo moderno.

11 Si no le incomoda, me agradaría que me los enseñara.

12 Tendré⁵ mucho gusto. En primer lugar pasemos al recibidor (cuarto de recibo).

13 Aquí veo un sofá, dos sillones, varias mesitas con sus lámparas y una bonita colección de cuadros.

---

effect; por, of *cause. Para* stands for: (a) *In order to,* as: *Comemos para vivir y no vivimos para comer;* We eat *to* (in order to) live, and we do not live *to* (in order to) eat. (b) *About to,* as: *Estoy para salir;* I am *about to* go out. (c) *Pur-*

Pronunciation	Translation
1 ... *vee'voh* ... *theew-dahd'* ¿ ... *vee'vayn* ... ?	I live in the city. Where do you (pl.) live?
2 *noh - soh'trohs vee - vee'mohs* ... *ah-fway'rahs* ... (*soo-boorr'bee-ohs*).	We live in the outskirts (in the suburbs).
3 ¿ ... *pee'sohs?*	Has your house many floors?
4 ... *kwa'troh* ... *bah'hoh.*	No, only four, including the ground floor.
5 ¿*kwarr'tohs* ... *ah-pahrr-tah-mayn'toh?*	How many rooms are there in your apartment?
6 ... *kohns'tah* ... *ah-bee-tah-thee-oh'nays* ...	My apartment consists of seven rooms: the living room, the dining room, two bedrooms, the kitchen, the bathroom and the library.
7 ¿*soo'bayn* ... *ays-kah-lay' rah?*	Do you go up to your floor by the staircase.
8 ... *soo-beerr'* ... *ahs-thayn-sohrr'.*	No, to go up we use the elevator.
9 ¿ ... *ah-mway-blah-dohs* ... *Loh'payth?*	Have the rooms been furnished by you, Mr. López?
10 ... *ah-yoo-doh'* ... *say-layk-thee-oh-nahrr'* ... *moh-dayrr' noh.*	Yes, but, of course, my wife helped me to select the furniture, which is in the modern style.
11 ... *een-koh-moh'dah* ... *ayn-say-niah'rah.*	If it is not inconvenient to you, I should like to have you show it to me.
12 *tayn-dray'* ... *loo-gahrr'* ... *rray-thee-bee-dohrr'.*	I shall be glad to. Let us go first into the living room.
13 ... *vay'oh* ... *vah'ree-ahs* ... *lahm'pah-rahs* ... *kwah' drohs.*	Here I see a sofa, two armchairs, several small tables with (their) lamps and a lovely collection of pictures.

pose, in expressing the object for which things are made or intended, as: *Esta pluma no sirve para escribir;* This pen is of no use *to* write with. (d) The English *for* when it indicates destination: *Saldré para Méjico mañana;* I shall leave *for*

14 Efectivamente. Y los muebles, como podrá observar, son de caoba, que es una madera tan bella como duradera.

15 ¿De qué son los muebles de su dormitorio?

16 La cama, el tocador, la cómoda, el armario (ropero) y la mesita de noche son de nogal. El tocador y la cómoda están adornados con dos espejos de luna.

17 ¿Son estas alfombras persas?

18 No, señor; son de fabricación nacional y muy buenas.

19 ¡Qué colchón más blando tiene la cama! Y la colcha y las sábanas son preciosas.

20 Pasemos al comedor, si gusta. La mesa del centro es grande porque a veces tenemos invitados. Hay en todo doce sillas y un aparador en el cual guardamos la vajilla y los cubiertos.

21 ¡Qué cocina tan amplia tiene usted! Mientras más[6] la miro, más[6] me gusta.

22 Efectimavente; es tan espaciosa que a veces solemos comer en ella. Tenemos también una refrigeradora moderna y un fregadero para los platos.

Mexico tomorrow. (e) When referring to time, as: *Esta es la lección para el jueves;* This is the lesson for Thursday. (f) Also, *in relation to, in comparison to,* as: *Juan es muy alto para su edad;* John is very tall *for* (in relation to) his age. **4. -ó is**

14 ... *mway'blays* ... *poh-drah'* ... *mah-day'rah* ... *doo-rah-day'rah.*

Yes indeed. And the furniture, as you may see, is of mahogany, which is a wood as beautiful as it is durable.

15 ¿ ... *dohrr-mee-toh'ree-oh?*

What is your bedroom furniture made of?

16 ... *ahrr-mah'ree-os* ... *noh-gahl'* ... *ays-pay'hohs* ... *loo'nah.*

The bed, the dresser, the chest of drawers, the closet (wardrobe) and the small night table are of walnut. The dresser and the chest of drawers (bureau) have two large mirrors.

17 ¿ ... *ahl-fohm'brahs payrr' sahs?*

Are these Persian rugs?

18 ... *nah-thee-oh-nahl'* ...

No, they are of domestic manu-facture, and very good.

19 ... *kohl-chohn'* ... *blahn'doh* ... *kohl' chah* ... *sah'bah-nahs* ...

What a soft mattress the bed has! And the bedspread and sheets are beautiful.

20 ... *thayn'troh* ... *vay'thays* ... *ah-pah-rah-dohrr'* .. *vah-hee'lliah* ...

Let us go into the dining room, if you please. The table in the center is large because some-times we have guests. There are, altogether, twelve chairs and a sideboard in which we keep our table service and silverware.

21 ... *koh-thee'nah* ... *ahm' plee-ah* ...

What a large kitchen you have! The more I look at it the better I like it.

22 ... *ays-pah-thee-oh'sah* ... *soh-lay'mohs koh-mayrr'* ...

Indeed; it is so roomy that we sometimes eat in it. We also have a modern refrigerator and a sink for the dishes.

---

the ending of the 3rd pers. sing., past tense, of the verbs of the 1st conjugation, and it is very important that the accent should not be omitted in writing, as *-o* without accent is the ending of the 1st pers. sing. of the present tense, viz: *yo ayudo,* I help; usted *ayudó,* you helped.   5. *Tendré, I shall have,* future of *tener. Tendrá,* he, she or you will have; *tendremos,* we shall have; *tendrán,* they (masc.

23. ¿Podría ver su cuarto de[7] baño?

24 Está usted en su casa y puede hacer como guste. Ahí[8] encontrará toallas, una jabonera y los demás artículos que necesite para su tocado.

and fem.) will have.   *6.* The English expressions, *the more—the less; the better —the worse,* etc. are rendered in Spanish by *mientras* or *cuanto* followed by the adverbs *más* or *menos,* as: *Cuanto más estudia, más aprende;* The more he studies, the more he learns. *Mientras más libros lee, menos sabe;* The more books he reads, the less he knows. *Tanto* can also be used to emphasize the degree of comparison, as: *Cuanto más tiene, tanto más desea;* The more he has, the more he wishes (to have). *Cuanto menos duerma, tanto mejor será para él;* The less he sleeps, the better it will be for him. *Mientras menos practique el idioma, tanto peor lo hablará;* The less he practices the language, the worse he will speak it.   *7. De* and

23 *¿poh-dree'ah vayrr . . . bah-nioh?*   May I see your bathroom?

24 *. . . goos'tay . . . ah-ee' . . . hah-boh-nay'rah . . . toh-kah' doh.*   You are at home and you may do as you please. There you will find towels, a soap dish and other articles that you may need for your service.

desde mean *of* as well as *from*. In the sense of *from: del* (de el) *principio al fin,* from beginning to end; *de arriba a abajo,* from top to bottom. When meaning "of," *de* implies possession, manner and quality, as: *la casa de Juan,* John's house; *sé la lección de memoria,* I know the lesson by heart; *la mesa de nogal,* the walnut table, etc.   8. *Ahí* and *allí* mean *there. Ahí* indicates a place near the person addressed, while *allí* means a place farther distant from the person speaking. *Acá,* hither, and *allá,* thither, are less specific, as *acá* implies any place around here, and *allá,* any place around there. Viz.: *¿qué sucede allá?* what is happening (around) there?; *acá todos estamos bien,* here we are all well.

11 LECCION UNDECIMA

Nuevo Vocabulario

la ventana (*vayn-tah'nah*)	the window
la corriente (*koh-rreeayn'tay*)	draught
hace buen tiempo	weather is fine
(*ah'thay bwayn tee-amy'poh*)	
hace mal tiempo (*-mahl-*)	weather is bad
sofocante (*soh-foh-kahn'tay*)	suffocating
agradable (*ah-grah-dah'blay*)	agreeable
a torrentes (*toh-rrayn'tays*)	pouring
asciende (*ahs-thee-ayn'day*)	it rises, climbs
a la sombra (*ah lah sohm'brah*)	in the shade
a menudo (*ah may-noo'doh*)	often

el paraguas (*pah-rah'gwahs*)	the umbrella
el impermeable	raincoat
(*eem-pairr-may-ah'blay*)	
los chanclos (*chahn'clohs*)	rubbers (shoes)

hace viento (*vee-ayn'toh*)	it is windy
coger un resfriado	to catch a cold
(*coh-hairr'rrays-free-ah'doh*)	

nublado (*noo-blah'doh*)	cloudy
relampaguea	it is lightning
(*rray-lahm-pah-ghay'ah*)	

hace sol (*ah'thay sohl*)	the sun shines	**la brisa** (*bree'sah*)	the breeze
hace fresco (*-frays'koh*)	it is cool	**la helada** (*ay-lah'dah*)	frost
hace calor (*-kah-lohrr'*)	it is warm	**la costa** (*kohs'tah*)	coast
desagradable (*days-*)	disagreeable	**el sol** (*sohl*)	sun
por lo tanto (*-tahn'toh*)	therefore	**los grados** (*grah'dohs*)	degrees

EL MAL y EL BUEN TIEMPO

THE BAD AND THE GOOD WEATHER (*ell mahl ee ell bwayn tee-aym'poh*)

el clima (*klee'mah*)	the climate
el frío (*free'oh*)	cold
el calor (*kah-lohrr'*)	heat
el aire (*ah'ee-ray*)	air
el viento (*vee-ayn'toh*)	wind

el hielo (*yay'loh*)	the ice
la lluvia (*llioo'vee-ah*)	rain
la nieve (*nee-ay'vay*)	snow
el fango (*fahn'goh*)	mud
el lodo (*loh'doh*)	mire

el termómetro (*tairr-moh'may-troh*)	thermometer
el barómetro (*bah-roh'may-troh*)	barometer
centígrado (*thayn-tee'grah-doh*)	centigrade

la tempestad (*taym-pays-tahd'*)	the tempest
la tormenta (*tohrr-mayn'tah*)	storm
la humedad (*oo-may-dahd'*)	humidity
la ventisca (*vayn-tees'kah*)	blizzard
el mercurio (*mairr-koo'ree-oh*)	mercury

FOOTNOTES: *1. Hace,* makes or does, comes from *hacer,* to make or to do, and is used in this case idiomatically instead of *to be* in English. *Hace calor,* it is warm; *hace frío,* it is cold; *hace viento,* it is windy; *hace sol,* it is sunny or the sun shines. etc. *2.* When *tiempo,* weather, is used in connection with adverbs or adjectives, the verb *estar* is used instead of *hacer;* viz.: *¿Cómo está el tiempo hoy?* How is the weather today?; *el tiempo está hermosísimo,* the weather is very beautiful; *el día está frío,* the day is cold; *la tarde está calurosa,* the afternoon is warm, etc. *3. Hace un sol espléndido,* or *el sol brilla espléndidamente.*

CONVERSATION

1 ¿Qué clase de tiempo hace?[1]

2 Hace un tiempo delicioso. El tiempo está hermosísimo.[2]

3 Abra usted la ventana y mire como está el tiempo.

4 Hace un sol espléndido,[3] pero hace mucho[4] frío.

5 ¿A cuántos grados está el termómetro? ¿Está bajo o sobre cero?

6 El termómetro está a cuatro grados bajo cero.

7 Me parece que vamos a tener mal tiempo; el barómetro señala lluvia.

8 El barómetro ha bajado (ha subido); temo que tengamos[5] una ventisca.

9 ¡Mire cómo relampaguea! La tormenta (la tempestad) se acerca; ya hace mucho viento. Hay mucho lodo (fango) en las calles.

10 ¿A cuántos grados llega el termómetro en Colombia?

11 En la costa hace mucho calor y el mercurio asciende[6] algunas veces hasta 40 grados centígrados a la sombra.

12 ¿Y hasta cuántos grados baja[7] en Buenos Aires?

---

4. Mucho is used instead of *muy* in connection with the verb *hacer* when referring to the weather, as: *Hace mucho frío,* it is very cold. Observe also that *muy,* though generally translated by *very* or *very much,* can never qualify a verb or stand alone in discourse; viz.: Is it very cold today? Yes, very; *¿Hace mucho frío hoy? Sí, mucho.* Does he speak very well? Very; *¿Habla él muy bien? Sí, muy bien.* 5. *Tengamos,* from *tener,* is the 1st pers. pl., present subjunctive. The subjunctive mood must be used after verbs denoting *fear, doubt, possibility, command, wish, permission,* and *desire.* 6. *Asciende,* is the 3rd pers. sing., present indicative, of the irregular verg *ascender,* to ascend. See Class I, irregular verbs, 2nd

PRONUNCIATION	TRANSLATION
1 ¿ . . . *tee-aym'poh* . . . ?	How is the weather?
2 *ah'thay* . . . *day-lee-thee-oh'* *soh* . . . *ayrr-moh-see'see-moh.*	We are having delightful weather. The weather is very beautiful.
3 . . . *vayn-tah'nah* . . . *mee'* *ray* . . .	Open the window and see how the weather is.
4 . . . *ays-playn'dee-doh* . . . *free'oh.*	The sun is shining brilliantly, but it is very cold.
5 ¿ . . . *grah'dohs* . . . *thay'roh?*	What is the temperature by the thermometer? Is it below or above zero?
6 . . . *tairr-moh'may-troh* . . .	The thermometer is at four degrees below zero.
7 . . . *say-niah'lah llioo'vee-ah.*	I think we are going to have bad weather; the barometer indicates rain.
8 . . . *bah-roh'may-troh* . . . *bah-hah'doh* . . .	The barometer has gone down (has gone up); I am afraid we may have a blizzard.
9 . . . *rray-lahm-pah-gay'ah* . . . *ah-thairr'kah* . . . *loh'doh* . . .	Look how it is lightning! The storm (tempest) is approaching; it is already very windy. There is much mud in the streets.
10 ¿ . . . *lliay'gah* . . . *Koh-lohm'bee-ah?*	How high does the thermometer rise in Colombia?
11 . . . *mairr-koo'ree-oh* . . . *sohm'brah.*	Along the coast it is very warm and the mercury climbs up sometimes to 40 degrees Centigrade in the shade.
12 ¿ . . . *bah'hah* . . . ?	And how low does it get in Buenos Aires?

model.   7. *Baja,* from *bajar,* to come down, to descend. *Descender,* synonymous with *bajar,* can also be used in this case. *Descender* is an irregular verb of the same class as *ascender.*   8. *Nunca, jamás,* are synonymous, and may be used in connection with *no* or without it. *No* always precedes the verb, as: *No desciende nunca,* but is omitted when the other negative precedes it, as: *Nunca desciende. Nunca* and *jamás* are always used in emphatic speech, as: *Nunca jamás desciende* or *no desciende nunca jamás.* When *jamás* is connected with *para siempre,* it means quite the opposite of *never* (ever), as: *para siempre jamás,* for ever and ever. In interrogations, *jamás* stands also for *ever* when no other negative is pres-

13 En Buenos Aires tenemos a menudo una temperatura muy agradable; aunque a veces llueve a torrentes.

14 En Caracas nunca[8] desciende la temperatura a más de veinte o veinticinco grados.

15 El invierno debe[9] ser, por lo tanto, muy agradable allí.

16 ¿No cree usted que va a llover?

17 Está muy nublado,[10] pero creo que hace demasiado frío para que llueva. Caerá más bien una helada.

18 Efectivamente; ya está nevando. Debe usted ponerse su impermeable,[11] puesto que[12] un paraguas[13] no le servirá[14] para nada.

19 ¿No tiene usted chanclos (zapatos de goma)?

20 No ha hecho tanto frío (calor) en todo el invierno (verano, primavera, otoño).

21 ¿No cree usted que hace demasiado[15] calor para la presente estación?[16]

22 El calor es sofocante. No[17] corre[18] ni[17] el más ligero viento.

---

ent, as: *¿Ha visto Ud. jamás eso?* Have you ever seen that?   9. *Deber* means *to owe, to be obliged to*; *deber de*, must, as: *debe de ser*, it must be. The imperfect indicative can be translated by *ought to*, as: *debía llegar hoy*, he ought to arrive today.   10. *Nube*, cloud; *nublado*, cloudy. The verb is *nublar*, to cloud. 11. *Impermeable* has the same meaning as in English, only that in Spanish it is also used as a noun and stands for a water-proof coat: *el impermeable*, the rain coat.   12. *Puesto que* is a CONJUNCTIVE ADVERB of cause meaning *since, as, insomuch as, in so far as*.   13. *Paraguas*, umbrella, a word derived from the Latin

13 ... *ah may-noo'doh* ... *taym-pay-rah-too'rah* ... | In Buenos Aires we often have a very pleasant temperature; although sometimes it rains in torrents.

14 ... *Kah-rah'kahs* ... *days-thee-ayn'day* ... | In Caracas the temperature never goes down to more than twenty or twenty-five degrees.

15 ... *tahn'toh* ... *ah-grah-dah' blay* ... | The Winter, therefore, ought to be very agreeable there.

16 ¿ ... *cray'ay* ... *llioh-vayrr'?* | Don't you think it is going to rain?

17 ... *noo-blah'doh* ... *cray'oh* ... *kah-ay-rah'* ... *ay-lah' dah.* | It is very cloudy, but I believe it is too cold to rain. Most likely we shall have frost.

18 ... *yah* ... *nay-vahn'doh* ... *eem-pairr-may-ah'blay* ... | Indeed; it is already snowing. You must put on your raincoat, as an umbrella would be of no use to you.

19 ¿ ... *chahn'klohs* ... *goh' mah?* | Have you no overshoes (rubber shoes)?

20 ... *een-vee-airr'noh* ... *pree-mah-vay'rah* ... | It has not been so cold (warm) throughout the Winter (Summer, Spring, Autumn).

21 ¿ ... *day-mah-see-ah'doh kah-lohrr'* ... ? | Don't you think it is too warm for the present season?

22 ... *soh-foh-kahn'tay* ... *vee-ayn'toh.* | The heat is suffocating. There is not even a breath of air.

---

parare (Spanish *parar*) to stop, to ward off, and *aquas*, waters. *Paraguas* is masc. sing.   14. *Servirá*, from *servir*, to serve, to be useful; 3rd pers. sing. of the future indicative: *esto no sirve para nada*, this is good for nothing.   15. *Demasiado*, too much, is alterable and agrees with the nouns in gender and number. *Demasiados libros*, too many books; *demasiadas plumas*, too many pens.   16. *Estación* means in this case, *season*.   17. *No—ni*, in this case is translated by *not even*, but it usually means *neither—nor*, as: *No hace frío ni calor*, it is neither cold nor warm.   18. *Corre*, from *correr*, to run, is used in this case idiomatically. The English expression *the wind blows* can also be translated in Spanish by *el viento sopla*, from *soplar*, to blow.   19. *Clima* is masculine, notwithstanding that it ends in *-a*.   20. *Humedad* is feminine, like all nouns ending in *-ad*.   21. *Mismo* (*misma, mismos, mismas*) means *same*, and in some cases *self*, as: *al mismo tiempo*, at the same time; *el hombre mismo*, the man himself. *Mismo* is used

23 El clima[19] aquí es muy húmedo y la humedad[20] hace el calor más intenso, lo mismo[21] que el frío.

24 Hay mucha niebla; pero creo que ahora se levanta una suave brisa.

25 Ya hace mucho[22] viento. Cierre usted la puerta; temo coger un resfriado.

26 Hay una corriente desagradable, y además[23] las corrientes son siempre peligrosas.

---

idiomatically in connection with some words, viz.: *hoy mismo,* this very day; *ahora mismo,* this very moment (just now); *aquí (allí) mismo,* in this (that) very place (right here, there); *mañana mismo* (tomorrow certain), etc. *Que* must follow after *mismo* in comparison, as in this instance; *lo mismo que el frío.* With the pronouns *yo, tú, él,* etc., it becomes reflexive; as, *yo mismo (misma),* I my-

23 ... *klee'mah* ... *oo'may-doh* ... *een-tayn'soh* ... The climate here is very damp and the humidity makes the heat, as well as the cold, more intense.

24 ... *nee-ay'blah* ... It is very foggy, but I think that a pleasant breeze is now arising.

25 ... *thee-ay'rray* ... *koh-hayrr'* ... It is already very windy. Shut the door; I am afraid I may catch a cold.

26 ... *koh-rree-ayn'tay* ... *pay-lee-groh'sahs.* There is a disagreeable draught, and besides draughts are always dangerous.

self; *tú mismo* (*misma*) you yourself (sing.); *él mismo,* he himself; *ella misma,* she herself; *nosotros* (*nosotras*) *mismos* (*mismas*), we ourselves; *vosotros* (*vosotras*) *mismos* (*mismas*), you (yourselves); *Uds. mismos* (*mismas*), you yourselves; *uno mismo, una misma,* one's self. 22. For the use of *mucho,* much, instead of *muy,* very, see note 4. 23. *Además* stands for *besides* or *moreover.*

12 LECCION DUODECIMA

Nuevo Vocabulario

la moda (*moh'dah*)	the fashion, style
la costura (*kohs-too'rah*)	seam
la cinta (*theen'tah*)	ribbon
las mangas (*mahn'gahs*)	sleeves
cortar (*kohrr-tahrr'*)	to cut
ancho (*ahn'choh*)	broad, wide

el género (*hay'nay-roh*)	the material
la tela (*tay'lah*)	light fabric

por medio de (*pohrr may'dee-oh*)	by means of
propio (*proh'pee-oh*)	proper, own
vistosos (*vees-toh'sohs*)	beautiful, showy

se ajusta (*say ah-hoos'tah*)	it is fitted
estrecho (*ays-tray'choh*)	tight, narrow

se cose (*-koh'say*)	it is sewn
¿cómo sienta? (*koh'moh see-ayn'tah*)	how does it fit?

los bordados (*bohrr-dah'dohs*)	the embroidery
la cintura (*theen-too'rah*)	waistline
el algodón (*ahl-goh-dohn'*)	cotton
el terciopelo (*tairr-thee-oh-pay'loh*)	velvet
los botones (*boh-toh'nays*)	buttons
el encaje (*ayn-kah'hay*)	lace

LA SASTRERÍA • LA MODISTA • LA MODA
(*la sahs-tray-ree'ah, la moh-dee's-tah, la moh-dah*)

The Tailor Shop, The Dressmaker, Styles

el estilo (*ays-tee'loh*)	the style	**el lino** (*lee'noh*)		the linen
el crepé (*kray-pay'*)	crepe	**la seda** (*say'dah*)		silk
el rayón (*rrah-yohn'*)	rayon	**la franela** (*frah-nay'lah*)		flannel

el sastre (*sahs'tray*)	the tailor
el patrón (*pah-trohn'*)	pattern
el adorno (*ah-dohrr'noh*)	trimming
el talle (*tah'lliay*)	waist
las tijeras (*tee-hay'rahs*)	scissors

la máquina (*mah'kee-nah*)	machine
la máquina de coser (*-koh-sairr*)	sewing machine
la aguja (*ah-goo'hah*)	needle
el hilo (*ee'loh*)	thread

FOOTNOTES: *1. Máquina de coser* or *para coser*, machine to sew or sewing machine. When a noun is employed to indicate a use or purpose, the prepositions *de* or *para* are used followed by the infinitive: *papel de escribir*, writing paper; *vaso para beber*, glass to drink (with). *2. Hacerse* is the reflexive form of the verb *hacer* and is used idiomatically in this case for *to have made, to order to be made. Mandar hacer* and *mandarse hacer* can also be used, and are like the English, *to have* with a past participle, as: *mandé hacer un traje*, I *had* a suit of

CONVERSATION

1 Señorita Rivera, ¿tendría usted la bondad de decirnos de cuántas piezas se componen los vestidos de las señoras?

2 Generalmente se componen de dos piezas: la blusa (el corpiño) y la falda. Hay también vestidos de una sola pieza.

3 Muy bien, señorita; y las partes del vestido que cubren los brazos ¿cómo se llaman?

4 Se llaman mangas; la parte alta del vestido es el cuello, y la parte que se ajusta a la cintura, el talle.

5 ¿Cuál es la moda actual para las mangas?

6 La moda o el estilo para las mangas varía frecuentemente. Unas veces se usan largas y otras cortas; algunas veces anchas y otras estrechas.

7 ¿De qué son hechos generalmente los vestidos?

8 Hay una gran variedad de telas con las cuales se hacen, pero las más usadas son: la seda, el crepé, el rayón, la franela, el lino, el algodón, el terciopelo y otras.

9 Usted debe saber bastante de costura, ¿no es verdad?

10 Sí, señor; lo suficiente para hacerme mis propios vestidos por medio de un patrón (figurín).

11 ¿Sería usted tan amable que nos explicase cómo se hace un vestido?

clothes *made.*   3. *Esquina,* corner, means *the outside corner,* while *rincón* is *the inside corner,* as: *la esquina de una calle,* the corner of a street; *el rincón de un cuarto,* the inside corner of a room.   4. *Pues* since, as, then, is a conjunctive adverb of cause which serves to link two sentences in a compound clause: *Leeré*

Pronunciation	Translation
1 ... *Rree-vay'rah, ¿ ... bohn-dahd' ... vays-tee-'dohs ...?*	Miss Rivera, would you kindly tell us how many pieces there are in a lady's dress?
2 ... *bloo'sah ... pee-ay'thah.*	Ordinarily they consist of two pieces: the blouse and the skirt. There are also dresses of only one piece.
3 ... *brah'thohs ¿ ... lliah' mahn?*	Very well, Miss; and the parts of the dress which cover the arms, what are they called?
4 ... *mahn'gahs ... ah-hoos' tah ... theen-too'rah ... tah' lliay.*	They are called sleeves; the top part of the dress is the collar and the part adjusted to the waistline is called the waist.
5 ¿ ... *ahk-too-ahl' ...?*	What is the current style for sleeves?
6 ... *ays-tee'loh ... fray-kwayn'tay-mayn'tay ... ahn' chahs ...*	The mode or style for sleeves varies frequently. Sometimes they are worn long, and other times short; sometimes wide and other times tight.
7 ¿ ... *ay'chohs ...?*	What are the dresses made of ordinarily?
8 ... *tay'lahs ... kray-pay' ... tayrr-thee-oh-pay'loh ...*	There is a great variety of fabrics with which they are made, but the most commonly used are: silk, crepe, rayon, flannel, linen, cotton, velvet and others.
9 ... *kohs - too'rah ¿vairr-dahd'?*	You must know a great deal about sewing, don't you?
10 ... *may'dee-oh ... pah-trohn' (fee-goo-reen').*	Yes sir; enough to make my own dresses with the aid of a pattern.
11 ¿ ... *ah-mah'blay ...?*	Would you be so kind as to explain to us how a dress is made?

---

este libro, pues usted me dice que es bueno, I will read this book, since you tell me it is good. 5. *Traje, terno* and *flux* are synonymous and they mean *a suit of clothes. Flux* is used mostly in South America. 6. *Me hace falta,* idiomatic expression for *I need.* Note that in this case *hacer* is used in a reflexive way; *me*

12 Con mucho gusto. En primer lugar se necesitan tres o más metros de tela; se corta ésta con las tijeras, de acuerdo con el patrón y las medidas y se cose con hilo y aguja, ya sea a mano o con una máquina de coser.[1]

13 Después supongo que se probará para ver cómo sienta.

14 Así es; y también se le añaden los adornos que consisten en encajes, cintas, bordados y botones vistosos.

15 ¿Para cuándo necesita su esposo ese dinero?

16 Lo necesita inmediatamente, pues tiene que comprarse alguna ropa hoy.

17 ¿En dónde piensa él hacerse[2] los trajes?

18 En la sastrería de la esquina[3] de la calle San Martín y Sucre. El Sr. Fuentes es un buen sastre.

19 Pues,[4] vamos allá. Aquí viene su esposo.

20 Buenos días, señor Fuentes. Deseo hacerme un traje.[5]

21 Le ruego me enseñe los géneros más nuevos para trajes.

---

hace, le hace (*a él, a ella, a usted*), *nos hace, les hace* (*a ellos, a ellas, a ustedes*). 7. *Trataré,* from *tratar* to try, 1st pers. sing. future indicative. When not followed by *de,* as in this case, *tratar* means also *to treat.* 8. *A Más tardar,* idiomatic expression for *at the latest.* 9. *Tan,* so, as, is used with adjectives,

12 ... *may'trohs* ... *korr'tah* ... *ah-kwayrr'doh* ... *tee-hay'rahs* ... *ah-goo'hah* ...	With pleasure. First, you need three or more meters of fabric, which you cut with scissors, according to the pattern and measurements, and then you sew it with needle and thread, either by hand or with a sewing machine.
13 ... *soo-pohn'goh* ... *see-ayn' tah.*	After that, I suppose you try the dress on to see how it fits.
14 ... *ah-niah'dayn* ... *ayn-kah'hays* ...	Exactly; and you also add the trimmings, which consist of lace, ribbons, embroidery, and colorful buttons.
15 ¿ ... *dee-nay'roh?*	When will your husband need that money?
16 ... *nay-thay-see'tah* ... *rroh' pah* ... *oh'ee.*	He needs it immediately as he has to buy himself clothes today.
17 ¿ ... *trah'hays?*	Where does he intend to have his clothes made?
18 ... *ays-kee'nah* ... *sahs'tray.*	At the tailor shop on the corner of San Martin Street and Sucre. Mr. Fuentes is a good tailor.
19 ... *ays-poh'soh.*	Then, let us go there. Here comes your husband.
20 ... *Foo-ayn'tays* ...	Good morning, Mr Fuentes, I wish to have a suit made.
21 ... *hay'nay-rohs* ... *nway' vohs* ...	Please show me the latest material (fabrics) for suits.

---

adverbs and nouns to denote a degree of comparison: *tan grande como*, as large as; *tan de prisa*, in such a hurry. Before a noun *tan* becomes *tanto* and agrees in gender and number with the noun, viz.: *tanto dinero*, so much money; *tanta leche*, so much milk; *tantos libros*, so many books; *tantas flores*, so many flowers.

22 Deseo hacerme un traje a la medida; los hechos nunca me sientan
bien.

23 Entonces permítame que le tome
la medida. ¿Desea usted el saco
ancho o estrecho?

24 Hágamelo ancho y cómodo, y no
olvide usted que me hace falta[6]
para la semana que viene.

25 Trataré[7] de que tenga usted todo sin falta para el martes
o miércoles a más tardar.[8]

26 Mándeme la cuenta al mismo tiempo para que la pague.

27 ¡Oh! No necesita usted estar tan[9] de prisa (o, tener tanta
prisa); hay mucho tiempo.

28 Yo tengo que comprar un vestido para mi hija mayor.

29 En la tienda de la esquina los venden baratos.

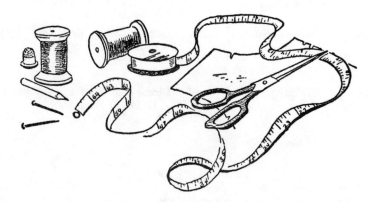

22 *. . . noon'kah . . . see-ayn' tahn . . .*	I want to have a suit made to order, the ready made ones never fit me well.
23 *. . . payrr-mee'tah-may . . . sah'koh . . .*	Allow me then to take your measurements. Do you want the coat to be loose or tight?
24 *. . . fahl'tah . . . say-mah'nah . . .*	Make it loose and comfortable, and do not forget that I need it for next week.
25 *trah-tah-ray' . . . tahrr-dahrr'.*	I will try to have everything ready for you without fail by Tuesday or Wednesday at the latest.
26 *mahn'day-may . . . pah'gay.*	Send me the bill at the same time so that I may pay it.
27 *' . . . pree'sah . . .*	Oh! you need not be in such a hurry; there is plenty of time.
28 *. . . ee'hah mah-yohrr'.*	I have to buy a dress for my oldest daughter.
29 *. . . tee-ayn'dah . . . vayn' dayn bah-rah'tohs.*	At the corner store they sell them reasonably.

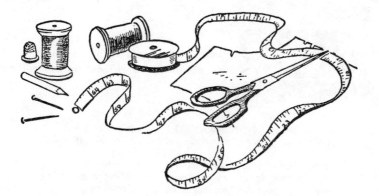

13 LECCION DECIMOTERCERA

Nuevo Vocabulario

los vehículos (*vay-ee'koo-lohs*)	the vehicles
la aglomeración (*ah-glo-may-rah-thee-ohn'*)	rush
el tipo de cambio (*tee'poh kahm'bee-oh*)	rate of exchange
los suburbios (*soo-boorr'bee-ohs*)	suburbs
la casa de correos (*kah'sah day . . .*)	post office

dormir (*dohrr-meerr'*)	to sleep
acostarme (*ah-kohs-tahrr'may*)	to put (myself) to bed

la película (*pay-lee'koo-lah*)	the film
el teatro (*tay-ah'troh*)	theatre
el cine (*thee'nay*)	movies

cambiar (*kahm-bee-ahrr'*)	to change
la aduana (*ah-doo-ah'nah*)	the Custom-House

dar un paseo (*dahrr- pah-say'oh*)	to go for a walk
preferiría (*pray-fay-ree-ree'ah*)	I should (or would) prefer
es admirable (*ahd-mee-rah'blay*)	it is wonderful
presentarme (*pray-sayn-tahrr'may*)	to introduce me
ahora mismo (*ah-oh'rah mees'moh*)	right now
celebro la ocasión (*thay-lay'broh . . .*)	I welcome the occasion
hasta ahora (*ahs'tah ah-oh'rah*)	until now
populosa (*poh-poo-loh'sah*)	densely populated
levantarme (*lay-vahn-tahrr'may*)	to get (myself) up
a sus órdenes (*ah soos ohrr'day-nays*)	at your service

116

EN LA CIUDAD • LA PRESENTACIÓN
(ayn la theew-dahd,   la pray-sayn-tah-thee-ohn')

IN THE CITY, THE INTRODUCTION

la calle (*kah'lliay*)	the street	**la esquina** (*ays-kee'nah*)	the corner
la acera (*ah-thay'rah*)	sidewalk	**el casino** (*kah-see'noh*)	club
la plaza (*plah'thah*)	square	**la iglesia** (*ee-glay'see-ah*)	church
el paseo (*pah-say'oh*)	walk	**el correo** (*koh-rray'oh*)	mail
el parque (*pahrr'kay*)	park	**la escuela** (*ays-kway'lah*)	school
el banco (*bahn'koh*)	bank	**el hospital** (*ohs-pee-tahl'*)	hospital
el bar (*bahrr*)	bar	**lavarme** (*lah-vahrr'may*)	to wash myself
la tarea (*tah-ray'ah*)	task	**vestirme** (*vays-teerr'may*)	to dress myself
la gente (*hayn'tay*)	people	**sentarme** (*sayn-tahrr'may*)	to sit (myself)
tantos (*tahn'tohs*)	so many	**tan grandes** (*-grahn'days*)	so large

el tráfico (*trah'fee-koh*)	the traffic
los habitantes (*ah-bee-tahn'tays*)	inhabitants
el policía (*poh-lee-thee'ah*)	policeman

los edificios (*ay-dee-fee'thee-ohs*)	buildings
el ayuntamiento (*ah-yoon-tah-mee-ayn'toh*)	city hall
la avenida (*ah-vay-nee'dah*)	avenue
el gusto (*goos'toh*)	pleasure, taste
el pavimento (*pah-vee-mayn'toh*)	pavement
el mercado (*mairr-kah'doh*)	market place

FOOTNOTES: *1. Se acostó*, 3rd pers. sing., past, of the reflexive verb *acostarse*, go to bed. The conjugation of the past definite tense of the verb *acostarse* is: **yo**

CONVERSATION

1 ¿A qué hora se acostó[1] usted anoche,[2] que está durmiendo todavía?

2 Me acosté muy tarde, y me he quedado dormida.[3]

3 No me pude[4] dormir hasta las cuatro de la mañana.

4 Mi criada no me llamó[5] y no me he despertado[6] hasta ahora.

5 Pero hágame el favor de sentarse;[7] voy a levantarme,[8] lavarme y vestirme inmediatamente.

6 Bueno, pues ya estoy lista[9] y a sus órdenes.

7 Vámonos cuando usted guste.

8 ¿A dónde desea usted que vayamos?

9 Si le parece nos iremos a dar un paseo[10] por el Parque Central.

10 Yo preferiría visitar algunos edificios públicos, como las escuelas, la casa de correos, el mercado, las iglesias y el ayuntamiento.

11 ¡Magnífica idea! Y después iremos al teatro o al cine. En esta plaza hay un cine en el cual[11] se dan las mejores películas.

12 Mientras más edificios visitemos tanto[12] mejor conoceremos la ciudad.

---

me acosté, *tú te* acostaste, *él, ella, Ud. se acostó, nosotros nos* acostamos, *vosotros os* acostasteis, *ellos, ellas, Uds. se* acostaron. 2. *Anoche* means last night; *esta noche,* to-night. 3. *Me he quedado dormida,* from *quedarse dormido* to oversleep. The reflexive pronouns, when in connection with the infinitive, gerund, and imperative affirmative, are joined to them as *one word,* but are *separated* and placed *before* the verb when in connection with *any other tense.* The gerund of

PRONUNCIATION	TRANSLATION

1 *¿ ... ah-kohs-toh' ... ah-noh' chay ...?* — At what time did you go to bed last night that you are still sleeping?

2 *... kay-dah'doh dohrr-mee' dah.* — I went to bed very late and overslept.

3 *...* — I was not able to fall asleep until four o'clock in the morning.

4 *... days-pairr-tah'doh ...* — My maid did not call me and I did not awaken until now.

5 *... sayn-tahrr'say ...* — But please sit down; I am going to get up, wash and get dressed immediately.

6 *... lees'tah ...* — Well, I am quite ready, and at your service.

7 *vah'moh-nohs ...* — Let us go when you please.

8 *¿ ... vah-yah'mohs?* — Where do you wish we shall go?

9 *... pah-say'oh ... Pahrr'kay Thayn-trahl'.* — If you like we shall go for a walk in Central Park.

10 *... ah-yoon-tah-meeayn'toh.* — I should rather visit some public buildings, like the schools, the post office, the market, the churches and the city hall.

11 *¡mahg-nee'fee-kah ee-day'ah!* *...* — A splendid idea! And afterwards we shall go to the theatre or to the motion picture. In this square there is a motion picture theatre in which the best pictures are shown.

12 *... theew-dahd'.* — The more buildings we visit, the better we shall know the city.

---

quedarse, to remain, is *quedándose,* and the imperative, *quédate tú; quédese él, ella,* or *Ud.; quedémonos nosotros; quedaos vosotros; quédense ellos, ellas,* or *Uds.* Note that the 1st pers. pl. of this tense loses the *-s* of the termination *-mos* before the particle-*nos: quedémonos instead of quedémosnos.*   4. *Could,* implying *power,* I was able, is translated by *podía* or *pude,* as: *no podía* or *no pude dormirme.* If used with the conjunction *si,* if, *could* is translated by *pudiera* or *pudiese,* as: *me dormiría si pudiera* or *si pudiese,* I would sleep if I could. But when the condition is implied, it is translated by *podría,* as: *podría dormirme si*

13 Es admirable ver como el policía dirige el tráfico. Hay tantos[12] vehículos, y la aglomeración de gente en las aceras y en medio de las calles es tan[12] grande, que a veces es una tarea difícil.

14 Buenos Aires es una ciudad muy populosa (tiene muchos habitantes), y sus calles, avenidas, parques y suburbios son modernos, amplios y bellos.

15 Yo necesito ir al banco para cambiar algunos dólares en moneda nacional.

16 El tipo de cambio es muy bajo. Siento no poder acompañarla. La esperaré en casa de la modista.

17 ¿No tendría usted la bondad de presentarme, antes de marcharse, a esa señora?

18 Con mucho gusto; voy a presentársela ahora mismo.

19 Amiga Doña[13] María, tengo el gusto de presentarle la señora Martínez.

20 Señora (Sra. Martínez), celebro la ocasión que me proporciona el gusto de conocerla.

---

quisiera, I could go to sleep if I wished. 5. It is very important not to confuse the *indirect object personal pronouns* with the *reflexive pronouns.* In this case, *me llamó, me* is the indirect object personal pronoun, as *llamó,* 3rd person, indicates that somebody other than *myself* called *me.* To be a reflexive form, *me,* first person, must be used in connection with the *first person* of the verb, the same as *te* with the *second, se* with the *third,* etc. 6. *Me he despertado,* from *despertarse,* to awake one's self. 7. *Sentarse,* to be seated. Many of the passive English verbs are reflexive in Spanish, viz.: *equivocarse,* to be mistaken; *engañarse,*

13 ... *poh-lee-thee'ah* ... *dee-ree'hay* ... *dee-fee'theel.*	It is wonderful to watch the policeman direct the traffic. There are so many vehicles, and the rush of people on the sidewalks and on the streets is so great, that sometimes it is a difficult task.
14 ... *ahm'plee-ohs* ...	Buenos Aires is a densely populated city, (it has many inhabitants), and its streets, avenues, parks and suburbs are modern, large and beautiful.
15 ... *nay-thay-see'toh* ...	I have to go to the bank in order to exchange some dollars into national currency.
16 *ell tee'poh* ... *seeayn'toh* ...	The rate of exchange is very low. I regret I cannot accompany you. I shall wait for you at the dressmaker's.
17 ¿ ... *mahrr-chahrr'say* ... ?	Would you be so kind as to introduce me, before you go, to that lady?
18 ... *prayn-sayn-tahrr'say-lah* ...	With much pleasure: I am going to introduce her to you right now.
19 *ah-mee'gah Doh'niah Mah-ree'ah* ... *Mahrr-tee'nayth.*	Friend Doña Maria, I have the pleasure to introduce to you Mrs. Martinez.
20 *say nioh'rah* ...	Madam, (Mrs. Martinez), I am glad the occasion affords me the pleasure of meeting you.

to be deceived; *disgustarse,* to be displeased, etc. Also those formed with *to get* and *to become,* viz.: *enriquecerse,* to become rich; *enfermarse,* to get sick, etc. 8. *Levantarme,* to rise myself, from *levantarse,* to get up; *lavarme,* to wash myself, from *lavarse,* to wash one's self; *vestirme,* to dress myself, from *vestirse,* to dress one's self, are reflexive verbs. See note 1. 9. *Listo, -a,* in connection with *estar,* means *ready,* while used with *ser* it means *clever* (smart). 10. *Dar un paseo* is an idiomatic expression meaning to *take a walk, ride or drive.* 11. *Such expressions* as *he who, she who, they who, the one who,* etc., are translated in Spanish by *el que, la que, los que, las que. That which* or *that what,* by *lo que,* as: *lo que es útil nunca está de más,* that which is useful is never in the way; *sucedió lo que yo le dije a Ud.,* it happened as (that what) I told you. *El cual, la cual, los cuales, las cuales,* who, which, are often employed instead of *que* or *quien,* for

21 Ese placer es mío, señora Calderón.

22 ¿Viene usted a pasar muchos días en la ciudad?

23 No; vengo sólo a pasar la tempo· rada de verano. Me han dicho que esta ciudad tiene muy lindas pla· yas.

24 Y además, bellos sitios de recreo. Tendré mucho gusto en acompa· ñarla a ellos.

25 Es usted muy amable y le quedo sumamente agradecida.

26 Mande como guste, y usted lo pase bien.

27 Adiós, pues. Hasta la vista.

---

clarity, as: *acabo de ver a Pedro con su madre, la cual no está bien,* I have just seen Peter with his mother, who is not well. *La cual* clearly refers to *the mother,* not to *Pedro.*   12. The adverbs *tanto* and *cuanto* lose the last syllable *-to* before an adjective or adverb, becoming *tan* and *cuan.* The comparative of *equality* is formed by placing the adverbs *tan,* so, as, *tantos, tantas,* so many, as many, before adjectives or adverbs, and *como,* as, after. Examples: *Castelar es tan elocuente como Gladstone;* Castelar is as eloquent as Gladstone. *La biblioteca de Brooklyn tiene tantos libros y tantos suscritores como la de Nueva York;* The Brooklyn library has as many books and as many subscribers as that of New York. *13. Don* (abbreviation *Dn.*), means *Mr.,* and *Doña* (abbreviation *Dña),* *Mrs.*

21 . . . *Kahl-day-rohn'.*	That pleasure is mine, Mrs. Calderón.
22 . . .	Are you going (do you come) to spend many days in the city?
23 . . . *leen'dahs plah'yahs.*	No, I am going (come) to spend only the summer season. They told me that this city has beautiful beaches.
24 . . . *rray-kray'oh* . . .	And also many amusement centers. I shall be glad to accompany you to them.
25 . . . *ah-grah-day-thee'dah.*	You are very kind and I am most grateful to you.
26 . . . *pah'say* . . .	Command as you please, and may you fare well.
27 *ah-deeohs'* . . . *ahs'tah* . . .	Goodbye. Till we meet again.

These appellations are used before given names only, while *señor* (abbrev. *Sr.*) and *señora* (abbrev. *Sra.*), Mr. and Mrs., respectively, are used before family names. Miss is rendered by *señorita* (abbrev. *Srta.*) and Master, by *señorito* (*Srto.*), and can be used either before a given name or a surname. Note that these abbreviations should always be pronounced in full. In addressing somebody by his or her full name, as for instance: Mr. John López, we say, *Sr. Dn. Juan López, Dn. Juan López,* or *Sr. López.* When speaking of a person, the appellatives *señor, señora,* and *señorita,* require the definite article before them, as: *el Sr. López está en casa,* Mr. López is at home; *la Sra. López y la Srta. García acaban de llegar,* Mrs. López and Miss García have just arrived. The article is not used when addressing a person directly.

14 LECCION DECIMOCUARTA

Nuevo Vocabulario

una cucharada (-koo-chah-rah'dah)	a spoonful
¿cuánto lleva? (kwahn'toh lliay'vah)	how much does he charge?
pasar adelante (pah-sahrr' ah-day-lahn'tay)	to come in
al contrario (ahl kohn-trah'ree-oh)	on the contrary
dentro de (dayn'troh day)	within
desalquilado (days-ahl-kee-lah'doh)	free (unhired)

el auto (ahw'toh)	the automobile
el conductor (kohn-dooc-tohrr')	driver

el timbre (teem'bray)	the electric bell
el taxi (tahk'see)	taxicab
el pulso (pool'soh)	pulse
de prisa (day pree'sah)	quickly
dése prisa (day'say-)	hurry!
lejos (lay'hohs)	far
cada (kah'dah)	each, every
sudando (soo-dahn'doh)	perspiring

el mareo (mah-ray'oh)	dizziness
el dolor de cabeza (doh-lohrr' day kah-bay'thah)	headache

la receta (rray-thay'tah)	the prescription
la farmacia (fahrr-mah'thee-ah)	drugstore

indispuesto (een-dees-pways'toh)	indisposed
grave (grah'vay)	grave, very ill
el apetito (ah-pay-tee'toh)	the appetite
el resfriado (rrays-free-ah'doh)	cold
la consulta (kohn-sool'tah)	visit (doctor's)
la clínica (klee'nee-kah)	doctor's office

UNA VISITA AL MÉDICO

A VISIT TO THE DOCTOR   (*oo'-nah vee see' tah al may-dee-koh*)

el médico (*may'dee-koh*)	the doctor
la lengua (*layn'gwah*)	tongue
los síntomas (*seen'toh-mahs*)	symptoms
las píldoras (*peel'doh-rahs*)	pills
la fiebre (*fee-ay'bray*)	fever, temperature
la medicina (*may-dee-thee'nah*)	medicine
la propina (*proh-pee'nah*)	tip
la portezuela (*pohrr-tay-thway'lah*)	car door, little door
la visita facultativa (*-fah-kool-tah-tee'vah*)	doctor's visit

buena cara (*bway'nah kah'rah*)	looking well
me siento bien	I feel well
(*may see-ayn'toh bee-yan'*)	
me siento mal (*-mahl*)	I feel sick

FOOTNOTES: *1. Tener buena cara,* lit. to have a good face, which means *to look* or *appear well.   2. Siento,* from *sentir,* to feel, is an irregular verb. *Me siento* belongs to the reflexive conjugation *sentirse,* to feel one's self.   *3.* The *direct* object of a verb, if an animate being, takes *a,* to, as: *busco al (a el) doctor, espero a Juan, llamo al (a el) perro.* If indeterminate, or preceded by a number, *a* is omitted, as: *busco un amigo,* I am looking for a friend; *a* is also omitted if the direct object is a thing, as: *espero el tren,* I await the train; *busco mi sombrero,* I am looking for my hat.   *4. Por* conveys the general idea of *cause.* It expresses: (a) *Price, exchange, equivalent* and *percentage,* as: *Quiero dos pesos*

CONVERSATION

1 ¿A cuántos estamos hoy?

2 Estamos a veintidós de septiembre.

3 Pero, ¿qué tiene usted? No tiene buena cara.[1]

4 No me siento[2] bien. He perdido el apetito y desearía ver a[3] un médico.

5 ¿Cuánto lleva el doctor Garrido por[4] hacer[5] una visita facultativa?

6 No sé; pero él vive muy lejos y probablemente pedirá mucho por venir aquí.

7 En ese caso tomaremos un taxi e[6] iremos a su clínica.

8 Le acompañaré a usted con mucho gusto. Aquí viene un auto.

9 Conductor (chófer), está su auto desalquilado?

10 Sí, señores; ¿a dónde desean ustedes ir?

11 Llévenos a la calle Montevideo, número 6, lo más aprisa posible. Cierre[7] la portezuela.[8]

---

por mi libro; I want two dollars *for* my book. *El dinero produce cuatro por ciento*; Money brings four *per* cent. (b) *Origin, direction,* and *duration of time,* as: *La mesa está hecha por el carpintero*; The table is made *by* the carpenter. *Estuve ausente por tres meses*; I was absent *for* three months. *Fui a España por Italia*; I went to Spain *by way of* Italy. (c) *Estimation,* and in such expressions as *to go for, to send for,* and *to ask for,* as: *Pasa por hombre instruido*; He passes *for* a learned man. *Envíe Ud. por el médico*; Send *for* the physician. *Vienen por mí*; They come *for* me. (d) It also stands for *on account of* (*a causa de*), or *owing to* (*debido a*), as: *Por* (*a causa de*) *su hermano de Ud., no concluí mi trabajo*; On account of your brother I did not finish my work. (e) *Instead of* (*en vez de*) or *in place of* (*en lugar de*), as: *Hágalo Ud. por mí*, Do it *for* me. (f) With the

PRONUNCIATION	TRANSLATION
1 ...	What day of the month is it?
2 ... *sayp-tee-aym'bray* ...	It is September twenty-second.
3 ...	But, what ails you? You don't look well.
4 ... *may'dee-koh.*	I don't feel well. I have lost my appetite and I should like to see a doctor.
5 ¿ ... *Gah-rree'doh* ... *fah-kool-tah-tee'vah?*	How much does Dr. Garrido charge for a professional visit?
6 ... *lay'hohs* ...	I don't know, but he lives very far and he will probably ask a good deal to come here.
7 ... *tahk'see* ... *klee'nee-kah.*	In that case we shall take a taxi and go to his office.
8 ... *ahw'toh.*	I shall be glad to go with you. Here comes a car.
9 *kohn-dook-tohrr'* (*choh'fairr*), ¿ ... *days-ahl-kee-lah'doh?*	Driver, is your car free (unhired)?
10 ...	Yes, gentlemen, where do you wish to go?
11 ... *Mohntay-vee-day'oh* ...	Drive us to No. 6 Montevideo Street as quickly as possible. Shut the door.

---

verb *estar* and an infinitive, when conveying the idea of *want* and *requirement,* as: *El taxi está por alquilar;* The taxi is for hire. *Estoy por salir;* I am *inclined* to go out. (g) In connection with adjectives and adverbs followed by *que* (*no matter how*); as, *Por mucho que estudie, nunca aprenderá;* No matter how much he may study he will never learn. 5. After prepositions the verb must be in the infinitive. 6. *Y,* and, before words beginning with -*i* or -*hi,* changes to *e* for the purpose of euphony, except before -*hie,* as: *padre e hijo,* father and son; *francés e inglés,* French and English, etc.; but, *nieve y hielo,* snow and ice. 7. *Cierre,* imperative of the irregular verb *cerrar,* to close. These verbs having an *e* in the syllable before the last take an -*i* before the -*e* in all persons *except the 1st and 2nd pl.* in the present indicative, subjunctive, and the imperative. See

12 Dése prisa y tendrá una buena propina.

13 Pare aquí; ésta es la casa y vamos a bajar.

14 Toque el timbre de la puerta.

15 ¿Está en casa el doctor?

16 ¿Tengo el gusto de hablar con el doctor Garrido?

17 Servidor de usted.[9] Hágame el favor de pasar adelante.[10]

18 ¿Desde cuándo se siente usted indispuesto?

19 Desde anoche; estaba sudando al salir[11] del teatro y cogí un fuerte resfriado.

20 Déjeme tomarle el pulso.[12] Enséñeme la lengua.

21 ¿Cree usted, doctor, que los síntomas son graves?

22 No, señor; el termómetro indica que tiene usted sólo una pequeña fiebre.

Class I, irregular verbs. **8.** The endings *-uelo, -uela,* form the diminutive, and usually convey the idea of *contempt* and *adversity,* but *portezuela* stands for the *small door of a carriage,* and is the usual expression employed. Diminutives generally end in *-ito* (masc..) and *-ita* (fem.). Besides expressing smallness they are sometimes used as terms of endearment. Diminutives follow the gender and number of the names from which they are formed, as: from *hermano, hermanito*; from *hermana, hermanita*; from *hermanos, hermanitos* and from *hermanas, hermanitas* (little brother, little sister, etc.). For words ending in *-co, -go* (masc.), or *-ca, -ga* (fem.), the suffixes *-quito, -guito, or -quita, -guita,* respectively, are substituted, as: from *chico, chiquito*; *chica, chiquita* (little boy or girl); *amigo, amiguito*; *amiga, amiguita* (little friend). Diminutives of words of one syllable, ending in **a**

12 *day'say . . . proh-pee'nah.*	Hurry, and you will receive a good tip.
13 *. . . bah-hahrr'.*	Stop here; this is the house and we are going to get out.
14 *toh'kay ell teem'bray . . .*	Ring the door bell.
15 *. . .*	Is the doctor at home?
16 *. . . ah-blahrr' . . .*	Have I the pleasure of speaking to Dr. Garrido?
17 *sairr-vee-dohrr' . . .*	At your service, sir. Please come inside.
18 *¿days'day . . . een-dees-pways' toh?*	Since when have you felt indisposed?
19 *. . . koh-hee' . . . rrays-free-ah'doh.*	Since last night. I was perspiring when I left the theatre, and I caught a violent cold.
20 *. . . pool'soh . . . ayn-say' niay-may lah layn'gwah.*	Let me take your pulse. Let me see your tongue.
21 *¿ . . . seen'toh-mahs . . . ?*	Do you think, Doctor, that the symptoms are serious (grave)?
22 *. . . pay-kay'niah feeay'bray.*	No, sir; the thermometer shows that you only have a slight fever.

consonant, are formed by adding *-ecito, -ecita,* as: from *pan, panecito; flor, florecita.* Words of more than one syllable, ending in a consonant, except *n* or *r,* add *-ito, -ita,* as: from *lápiz, lapicito; señal, señalita.* When the word ends in *-e, -n,* or *r,* add *-cito, -cita,* as: from *hombre, hombrecito; mujer, mujercita; jardín, jardincito.* From *mano,* we get *manecita,* and from *pie, piececito,* little hand and foot, respectively. Other diminutive endings implying beauty, grace and endearment, are: *-illo, -illa* and *-ico, -ica.* Common endings for proper names are *-ito, -ita,* as: *Juan, Juanito; Ana, Anita.* 9. People wishing to be polite, either in social or business life, will answer by *servidor de usted,* your servant, instead of *that is my name.* 10. *Pasar adelante* means *to walk in.* 11. *Al salir,* upon leaving. *al* with the infinitive is often used with the same meaning as *on* and *upon,* plus the present participle in English, as: *al venir aquí,* on coming here; *al llegar a Méjico,* upon arriving in Mexico; *al entrar en casa, me encontré su carta,* on entering the house, I found your letter. 12. *El pulso,* the pulse. In Spanish when

23 Siento un gran dolor de cabeza y mareo.

24 Tome usted estas píldoras y se le pasará el dolor.

25 ¿No se siente usted mejor[13] ahora?

26 Al contrario, me siento peor.[14]

27 En ese caso envíe esta receta a la farmacia (botica) y tome una cucharada[15] de la medicina cada[16] dos horas.

28 Si no se siente mejor, hágame el favor de volver[17] dentro de tres días.

referring to any part of the body, the definite article *el* or *la* is used instead of the possessive adjective. *Déme usted el pulso,* for instance, is said instead of *su pulso; enséñeme la lengua,* instead of *su lengua.* 13. *Mejor,* better, is the irregular comparative of the adjective *bueno,* good, and of the adverb *bien,* well. 14. The adverbs irregularly compared are: *Bien,* well; *mejor,* better; *lo mejor,* the best. *Mal,* badly; *peor,* worse; *lo peor,* the worst. *Mucho,* much; *más,* more; *lo más,* the most. *Poco,* little; *menos,* less; *lo menos,* the least. 15. *Cuchara,* spoon; *cu-*

23	... *kah-bay'thah ee mah-ray' oh.*	I have a violent headache and I feel dizzy.
24	... *peel'doh-rahs ...*	Take these pills and you will get rid of your pain.
25	¿ ... *may-hohrr' ah-oh'rah?*	Don't you feel better now?
26	... *pay-ohrr'.*	On the contrary, I feel worse.
27	... *rray-thay'tah ... fahrr-mah'theeah (boh-tee'kah) ...*	In that case send this prescription to the pharmacy (drugstore) and take a spoonful of the medicine every two hours.
28	... *vohl-vairr' dayn'troh ...*	If you don't feel better, please return within three days.

---

charita, teaspoon; *cucharada,* spoonful; *cucharadita,* teaspoonful.   16. *Cada* is invariable, and means *each* as well as *every,* as: *cada uno,* each one or every one; *cada hombre, cada mujer,* etc. It is used in the plural when numerals are introduced as is *every* in English: *cada dos horas,* every two hours; *cada dos días, cada veinticinco años,* etc.   17. *Volver,* to return, to turn, to come back, is an irregular verb, Class II. *Volver a hacer algo,* to do something again; *vuelva Ud.,* come again. The expression *again* has no literal equivalent in Spanish, but it is translated by *volver a* or *otra vez,* another time.

15 LECCION DECIMOQUINTA

Nuevo Vocabulario

por semana (*say-mah'nah*)	by the week
por trimestre (*tree-mays'tray*)	every three months
con vista a (*kohn vees'tah ah*)	overlooking
por supuesto (*pohrr soo-pways'toh*)	of course
pago adelantado (*pah'goh ah-day-lahn-tah'doh*)	advance payment
alquilar (*ahl-kee-lahrr'*)	to hire
rentar (*rrayn-tahrr'*)	to rent
arrendar (*ah-rrayn-dahrr'*)	to lease

me mude (*may moo'day*)	that I move
desamueblado (*days-ah-mway-blah'doh*)	unfurnished

importe (*eem-pohrr'tay*)	amount, payment
mostrarle (*mohs-trahrr'lay*)	to show you (him, her)
me enseñe (*may ayn-say'niay*)	that you show me
equivalentes (*ay-kee-vah-layn'tays*)	equivalent
espacioso (*ays-pah-thee-oh'soh*)	roomy, spacious
amueblado (*ah-mway-blah'doh*)	furnished

el agua fría (*ah'gwah free'ah*)	the cold water
el agua caliente (*-kah-lee-ayn'tay*)	hot water

la calefacción (*kah-lay-fahk-thee-ohn'*)	the heating
la crema (*kray'mah*)	cream
la esponja (*ays-pohn'hah*)	sponge
la regadera (*rray-gah-day'rah*)	sprinkler
el lavabo (*lah-vah'boh*)	wash basin
la pasta de los dientes (*pahs'tah ... dee-ayn'tays*)	toothpaste

132

Alquilando un Cuarto • Objetos de Tocador
(*ahl-keelah'n-doh oon kwah'rr-toh, ob-hay-tohs de toh-kah-do'hr*)

RENTING A ROOM, TOILET ARTICLES

dar a (*dahrr ah*)	to face, (to front)	**las piezas** (*pee-ay'thahs*)	the rooms
por mes (*mays*)	by the month	**el recibo** (*rray-thee'boh*)	receipt
el pago (*pah'goh*)	the payment	**los polvos** (*pohl'vohs*)	powder

el cepillo (*thay-pe'llioh*)	the brush
el peine (*pay'ee-nay*)	comb
el perfume (*pairr-foo'may*)	perfume

la electricidad (*ay-layk-tree-thee-dahd'*)	the electricity
el gas (*gahs*)	gas

FOOTNOTES: *1.* The present subjunctive must be used after impersonal phrases such as, *es necesario que, es preciso que, es menester que,* it is necessary; *puede ser que,* it may be; *es imposible que,* it is impossible; *es natural que,* it is natural; *es tiempo de que,* it is time, etc. Examples: *Es menester que venga Ud. a verme;* You must come to see me. *Es preciso que haga Ud. eso en seguida;* It is necessary for you to do that at once. *Es necesario que empiece Ud. a trabajar cuanto antes;* You must begin to work as soon as possible. *Puede ser que venga;* It may be that he is coming. *Es tiempo de que Ud. hable;* It is time for you to speak. When *que*

CONVERSATION

1 Es necesario que[1] me mude hoy mismo[2] de mi hotel.

2 ¿Desea usted una habitación amueblada o desamueblada?

3 Preferiría tres piezas sin amueblar; un saloncito,[3] un dormitorio y un cuarto de baño.

4 Sírvase pasar y tendré el gusto de mostrarle[4] lo que usted desea.

5 Quiere usted que el salón dé[5] a la calle o al mar?

6 Si es posible elegiré uno con vistas al mar.

7 El cuarto de dormir puede dar[5] a la calle o al mar; no me importa.

8 ¿Cuál es el precio de este cuarto?

9 ¿Cuánto rentan estas habitaciones?

10 ¿Alquila usted por mes o por semana?

11 ¿Cuánto lleva usted por cuarto y comida?

12 ¿Se sirven también las comidas a la carta?

does not follow the expressions *es menester, es preciso, es necesario,* the verb must be used in the infinitive, viz.: *es menester* (*es necesario, es preciso*) *escribir una carta, y es necesario* (*es menester, es preciso*) *hacerlo en seguida,* it is necessary to write a letter, and it must be done at once.   2. The expression *hoy mismo* is idiomatic, and means *this very day.* The indefinite pronoun *mismo* (self, is often used to give emphasis to the word placed *before it,* as: *él me lo dijo a mí mismo,* or, *a mí mismo me lo dijo él,* lit. he told it to my own self.   3. *Saloncito* is the diminutive of *salón.* The *augmentatives* are formed by adding *-on, -ote, -azo*

PRONUNCIATION	TRANSLATION
1 ... *moo'day* ... *oh-tayl'*.	It is necessary that I move from my hotel this very day.
2 ¿ ... *ah-mway-blah'dah* ... ?	Do you wish a furnished or an unfurnished room?
3 ... *sah-lohn-thee'toh* ...	I should prefer three unfurnished rooms: a sitting room, a bedroom, and a bathroom.
4 ... *mohs-trahrr'lay* ...	Please step inside and I will gladly show you what you wish.
5	Do you like the sitting room facing the street or the sea?
6 ... *ay-lay-hee-ray'* ...	If it is possible, I will choose one with a view to the sea.
7 ... *dohrr-meerr'* ...	The bedroom may face the street or the sea; I don't care.
8 ¿ ... *pray'theeoh* ... ?	What is the price of this room?
9 ¿ ... *rrayn'tahn* ... ?	How much is the rent of this apartment (rooms)?
10 ¿*ahl-kee'lah* ... ?	Do you rent by the month or by the week?
11 ...	How much do you charge for room and board?
12 ¿ ... *kahrr'tah?*	Are the meals also served a la carte?

(masc.), and -*ona*, -*ota*, -*aza* (fem.), and they imply *contempt, aversion,* or *unnatural size,* as: from *salón, salonzote, salonzazo,* unnecessarily large room; from *hombre, hombrón, hombrote, hombrazo,* a big, strong man; from *mujer, mujerona,* a big, strong woman. The suffix -*azo,* when applied to nouns of the neuter gender in English, such as *stick, sword,* etc., means a *blow struck,* as: from *bastón,* cane; *bastonazo,* a blow struck with a cane; from *sable,* sabre, *sablazo.* The suffix -*ada* is similarly applied, asó from *puñal,* poniard, *puñalada,* a stab with a poniard; -*azo* applies to blunt instruments, and -*ada* to sharp ones. The simple idea of *large* or *small* size is expressed, as in English, by the adjectives *grande* and *pequeño.* 4. *Mostrar,* to show, and *enseñar,* to show or to teach are synonymous in

13 Deseo alquilar un cuarto amueblado y espacioso.

14 Debo informarle que el pago es por adelantado.

15 Entendido; pero preferiría pagarle por semana.

16 Dispénseme usted, pero todos[6] mis arreglos son por mes y no puedo arrendar en otras condiciones.

17 En ese caso le pagaré por quincena adelantada; es lo más[7] a que puedo comprometerme.

18 El cuarto tiene, por supuesto, lavabo y baño.

19 Sí, señor; nuestros cuartos están provistos de todas las comodidades modernas: gas, electricidad, calefacción, agua fría y agua caliente.

20 Bien; deseo mudarme[8] cuanto antes, y si me lo permite, tomaré los cuartos desde[9] ahora.

21 Dentro de una hora estará aquí el equipaje.

22 Aquí tiene el importe de una quincena. Hágame el favor de darme un recibo.

23 Aquí tiene el recibo firmado.

24 Tenga la bondad de leérmelo.[10]

---

this sense. 5. *Dé*, present subjunctive of *dar*, is used idiomatically, meaning *to face*. 6. *Todo, todos, toda, todas*, whole, all, every, everything; as: *todo el día*, the whole day; *todos los días*, every day; *toda la noche*, the whole night; *todas las noches*, every night; *todas las veces*, *every time*. 7. The superlative is formed by means of *más, menos*, and the article *el, la, lo, los, las*, as: *estas casas son las más hermosas de la cuidad*. It sometimes relates an idea, as in the sentence *es lo*

13 . . . *ays-pah-theeoh'soh.*	I want to rent a large (sized), furnished room.
14 . . .	I must inform you that the payment is in advance.
15 *ayn-tayn-dee'doh* . . .	I understand, but I should prefer to pay you by the week.
16 . . . *ah-rray'glohs* . . .	I am sorry, but all my arrangements are monthly, and I cannot rent under any other conditions.
17 . . . *keen-thay'nah* . . .	In that case I will pay you every fortnight in advance; that is the most I can promise to do.
18 . . . *pohrr soo-pways'toh,* . . .	The room has, of course, a wash basin and bath.
19 . . . *proh-vees'tohs* . . .	Yes, sir; our apartments are provided with all the modern conveniences: gas, electricity, heat, hot and cold water.
20 . . . *moo-dahrr'may* . . .	All right, I wish to move as soon as possible, and if you will permit me, I shall take the rooms right now.
21 . . . *ay-kee-pah'hay.*	Within an hour my luggage will be here.
22 . . . *keen-thay'nah* . . .	Here is the payment for a fortnight. Please give me a receipt.
23 . . .	Here is the receipt signed.
24 . . . *bohn-dahd'?*	Please read it to me.

---

más a que puedo comprometerme. *8. Mudarse,* to move, means to change one's *place* in the sense of going to live elsewhere, while *mover,* to move, implies movement only. *9. Desde,* from, points out the *beginning* of *time* or *place,* as: *Desde la creación del mundo;* From the creation of the world. *Desde Nueva York a Filadelfia;* From New York to Philadelphia. For this reason it forms part of several adverbial expressions which signify time or place, viz: *desde ahora,* from this time; *desde aquí,* from hence, etc. *10.* In Spanish a sentence is never constructed, as in English, by placing *para mi* after the verb, but by using the accusative pro-

25 "Recibí de don Fulano de Tal[11] la cantidad[12] de cincuenta pesos ($50.00) equivalentes a una quincena adelantada en pago de los cuartos que ocupa en la calle del Pez,[13] número *15* Ciudad de Méjico, 15 de enero . . ."

26 Las comidas se sirven: de siete y media a nueve de la mañana, el desayuno o almuerzo; la comida, de doce a una, y la cena desde las siete en punto[14] a las nueve de la noche.

27 Le ruego me enseñe el cuarto de baño.

28 Aquí está. Como puede observar, está provisto de regadera, esponja, toallas y un estante para el peine, el cepillo, el perfume, los polvos, la crema, la pasta de los dientes, etc.

---

noun *me* before or after the verb, according to the tense in use. In the present instance it is not permissible to say, *sírvase Ud. leerlo para mí,* but *leérmelo,* viz.: *¿quiere Ud. alcanzarme* (lit. reach me) *eso?* instead of *¿quiere Ud. alcanzar eso para mí?* will you please get that *for me?* Unless the sentence should begin with a preposition, then it must be mentioned in the answer, and the construction will be as in English, viz.: *¿para quién lo alcanzo? le suplico que lo alcance Ud. para mí.* 11. *Don Fulano de Tal,* Mr. Such-a-Person, Mr. So-and-So. *Tal (tales,* pl.), such, such a, refers to persons and things, as: *no conozco a tal persona,* I don't know such a person; *tal individuo no vive aquí,* such an individual does not live

25 ... *Joo-lah'noh day Tahl* ...   "Received from Mr. So-and-So the sum of fifty pesos ($50.00), in payment of (equivalent to) a fortnight's rent in advance for the rooms he occupies at No. 15 Pez Street, City of Mexico, January 15th ..."

26 ... *say seerr'vayn* ...   Meals are served: breakfast from 7:30 to 9:00 a.m.; lunch from 12:00 to 1:00, and dinner from 7:00 o'clock sharp until 9:00 p.m.

27 ... *rrway'goh* ...   Please show me the bathroom.

28 ... *ohb-sayrr-vahrr'* ...   Here it is. As you can see, it is provided with a sprinkler, a sponge, towels and a stand for a comb, brush, perfume, powder, cold cream, toothpaste, etc.

here; *tal amo, tal criado*, like master, like servant. *Un tal, una tal*, means *a certain*; *un tal Fernández estuvo aquí*, a certain Fernández was here. *Tal cual* means *so so*, as: *¿cómo está Ud.? tal cual*. *Con tal que* means *on condition that*, as: *se lo prestaré a Ud. con tal que me lo devuelva*, I shall lend it to you on condition that you return it to me.   12. *Cantidad* or *suma*, sum, are equally correct.   13. *Pez*, fish. In Spanish the word *calle* is always placed before the noun. *La calle del Pez*, the Street of the Fish, Fish Street.   14. The combination of the words *en punto*, used *only* in connection with the hour, is idiomatic, and synonymous with *exactamente*, sharp.

16 LECCION DECIMOSEXTA

Nuevo Vocabulario

el directorio (*dee-rayk-toh'reeoh*)	the directory
las sucursales (*soo-koorr-sah'lays*)	branch stores
papel carbón (*pah-payl'kahrr-bohn'*)	carbon paper
papel de cartas (. . . *cahrr'tahs*)	writing paper
papel secante (. . . *say-kahn'tay*)	blotting paper
hacer efectiva (. . . *ay-fayk-tee'vah*)	to cash
sitio céntrico (*see'teeoh thayn'tree-koh*)	central location

correo aéreo   air mail
  (*koh-rray'oh ah-ay'ray-oh*)
la carta (*kahrr'tah*)   the letter

sección comercial (. . . *ko -mayrr-thee-ahl'*)	business section
últimamente (*ool'tee-mah-mayn'tay*)	lately
realizar (*rray-ah-lee-thahrr'*)	to make
ocupados (*oh-koo-pah'dohs*)	busy
en seguida (*ayn say-ghee'dah*)	at once
suficiente (*soo-fee-thee-ayn'tay*)	enough, sufficient

el lápiz (*lah'peeth*)   the pencil
la regla (*rray'glah*)   ruler

el escritorio (*ays-kree-toh'reeoh*)	the writing desk
la máquina de escribir (*mah'kee-nah day ays-kree-beerr'*)	typewriter
las circulares (*theerr-koo-lah'rays*)	circular letters
el conocimiento (*koh-noh-thee-mee-ayn'toh*)	bill of lading
la mercancía (*mayrr-kahn-thee'ah*)	merchandise
la papelería (*pah-pay-lay-ree'ah*)	stationery store
hoja de papel (*oh'hah day pah-payl'*)	sheet of paper
contabilidad (*kon-tah-bee-lee-dahd'*)	accounting

LAS RELACIONES COMERCIALES
(lahs ray-lah-thee-oh'-nays koh-mer-thee-a'h-lays)

COMMERCIAL RELATIONS

al menos (*ahl may'nohs*)	at least	**la copia** (*koh'peeah*)	the copy
cierto (*thee-ayrr'toh*)	certain, sure	**la tinta** (*teen'tah*)	ink
por cierto (*pohrr . . .*)	incidentally	**el tintero** (*teen-tay'roh*)	inkstand
en punto (*ayn poon'toh*)	exactly	**la letra** (*lay'trah*)	draft
el sobre (*soh'bray*)	the envelope	**el mapa** (*mah'pah*)	map
la pluma (*ploo'mah*)	pen	**el agente** (*ah-hayn'tay*)	agent

diario (*dee-ah'reeoh*) the journal
libro mayor (*lee'broh mah-yohrr'*) ledger
libro de caja (*lee'broh day kah'hah*) cash book

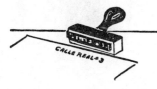

el sello (*say'llioh*) the stamp, seal
sellos de goma rubber stamps
    (*say'lliohs day goh'mah*)

FOOTNOTES: *1. Ha*, he or she has, you have, is the 3rd pers. sing., present indicative, of the auxiliary verb *haber*, to have; *he*, I have; *hemos*, we have; *han*, they have. This verb, when used as an auxiliary, must always be followed by the past participle of the principal verb, as in English.   *2. Escrito, written*, is the past part. of the irregular verb *escribir*.   *3. Hecho*, made, done, is the past part. of the irregular verb *hacer*, to make, to do.   *4. Se habla*, an impersonal expression

CONVERSATION

1 ¿Qué ha[1] hecho usted hoy?

2 ¿Han trabajado ustedes mucho?

3 Sí, señor; hemos estado muy ocupados escribiendo la correspondencia para nuestras sucursales en Hispano América.

4 ¿Ha escrito[2] usted las cartas en español?

5 Naturalmente, así lo he hecho.[3] En esos países se habla[4] español y hay que escribir las cartas en ese idioma.

6 ¿Escriben ustedes sus cartas a máquina?

7 Sí, toda casa moderna escribe hoy sus cartas a máquina y generalmente se sacan dos copias.

8 ¿Tiene[5] usted relaciones comerciales con Perú y Chile?

9 Sí; tenemos negocios con esos países y también con Venezuela, Bolivia, Colombia y Méjico.

10 Deseo hacer efectiva una letra. Necesito dinero norteamericano y no tengo sino pesos colombianos.

11 Yo he hecho hoy efectiva una letra de Méjico.

---

meaning *it is spoken* or *they speak.*   5. *Tiene,* from *tener,* to have, to possess, to hold. *Tengo,* I have; *tenemos,* we have; *tienen,* they have. There are two verbs in Spanish, *haber* and *tener,* corresponding to the English *to have.* Tener is an active verb, while *haber* is an auxiliary, which must always be followed by the

PRONUNCIATION	TRANSLATION
1 ¿ ... ?	What have you done today?
2 ¿ ... trah-bah-hah'doh ... ?	Have you (pl.) worked hard?
3 ... soo-koorr-sah'lays ...	Yes, we have been very busy writing the correspondence for our branches in Spanish America.
4 ¿ ... ays-kree'toh ... ?	Have you written the letters in Spanish?
5 ... pah-ee'says ...	Naturally, I did so. In those countries they speak Spanish and the letters must be written in that language.
6 ¿ ... ?	Do you typewrite your letters?
7 ... sah'kahn ...	Yes; today every modern (business) house types its letters, and ordinarily they make two copies.
8 ¿ ... rray-lah-theeoh'nays ... ?	Have you business relations with Peru and Chile?
9 ... nay-goh'theeohs ...	Yes, we do business with those countries and also with Venezuela, Bolivia, Colombia and Mexico.
10 ... nohrr-tay-ah-may-ree-kah' noh ...	I want to cash a draft. I need American currency and I only have Colombian pesos.
11 ... May'hee-koh.	I have cashed a Mexican draft today.

past participle of the active verb being conjugated, as: *he tenido dinero,* I have had money. *He,* present indicative, of the auxiliary verb *haber; tenido,* past participle of the active verb *tener,* to possess, to hold. To be more explicit, *tengo un libro,* I have a book, can not be expressed by *yo he un libro.*   6. If the verb *haber* is followed by *de,* it is synonymous with the English *to have to, to be obliged to,* and it must then precede the infinitive of the principal verb, as: *hemos de,* we have to, *he de,* I have to, etc.   7. *Cierran,* they close, from *cerrar,* a radical changing verb.   8. *Mandar* means both to *command* or *to send.*   9. Nouns ending in *-e* are for the most part masculine, with some exceptions, as: *la noche,*

12 ¿Hemos de[6] ir al banco inmediatamente?

      13 Sí, señor; hemos de ir en seguida porque los bancos cierran[7] a las tres en punto.

      14 ¿Cuándo tiene usted que enviar estos artículos?

      15 ¿Tiene usted que mandar[8] las mercancías en seguida?

      16 ¿No desearía usted enviar antes un radiograma a su agente?

17 No; una carta por correo aéreo será suficiente. El la recibirá el lunes.

18 Yo también tengo que escribirle una carta a mi agente en Buenos Aires esta noche.[9]

19 ¿Qué[10] día sale el correo para Chile? ¿Hay que[11] esperar mucho?

20 El vapor sale al menos una vez por semana; pero hay servicio de correo aéreo todos los días.

21 ¿Realiza usted muchas transacciones comerciales con Centro América?

---

night; *la calle,* street; *la carne,* meat, flesh; *la clase,* class; *la frase,* phrase; *la fiebre,* fever; *la leche,* milk; *la llave,* key; *la tarde,* afternoon; *la muerte,* death; *la parte,* part; and a few others. *La frente,* forehead, is feminine, but *el frente,* front, is masculine. Nouns ending in *-umbre* are feminine, as: *la lumbre,* fire; *la pesadumbre,* sorrow, etc. **10.** The relative pronouns *¿qué?* what? *¿quién?* who? and *¿cuál?* which?, are accented when used in interrogations or exclamations, as: *¿Qué tiene Vd.?* What is the matter with you? *¡Qué felicidad!* What happiness! *¡Qué bonito!* How pretty! *¿Quién llama?* Who knocks? *¿Cuál desea*

12 ¿ ... ?	Must we go to the bank immediately?
13 ... *ayn-say-ghee'dah* ... *theeay'rrahn* ...	Yes, we must go right now, because the banks close at three o'clock sharp.
14 ¿ ... *ayn-vee-ahrr'* ... ?	When do you have to send out these articles?
15 ¿ ... *mairr-kahn-thee'ahs* ... ?	Do you have to ship the merchandise immediately?
16 ¿ ... *ah-hayn'tay?*	Wouldn't you like first to. send a radiogram to your agent?
17 ... *koh-rray'oh ah-ay'ray-oh* ...	No, an air mail letter will be sufficient. He will receive it by Monday.
18 ...	I also have to write a letter tonight to my agent in Buenos Aires.
19 ¿ ... *ays-pay-rahrr'* ... ?	On what day does the mail leave for Chile? Does one have to wait long?
20 *ell vah-pohrr'* ...	The boat leaves at least once a week, but there is air mail service every day.
21 ¿ ... ?	Do you do much business with Central America?

Ud.? Which one do you wish?   *11. Hay que,* it is necessary, is the present of the impersonal verb *haber que. Haber,* as impersonal, means *there* (to) *be;* and if followed by *que,* it is idiomatically translated *to be necessary,* synonymous with *ser necesario. 12.* For the days of the month the cardinal numbers are used instead of the ordinal in Spanish. *Primero,* first, is the only exception, viz.: *hoy es el primero de mayo,* today is the first of May. The second, third, etc., are named *el dos, el tres,* etc., the two, the three, etc. *13. libro mayor,* means *ledger,* but the word *mayor* by itself means *larger* and is the comparative of the adjective *grande,* large. The following adjectives are compared irregularly:

ADJECTIVES	COMPARATIVES	SUPERLATIVES
Grande, large;	*mayor,* larger;	*el, la, lo mayor,* the largest.
Pequeño, small;	*menor,* smaller;	*el, la, lo menor,* the smallest.
Bueno, good;	*mejor,* better;	*el, la, lo mejor,* the best
Malo, bad;	*peor,* worse;	*el, la, lo peor,* the worst.

Mayor also means *older,* and *menor,* younger. *El* or *la mayor* (the largest), means also *the eldest,* and *el* or *la menor* (the smallest), the youngest.

22 Ultimamente hemos vendido bastante mercancía a Guatemala, Costa Rica y Panamá.

23 En ese caso necesitará usted abrir una oficina mayor en Nueva York, ¿no es cierto?

24 Pienso abrir una nueva oficina en un sitio céntrico de la ciudad, en la sección comercial, el quince[12] de este mes.

25 ¿Ha comprado ya los artículos que necesita para su oficina?

26 Todavía no; pero mañana compraré nuevos escritorios, varias mesas, seis máquinas de escribir, tinteros, tinta, papel de cartas, sellos de goma, circulares, mapas, un directorio comercial, etc.

27 Y para contabilidad necesitará seguramente un diario, un libro mayor,[13] un libro de caja y libros auxiliares.

22   . . . *Gwah-tay-mah'lah, Kohs' tah Rree'kah ee Pah-nah-mah'.*

Lately we have sold a great deal of merchandise to Guatemala, Cost Rica and Panama.

23   . . .

In that case you will have to open a larger office in New York. Is it not so?

24   . . . *see'teeoh   thayn'tree-koh* . . .

I intend to open a new office centrally located in the business section of the city, on the 15th of this month.

25   ¿ . . . *nay-thay-see'tah . . . ?*

Have you already purchased the articles that you need for your office?

26   . . .

No, I haven't yet, but tomorrow I am going to buy new writing desks, several tables, six typewriters, inkstands, ink, writing paper, rubber stamps, circular letters, maps, a commercial directory, etc.

27   . . . *kohn-tah-bee-lee-dahd'* . . .

And for your accounting department you will need a journal, a ledger, a cash book and auxiliary books.

17 LECCION DECIMOSEPTIMA

VIAJE POR HISPANO AMÉRICA

Las estrechas relaciones de amistad y comercio que existen entre los pueblos que ocupan el Hemisferio Occidental son cada vez mayores, más íntimas y cordiales y, por esta razón, nada

puede agradar más a los habitantes de la gran República Norteamericana que un viaje a través de las naciones de habla española que, junto con el Brasil, ocupan el área mayor del Continente Americano.

Estos países, tan pintorescos, tan llenos de curiosidades geológicas e históricas, son hoy, gracias a los rápidos medios modernos de comunicación, sumamente accesibles al viajero norteamericano.

Hay varias vías de comunicación para llegar a ellos: por aeroplano, por automóvil, ferrocarril o vapor.

Emprendamos, pues, nuestro viaje saliendo de Nueva York en dirección a la vecina república de Méjico.[1]

FOOTNOTES: *1. Méjico* constituye los extremos S. O. y S. de la América del Norte, y ocupa una porción del Istmo de Tehuantepec, que con el de Panamá, pone en comunicación los dos grandes continentes americanos. Fué conquistado por Hernan Cortés en 1519, cuando ocupaba el trono azteca el emperador Moctezuma. En 1540 formó parte de la monarquía española bajo el nombre de Nueva España, continuando así hasta 1810, en que tuvo lugar la primera insurrección capitaneada por el cura Hidalgo, quien se aprovechó de la oportunidad que ofrecía a sus planes la guerra napoleónica en la Península. Más tarde Guerrero e Iturbide dieron el grito de rebelión, y el último se constituyó emperador hasta 1824, en que fué declarada la Independencia; quedando establecida una forma republicana federal

Partiendo de Nueva York se puede ir directamente a Méjico por vapor hasta el puerto de Veracruz, o podemos ir por ferrocarril hasta Laredo, en el estado de Tejas, ciudad ésta que fué fundada por los españoles y hoy se encuentra en la línea divisoria de ambas naciones, frontera que forma casi en su totalidad el famoso Río Grande.

Cruzando este río se llega a Nuevo Laredo, Estado de Tamaulipas, Méjico. Siguiendo el viaje hacia la capital mejicana, se atraviesa por una gran planicie, la cual se convierte, poco a poco, en terreno montañoso, presentando el paisaje más pintoresco.

El viajero distingue en el curso de su camino la célebre Mesa de los Cartujos, la cual se halla en una montaña que tiene la

---

con un Presidente. En 1841, al dimitir Bustamante, el general Santa Ana tomó las riendas del gobierno declarándose dictador. En 1845, Méjico se vió obligado a reconocer la independencia de Tejas, que fué incorporado a los Estados Unidos, declarándose entonces la guerra entre ambos países, que duró hasta que en 1848 se firmó la paz. Después de esta fecha, el país estuvo sucesivamente en manos de Herrera, Cevallos, Santa Ana (segunda vez), Alvarez, Comonfort, Zuvalgo, Robles y Juárez, al que se opuso el general Miramón, jefe del partido conservador. Declarada la guerra entre embos partidos, necesitaron intervenir Inglaterra, España y Francia en apoyo de sus súbditos, concluyendo la intervención con un tratado al que se adhirieron y confirmaron las dos primeras naciones. Francia declaró entonces la guerra al gobierno de Juárez constituído poder, y su ejército, al mando primero del general Forey y luego al de Bazaine, continuó las hostilidades. Poco después

particularidad de ser inaccesible, excepto por un solo punto.

A pocas horas de viaje se encuentra la bonita ciudad de Monterrey,[2] que por su situación es considerada como de las más lindas del país.

La ciudad, enclavada en la Sierra Madre, se levanta entre dos montañas llamadas, una La Silla, por su parecido a una silla de montar española, y la otra Las Mitras, por su semejanza a la prenda de este nombre que usan los obispos católicos.

Entre otras cosas notables llaman la atención en Monterrey su hermosa catedral y su bonita y bien cuidada plaza.

A poco de salir de Monterrey, el viajero se encuentra a una altura de 5,300 (cinco mil trescientos) pies, y admira el panorama más bello que la naturaleza puede presentar.

Más tarde pasa el tren por Saltillo[3] y a corta distancia de Buena Vista, pueblo célebre por la famosa batalla de su nombre librada en febrero de 1847 (mil ochocientos cuarenta y siete) entre las tropas de Estados Unidos y Méjico; para después el

se decidió, en unión de los conservadores de Méjico, mandar una diputación a afrecer el trono al Archiduque Maximiliano de Austria, quien se presentó en Méjico a tomar posesión el 12 de Junio de 1864, ocupándolo hasta el trágico fin del Cerro de las Campanas. 2. Monterrey ocupa una preciosa situación en uno de los valles más fértiles de Méjico. Como a unas tres millas de la ciudad, se hallan los celebrados baños calientes de *Topo Chico,* cada día más conocidos por sus propiedades medicinales. El clima allí es muy agradable, y los manantiales poseen la ventaja de ser tan accesibles en verano como en invierno. 3. *Saltillo,* capital del estado de *Coahuila,* es uns población bastante atractiva. Sus calles están trazadas a cordel; posee una preciosa plaza y algunos edificios de cierto mérito arquitectónico. 4. Las primeras minas de plata fueron descubiertas en 1780. La ciudad dista ocho millas de la estación, y por esta razón, *Catorce,* que es muy interesante, no es nunca visitada por turistas. El número de sus habitantes varía según las condiciones de las minas. Las calles están por lo general bien cuidadas, pero son en extremo pendientes, algunas de ellas formando un ángulo de 45 grados. 5. *San Luis Potosí,* capital del estado de su nombre, está bien construída

tren en Catorce,[4] el distrito minero por excelencia de la República, entrando por último en Şan Luis Potosí,[5] ciudad de gran importancia.

Allí es digna de visitarse la vieja catedral de San Francisco. Desde San Luis corre el tren por campos fertilísimos, donde la naturaleza se nos presenta en todo su esplendor, y a su paso se ven: el histórico pueblo de Dolores Hidalgo,[6] nombre que le fué dado en honor de Don Miguel Hidalgo; Celaya,[7] famosa por sus dulces, y otras poblaciones.

A corta distancia de la última nombrada se encuentra Querétaro,[8] célebre por haber sido allí fusilado el emperador Maximiliano, el 19 (diez y nueve) de junio de 1867 (mil ochocientos sesenta y siete). El sitio en donde el infortunado emperador concluyó sus días se denomina Cerro de las Campanas.

Antes del término del viaje se pasa por Toluca, capital del Estado de Méjico, situada al pie del volcán El Nevado de Toluca.[9]

---

y situada a unos 6,350 pies sobre el nivel del mar. Sus calles son en general estrechas, pero en extremo pintorescas. *6.* El pueblo es pequeño siendo una de las cosas más interesantes de ver en él las reliquias de su héroe, conservadas en la casa que habitaba. *Don Miguel Hidalgo,* nacido en la América del Sur, pero residente en Méjico, murió ajusticiado el 27 de Julio de 1811. Su elocuencia tenía un poderoso efecto en la clase del pueblo, y el vigor de sus palabras lo acompañaba mostrando a la virgen de Guadalupe, patrona de Méjico, dando de este modo a la insurrección el carácter de cruzada. En esta forma y capitaneando sus fuerzas llegó a las puertas de la capital, pero excomulgado entonces por el arcipreste, sus partidarios perdieron su confianza, completando su ruina y la de todas sus fuerzas dos derrotas sucesivas que sufrió. *7. Celaya* está edificada en un llano en el valle de *La Laja.* Es famosa esta ciudad por la batalla librada en ella entre las fuerzas de los generales Villa y Obregón durante la revolución mejicana. *8. Querétaro* es la capital de su Estado. La ciudad está construída sobre un plano regular. Contiene algunos edificios ricamente decorados y un magnífico acueducto que surte de agua a la ciudad. *9.* La montaña tiene una altura de 15,000 pies, y la ciudad se alza

La ascensión al volcán es fácil, y una vez en su cráter, donde se extiende un lago de gran profundidad, puede disfrutarse de uno de los más sorprendentes panoramas del país.

Méjico,[10] la gran ciudad de los aztecas, cuya historia romántica y llena de tradiciones no desmerece de la bellísima posición que ocupa, está situada en el valle de Tenochtitlán cerca del Lago Tezcoco.  Sus calles principales son rectas, bien trazadas y todas en dirección a la gran plaza de armas, llamada el Zócalo,[11] dos lados de cuyo cuadrado lo ocupan la catedral, erigida sobre las ruinas del gran teocalli o templo azteca, y el Palacio Nacional.

Méjico contiene además hermosos paseos, como los de La Alameda y La Reforma, plantados con doble hilera de árboles; magníficos edificios y casas particulares. Su Academia de Bellas Artes posee una rica colección de antigüedades aztecas, y sus escuelas e iglesias son notables por su arquitectura.

Cerca de la capital se halla Chapultepec, fortaleza bellamente situada sobre un montículo de roca de unos doscientos pies de altura que resguarda a un castillo construído en el centro, el cual sirvió de residencia al malogrado emperador Maximiliano I.

Este castillo, destinado hoy a Observatorio Astronómico, es de las cosas más dignas de visitarse en Méjico, tanto por las curiosidades que encierra como por el dilatado y grandioso panorama que desde allí se descubre.

---

a 8,600 sobre el nivel del mar. *Toluca* se extiende en un valle muy feraz al oeste de Sierra Madre, donde termina la *Tierra caliente.* *10.* La ciudad de Méjico, antigua *Tenochtitlán* del imperio Azteca, está situada a 7,500 pies sobre el nivel del mar, y tiene 1,750,000 habitantes. *11. Zócalo*, palabra que en arquitectura designa el cuerpo inferior de un edificio, o la parte inferior de un pedestal, es el nombre de la plaza principal de Méjico. *12. Guatemala.* Area: 125,071 kms.

El Teatro Nacional es un hermoso edificio decorado con un lujo extraordinario.

Los hoteles son cómodos, buenos y elegantes, contándose entre los principales el de Iturbide y el del Jardín.

En Méjico, por su elevación que es de siete mil quinientos pies sobre el nivel del mar, se respira un aire muy puro, y el promedio de su temperatura durante el año es de 60 grados.

Desde Méjico pasamos a Guatemala,[12] no sin antes haber cruzado por Yucatán, donde pueden admirarse las ruinas de la esplendorosa civilización Maya, que pueden compararse en interés histórico con las de Egipto.

En Guatemala visitamos la capital de la república, Guatemàla, y las ciudades de Quiriguá, Quezaltenango, Totonicapán, Cobán y Zacapa, todas ellas sumamente interesantes por su situación y las diversas fiestas que en ellas se celebran.

De Guatemala podemos salir para El Salvador[13] por ferrocarril, llegando a Santa Ana, en la frontera salvadoreña, y tomando aquí el tren para San Salvador, la capital de la república.

Visitamos en esta adelantada nación, además de la capital, las ciudades de Santa Tecla, Sonsonate, San Miguel y San Vicente. También el bello lago de Ilopango, a 10 (diez) millas de San Salvador, y el volcán de Izalco, que hace unos 120 (ciento veinte) años se levantó de una planicie y ya alcanza una elevación de 6,000 (seis mil) pies.

---

cuadrados (48,290 millas cuadradas). Población: 3,500,000 habitantes. Con excepción de las tierras bajas de la costa, el país es sumamente montañoso y elevado. Sus mesetas son muy saludables y fértiles y en ellas se dan todos los frutos tropicales y de las zonas templadas. El café que se cultiva en Guatemala es excelente. Otros productos del país son el azúcar, el cacao, el tabaco y los plátanos.

De El Salvador cruzamos a la República de Honduras,[14] donde visitamos la capital, Tegucigalpa, y las ciudades de San Pedro de Sula y Santa Rosa de Copán, junto con los puertos de La Ceiba, Tela y Trujillo.

Nuestra próxima visita es a Nicaragua,[15] donde podemos admirar el gran Lago de Nicaragua, la capital, Managua, y las ciudades de León, Corinto, Granada y Chinandega.

En Costa Rica[16] entramos por el bello puerto de Puntarenas, en el Pacífico, y visitamos también la capital de esta república, San José, donde admiramos magníficos edificios públicos y bellas residencias, y las ciudades de Cartago, Heredia y Alajuela.

En Puerto Limón, Costa Rica, tomamos el vapor para Colón, puerto de la República de Panamá.[16a] Esta nación ofrece muchos atractivos al viajero, particularmente el de su canal, maravilla de ingeniería moderna, que permite el paso de grandes vapores de uno al otro océano.

Después de una visita a la capital, Panamá, tomamos en el puerto de Balboa el vapor que nos conduce a Buenaventura, el

---

Tiene abundancia de minerales, maderas y caucho. *13. El Salvador* tiene un área de 34,126 kms. cuadrados (13,176 millas cuadradas) y una población de 2,000,000 de habitantes. El país está cruzado por dos cordilleras de considerable altitud, en las que se encierran numerosos y fértiles valles. En estos se cultiva el café, el cacao, el tabaco, la goma y el henequén. Hay minas de oro, plata y otros metales de considerable importancia. *14. Honduras* tiene un área de 120,000 kms. cuadrados (46,332 millas cuadradas) y una población de más de 1,175,000 de habitantes. El país es en su mayor parte montañoso y abunda en grandes y fértiles mesetas y valles, entre ellos el llano de Comayagua que tiene 64,000 kilómetros de extensión. En estos valles y llanuras se produce excelente pasto para el ganado y son tierras excelentes para todos los productos agrícolas. El país es notable por sus maderas, especialmente la caoba. Otros productos de su exportación son el azúcar, el café, el caucho, los cocos, el ganado y las pieles. El plátano se exporta en cantidades considerables. *15. Nicaragua* tiene un área de 127,428 kms. cuadrados (49,200 millas cuadradas) y una población de 1.500,000 habitantes. El país está atravesado por una cordillera de muchos picos volcánicos, que corre del noroeste al sudeste. Entre esta cordillera y las montañas volcánicas situadas al oeste, se encuentra el Lago de Managua, que tiene 48 kilómetros de largo por 24 de ancho. Aunque existen algunos yacimientos auríferos y de otros metales, el país es esencialmente agrícola. Sus principales productos de exportación son el plátano, el café, el azúcar y la caoba. *16. Costa Rica* tiene un área de 59,570

puerto principal de Colombia[17] en el Pacífico. Aquí tomamos el tren que nos lleva a Bogotá, la capital de dicha república, de donde partimos para Medellín, importante ciudad comercial, visitando también los puertos de Cartagena, Barranquilla y Santa Marta.

De Colombia pasamos a Venezuela,[18] la patria del Libertador, Simón Bolívar, el "Jorge Washington" de Sud América.

Además de Caracas, la capital, visitamos las interesantes ciudades de Mérida, donde se halla una de las más antiguas Universidades del Continente, Trujillo, Valencia, Maracay, Ciudad Bolívar y Maracaibo, ciudad ésta situada en el lago de su nombre y famosa por sus explotaciones petroleras.

De Venezuela damos un gran salto hasta llegar al Uruguay,[19] donde visitamos la capital, Montevideo, famosa por sus bellos

---

kms. cuadrados (23,000 millas cuadradas) y una población de 750,000 habitantes. Una parte de la Cordillera de los Andes atraviesa el país del noroeste al sudeste. Sus productos principales de exportación son el plátano, el cacao, el coco, el azúcar, las maderas preciosas y las frutas. Costa Rica tiene bellas ciudades modernas y en todas ellas se admira el adelanto de esta nación. *16a. Panamá* ocupa un área de 88,500 kms. cuadrados (34,170 millas cuadradas) y tiene una población de 625,000 habitantes. Dos sistemas de Cordilleras atraviesan el país, las que dan origen a un gran número de planicies y valles de tierra excelente para el cultivo y la ganadería. Sus principales productos de exportación son el plátano, el coco, las pieles, el caucho, el cacao, la madreperla, el carey y las maderas preciosas. Se explotan el oro y el manganeso y hay depósitos de plata, alumninio, carbón, plomo, hierro y asbesto. *17. Colombia* tiene un área de 1.235,214 kms. cuadrados (476,916 millas cuadradas) y una población de 10.000,000 de habitantes. Los Andes atraviesan el país en tres direcciones distintas: las Cordilleras Central, del Norte y del Este. Su río principal es el Magdalena, navegable en una gran extensión y el cual desagua en el Mar Caribe. Productos importantes del país son el café, el cacao, el azúcar, el tabaco y el plátano. La riqueza mineral del país no ha sido aún muy explotada, aunque sus minas de esmeralda son conocidas en el mundo entero y la producción del petróleo ha aumentado considerablemente en los últimos años. El oro, la plata, el platino, el azogue, el hierro y el plomo abundan en sus yacimientos. *18. Venezuela* tiene un área de 1.020,400 kms. cuadrados (393,976 millas cuadradas) y una población

y modernos edificios, y las ciudades de Paysandú, Florida y Colonia.

Tras una pequeña travesía desde Montevideo, llegamos a Buenos Aires, la gran metrópoli y capital de la República Argentina.[20] Esta moderna y populosa urbe tiene una población de más de dos millones y medio de habitantes, y es sólo superada en el resto del Continente Americano por Nueva York y Chicago.

Una visita a esta gran ciudad requeriría, para ser completa, mucho más tiempo del que disponemos, por cuya razón, después de admirar sus amplias avenidas y modernos y lujosos edificios, partimos hacia el interior de la república, visitando, entre otras, las ciudades de Rosario, Córdoba, La Plata, Tucumán y Mendoza.

Desde este último punto entramos en Chile,[21] donde visitamos la capital, Santiago, y las interesantes ciudades de Valparaíso,

---

de 3.850,000 habitantes. La región de los llanos ocupa una extensión de unas 100,000 millas cuadradas y se extiende desde la frontera de Colombia hacia el este a lo largo del gran río Orinoco, el cual tiene una longitud de 1,100 millas y es navegable hasta Puerto Ayacucho, a 1,000 millas de la desembocadura en el Atlántico. El principal producto de exportación del país es el petróleo, que constituye la riqueza nacional por excelencia. Venezuela ocupa el tercer lugar en la producción mundial del petróleo. También se exportan en grandes cantidades el café y la pluma de garza. Otros productos del país son el oro, las perlas, el hierro, el carbón, etc. *19. El Uruguay* tiene un área de 186,876 kms. cuadrados (82,153 millas cuadradas) y una población de 2.200,000 habitantes. El país es eminentemente agrícola y ganadero, produciendo cerca de un millón de toneladas métricas de cereales, entre los cuales son los más importantes el trigo y el maíz. Su principal industria es la carne congelada y los saladeros, las pieles y demás productos derivados del ganado vacuno. *20. La Argentina* tiene un área de 2.797,113 kms. cuadrados (1.079,965 millas cuadradas) y una población de 14.000,000 de habitantes. Extensas y fértiles llanuras (pampas) han hecho de la Argentina un país eminentemente agrícola y ganadero. El promedio de sus cosechas en los últimos años ha sido: Trigo, 6.500,000 toneladas métricas; maíz, 10.000,000 de toneladas métricas; linaza 2.000,000 de toneladas métricas. También son muy importantes las

Concepción, Antofagasta e Iquique.

El ferrocarril de Antofagasta a La Paz nos lleva a dicha capital de Bolivia,[22] situada a 11,910 (once mil novecientos diez) pies de altura. Después de visitar las ciudades de Sucre, Oruro, Santa Cruz y Potosí, famosa esta última por sus minas

de plata, tomamos el tren que nos conduce al famoso Lago de Titicaca, el mayor de los lagos en Sud América y el de mayor elevación en el mundo.

De Bolivia pasamos al Paraguay,[23] donde visitamos la capital, Asunción, y las ciudades de Villa Rica y Villa Concepción, ambas importantes por su comercio e industria.

El aeroplano que sale de Asunción nos lleva de nuevo a Buenos Aires, donde hacemos nuevos transbordos, que finalmente nos dejan en el Perú.[24]

En este interesante país visitamos la bella capital, Lima, y las históricas ciudades de Cuzco, Trujillo, Callao y Mollendo, estas

cosechas de azúcar de caña, algodón, centeno, cebada y otros productos agrícolas. La ganadería y la industria derivada de ésta ocupan lugar importantísimo en la economía mundial. El país es también importante en la producción de petróleo. *21. Chile* tiene un área de 741,765 kms. cuadrados (286,396 millas cuadradas) y una población de 5.300,000 habitantes. El país es sumamente rico en yacimientos minerales, en los que se explotan el cobre, el oro, la plata, el cobalto, el níquel, el plomo, el hierro y el manganeso. En la zona sur se encuentran sus famosos y vastos yacimientos de nitrato, azufre y bórax. La agricultura también se halla muy desarrollada. *22. Bolivia* tiene un área de 1.086,427 kms. cuadrados (419,470 millas cuadradas) y una población de 3.500,000 habitantes. La fuente principal de riqueza del país es la minería, y los minerales más importantes que se explotan son el estaño, la plata, el plomo, el wolframio, el zinc, el antimonio y el cobre. El caucho, la quina y la coca se exportan en cantidades considerables. *23. El Paraguay* tiene un área de 457,000 kms. cuadrados (154,165 millas cuadradas) y una población de 1.600,000 habitantes. La agricultura y la ganadería son las fuentes principales de riqueza del país. Sus cosechas más importantes son de yerba mate, algodón y tabaco. Una de sus principales exportaciones es el quebracho, del cual se extrae el tanino para el curtido de pieles. *24. El Perú* ocupa un área

dos últimas, importantes puertos del Pacífico.

Del Perú pasamos a la República del Ecuador,[25] donde hacemos una visita a la capital, Quito, y a las ciudades más importantes del país: Cuenca, Riobamba, Loja y Guayaquil, puerto éste del Pacífico en el cual tomamos el vapor que nos conduce a través del Canal de Panamá y nos lleva a La Habana, capital de la República de Cuba,[26] la isla mayor de las Antillas.

Después de admirar los numerosos y notables edificios que hermosean a la capital cubana,[27] hacemos un recorrido de la isla, visitando las ciudades de Santiago de Cuba, Camagüey, Matanzas y Santa Clara.

El vapor nos conduce más tarde a la República de Santo Domingo,[28] la cual, junto con Haití, forma la Isla Española, nombre con que esta isla es tradicionalmente conocida.

En Santo Domingo visitamos la capital, Ciudad Trujillo, y las ciudades de Santiago de los Caballeros, San Pedro Macorís y Puerto Plata.

---

de 1.249,048 kms. cuadrados (482,258 millas cuadradas) y una población de 7.000,000 de habitantes. El Perú es tradicionalmente conocido por sus riquezas minerales. Se explotan en cantidades considerables el petróleo, el cobre, el oro, la plata, el vanadio, el antimonio y el bismuto. Uno de los principales productos de exportación es el guano que se usa para el abono de las tierras de labranza. La agricultura se halla también hastante desarrollada. 25. *El Ecuador* tiene un área de 873,844 kms. cuadrados (337,392 millas cuadradas) y una población de 3.500,000 habitantes. Sus principales productos de exportación son el cacao, el marfil vegetal, los sombreros de paja, el caucho, el café, las pieles, el oro, la quina y otros. 26. *Cuba* tiene un área de 114,385 kms. cuadrados (44,164 millas cuadradas) y una población de 4.800,000 habitantes. Sus principales productos de exportación son el azúcar, el tabaco, el plátano, la piña y otras frutas. *La Isla de Cuba* está situada en el golfo de Méjico, entre las penínsulas de Yucatán y Florida y a la misma distancia (50 millas) de ambos estrechos. Cuba es la mayor de las Antillas. Fué descubierta el año 1492, en el primer viaje de Cristóbal Colón. De Cuba fué de donde salió la expedición para la conquista de Méjico al mando de Cortés. La situación de la Isla es en extremo favorable para el comercio, mientras que la extraordinaria feracidad de su suelo y naturaleza de sus productos, le dan ventajas inmensas. De 250 ríos aproximadamente que tiene la Isla, sólo uno, *El Cauto*, es navegable. El más interesante de ellos es el *Ay*, que se parte en varios lugares formando pintorescas cataratas, algunas de ellas de 200 pies de altura. El termómetro rara vez asciende a 100 grados F. o baja de 50. El clima es sano, especialmente durante seis meses del año, tanto en la costa como en el interior.

Y con esto damos por terminado nuestro largo, interesante e instructivo viaje a través de la América de habla española, donde tuvimos ocasión de practicar el idioma que hemos aprendido en este Método.

---

27. La Habana, capital de la *Isla de Cuba,* es una bonita ciudad, preciosamente situada, con excelente puerto, buenos teatros, etc. Sus calles en la parte vieja son estrechas, pero en la parte nueva están construídas regularmente, son anchas y con espaciosas aceras. Los paseos son hermosísimos, distinguiéndose los de *La India, La Punta, El Parque Central* y *El Prado.* Las casas son bajas, sólidamente construídas, y muy parecidas a las del Mediodía de España. A causa del excesivo número de vehículos en la ciudad, las calles se hacen a veces intransitables.
28. La *República Dominicana*. Area: 50,050 kms. cuadrados (19,325 millas cuadradas). Población: 2.000,000 de habitantes. Sus principales productos de exportación son el azúcar, el coco, el café y el tabaco. El país es principalmente agrícola, pero también se benefician algunos minerales.

18 LECCION DECIMOCTAVA

VIAJE POR ESPAÑA[1]

Irún[2] es el primer pueblo de España en la frontera de Francia, en los Pirineos occidentales. Los carabineros[3] registran allí el equipaje.

Suena la campana de la estación; el tren parte cruzando por parajes en extremo pintorescos y llega a San Sebastián,[4] lindí-

simo y aristocrático sitio de veraneo, que tiene una preciosa y bien situada playa, la cual se ve favorecida por distinguidos bañistas del país y del extranjero.

Cerca de San Sebastián se halla Azpeitia, hermoso pueblecito rodeado de las pintorescas montañas de Guipúzcoa,[5] y célebre por haber sido la cuna[6] de San Ignacio de Loyola, el fundador de la Compañía de Jesús. Allí se levanta el famoso monasterio de Loyola dedicado a su patrono.

FOOTNOTES: *1. España.* Estado de Europa que forma con Portugal la Península Ibérica. Limita al Norte con el Mar Cantábrico y Francia, al Este con el Mar Mediterráneo, al Sur con el mismo mar, el Estrecho de Gibraltar y el Océano Atlántico, y al Oeste con Portugal y el Atlántico. Tiene un área de 505,196 kilómetros cuadrados y una población de 26.000,000 de habitantes. El clima es vario, pero saludable y su suelo es muy fértil, produciéndose en grandes cantidades la aceituna y el aceite, los vinos, los cereales y las frutas. También se explotan casi todos los minerales conocidos, entre ellos el azogue, el cobre, el hierro, el plomo, la plata, el azufre, el carbón, etc. *2. Irún* es un pueblecito pequeño, de construcción moderna. *3. Carabinero*, nombre con que se designa al soldado cuya ocupación es la de perseguir el contrabando. *4. San Sebastián*, puerto de mar perteneciente a *Guipúzcoa*. Está situado en una península en la base del *Monte Orgullo*, defensa de tan bella y fuerte posición que ha merecido

La locomotora, emprendiendo otra vez su interrumpida marcha en dirección a Castilla[7] la Vieja, pasa por Vitoria, la alegre y bonita ciudad capital de la provincia de Alava, que siempre será memorable por la decisiva e importante victoria que obtuvieron allí los españoles sobre los franceses capitaneados por José Bonaparte y Jourdan, el 21 (veintiuno) de junio de 1813 (mil ochocientos trece). El tren detiénese luego en Burgos,[8] la patria del Cid Campeador, con su antigua y célebre catedral, inestimable modelo de arquitectura gótica, y cuyas capillas guardan riquísimos tesoros en esculturas y sepulcros.

---

el nombre de *Gibraltar del Norte*. *San Sebastián* fué casi totalmente destruída en 1913 durante la guerra entre Francia y España, pero fué posteriormente reedificada sobre un plano rectangular perfecto. 5. *Guipúzcoa* es una de las tres provincias vascongadas: *Vizcaya, Guipúzcoa* y *Alava*. Las tres forman una especie de triángulo cuya base al norte es la bahía de Vizcaya. El aspecto general de estas provincias es montañoso, pero excesivamente pintoresco. 6. *Cuna* se llama la cama para niños, pero en lenguaje figurado se aplica este nombre a la patria o lugar de nacimiento de alguno. 7. *Castilla* es, considerándola desde el punto de vista geográfico y político, el distrito central de la península española. Se divide en *Castilla la Nueva* y *Castilla la Vieja*, que son los dos antiguos reinos. La capital de *Castilla la Vieja* era Valladolid, y Madrid la de *Castilla la Nueva*, subdividiéndose ahora ambos reinos en varias provincias. *Castilla la Vieja* comprende las provincias de Burgos, Logroño, Santander, Soria, Segovia, Avila, Palencia y Valladolid. A *Castilla la Nueva* pertenecen Madrid, Guadalajara, Cuenca, Toledo, y Ciudad Real. 8. *Burgos*, capital de la provincia del mismo nombre, perteneciente al antiguo reino de Castilla la Vieja, está situada en un fértil valle al pie de la *Sierra de Oca* y a la derecha del río *Arlanzón*. Burgos es una de las ciudades más antiguas de

El carácter de los españoles es en general franco, entusiasta y expansivo. Apenas se pone el tren en movimiento, entablan conversación que poco a poco se hace más interesante y amistosa. Valladolid[9] fué capital y corte del reino de Castilla la Vieja. Allí nació Felipe II, y allí está el célebre Colegio del Arma de Caballería. Su museo es un elegante edificio lleno de cuadros y de esculturas, siendo las últimas el tesoro de más valor que encierra, no obstante haber entre los cuadros varios firmados por Murillo, Rubéns y otros artistas de nombre.

Después de Valladolid pasa el tren por Segovia.[10] En esta ciudad se halla el gran acueducto que se supone fué construído por Trajano, y que está considerado como la obra más importante de estilo romano en la Península Ibérica. Luego puede el viajero detenerse en Avila, cuna de dos glorias patrias: Santa Teresa de Jesús, nombrada por Felipe II patrona de España, y Alfonso Tostado de Madrigal, cuyas doctrinas, según sus biógrafos, eran tan sabias e ilustradas que "hacían ver a un ciego."

España, habiendo sido fundada el año 844, y en ella existen aún muchas casas que fueron construídas hace varios siglos. En el castillo de Burgos se casó Eduardo I de Inglaterra con Da. Leonor de Castilla. *9. Valladolid* es la capital de su provincia, y está situada a la orilla izquierda del río Pisuerga. Cerca del palacio real existen dos edificios religiosos modelos de la más hermosa arquitectura gótica, y se consideran como los más puros de este género en el mundo: el convento de San Pablo y el colegio de San Gregorio; ambos rica y hermosamente decorados. Los alrededores de Valladolid son notablemente fértiles y están admirablemente situados, lo mismo que la ciudad, para toda clase de manufacturas. *10. Segovia,* capital de su provincia, es una ciudad muy interesante. Ocupa una preciosa situación en la cima de una colina roqueña a unos 3,300 pies sobre el nivel del mar, y está rodeada en parte por pintorescas murallas adornadas con varias torres circulares. El Alcázar o castillo está edificado en la extremidad oeste de la montaña, y aunque de origen árabe, fué posteriormente reconstruído de una manera magnífica en 1452. La Catedral es uno de los modelos más bellos de estilo gótico en España. *11. El Escorial* o *El Real sitio de San Lorenzo,* debe su origen a un voto hecho por Felipe II durante la batalla de San Quintín (Ag. 10, 1557), durante la cual imploró el monarca la ayuda de San Lorenzo, y prometió dedicar al santo un monasterio si conseguía la victoria. El Escorial está construído en forma de parrilla, en alusión

Después se entra en el Escorial,[11] templo y mausoleo, bajo cuyas bóvedas yacen los restos de Carlos V, Felipe III y la larga línea de sus no tan poderosos sucesores. El Escorial es célebre por su monasterio, colosal y grandiosa obra de arquitectura considerada como la octava maravilla del mundo. El área que ocupa es casi tan grande como la de la Gran Pirámide

de Egipto. Su biblioteca, antes de ser saqueada por los franceses, contenía 34,300 (treinta y cuatro mil trescientos) volúmenes, casi todos ellos tesoros de la literatura arábiga. La colección de monedas, medallas y pinturas era también notable.

Dos horas más de tren y el viajero se encuentra en la Estación del Norte de la capital de España.

¡Madrid![12] dicen desde el andén los empleados de la estación abriendo las puertas de los coches. Un taxi lleva al viajero por el Campo del Moro, Plaza de Oriente y calle Mayor a la Puerta del Sol, a la que afluyen nueve calles diferentes. En esta histórica plaza, que puede compararse con la Plaza de Trafalgar de Londres, o la Plaza de la Opera de París, se encuentran algunos

---

al instrumento de martirio de San Lorenzo. Forma un vastísimo paralelógramo rectangular dividido en largos patios que indican los intervalos de las barras de la parrilla, y representan los pies una torre en cada uno de los ángulos del paralelógramo. Del centro de uno de los lados sale una hilera de edificios unidos unos a otros, que es la residencia real y representa el mango de la parrilla. Posee una magnífica capilla con tres naves. El *panteón* o tumba real, es una cámara octógona, espléndida y suntuosamente decorada, en cuyos ocho lados existen numerosos sarcófagos de mármol negro. El costo del colosal edificio, que tiene 14,000 puertas y 11,000 ventanas, fué de 6.000,000 de ducados. *12. Madrid*, capital de España, de la provincia del mismo nombre y del reino de Castilla la Nueva. Está situada en el centro de la Península Ibérica, a la orilla del río Manzanares. La temperatura en Madrid es bastante variable. La ciudad posee muchos palacios. *El Palacio Real,*

de los principales hoteles, tiendas, cafés, etc.

Los hoteles Palace y Ritz, que se encuentran en el Paseo del Prado, son hoy los más afamados.

Uno de los principales atractivos del transeúnte en Madrid es visitar su célebre museo del Prado, cuya colección de pinturas es considerada como la mejor y más rica del mundo. Allí se ven

obras de los principales artistas españoles y extranjeros, y pueden leerse con frecuencia los nombres de Rafael, Murillo, Velázquez, Miguel Angel, el Greco, el Ticiano, Tintoretto, Paolo Veronese, Van Dyck, Rubéns, el divino Morales, Goya, Luis de Vargas, Fortuny, Domingo, Villegas, Jiménez, Serra, Garrido, Casanova, Casado, Zamacois, José Benlliure, y otros muchos.

Además del museo, es interesante visitar la Armería Real, considerada como la más notable que existe; el Museo de Historia Natural, el Congreso o Parlamento, el Palacio Real, el teatro de La Comedia, el de La Zarzuela,[13] el Real u Opera, las plazas de to-

---

por ejemplo, es un espléndido edificio rectangular, todo de granito y piedra parecida al mármol blanco. El aspecto general de Madrid es el de una ciudad nueva; tiene magníficas casas, buenas calles y hermosos paseos y plazas. En éstas hay numerosas estatuas, como la ecuestre de Felipe IV en la Plaza de Oriente, la de Cervantes frente al Congreso, etc. Madrid dió el ejemplo para el levantamiento general contra Murat el 2 de Mayo de 1808, cuando la guerra napoleónica, jornada en la que perdieron la vida 1,500 vecinos de la heroica ciudad. *13.* El dar el nombre de *zarzuela* a la *ópera cómica*, viene de haberse representado las primeras obras de esta clase en *La Zarzuela*, sitio de recreo de los reyes próximo al *Pardo*, nombre de la casa real de campo cerca de Madrid. *14. Las plazas de toros* son unos edificios redondos u ovalados parecidos a un circo, pero sin techado, donde las gradas se levantan unas sobre otras, formando una escalera terminada en su parte superior por una galería dividida en palcos. El espectáculo que se celebra allí se llama *Corrida de Toros*, en el que toman parte hombres a pie y a caballo. Uno de los mayores atractivos de esta fiesta, es la salida de la *cuadrilla* o compañía, que ofrece un indescriptible golpe de vista. En primera fila van los *matadores*, o

ros,[14] magníficos edificios de piedra y ladrillo, especie de anfiteatros parecidos a aquéllos en que los romanos celebraban los combates de gladiadores y otros espectáculos.

Por la tarde debe ir el visitante a los paseos de la Castellana, Recoletos y al Parque del Retiro, donde puede admirar, entre otras cosas, a las bellas señoritas dando un paseo en lujosos automóviles.

Por la noche, si es verano, las madrileñas salen a pasear por los parques y jardines en que abunda la ciudad. Si es invierno, los teatros antes nombrados dan una idea de la altura a que están el drama, la comedia, la zarzuela y aun la ópera española.

Toledo,[15] ciudad morisca que tantos recuerdos notables encierra, se encuentra cerca de Madrid. El río Tajo, rodeándola casi completamente, hizo de esta ciudad una ciudadela inexpugnable. Es digna de visitarse también por su grandiosa catedral, mezcla de estilo gótico y mozárabe; por la fábrica de armas, donde se forjan las

cabezas de las respectivas cuadrillas; después, los *banderilleros,* o los que colocan las *banderillas* (palos de unos dos pies de largo terminados en una punta de hierro en forma de anzuelo (*fish-hook*); luego, los *chulillos* o los que no tienen otra obligación que correr o preparar a los toros con sus capas; detrás, los *picadores* u hombres a caballo armados con *picas* a lanzas, y por último las *mulillas,* o sea, tres mulas preciosamente enjaezadas, que tienen por objeto despejar la plaza de los animales muertos después de terminada la corrida de cada toro. Una vez que la cuadrilla formada así ha saludado al presidente, la plaza se despeja, se retiran las mulillas, y sale el primer toro. En primer lugar entran en combate los *picadores,* castigando al toro con la pica siempre que el animal trata de embestir al caballo. Sucede muy amenudo que el picador no puede contener el poderoso ímpetu de aquellas fieras, criadas exclusivamente con este objeto, y picador y caballo caen a la arena, siendo el deber de los de a pie salvar a su compañero. Entonces se ven muy frecuentemente actos de gran valor de parte de los *toreros,* especialmente de los *matadores,* que están generalmente cerca, y siempre dispuestos a salvar aún a costa de su propia vida, la de uno de sus subordinados. En el segundo *tercio* de la *lidia* o combate contra el toro, toman parte los *banderilleros,* y es este el acto

celebradas hojas de Toledo; por la Plaza de Zocodover (plaza cuadrada) cuyo estilo, lo mismo que el primitivo nombre que ha conservado, es del más puro carácter morisco; y finalmente, por otros edificios, como el Alcázar, hospitales, fábricas, etc.

Para tomar el tren de Andalucía es necesario ir a Alcázar de San Juan. Por la mañana llega el tren a Córdoba,[16] la ciudad del Gran Capitán, en donde hay que ver la célebre Mezquita, inmensa estructura del siglo VIII, citada como el mejor y más genuino modelo de arquitectura en su clase en Europa. Este templo árabe, hoy convertido en catedral, posee 850 (ochocientas cincuenta) columnas de mármol y jaspe de varios colores, formando la columnata más perfecta que en el mundo puede admirarse. Otro edificio de interés para el visitante es el Casino;

más interesante, consistiendo en poner las banderillas en el morrillo del toro en el momento de bajar éste la cabeza para embestir o acometer al torero. Por último entra en acción el *matador* o jefe de los lidiadores, para completar el tercer tercio, que es el de más habilidad y de más interés para los aficionados, y que concluye con la vida del bruto. El *matador* va vestido con *traje de luces,* tan original como vistoso; su mano derecha armada de una espada desnuda y la izquierda de la *muleta,* pequeño palo del que pende una pieza de tela de seda encarnada, con que llama la atención del animal. La importancia de esta suerte consiste en que el *matador* mate al toro metiéndole la espada por cierto punto determindo de la *cruz,* y una vez en el suelo es rematado por el *puntillero,* torero destinado y experimentado en dar el golpe *de gracia.* Rara vez, a pesar del peligro en que constantemente están toreros y picadores, hay que lamentar la muerte de alguno de ellos, siendo de admirar la destreza del hombre sobre la fuerza bruta de la fiera. *15. Toledo,* la famosa y vetusta ciudad morisca, capital de su provincia, está situada en un grupo de colinas a la orilla norte del río Tajo, y tiene una elevación de 2,400 pies sobre el nivel del mar. El Tajo, que corre por entre rocas escarpadas y precipicios, forma la gran fortaleza de la ciudad a la que rodea casi por completo. Las otras fortificaciones construídas, unas por el rey godo Wamba en el siglo VII, y otras por Alfonso VI en el XII, son dignas de admirarse por la profusión y belleza de sus torres y puertas. La vista de Toledo desde cierta distancia es de imponente apariencia; dentro, es interesante y pintoresca. En general sus calles son muy estrechas, irregulares y pendientes. *16. Córdoba,* capital de la provincia del mismo nombre en la región de Andalucía, está situada en medio de

pero todo en aquella vetusta ciudad arábiga es atractivo e interesante.

Cuatro horas más de ferrocarril y se llega a Sevilla,[17] la patria de Murillo y reina del Guadalquivir, el río poético por excelencia.

Antes de llegar se distingue su famosa Giralda, torre morisca construída en el siglo XII, y que tiene 350 (trescientos cincuenta) pies de altura. Más tarde se ve la renombrada Torre del Oro; y el tren, por último, llega a la capital de Andalucía atravesando un edén de flores y naranjales.

Dentro de Sevilla se halla la famosa catedral, una de las más bellas, más extensas y más grandiosamente decoradas de España. Puede verse también el Alcázar, antiguo palacio de los reyes, cuyos salones son tan suntuosos y de tan delicada ornamentación, que pueden muy bien rivalizar con los de la Alhambra.

---

un bosque de olivos y Palmeras, a orillas del río Guadalquivir. La ciudad está rodeada de jardines que le dan aspecto oriental. Entre sus principales edificios se halla la catedral, en otro tiempo *mezquita*, nombre que los mahometanos dan al lugar donde se reunen para adorar a Alá. Antiguamente esta ciudad era la capital del imperio árabe en España y fué tomada por Fernando III de Castilla, en 1236. Córdoba ha sido el lugar de nacimiento de varios hombres célebres, entre ellos los dos Sénecas, el poeta Lucano, los filósofos Maimónides y Averroes, y de ella tomó el nombre el *Gran Capitán* Gonzalo Fernández *de Córdoba*. 17. *Sevilla*, la *Hispalis* de los romanos, *la reina de Andalucía* según los sevillanos, quienes agregan que,

> Quien no ha visto a Sevilla
> No ha visto maravilla,

es la capital de la moderna provincia de su nombre y antiguamente del reino. Las casas son anchas, espaciosas, bien ventiladas por amplios patios consuelo de mármol, y perfectamente adecuadas al clima. Entre sus edificios notables cuéntase la Catedral, que fué concluída en 1519, y que tiene 431 pies de largo por 315 de ancho. Tiene siete naves, y un excelente órgano con 5,400 tubos. Uno de sus tesoros es el gran número de pinturas de Murillo, Vargas, los Herreras, etc., que contiene. Su notable torre es una de las más célebres del mundo; se llama la *Giralda*, por la forma de su cúspide, que es una figura de mujer en bronce, y de 14 pies de altura. Otro de los edificios notables es *El Alcázar*, del árabe *Al-Kasar*. Entre los edificios nuevos merecen especial mención el palacio de San Telmo, la fábrica de tabaco,

La época en que Sevilla presenta más atractivos al viajero es la de Semana Santa, cuyas fiestas se consideran superiores a las de Roma. A estas fiestas suceden con breve intervalo las de su renombrada feria.

De Sevilla a Granada[18] tarda el tren ocho horas, aproximadamente, encontrándose uno en la morada de Boabdil el Chico, el último rey moro granadino.

La célebre y ponderada Alhambra[19] corona la cumbre del monte del mismo nombre. Este edificio fué construído para satisfacer los sueños de los árabes que lo habitaron, y respira por doquier un lujo oriental. Sus patios, corredores, jardines, fuentes, torres y almenas presentan con el mayor realismo las creaciones fantásticas de Las Mil y Una Noches.

Desde ella puede disfrutarse la vista encantadora de Granada, con sus pintorescas calles y plazas, y el famoso barrio del Albaicín dominando la opuesta colina.

---

la universidad, el museo, que encierra inapreciables pinturas, especialmente de Murillo, el hijo predilecto de la ciudad; la plaza de toros, soberbio circo de piedra que puede contener 12,000 personas, etc., etc. Los edificios históricos son muchos, y entre ellos está la casa en donde nació y murió Murillo que se conserva aún en buen estado. Sevilla fué conquistada de los moros en 1248, por Fernando III de Castilla. Desde esta fecha hasta el traslado de la corte a Valladolid por Carlos V, fué la capital de España.   *18. Granada*, antigua capital de su reino y hoy de la provincia del mismo nombre, está edificada al norte de la Sierra Nevada y a una elevación de 245 pies sobre el nivel del mar. La bañan los ríos Genil y Darro, y el último da el riego para la fértil y extensa *Vega* o llanura de Granada. En la cima de una de las colinas sobre las que está situada la ciudad, se levanta la ponderada *Alhambra*, y en la otra el interesante barrio del *Albaicín*, la parte más antigua, ahora casi en su totalidad habitada por *gitanos*. La Alhambra está rodeada de altas murallas y fuertes ciudadelas. Las calles de Granada son estrechas y tortuosas; las casas buenas, espaciosas y bien adecuadas al clima; todas conservan el estilo de arquitectura morisca. La catedral, de espléndida estructura, está profusamente decorada con jaspe y mármol de colores. El altar mayor, que lo sostienen 22 pilares, contiene los restos mortales de los reyes católicos Fernando e Isabel.

La lindísima Vega, que se extiende al frente de la ciudad, ofrece el más hermoso e interesante golpe de vista.

A poca distancia de Granada está Málaga,[20] célebre por su puerto, desde donde se va a Cádiz por tren, o en vaporcitos que hacen la travesía a menudo.

Cádiz[21] es un precioso puerto de mar, limpio, atractivo e interesante. La vista de Cádiz desde el faro de San Sebastián, presenta uno de los más bellos y grandiosos panoramas que pueden disfrutarse en Europa. A un lado, sus miles de casas blancas como la espuma de las azules ondas,

entre las cuales se divisan su frondosa Alameda de Apodaca, sus tres calles principales: Ancha, San Rafael y San Fernando, y la playa; y, al otro, la imponente y siempre fascinadora inmensidad del océano.

De Cádiz a Barcelona puede hacerse el viaje en vapor, pene-

Tiene además la ciudad otros monumentos notables, preciosas plazas públicas, una famosa universidad, etc. Granada fué fundada por los moros, conquistándola los Reyes Católicos en 1492, después de un sitio de doce meses.   *19. La Alhambra,* suntuoso palacio habitado por los reyes árabes de Granada, fué construído entre los años 1248 y 1354. Desde ella se domina por completo toda la ciudad y sus alrededores. Los recintos más notables del vetusto alcázar son: *el Patio de los Leones,* el de *la Alberca,* la sala de *Embajadores,* la *Plaza de los Aljibes* y otros muchos. La galería de las *Dos Hermanas* posee la fuente más linda que jamás ha hecho la mano del hombre, y el techo de la gruta en que se halla está construído con 5,000 estalactitas de las formas más esbeltas. No obstante los desperfectos causados por el tiempo y los temblores de tierra, la Alhambra es el palacio árabe más hermoso que se conoce en nuestros días; y el bello paisaje que la rodea no tiene rival en el mundo.   *20. Málaga,* puerto del Mediterráneo y capital de la provincia del mismo nombre, a 70 millas de Gibraltar. En Málaga, pueblo exclusivamente comercial, hay poco notable con excepción de las reliquias árabes que todavía se conservan. Tiene una preciosa *Alameda* o paseo público, y es célebre por sus vinos dulces y las uvas que en sus alrededores se cultivan. Es una ciudad muy antigua fundada por los fenicios y conocida por los romanos con el nombre de *Malacca.*   *21. Cádiz,* antiguamente Gadez, importante puerto del Atlántico y capital de su provincia. El mar baña su lado oeste y parte del sur. La ciudad

trando en el Mediterráneo y pasando por frente a Málaga, después por Almería, antiguamente la ciudad más rica e importante del reino de Granada; Cartagena, antiguamente Cartago Nova, fundada por los cartagineses procedentes de la célebre y gran ciudad de Cartago, en el Norte de Africa. Cartagena posee un excelente puerto en donde estuvo el más importante arsenal de Europa. Luego se encuentra Valencia, la preciosa ciudad que fué conquistada por el Cid.

Valencia,[22] ciudad encantada, como la ha llamado uno de nuestros escritores, está casi rodeada de su Huerta, delicioso jardín en donde se crían con increíble exuberancia toda clase de frutas, especialmente naranjas y limones.

Apenas se sienta el pie en tierra, se ve uno rodeado de tartaneros que ofrecen su típico vehículo, la tartana.

Una vez en uno de aquellos coches, se entra en la ciudad por el camino del Grao, que es un verdadero paraíso, en donde se respira el más delicioso perfume de azahar.

Barcelona[23] tiene todo el aspecto de una gran ciudad. Los edificios son magníficos. La parte nueva es grandiosa. La Rambla divide a la población en dos partes iguales: A un extremo, lo que se denomina el Ensanche, al otro, la magnífica muralla que sirve de anchuroso paseo; el puerto, con su gran variedad de

---

rodeada de murallas, forma casi un cuadrado como de una milla y media de lado. Sus calles son regulares, bien empedradas y claras. Tiene varios bonitos paseos públicos, siendo el más frecuentado *La Alameda*. Sus dos catedrales son los edificios más notables. Estas contienen algunos cuadros famosos, especialmente de Murillo. Cádiz es una de las ciudades más antiguas de Europa habiendo sido originalmente construída por los fenicios con el nombre de *Gaddir*, 347 años antes de la fundación de Roma o 1100 antes de Cristo. En 1262 fué tomada por los españoles después de haber estado sucesivamente en manos de cartagineses, romanos y moros. *22. Valencia del Cid*, capital del antiguo reino del mismo nombre, hoy de la provincia, está pintorescamente rodeada de jardines, y el interior es curioso y agradable. Su catedral, llamada *La Seo*, es de estilo clásico en el interior, perteneciendo el exterior al estilo gótico. Desde lo alto de su torre, llamada *El Miguelete*, se descubre el panorama de más sorprendente belleza que puede imaginarse. *El Cid* fué el conquistador de Valencia en 1094, antes en poder de los árabes desde el año 712, los que a su vez la conquistaron de los godos. *23. Barcelona* (Cataluña), la ciudad industrial más importante de España, capital del

buques, y el mar. Dominándolo todo, y como vigilándolo todo, se levanta imponente el antiguo castillo de Montjuich.

La parte monumental de la ciudad tiene grandes encantos para el artista. La catedral, de arquitectura gótica, la iglesia de Santa María del Mar, el interior de la Audiencia, la Universidad y otros monumentos no menos notables.

El tren parte de Barcelona para Francia llegando en pocas horas a Gerona.[24] Tres horas después se atraviesan los Pirineos y se llega a Perpiñán, encontrándose el viajero fuera de España, pero sin que de su imaginación puedan borrarse los dulces recuerdos de las felices horas que ha pasado en la patria de Cervantes, Calderón y Benavente.

---

antiguo condado y hoy de su reino y provincia. Está conveniente y bonitamente situada en el Mediterráneo, entre las bocas del Llobregat y el Besó, y en medio de un distrito muy fértil y abundante. Tiene una ciudadela bajo la jurisdicción de la fortaleza de *Montjuich* que se levanta al oeste. Barcelona está dividida por la *Rambla* (river-bed), de la que se ha hecho un bulevar delicioso, en dos partes, *nueva* y *vieja*. Tiene varios colegios, muchas escuelas, bibliotecas públicas, etc.; también posee bellos teatros, siendo uno de los mejores *El Liceo*. El puerto de la ciudad es magnífico y de gran movimiento. Sus calles en la parte nueva son regulares, anchas y espaciosas. El nombre Barcelona, antiguamente *Barcino*, viene de su refundador Amílcar Barca, padre de Aníbal. Barcelona fué muy importante bajo los godos, romanos y *árabes*. En 878 se hizo estado independiente, apellidándose sus soberanos Condes de Barcelona, hasta el siglo 12, en que su jefe tomó el título de rey de Aragón y lo incorporó a dicho reino. En Barcelona fué en donde los reyes católicos recibieron a Colón después del descubrimiento de América.
24. *Gerona*, antiguamente *Gerunda*, capital de la provincia del mismo nombre, está situada a 60 millas de Barcelona. Su hermosa catedral de estilo gótico, data del año 1316. Gerona es de origen romano y en un tiempo fué la residencia de los reyes de Aragón. Es célebre por las heroicas defensas que realizó durante los numerosos sitios que ha sufrido; el más notable de ellos, el de los franceses en 1809. Los sitiados desprovistos de todo, aun de municiones, mantuvieron en su poder la plaza por siete meses y cinco días, capitulando solamente a la muerte de su heroico gobernador, que fué víctima del hambre.

19 LECCION DECIMONONA

LITERATURA CLÁSICA ESPAÑOLA

—En primer lugar distingo entre los libros de usted la obra universal del inmortal Miguel de Cervantes.[1]

—Sí, el *Quijote;* y además tengo el *Viaje al Parnaso,* sus *Novelas Ejemplares,* la *Galatea* y *Persiles y Segismunda. Don Quijote* es su obra maestra y fué concebida por el ilustre Manco[2] estando prisionero y encerrado en una obscura mazmorra.[3] Otro escrito importante de Cervantes es la última y elocuentísima carta que dirigió al Conde de Lemos, dedicándole *Los Trabajos de Persiles y Segismunda,* postrera obra de tan insigne autor.

—En un anaquel próximo de este estante leerá usted los nombres de Lope de Vega, Calderón, Tirso de Molina, Alarcón, Rojas y Moreto.

—Dígame, le ruego, ¿cuáles son las obras más notables de Lope?

FOOTNOTES: *1.* Don Miguel de Cervantes nació en Alcalá de Henares el 9 de octubre de 1547. Sus padres, descendientes de ilustres familias, fueron Don Rodrigo de Cervantes y Doña Leonor de Cortinas. Sus primeros estudios los hizo en Madrid, en el colegio de Humanidades de Juan López de Hoyos. En 1571, Cervantes se alistó como soldado en las tropas que con el nombre de *Santa Liga* formaron el Papa, Felipe II de España, y Génova, contra el turco. Formando parte de tal expedición se encontró en la memorable batalla naval de Lepanto. donde recibió una herida en un brazo que le dejó manco. En 1575, estando de guarnición en Nápoles, se embarcó para volver a España, y fué hecho prisionero por el famoso corsario Arnaute Mamí. Cinco años y medio duró su cautiverio, y cuando volvió a España en 1580, Cervantes se encontró sin padres, sin amigos y sin

—Lope⁴ es el maestro y creador del teatro moderno. Cervantes, ponderando su talento, lo apellidó *Monstruo de la Naturaleza*. Sus obras teatrales se dividen en tragedias, dramas y comedias. Entre las tragedias figuran en primer lugar: *El Castigo sin Venganza, La Judía de Toledo* y *Los Siete Infantes de Lara*. Sus dramas son *históricos, legendarios*⁵ y *novelescos*. Entre los históricos le citaré como más importantes: *Los Tellos de Meneses, El Nuevo Mundo de Cristóbal Colón* y *El Mejor Alcalde, el Rey*.⁶ Sus comedias⁷ más notables son: *Lo Cierto por lo Dudoso*,⁸ *El Acero de Madrid*⁹ y *La Moza de Cántaro*.¹⁰ De sus comedias de capa y espada deben mencionarse: *La Hermosa Fea, Dineros son Calidad, El Perro del Hortelano, La Dama Boda*, etc.

fortuna. Rodeado de miseria y privaciones pasó su vida este gran hombre y murió el 23 de Abril de 1616, siete días después de Shakespeare. 2. *Manco* se aplica a la persona a quien falta un brazo o una mano. 3. *Mazmorra*, prisión subterránea. 4. Fray Lope de Vega, *"Fénix de los ingenios,"* como le llamó su siglo, nació en Madrid el 25 de Noviembre de 1562. Antes de saber leer ni escribir, repartía sus juguetes entre sus compañeros de escuela mayores de edad para que escribieran los versos que él les dictaba. Como Cervantes y Calderón fué también militar, tomando parte en la expedición naval de la *Armada Invencible* que Felipe II envió contra Inglaterra, y después de una vida agitada y llena de peripecias, se retiró a gozar de la tranqûilidad que sólo el claustro le brindaba y se ordenó sacerdote, muriendo el 25 de agosto de 1635. Difícilmente registrará la historia un poeta de tanta popularidad como Lope de Vega. En vida se vió obsequiado y aplaudido por hombres de todas las condiciones, desde el Pontífice y los monarcas, hasta la clase más baja del pueblo. A su muerte, aun en los países extranjeros se hicieron honras a su memoria. Respecto a su fecundidad, puede

—Y ¿qué me dice usted de las obras de Tirso de Molina?

—Tirso de Molina,[11] o Fray Gabriel Téllez, pues éste era su verdadero nombre, fué discípulo del gran Lope y acérrimo propugnador de sus innovaciones teatrales. Entre las tragedias de este autor se citan como más notables: *Los Amantes de Teruel* y *El Burlador de Sevilla y Convidado de Piedra*. De este último

drama sacó José Zorilla su *Don Juan Tenorio*, y, con más o menos éxito, Moliere, Shawell, Mozart, Rostand y muchos otros también lo llevaron en distintas formas a la literatura y a la ópera. El *Don Juan* de Lord Byron y *El Estudiante de Salamanca* de Espronceda no son sino pálidas evocaciones de este personaje legendario creado por el insigne fraile mercedario español.

Entre los dramas históricos y legendarios que le aseguran gloria imperecedera cuéntanse: *La Prudencia en la Mujer, Antona García* y *Hazaña de los Pizarros*; y de las comedias, que es donde más ingenio y donaire manifiesta, le citaré: *Don Gil de las Calzas Verdes, La villana de Vallecas* y *El Vergonzoso en Palacio*.

---

decirse de Lope, que él solo escribió más que todos los poetas juntos de su tiempo. A los once años de edad, compuso su primer drama; a los cuarenta y uno, tenía escritos 230, número que seis años más tarde se elevaba al de 483. A los cincuenta años, era Lope autor de 900 comedias, y a su muerte, tenía repartidas en los teatros del reino 1,500 piezas teatrales. Asegúrase que en el espacio de 24 horas, mitad en un día y mitad en otro, componía Lope un drama de 2,400 versos o más, agigantado e increíble esfuerzo que repitió en su vida más de cien veces. 5. *Legendario,* perteneciente a la *leyenda* épica. 6. Este drama está reputado como la mejor obra de Lope, y está tomado de la cuarta parte de la *Crónica General* de Alfonso el Sabio. 7. Entre las comedias de Lope las hay *religiosas,* como *El Nacimiento de Cristo, La Creación del Mundo, San Diego de Alcalá,* etc., de *caracteres* y de *costumbres,* y *de capa y espada.* 8. En esta bella producción de Lope, una de las mejores en su género, son los protagonistas o héroes, el célebre Don Pedro I de Castilla apellidado *el cruel,* y su hermano y matador el Conde de Trastamara. 9. Este nombre está tomado de la preparación que del acero se hacía en aquella época para curar ciertas enfermedades. Molière trató

—También tiene usted aquí al gran Calderón,[12] último luminar del teatro de la Edad de Oro, verdadero maestro del drama filosófico y a quien, según tengo entendido, se ha comparado con el gran Shakespeare.

—En efecto, Calderón es el más profundo en ideas de nuestros autores dramáticos, y quizás el más grande en la admirable personificación de lo abstracto y simbólico, elementos éstos que más tarde habían de hacer de Goethe su más ferviente panegirista. Sus obras se dividen, como las de sus grandes antecesores, en dramas (filosóficos y teológicos) como: *La Vida es Sueño, La Devoción de la Cruz* y *El Mágico Prodigioso;* tragedias, como: *El Médico de su Honra, A Secreto Agravio, Secreta Venganza* y *El Alcalde de Zalamea,* y comedias de *capa y espada* como: *La Dama Duende, Casa con dos Puertas Mala es de Guardar* y *Guárdate del Agua Mansa.*[13]

Pero donde impera su ingenio y profundidad teológica es en los *Autos Sacramentales,* género dramático genuinamente

---

de imitarla en su *Médico a Palos.* 10. Esta es una de las obras más caracterizadas en el género de las de *capa y espada.* Llevan este nombre de *comedias de capa y espada,* las comedias de costumbres con trajes de la edad media. 11. El maestro Tirso de Molina o *Gabriel Téllez,* nació en Madrid el año 1583, muriendo en 1648. Además de las obras citadas de este autor, pueden mencionarse como figurando en primera línea, las tragedias: *El Condenado por Desconfiado,* y *La Venganza de Tamar;* los dramas históricos y legendarios: *Próspera fortuna de Don Alvaro de Luna, Las Quinas de Portugal, El Cobarde más Valiente* y la comedia *Marta la Piadosa.* 12. Don Pedro Calderón de la Barca, el primero y más grande de los poetas cristianos, como le llamó Schlegel, nació en Madrid el 17 de enero de 1600. A la edad de quince años fué a Salamanca en cuya célebre universidad, dicen sus biógrafos, aprendió en cinco años todo lo que en ella se enseñaba. En 1625, entró en la carrera de las armas donde continuó hasta 1635 en que Felipe IV le nombró poeta cortesano en reemplazo del difunto Lope de Vega. Calderón se ordenó sacerdote en 1651, dejando de existir treinta años más tarde "con llanto universal," como dice uno de sus biógrafos. A ciento veinte ascienden los dramas escritos por Calderón, entre los que mencionaremos, además de los del texto, *En*

español en el cual es el más alto exponente. Ejemplos: *La Cena de Baltasar, A Dios por Razón de Estado y Las Espigas de Ruth.* Escribió también zarzuelas como: *El Laurel de Apolo, La Púrpura de la Rosa* y otras.

Al lado de estos tres próceres del teatro están Alarcón, Rojas y Moreto.

Alarcón[14] escribió poco, pero sobresale por su sobriedad y sentido moralizador. Entre sus comedias están: *Las Paredes Oyen y La Verdad Sospechosa.*[15] La última, traducida y adaptada por Corneille en su célebre *Le Menteur,* extendió la fama de Alarcón por toda Europa. De sus dramas, figuran en primer lugar: *El Tejedor de Segovia y Quien Mal Anda, en Mal Acaba.*[16]

De Francisco de Rojas[17] existen ochenta piezas teatrales. Principales entre ellas son: *Del Rey Abajo, Ninguno o García del Castañar, Entre Bobos el Juego,* que tradujo también Corneille, *Donde Hay Agravios no Hay Celos,* traducida por Scarron, *No Hay Ser Padre Siendo Rey,* imitada por Rotrou y *Casarse por Vengarse,* que redujo a novela Lesage e

esta vida todo es verdad y todo es mentira, drama que sirvió a Corneille para su *Heraclio,* y, *El Mayor monstruo los celos* (tragedia). Entre las comedias, *El escondido y la tapada, Dar tiempo al tiempo, El Secreto a voces, El Alcaide de sí mismo,* que fué imitado por Corneille con el título de *El Carcelero de sí mismo,* etc., etc. 13. Molière la tomó por modelo para su *Escuela de los maridos.* 14. Don Juan Ruiz de Alarcón nació en Méjico, en donde su padre estaba empleado por el gobierno español, el año 1581. Cursó sus primeros estudios en la universidad de dicha ciudad, y en 1600, llegó a la Península con objeto de continuar sus estudios en la célebre Universidad de Salamanca. Hacia 1614, después de otro viaje a Méjico, comenzó Alarcón a dar comedias a los teatros de Madrid, mereciendo muchos favores de la Corte y la nobleza hasta su muerte, acaecida en 1639. Se conservan de él 26, publicadas en dos partes: en 1628 y 1634

imitaron Thompson, Saurin y Goldoni.

Otro continuador y propulsor del teatro de Lope fué Agustín Moreto,[18] cuyas composiciones dramáticas ascienden a ciento tres. Su obra maestra es *El Desdén con el Desdén*, imitada sin éxito por Moliere en su *Princesse d'Elide*. Síguenle en importancia *El Lindo don Diego, Trampa Adelante* y *La Reliquia.*

No hay que olvidar al célebre Guillen de Castro,[19] autor, entre otras obras de fama mundial, de *Las Mocedades del Cid,* drama que sirvío a Corneille para su famosa tragedia *Le Cid.*

—¿Y dónde me deja usted al inimitable crítico de costumbres y autor de *El Diablo Cojuelo,* LUIS VELEZ DE GUEVARA?[20]

Es verdad; y no será mal recordar que *El Diablo Cojuelo* fué también traducido por Lesage con el nombre de *Le Diable Boiteux.* Se le conoce aún más como dramaturgo, contándose entre sus dramas: *Más Pesa el Rey que la Sangre,* en el que pinta la heroica hazaña de Guzmán el Bueno en Tarifa; *Reinar Después de Morir, El Diablo Está en Cantillana* y otros. [21]

---

respectivamente. *15. Corneille* declara que porque *La Verdad Sospechosa* fuera suya, diera las dos mejores que ha escrito, y confiesa, que además de éste, tomó otros asuntos de los españoles, como por ejemplo el del Cid, lo que Voltaire confirma en su comentario de *Le Menteur* diciendo: "Preciso es confesar que debemos a España la primera tragedia interesante y la primera comedia de carácter que ilustraron a Francia." *16.* También son dignas de mencionarse: *El Examen de Maridos, Mudarse por Mejorarse,* y *No hay mal que por bien no venga. 17.* Don Francisco de Rojas Zorrilla nació en la pintoresca Toledo el año 1607, y cursó su carrera literaria en las universidades de dicha ciudad y probablemente, en Salamanca. A la temprana edad de veinticinco años era ya conocido y celebrado como autor dramático. *Rojas* murió en Madrid en 1648. *18.* Don Agustín Moreto nació en Madrid el año 1618, e hizo sus estudios en Alcalá de Henares, como varios de sus predecesores. Perteneció a la *Academia de Madrid,* fué sacerdote, y murió el año 1669, a los 51 años de edad, dejando todos sus bienes a los pobres. Podrían además citarse como muy buenas obras de este autor *Antíoco y Seleuco, Como se Vengan los Nobles, De fuera vendrá quien de casa nos echará,* y otras.

—¿Y quién es ese Francisco de Quevedo[22] del cual he oído tantos chistes?[23]

—Es el escritor que llevó la sátira a su apogeo.

A sus escritos satíricos, morales y festivos debe este gran escritor principalmente su celebridad, aunque no hay que olvidar sus obras políticas y filosóficas, en las que descuella por su elevación de ideas y una rara visión profética del porvenir de España. Entre sus obras satíricas deben destacarse sus *Sueños,* que fueron imitados frecuentemente. En el género picaresco, característico de la novela realista española de la Edad de Oro, escribío la *Vida del Buscón,* considerada como una de las mejores de su época. De sus obras festivas citaremos: *Las Cartas del Caballero de la Tenaza* y *El libro de todas las cosas y otras muchas más.* Y de sus admirables poesías: *La Epístola al Conde-Duque de Olivares,* y la letrilla, *Poderoso Caballero es Don Dinero.*

—Hablar de la Edad de Oro parece el cuento de nunca acabar.

—Así es, pues aun no hemos mencionado a los grandes humanistas, como: *Raimundo Lulio, Luis Vives, Antonio de Ne-*

<hr />

19. Don Guillén de Castro, uno de los más célebres de la escuela de Lope de Vega, nació de familia ilustre, en Valencia, el año 1569. Su vida fué trágica y agitada, a causa de su genio altivo e inquieto, y tuvo protectores como el duque de Osuna y el conde duque de Olivares, terminando sus días en Madrid el año 1631. *20.* Don Luis Vélez de Guevara, uno de los sostenedores del teatro de Lope, de la escena sevillana, nació en Ecija, provincia de Sevilla, en 1579. Después de estudiar Humanidades en Osuna, pasó a Madrid, en donde bien pronto se hizo célebre por su elocuencia y su carácter agradable y festivo. Murió en dicha ciudad el año 1644. *21.* El número de sus obras asciende a unas 400, entre las que también pueden citarse: los dramas históricos *Doña Inés de Castro; El Valor no Tiene Edad,* que es la relación de los hechos de Don Diego García de Paredes; y *Los Amotinados de Flandes.* Entre sus más notables comedias se cuentan; *Los Hijos de la Barbuda, La Luna de la Sierra,* y *La Niña de Gómez Arias.* *22.* Don Francisco de Quevedo

brija, *Juan Valdés, Arias Montano, Gracián,* etc., o a historiadores, como: *Solís, Mariana, Gómara, Hurtado de Mendoza,*[24] *Cabeza de Vaca, Bernal Díaz del Castillo, Antonio de Herrera* y otros, o a los escritores místicos, como: *Teresa de Jesús, Juan de la Cruz, Fray Luis de León* y *Fray Luis de Granada;* o a los autores épicos, como: *Ercilla, Diego de Ojeda, Bernardo de Valbuena,* etc.

—Debemos, sin embargo, mencionar a Juan Boscán, famoso por su excelente versión de *Il Cortegiano* de Castiglione, aclamada como la mejor obra en prosa del reinado de Carlos V; a Garcilaso de la Vega, notable no sólo por sus *Eglogas,* sino por haber introducido, en colaboración con Boscán, el endecasílabo italiano en la métrica española, y también a Fernando de Herrera, apellidado "El Divino" por sus admirables poesías.

---

y Villegas nació el 28 de septiembre de 1580, y era hijo de Don Pedro Gómez de Quevedo, secretario de la princesa María (hija de Carlos V y mujer de Maximiliano de Alemania), y de Doña María Santibáñez. Hizo sus primeros estudios en la universidad de Alcalá. Después de ser secretario del duque de Osuna y de arreglar diplomáticamente varios tratados con la corte de Roma, con los duques de Saboya, y con la república de Venecia, volvió a Madrid y fué nombrado secretario del rey, muriendo el 8 de septiembre de 1645. Como escritor recorrió Quevedo todos los géneros así en prosa como en verso. Las persecuciones que por sus sátiras sufrió de parte del gobierno, que se apoderó en varias ocasiones de sus papeles, fueron sin duda, la causa a que se debe la pérdida de muchos de sus escritos. 23. Como definición bonita y original, al mismo tiempo que expresiva y verdadera de la palabra *chiste,* trasladamos aquí la que hizo de él uno de nuestros más insignes literatos contemporáneos en su discurso de recepción en la Academia de la Lengua. "El *chiste*—dijo—es todo acto, expresión o figura que, conteniendo una absoluta conveniencia de fondo, aparece con absoluta disconveniencia de forma." 24. Don Diego Hurtado de Mendoza nació en Granada el año 1503, y era hijo de los Condes de Tendilla y Marqueses de Mondéjar. Cursó sus primeros estudios en Granada y los continuó en la universidad de Salamanca, entrando después en la carrera de las armas al servicio del Emperador Carlos V. Murió en Madrid el año 1575.

20 LECCION VIGESIMA

LITERATURA ESPAÑOLA MODERNA

—Examinemos ahora la sección de literatura española moderna de su biblioteca, y detengámonos primero en los poetas líricos.

—Aquí está Quintana,[1] una de las glorias más grandes de nuestra literatura. Vea usted de él la *Colección de Poesías de los tiempos de Juan de Mena*, las *Vidas de Españoles Célebres*, su tragedia *Pelayo*, y sobre todo, sus *Odas*.

—A continuación veo los nombres de Nicasio Gallego,[2] autor de la célebre oda *El Dos de Mayo* y otras poesías de gusto neoclásico; del Duque de Rivas (Angel Saavedra) político y literato, y junto a éste veo a Martínez de la Rosa,[3] autor del drama romántico *La Conjuración de Venecia*, de escritos pedagógicos como *El Libro de los Niños*, de ensayos históricos, como

---

FOOTNOTES: *1.* Don Manuel José Quintana, nació en Madrid el año 1772, y cursó en Salamanca la carrera de derecho. En 1814 ingresó en las *Academias de San Fernando* y *Española*. Después de la muerte de Fernando VII fué senador vitalicio, ayo de Isabel II, y presidente del Consejo de Instrucción Pública. En 1855 fué coronado pública y solemnemente en el Senado, y murió dos años después de haber recibido esta prueba de admiración y cariño por parte de sus contemporáneos. *2.* Don Juan Nicasio Gallego nació en Zamora en 1777. Debe ser contado como muy ilustre entre los restauradores de nuestra poesía en el siglo XIX. Fué consejero de Estado, senador, secretario perpetuo de la Academia Española y presidente de la de la Historia. Murió en 1853. Como poeta nos ha dejado muchas *odas*, *elegías*, y *sonetos*, verdaderos modelos por la pureza de la forma y por su alto espíritu poético. *3.* Nació Don Francisco Martínez de la Rosa en Granada en 1787, provincia que lo eligió diputado en 1812. Fué ministro

Hernán Pérez del Pulgar y *El Espíritu del Siglo,* y finalmente, épico consumado por su tragedia neo-clásica *Epido.*

—Dígame usted algo sobre el Duque de Rivas,[4] pues he oído decir que es el iniciador del Romanticismo en España.

—Es muy difícil determinar quién fuera el iniciador de este movimiento literario, aunque, en efecto, el Romanticismo hizo su aparición entre nosotros con *El Moro Expósito.* Parece más acertado decir que este movimiento logró su triunfo definitivo con su *Don Alvaro o la Fuerza del Sino,* obra que más tarde convirtió Verdi en una de sus mejores óperas. Debemos recordar también sus bien conocidos *Romances Históricos,*

---

desde 1820 hasta 1823, en que emigró a Francia, en donde vivió hasta 1831. Desde esta época, su importancia política fué grande, unas veces embajador, otras ministro, ya presidente del Consejo de Estado, ya del Congreso. Además fué director de la Academia Española. *4.* Don Angel de Saavedra, duque de Rivas, nació en Córdoba el año 1791. Militar desde muy joven por gracia especial, hallóse en la gloriosa batalla de Bailén y en la de Ocaña, donde cayó con once heridas gravísimas. Una emigración posterior de diez años, durante los cuales residió en Gibraltar, en Londres, en varios puntos de Francia y en Malta, le dió oportunidad para tartar con los literatos extranjeros, y para estudiar las obras de los grandes escritores modernos de los varios países donde habitó. Walter Scott y Byron, Lamartine y Victor Hugo, además del estudio de Shakespeare, dieron nuevo y seguro rumbo a su inspiración y genio literario. Murió en Madrid en 1865.

verdaderos cuadros histórico-legendarios trazados con pincel de artista.

—¡Ah! por fin llegamos al poeta popular, al autor de *El Diablo Mundo* y *El Estudiante de Salamanca*, al Byron, Goethe y Leopardi español, a JOSÉ DE ESPRONCEDA,[5] en cuya historia estoy tan interesado.

La verdadera biografía de Espronceda está en sus obras. En la *Canción del Pirata* pinta su amor al peligro; su espíritu bélico, en el *Canto del Cosaco;* su acendrado patriotismo, en la *Despedida del Joven Griego*, de la *Hija del Apóstata;* sus sueños de reformador social, en *El Mendígo* y en *El Verdugo;* en el *Himno al Sol,* su elevación de ideas. Cuando canta *a* ilusiones; cuando en una *Orgía* se dirige *A Jarifa*, el hastío lo devora; cuando compone *El Estudiante de Salamanca*, dibuja en Don Félix de Montemar su propio retrato.

—Aquí veo un volumen de la gran poetisa cubana, GERTRU-

---

5. Don José de Espronceda nació en Almendralejo (Extremadura) en 1808, e hizo sus estudios en Madrid en el famoso colegio de San Mateo, dirigido por el no menos célebre Don Alberto Lista. A los catorce años escribió su poema *Pelayo*, y más tarde, estando desterrado en Londres, estudió a Shakespeare, a Milton y a Byron, y compuso muchas de sus poesías, entre ellas su hermosa elegía *A la Patria*. De Londres pasó a París, y se batió en las barricadas de 1830. Al volver a España entró en el cuerpo de Guardias de Corps, destinado a hacer la guardia a la reina. A consecuencia de unos versos que escribió contra el gobierno, fué segunda vez desterrado, componiendo entonces su novela *Sancho Saldaña*, colección de bellos cuadros. En 1841, fué nombrado secretario de la legación española en El Haya (Holanda), de donde volvió a poco para tomar asiento en las Cortes como diputado. Murió en 1842, cuando contaba treinta y cuatro años de edad.   6. Doña Gertrudis Gómez de Avellaneda nació en Puerto Príncipe, Cuba, en 1814. Siendo muy joven fué a España, estableciéndose en Madrid, y haciendo su aparición en nuestro Parnaso con la publicación, en 1841, de sus Poesías Líricas. Después, hasta 1846, en que se casó, escribió varias novelas y tragedias. A los pocos meses perdió a su esposo y se retiró a un convento, de donde salió al cabo de algunos años

DIS GÓMEZ DE AVELLANEDA.[6] Esta escritora fué muy notable en la lírica y en el drama. Dignas de mención son sus *Odas*, en las que pretende imitar a Quintana; y entre sus obras teatrales deben recordarse por su fuerza dramática y perfección de forma, *Baltasar*, *Saúl*, *Munio Alfonso* y otras.

—Como cantor de la montaña, de sencillo y candoroso estilo, cuyas *Narraciones Populares*, *Cuentos* y *Cantares* llegaron al alma del pueblo, puedo enseñarle a DON ANTONIO DE TRUEBA.[7]

—Otro autor que veo figura entre sus libros es JOSÉ SELGAS.[8]

—Este escritor es notable por sus delicadas poesías líricas, como *La Modista*, *La Cuna Vacía*, y otras; así como por sus admirables bocetos, llenos de filosofía y sano optimismo, publicados con el título de *Hojas Sueltas* y *Más Hojas Sueltas*.

—La edición que usted tiene aquí de BÉCQUER[9] es preciosa, pero yo creía que sus poesías eran más numerosas.

—Bécquer murió muy joven y sus obras no son muchas. Puede usted leer con deleite sus *Cartas desde mi Celda*, sus preciosas leyendas, como, *El Bandido de las Manos Rojas*, *Los Ojos Verdes*, *El Collar de Perlas*, *El Rayo de Luna*; y de sus poesías, cualquiera de sus famosas *Rimas* le ha de gustar.

dedicándose con más ardor a las letras, hasta 1873 en que murió. 7. Don Antonio de Trueba nació cerca de Bilbao en 1819, y murió en 1889. Ni la vida de la corte a donde fué muy joven, ni las angustias de la lucha por la existencia, consiguieron debilitar en su alma el amor a los poéticos valles nativos. Fué periodista, literato, cronista, novelista, y de todos modos un escritor notable. Su estilo es sencillo y natural, lo mismo en prosa que en verso. 8. Don José Selgas nació en Murcia en 1822, y murió en Madrid en 1882. Hombre de mucho talento y de una gran imaginación, llegó a ser un notable estilista. El estilo de Selgas es propio, personalísimo, nuevo. Fué además uno de los escritores más fecundos de nuestro tiempo; su laboriosidad fué tan grande como su modestia. 9. Don Gustavo Adolfo Bécquer nació en Sevilla en 1836, y murió en Madrid en 1870. Huérfano desde su más tierna infancia, pasó su niñez bajo la protección de su madrina, hasta que al cumplir diez y ocho años lo trajeron a Madrid sus ilusiones de escritor y de poeta, y el afán de conquistarse una posición. Su vida fué una constante lucha con la miseria, con la horrible miseria del pobre caballero, del carácter independiente, del hombre que no encuentra camino ni acierta con la ocasión ni con el modo de abrírselo, apesar de sentirse con alientos y con voluntad

—Por fin llegamos al último trovador español, Don José Zorrilla,[10] poeta popularísimo y fecundo, que vivió y sobrevivió al movimiento Romántico. Este simpático poeta escribió muchas obras teatrales, tales como: *Don Juan Tenorio, El Zapatero y el Rey, El Puñal del Godo*, que lo han inmortalizado. De sus muchas *leyendas* en verso me encantan *Margarita la Tornera, El Cristo de la Vega, La Pasionaria y El Alcalde Ronquillo.*

—Y ¿qué me dice usted de Don Ramón de Campoamor?[11]

—Este interesantísimo escritor inventó varias formas poéticas que definió y dividió en *Pequeños Poemas, Doloras y Humoradas.* Fué médico, estadista, filósofo y el primer poeta de temas no románticos. Su lema constante fué "el arte por la idea", y fiel a su teoría innovadora, es uno de los pocos que han sabido expresar en poesía un pensamiento filosófico empleando el menor número de palabras posible.

para el trabajo. *10.* Don José Zorrilla nació en Valladolid (1817), y fué el año 1889 coronado en La Alhambra como poeta nacional. Murió en 1893. *11.* Don Ramón de Campoamor de la Academia Española, nació en Asturias el año 1817, y concluyó sus estudios en Madrid, graduándose de doctor en medicina, profesión que nunca ejerció, dedicándose en absoluto a la literatura. Sus escritos son poéticos y fiilosóficos. Entre los primeros, además de los mencionados, se encuentran sus *Fábulas Políticas, Suspiros del Alma*, etc. Entre los segundos: *Filosofía de la Ley, Personalidad* y *El Absoluto.* Murió en 1901. *12.* Don Gaspar Núñez de Arce nació en Valladolid en Agosto de 1834. Después de ensayarse en el drama, produciendo algunas piezas notables, se dedicó en absoluto al género lírico. Su vida fué absorbida en gran parte por la política, en la que tomó parte muy activa, habiendo sido diputado y ministro varias veces. Fué miembro de la Real Academia, presidente de varias asociaciones literarias, etc., etc. muriendo en

—Y ¿qué autor es ése que tiene usted sobre la mesa?

—Nunez de Arce,[12] otro gran poeta que se separa del Romanticismo. Lea usted su colección de poesías *Gritos del Combate*, y sus bellísimos poemas narrativos: *Un Idilio y una Elegía, La Pesca, El Vértigo, La última lamentación de Lord Byron*, etc.

—Entre los autores dramáticos del siglo XIX (diez y nueve) no deje de leer las obras de: *Gil y Zárate*,[13] *Bretón de los Herreros*,[14] *Hartzenbusch*,[15] *Ventura de la Vega, García Gutiérrez*,[16] (cuyo drama *El Trovador* llevó Verdi a la ópera), *Adelardo López de Ayala*,[17] *José Echegaray, Tamayo y Baus, Joaquín Dicenta, Eduardo Gorostiza, Florentino Sanz, Enrique Gaspar y Benito Pérez Galdós*.

—Como el tiempo que nos queda es ya demasiado corto le agradecería me diese una idea de las principales obras del resto de los autores más importantes.

1903. *13*. Don Antonio Gil y Zárate nació en el Escorial en 1796; recibió en Francia su primera educación, de donde regresó a España en 1811, y murió en Madrid, en 1861. Fué escritor fecundo, y su personalidad literaria tiene mayor importancia en el género dramático que en los demás que cultivó. *14*. Don Manuel Bretón de los Herreros nació en 1796. En 1824, se representó su primera comedia *A la Vejez Viruelas*. Fué militar cuando la invasión francesa, y posteriormente secretario de la Academia Española hasta su muerte acaecida en 1873. *15*. Don Juan Eugenio Hartzenbusch nació en Madrid en 1806. Hijo de un ebanista, y huérfano desde muy niño, ejerció el oficio de su padre y dividió su juventud entre el estudio y sus trabajos manuales. En 1837, se estrenó su magnífico drama *Los Amantes de Teruel*, que le sacó de la oscuridad y le conquistó en una noche la celebridad y la gloria. En 1847, fué elegido académico de la Española, corporación que a su muerte en 1880, le proclamó autoridad de la lengua patria. Cualquiera de sus composiciones, en prosa o en verso, puede servir de modelo para aprender a escribir en castellano. *16*. Don Antonio García Gutiérrez nació en la provincia de Cádiz en 1813. Su padre, pobre artesano, quiso darle una educación esmerada y le envió a estudiar medicina a la capital de la provincia; pero descontento el futuro autor de *El Trovador* de estos estudios, dejó a Cádiz y fué a Madrid, haciendo a pie gran parte del viaje. Sujeto a grandes privaciones se vió en la necesidad de ingresar como voluntario en un regimiento. Aprendiendo el ejercicio se encontraba cerca de Madrid cuando se anunció la representación de su drama, entregado hacía tiempo y sin esperanza de ser puesto en escena. Murió en Madrid en 1884. *17*. Don Adelardo López de Ayala nació en la provincia de Sevilla, en 1828. Estudió en esta capital hasta que, muy joven, fue a Madrid, donde

—Pues ahí tiene usted a ALBERTO
LISTA,[18] preceptor famoso de Espronceda, Ventura de la Vega y otros literatos del siglo XIX (diez y nueve); a
Alcalá Galiano,[19] célebre orador y poeta de gran mérito, autor de *Estudios
Críticos,* del *Prólogo* al *Moro Expó-
sito* del Duque de Rivas y de epísto-
las y odas de gusto neo-clásico; a *Agustín Durán,*[20] compilador
de romances viejos españoles y crítico de gran mérito; a *Manuel
Milá y Fontanals,* otro crítico de métodos más modernos, notable por sus investigaciones y estudios sobre los orígenes de la
epopeya y romancero español y catalán; a *Modesto Lafuente;*[21]
autor de la monumental *Historia de Epaña;* a *José Amador de
los Ríos,* famoso por sus eruditos estudios medioevales; a *Pas-
cual Gayangos,* arabista 'de nota y editor de obras antiguas; a
Cayetano Alberto de la Barrera, erudito y paciente bibliógrafo
del drama; a *Ceán Bermúdez,* bien conocido por su admirable
Diccionario de las Bellas Artes; a *Diego Clemencín,* el primer
comentarista de nota del *Quijote;* a *Bartolomé José Gallardo,* el
más grande de los bibliógrafos españoles por su *Ensayo;* a

---

se dió muy pronto a conocer. Fué político activo, ministro de Ultramar, y murió
en 1879, siendo presidente del Congreso.   *18.* Don Alberto Lista nació en Sevilla
en 1775. Fué catedrático de matemáticas primero; después de Retórica y Poética,
rector del célebre colegio de San Mateo de Madrid y director de la *Gaceta de
Madrid.* Murió en Sevilla en 1848.   *19.* Don Antonio Alcalá Galiano nació en
Cádiz en 1789. Fué diputado en varias ocasiones, y últimamente ministro de
Fomento en 1864. Murió en 1865.   *20.* Don Agustín Durán nació en Madrid en 1793,
y estudió en el *Seminario de Vergara* y en la universidad de Sevilla. Las fechas
principales de su biografía son las de la publicación de sus obras. Murió en 1862.
21. Don Modesto Lafuente nació en 1806. Hizo sus estudios en León, Santiago y
Valladolid. En 1845, comenzó a publicar el *Teatro Social del Siglo XIX,* que
abandonó más tarde para dedicarse a reunir los materiales para su *Historia de
España.* Diputado varias veces, señalóse en el Parlamento como orador fácil y
elegante y de palabra enérgica y persuasiva. Fué vicepresidente del Congreso,
individuo de las academias Española y de la Historia, y director de la Escuela de
Diplomacia. Murió en 1866.   *22.* Don Ramón de Mesonero Romanos nació en
Madrid en 1803, y murió en 1882. Su posición independiente y lo apacible de su
carácter, alejáronle por completo de las agitaciones políticas en que vivieron la
mayor parte de los escritores contemporáneos suyos, y le permitieron consagrar

Mesonero Romanos,[22] *Larra,*[23] *Estébanez Calderón,* costumbristas de primera línea, etc., etc.

—Y ¿quién fué JAIME BALMES?[24]

—Fué uno de los filósofos cristianos más grandes de su época. Hallará usted sus ideas filosóficas en: *Filosofía Fundamental, Cartas a un Escéptico en Materias de Religión, El Criterio* y otras. Como filósofo de la historia descuella por su obra magistral *El Protestantismo Comparado con el Catolicismo* . . .

Vea usted también a *Nocedal*[25] entre los oradores; a *Cristóbal Pérez Pastor* entre los bibliógrafos de Cervantes, Lope de Vega y Calderón; a *Emilio Cotarelo y Mori,* de vastísima erudición en materias del teatro; a *Francisco Rodríguez Marín,* folklorista, investigador y autor de la mejor edición moderna del *Quijote.*

—Y ¿dónde me deja usted a MENÉNDEZ y PELAYO?[26]

—Menéndez y Pelayo es el crítico más grande de su siglo,

---

su vida a los trabajos literarios. Sus obras todas contribuyen a justificar el alto puesto que el autor tiene en nuestra literatura. **23.** Don Mariano José de Larra nació en Madrid en 1809. Recibió en París parte de su educación, y volvió a España ingresando en el colegio de San Antonio Abad de Madrid. Comenzó a dar muestras de su afición literaria, traduciendo del francés *La Ilíada* y *El Mentor de la juventud.* Murió en 1837, disparándose un pistoletazo, con lo que puso fin a una existencia que pudo ser muy provechosa para su patria. **24.** Don Jaime Balmes nació en Vich en 1810. Estudió en el seminario de su ciudad natal y luego en la universidad de Cervera, donde fué profesor y desempeñó varias cátedras. En 1839, se dió a conocer como escritor, con *Memorias sobre el Celibato.* Murió en Vich en 1848. **25.** Don Cándido Nocedal nació hacia la mitad del primer tercio del siglo XIX. Fué Ministro de la Gobernación en 1856, y murió en Madrid, en 1885, siendo jefe del partido carlista. **26.** Don Marcelino Menéndez y Pelayo nació en 1856. Fué asombro de erudición e inteligencia. A los veinticuatro años era miembro de la Real Academia. Murió en 1912. **27.** Don Benito Pérez Galdós nació en Canarias en 1843. Además de novelista, fué legislador y miembro de la Cámara de Diputados. Vivió en Madrid, donde publicó sus obras, desde su llegada a la capital

no sólo por lo acertado de sus juicios y asombrosa erudición sino por el gran número de obras que escribió. Humanista, filósofo, poeta, crítico, polígrafo y mentor de toda una generación literaria, escribió incansablemente, contándose entre sus principales obras: *La Verdadera Ciencia española, Historia de Los Heterodoxos Españoles, Los Orígenes de la Novela, Horacio en España, Calderón y su Teatro, Edición de las Obras Dramáticas de Lope de Vega, Antología de Poetas Líricos Castellanos de la Edad Media,* y sobre todo, su obra maestra, *Historia de las Ideas Estéticas en España,* que es más bien un estudio crítico-literario de las bellas letras en Europa hasta la fecha de la aparición de la obra.

—¿No podría usted nombrarme algunos de sus discípulos más destacados?

—Ya he mencionado a Rodríguez Marín y Emilio Cotarelo y Mori; otro discípulo y colaborador del "Maestro" fué *Adolfo Bonilla San Martín,* abogado, filósofo, historiador, literato y humanista de vastísima erudición. Entre las magníficas contribuciones de este autor cuéntanse: *Luis Vives y la Filosofía del Renacimiento,* su obra maestra, y la *Historia de la Filosofía Española.*

siendo aún muy joven. Murió en esta ciudad en 1920. *28.* Don Juan Valera, de la Academia Española, nació en 1827. Perteneció a ilustre familia y era hermano de la Duquesa de Malakoff que vivía en París ocupando uno de los primeros puestos en la antigua aristocracia de la cíudad a la moda. Fué senador del reino y miembro del Cuerpo Diplomático. Murió en 1905. *29.* Don Pedro Antonio de Alarcón nació en Guadix (Granada) en 1833. Estudió en la universidad de la capital donde se graduó a los catorce años, y fundó a los veinte, un periódico literario semanal. Poco después pasó a Madrid. Como crítico era tan extremadamente severo que, cuando él publicó su primer drama, *El Hijo Pródigo,* cayeron por vanganza sobre él tantas críticas, que aunque obra de no escaso mérito tuvo que retirarla del teatro. Murió en Madrid el año de 1891. *30.* Don Emilio Castelar nació el año 1832. Cuando contaba sólo veinticuatro años de edad ganó por oposición la cátedra de historia crítica y filosófica de la universidad de Madrid.

Y ahora, para concluír, voy a darle a usted una idea sucinta de los escritores modernos y el rasgo principal que los caracteriza. Pues bien; de *Zorrilla* puedo decirle que representó el españolismo; *Tamayo y Baus*, el buen gusto; *Echegaray*, la fuerza dramática; *Galdós*,[27] el talento narrativo y celo de reforma social; *Valera*,[28] la elegancia clásica y la crítica acogedora; *Alarcón*,[29] la exuberancia del espíritu meridional; *Campoamor*, la incredulidad amable y sonriente; *Pereda*, la "realidad idealizada" y el espíritu tradicional; *Núñez de Arce*, el dominio de la forma y la tolerancia; *Castelar*,[30] la sublimidad y grandilocuencia oratoria; *Fernández Flores*, la fina sátira del espíritu moderno; *Leopoldo Alas* (*Clarín*), la sátira literario-social; *Blasco Ibáñez*, la vida de la *Huerta*, y el dinamismo épico moderno; *Palacio Valdés*,[31] el ingenio, la gracia y la indulgencia; *Pérez Escrich*,[32] la invención, *Emilia Pardo Bazán*, el naturalismo españolizado; *Concha Espina*, el buen gusto literario y fuerza de estilo; *Menéndez Pidal*, la erudición precisa y sistemática; *Vicente Medina*, el alma murciana; *Gabriel y Galán*, el alma de la tierra extremeña y castellana; *Angel Ganivet*, el espíritu cosmopolita y un acendrado españolismo; *Joaquín Costa*, el celo de europeización; *Giner de los Ríos*, la reforma en la enseñanza; *Jacinto Benavente*, el arte de la sátira social en el teatro; *Linares Rivas*, la comedia de la vida; *Eduardo Marquina*, el teatro épico-lírico; los *Hermanos Quintero*, el gracejo y la

---

Después de una ardorosa campaña parlamentaria en favor de la república, se opuso vigorosamente al proyecto de una regencia. El gobierno elegido por las Cortes después de la abdicación de Don Amadeo I, le nombró ministro de Estado. En Agosto de 1873 fué elegido presidente de las Cortes, cargo de que hizo dimisión al ser nombrado Presidente de la República, el 6 de septiembre del mismo año. La muerte sorprendió a este autor en Madrid, en 1899, cuando su incansable y finísima pluma no cesaba de dar originales y tener ocupados a impresores y cajistas con la energía y fecundidad que le eran características. *31*. Don Armando Palacio Valdés nació en un pueblo de Asturias en 1853. Sus novelas han adquirido gran celebridad, no sólo en España, sino en toda Europa y América; se han traducido a varios idiomas y son objeto de estudio para los principales críticos extranjeros. *32*. Don Enrique Pérez Esrich nació en 1829. Autor de *El Mártir del Gólgota*, obra traducida al inglés, fué un escritor fecundísimo cuya biografía, se obtiene leyendo su preciosa novela *El Frac Azul*, en donde hace su más exacto retrato. Murió en 1897.

sal andaluza; *Martínez Sierra,* el alma femenina; *Pío Baroja,* el paisaje y el pesimismo exótico; *Valle-Inclán,* el culto a la filigrana y el estilismo dilettante; *Unamuno,* el eclecticismo y culto neopagano; *Azorín,* el impresionismo; *Altamira,* la erudición y el progresismo histórico; *Ortega y Gasset,* la filosofía social y el liberalismo moderno; *Pérez de Ayala,* el pesimismo y la correción de estilo; *Manuel Machado,* el modernismo amable; *Antonio Machado,* el paisaje y la serenidad artística; *Villaespesa,* la belleza lírico-dramática; *Ricardo León,* el misti cismo tradicional; *Ramón Jiménez,* un arte consumado con elegancia exquisita y, finalmente, *Federico de Onís,* la erudición y la pedagogía.

—Algún día pienso dedicarme a la lectura detenida y concienzuda de los autores que usted acaba de mencionar.

—Como puede comprender, no están incluídos en esta reseña todos los escritores de nota; pero en ella encontrará al menos los más representativos de la literatura española.

Reference Grammar

Although all the necessary grammatical explanations for each of the 20 Lessons have been provided in the footnotes of the lessons, a complete Reference Grammar is provided here for the convenience of the student. Each part of speech (the article, the noun, the verb, etc.) is explained thoroughly in all its uses. Therefore, should the student wish complete information about any point of grammar he can easily find it in the handy Reference Grammar.

PLAN FOR STUDY

Since the material of the *Reference Grammar* is not arranged in order of difficult or frequency of occurrence but is *classified by subjects* (the Article, Noun, Adjective, etc.), it is suggested that the student refer to and study the following paragraphs along with each lesson. The easiest way of locating any paragraph (§) is to flip through the pages watching for the § number which is in **bold face.**

Lesson 1 The definite article, §1. Conjugation of verbs, §46. The present tense of verbs, §47. Subject personal pronouns, §22. Possessive adjectives, §20

Lesson 2 Conditional, §51. Object personal pronouns, §23. The present tense of *tener*, §68. Adjectives, §11. Prepositions, §32.

Lesson 3 Nouns, §6-7. The imperfect tense, §48. Position of adjectives, §12. Demonstrative adjectives and pronouns, §17 and §28. Expressions of possession, §8.

Lesson 4 Prepositions, §33. Position of indirect object pronouns, §23.2-§24. Verbs changing *o* into *ue*, §83, class 7.

Lesson 5 The numerals, §21. Comparison of equality, §15. Comparison of adjectives, §14.1. The present of *saber*, §84.

Lesson 6 The verbs *estar* and *ser*, §70—§74.

Lesson 7 The imperative, §59. Interrogatives, §27. Possessive pronouns, §30. Relative pronouns, §29.

Lesson 8 The present of *venir*, §84. Indefinite pronouns, §31.

Lesson 9 Reflexive verbs, §75—§77. The present of *hacer*, §84. The absolute superlative, §15.

Lesson 10 Uses of *para*, §36. The future tense, §49.

Lesson 11 Verbs changing *e* to *ie*, §83, class 3. The perfect tense, §52. Reflexive pronouns, §25.

Lesson 12 The adverb, §39—§41. Past participle, §62. Orthographic changes in the stems of regular verbs, §64.

Lesson 13 The preterite tense, §50. The gerund, §61. Diminutives, §9.

Lesson 14 Uses of *por*, §37. The verb *dar*, §84. Irregular comparatives, §14.3

Lesson 15 The present subjunctive, §55. Impersonal expressions, §80—§81. Augmentatives, §9. Formation of the superlative, §14.2.

Lesson 16 The verb *haber*, §65—§67. Irregular comparatives and superlatives, §15. Interrogative pronouns, §27.

Lesson 17 Interjections, §44. Conjunctions, §42—§43.

Lesson 18 Irregular verbs, §82—§83.

Lesson 19 Passive voice, §78.

Lesson 20 Irregular verbs, §84.

REFERENCE GRAMMAR

	PAGE
Plan for Study	193

The Article

§1 The Definite Article	199
§2 Uses of the Definite Article	199
§3 The Indefinite Article	201
§4 Omission of the Indefinite Article	201
§5 The Neuter Article *lo*	202

The Noun

§6 Gender of the Noun	204
§7 Plural of Nouns	206
§8 The Use of Prepositions	207
§9 Diminutives and Augmentatives	207
§10 Cognate Suffixes	209

The Adjective

§11 Classes and Forms of the Adjective	210
§12 Position of Adjective	211
§13 Substantivised Adjectives	213
§14 Comparison of Adjectives	213

*§ *is the symbol for paragraph*

§15 The Absolute Superlative   213
§16 Pronominal Adjectives   214
§17 Demonstrative Adjectives   215
§18 Indefinite Adjectives   215
§19 Interrogative Adjectives   216
§20 Possessive Adjectives   216
§21 The Numerals   217

The Pronoun

§22 Subject Pronouns   218
§23 Object Pronouns   219
§24 Two-object Pronouns   220
§25 Reflexive Pronouns   221
§26 Additional Uses of *Se*   221
§27 Interrogative Pronouns   222
§28 Demonstrative Pronouns   222
§29 Relative Pronouns   223
§30 Possessive Pronouns   224
§31 Indefinite Pronouns   225

The Preposition

§32 Uses of Prepositions   227
§33 Common Simple Prepositions   227
§34 The Preposition *a*   227
§35 The Preposition *de*   228
§36 The Preposition *para*   229
§37 The Preposition *por*   230
§38 Compound Prepositions   231

The Adverb

§39 Formation of Adverbs   232
§40 Comparison of Adverbs   232
§41 Classes of Adverbs   233

The Conjunction

§42 Co-ordinating Conjunctions   235
§43 Subordinating Conjunctions   235

The Interjection

§44 Interjections   237

The Verb

§45 Nature of the Spanish Verb   238
§46 General Remarks about the Conjugations   238
§47 The Present Indicative   238
§48 The Imperfect Indicative   240
§49 The Future Indicative   242
§50 The Preterite Indicative   243
§51 The Conditional   244
§52 The Perfect Indicative   245
§53 The Pluperfect Indicative   246
§54 The Future and Conditional Perfect   247
§55 The Present Subjunctive   248
§56 The Imperfect Subjunctive   249
§57 Uses of the Subjunctive   250
§58 The Subjunctive—Sequence of Tenses   252
§59 The Imperative Mood   254
§60 The Infinitive   254
§61 The Present Participle or Gerund   258
§62 The Past Participle   258
§63 Government of Verbs   259
§64 Orthographic Changes   262
§65 Conjugation of Auxiliary Verb *haber*   264
§66 Uses of Auxiliary Verb *haber*   265
§67 Conjugation of Impersonal Verb *haber*   266
§68 Conjugation of the Verb *tener*   268
§69 Uses of the Verb *tener*   270
§70 Conjugation of the Verb *ser*   272
§71 Uses of the Verb *ser*   274
§72 Conjugation of the Verb *estar*   276
§73 Uses of the Verb *estar*   278
§74 Comparison of the Verbs *ser* and *estar*   280
§75 Reflexive Verbs   281
§76 Conjugation of the Reflexive Verbs   281
§77 Types of Reflexive Verbs   285
§78 The Possessive Voice   289
§79 Uses of the Passive Forms   289
§80 Impersonal Verbs   291
§81 Verbs Functioning as Impersonal Verbs   292
§82 Nature of Irregular Verbs   295
§83 Classes of Irregular Verbs   295
Irregular Verb list   297
Spanish Letter Form   300

APPENDIX

Vocabularies

The Family (continuation from page 27)   303
Holidays of the Year   303
Countries of the World   304
Colors   305
The Fireplace and its Appurtenances   305
The Country and the Sea   306
The Human Body   306
The Senses and Bodily Sensations   307
Agriculture   308
    The Farm   308
    The Trees   308
    The Fruits   308
    The Vegetables   309
    The Flowers   309
Quadrupeds and Birds   309
Numeral Adjectives
    Cardinal Numbers   310
    Ordinal Numbers   311
    Fractional Numbers   312
    Collective Numbers   312
Multiple Adjectives   313
Adverbs of Time   313
    of Doubt   314
    of Order   314
    of Comparison   314
    of Place   314
    of Quantity   315
    of Manner   315
    of Affirmation   315
    of Negation   315
Conjunctions   315
Interjections   316
Prepositions   316
Indefinite Pronouns   317
Usual Phrases   318
Spanish Idioms and Proverbs   320

DICTIONARIES

English-Spanish   329
Spanish-English   349

CHAPTER 1

THE ARTICLE

§1. The Definite Article

1. The definite articles in Spanish are:

	Singular	Plural
Masculine	el	los
Feminine	la	las

El and *los* (the) are placed before masculine nouns, singular and plural respectively:

el hombre	los hombres
the man	the men

La and *las* (the) are placed before feminine nouns, singular and plural respectively:

la mujer	las mujeres
the woman	the women

2. Contractions of the masculine singular definite article are formed with the prepositions *a* and *de*:

al (a el) hombre	del (de el) hombre
to the man	of the man

§2. Uses of the Definite Article

The definite article agrees in gender and number with the noun it modifies.

Note. *El* is used instead of *la* for euphony immediately before a stressed *a* or *ha;* e.g. *el ala* (the wing), *el hacha* (the axe).

The definite article in Spanish is used more often than in English. Its additional uses are:

1. Before nouns used in a general sense, including abstract and collective nouns, when they are used to denote all of the class named:

La honradez es una de las cosas que más me gustan
Honesty is one of the things I like most
El aluminio es un metal útil   Aluminium is a useful metal

199

2. Before the names of continents, countries, and all other geographical divisions when they are modified:

Toledo era la capital de la España antigua
Toledo was the capital of old Spain

3. Before the names of certain countries, cities, states, such as *los Estados Unidos, el Canadá, el Japón, la Argentina,* and all other South American countries except Bolivia, Chile, Colombia and Venezuela; *la Habana; la Carolina.*

Lima es la capital del Perú   Lima is the capital of Peru

4. Before the names of avenues, streets, and squares:

Viven en la calle Mayor   They live in Main Street

5. Before titles or names of professions followed by a person's name, but *not* before *don, doña, san(to), santa* and in direct address:

El Sr. Pérez está en Francia   **El presidente Martínez no está aquí**
Mr. Pérez is in France.   President Martínez is not here
But: **Buenos días, Sr. Pérez**
Good morning, Mr. Pérez

6. Before a proper noun when modified:

La pobre María no fué allá   Poor Mary did not go there

7. Before names of languages, except when the name of the language is directly preceded by the verb *hablar* (and occasionally by the verbs *aprender, escriber, estudiar*) or the prepositions *en* or *de.*

8. In a series of nouns, before each of these nouns:
Mande a mi madre los libros, los discos y los cuadros que compré ayer
Send my mother the books, records, and pictures I bought yesterday

9. Before designations of time such as the year, the week, and the hour, as well as before the names of the seasons and the days of the week, except when they follow some form of the verb *ser* and are unmodified:

El tren parte a las tres   **Ella venía los lunes**
The train leaves at three o'clock   She used to come on Mondays
But: **Ayer fué domingo**
Yesterday was Sunday

10. Before expressions of measure and weight, instead of the indefinite article used in English:

Este material cuesta dos pesos el metro
This material costs two pesos a yard

11. Before nouns designating parts of the body or personal articles of clothing, instead of the possessive adjective used in English, when there is no ambiguity as to the possessor, and sometimes also with other things closely associated with the subject of the sentence when the noun designating the thing is the object of a verb or a preposition:

María siempre tiene *las* **manos frías**
Mary's hands are always cold

Me compró *el* **coche**   **Le robaron** *el* **dinero**
He bought my car   They stole his money

12. In certain idiomatic expressions in which they contracted with the preceding preposition (*de+el→del*), and before the infinitive when it functions as a noun and is not after a form of the verb *ser* (to be):

El **manejar cuidadosamente promueve la seguridad** *del* **tráfico**
Careful driving promotes road safety

§3. The Indefinite Article

The forms of the indefinite article are:

	Singular	Plural
Masculine	un	unos
Feminine	una	unas

Un (a, an) and *unos* (some) are placed before masculine nouns, singular and plural respectively:

un hombre   **unos hombres**
a man   some men

Una (a, an) and *unas* (some) are placed before feminine nouns, singular and plural respectively:

una mujer   **unas mujeres**
a woman   some women

§4. Omission of the Indefinite Article

The indefinite article is not used in Spanish as often as in English. It is omitted:

1. Before an *unmodified* predicate noun expressing nationality, occupation, profession, religion or political point of view of a person:

Es español
He is a Spaniard

Es abogado
He is a lawyer

Es nacionalista
He is a Nationalist

Es socialista
He is a Socialist

But:

Es un abogado hábil   He is a smart lawyer

In the last example the noun is modified by an adjective.

2. Before a noun used in apposition, i.e. a relation of two words, the second of which serves to explain or describe the first:

Este es Juan, amigo de mi hijo   This is John, a friend of my son

However, the indefinite article is used when it is required for emphatic identification, to show clearly that the appositional noun indicates just *one* of various persons or things.

3. Before the numerals *cien(to)* (a hundred) and *mil* (a thousand):
He leído más de cien libros   I have read more than a hundred books

4. Before the adjectives *cierto* (a certain), *otro* (another), *medio* (half a), *tal* (such a) and *qué* (what a):

No tengo tal libro
I don't have such a book

¡Qué lástima!
What a pity!

§5. The Neuter Article lo

1. *Lo* is used with the masculine singular form of an adjective or a past participle to convert it into a noun and to give it an abstract or general sense. It translates the English *that which is;* for example:

With participles:
lo dicho that which is said *or* what has been said

With adjectives used as nouns espressing something in an indefinite sense:

lo útil that which is useful *or* the useful one
lo bueno that which is good *or* the good one

With pronominal adjectives:

lo nuestro that which is ours *or* ours

With phrases:

lo bueno del negocio	the good side of the business
lo de la niña	the story about the girl
lo de ayer	yesterday's affair

2. *Lo* is also used:

a) With the inflected (feminine or plural) forms of adjectives and participles which modify a noun or pronoun in the following relative clause to express the idea of the extent or degree to which a certain quality is possessed:

Sabemos lo útil que es esto	**Me sorprende lo buena que es**
We know how useful this is	I am surprised at how good she is

b) With adverbs:

¿Ha oído Vd. lo bien que canta?   Have you heard how well he sings?

c) In a number of idiomatic expressions:

por lo menos	at least	**en lo futuro**	in the future
los más pronto posible	as soon as possible		

d) With subordinate relative clauses:

lo que me dijo   that which (*or* what) he told me

CHAPTER 2

THE NOUN

§6. Gender of the noun

All nouns in Spanish are either masculine or feminine. There is no neuter gender.

In determining the gender of nouns it is generally true that nouns ending in -o are masculine, and those ending in -a, -dad, -tad, -tud, -ión, -umbre and -ie are feminine:

el muchacho	boy	**la muchacha**	girl
la verdad	truth	**la libertad**	liberty
la juventud	youth	**la región**	region
la lumbre	hearth	**la serie**	series

There are some exceptions to this general rule. The word *la mano* (hand) is feminine although it ends in -o. The words *el día* (day), *el mapa* (map), *el sofá* (sofa) and a few others not in frequent use are masculine even though they end in -a. The words *el pie* (foot), *el avión* (aeroplane), *el gorrión* (sparrow), and *el sarampión* (measles), although they end in -ie and -ión, are masculine.

Nouns of Greek origin ending in -ma or -ta are masculine. The most important of these are:

el aroma	aroma	**el clima**	climate
el diagrama	diagram	**el diploma**	diploma
el drama	drama	**el idioma**	language
el monograma	monogram	**el panorama**	panorama
el poema	poem	**el prisma**	prism
el problema	problem	**el programa**	programme
el síntoma	symptom	**el sistema**	system
el telegrama	telegram	**el tema**	theme
el déspota	despot	**el idiota**	idiot
el planata	planet	**el poeta**	poet
el profeta	prophet		

Nouns ending in -ista are masculine or feminine according to whether they denote male or female beings:

el or **la dentista**	dentist	**el** or **la organista**	organist
el or **la nacionalista**	nationalist	**el** or **la pianista**	pianist
el or **la novelista**	novelist	**el** or **la socialista**	socialist

Nouns denoting names of male beings and female beings, regardless of endings, are usually masculine and femine respectively.

el artista   the artist (*male*)   **la modelo**   the model (*female*)

Nouns ending in *-e* are for the most part masculine, with some exceptions, such as *la noche* (night), *la calle* (street), *la carne* (meat), *la clase* (class), *la frase* (phrase), *la fiebre* (fever), *el hambre*[1] (hunger), *la tarde* (afternoon), and some others.

Nouns ending in *-l* are masculine as *el baúl* (trunk). The exceptions to this rule are: *la cal* (lime), *la capital* (capital [of a country]), *la cárcel* (jail, *la col* (cabbage), *la miel* (honey), *la piel* (skin), *la sal* (salt), *la señal* (sign, signal), *la vocal* (vowel), and *la moral* (moral).

Nouns ending in *-z* are masculine, with the exception of *la cruz* (cross), *la luz* (light), *la nariz* (nose) *la raíz* (root), *la paz* (peace), *la vez* (turn, time), and *la voz* (voice). All *abstract* nouns ending in *-ez* are, however, feminine as *la niñez* (childhood), *la vejez* (old age), *la embriaguez* (intoxication), etc.

Nouns ending in *-s* are masculine, with the exception of *la tos* (cough), *la bilis* (bile), *la tisis* (tuberculosis) and all such nouns derived from the Greek. *Cutis* (skin, of human beings) and *análisis* (analysis) are either masculine or feminine.

Nouns denoting the names of seas, oceans, rivers, mountains, and ships and infinitives and other indeclinable words used as nouns are usually masculine:

el Mediterráneo	the Mediterranean	**los Alpes**	the Alps
el Pacífico	the Pacific	**el Santa María**	(name of ship)
el Guadalquivir	the Guadalquivir	**el ver**	seeing

The names of the days of the week and of the months (written with small letters in Spanish) are masculine:

el domingo   Sunday   **enero**   January

There are certain nouns which vary in meaning according to gender:

el calavera	madcap	**la calavera**	skull
el capital	capital (money)	**la capital**	capital (city)
el cólera	cholera	**la cólera**	anger, passion, rage
el cometa	comet	**la cometa**	kite
el cura	priest	**la cura**	cure
el corte	cut (in tailoring)	**la corte**	court
el frente	front	**la frente**	forehead
el guía	guide	**la guía**	guide-book
el haz	bundle	**la haz**	face, surface

[1] *Hambre* is feminine but uses **el** in the singular (see §2).

el orden	order (arrangement)	la orden	order (command)
el Papa	the Pope	la papa	potato
el parte	message	la parte	part

In the case of nouns ending in other consonants, the gender must be learned individually:

| el rey | la ley | el pan | la flor |
| the king | the law | the bread | the flower |

Note. Mar (sea) can be either masculine or feminine; in geographical designations, as stated above, it is masculine (*el mar Mediterráneo*); in compound forms, where it means tide, it is feminine: *la pleamar* (high tide), *la bajamar* (low tide).

Nouns denoting names of countries except those ending in unstressed -*a*, are usualy masculine.

| el Canadá | el Perú | el Japón |
| Canada | Peru | Japan |

§7. Plural of Nouns

1. The plural of nouns in both genders ending in an unstressed vowel is formed by adding *s*:

| el caballo | los caballos | la yegua | las yeguas |
| the horse | the horses | the mare | the mares |

2. If the noun ends with a consonant or with a stressed vowel, the plural is formed by adding *es*:

| la flor | las flores | el rubí | los rubíes |
| the flower | the flowers | the ruby | the rubies |

Note. If the final consonant is a *z*, this is changed to *c* before adding *es*:

| la voz | las voces |
| the voice | the voices |

3. Nouns ending in unaccented -*es* or -*is* and compound nouns in -*s* have the same form for the singular and the plural:

el jueves	Thursday	los jueves	(on) Thursdays
la crisis	crisis	las crisis	the crises
el sacacorchos	corkscrew	los sacacorchos	the corkscrews

§8. The Use of Prepositions to Indicate Possession and Object

1. In Spanish the nouns are not inflected for case, which means that no different endings are used to indicate the relation of possession or the object of a verb.

2. Possession is always expressed by the preposition *de* preceding the noun which designates the possessor:

el libro de Juan   John's book

3. If the direct and indirect object denote a person, or an animal they are preceded by the preposition *a*, which is called the "personal *a*." Compare the following examples:

Visitaremos *a* la tía de Pedro   We shall visit Peter's aunt
Visitaremos la ciudad   We shall visit the city

This personal *a* is also used for a personified entity:

Es un científico que honra *a* su nación   He is a scientist who honours his country

The personal *a* should, however, be omitted before the object if the person indicated by it has no definite identity. In the following sentence, for instance, the speaker does not have any *particular* policeman in mind, so that the reference is not "personal":

Llamamos un policía   We called a (=any) policeman

Note 1. The personal *a* is generally omitted if it could cause confusion with another *a* used as a true preposition:

Mandaremos Roberto a casa   We'll send Robert home

Note 2. When the verb has both a direct and an indirect object, the personal *a* is omitted before the direct object for greater clarity:

Presentaré Alicia al Sr. Ramírez   I'll introduce Alicia to Mr. Ramírez

§9. Diminutives and Augmentatives

Spanish speakers use a great number of diminutives and augmentatives, especially in colloquial speech. These diminutives and augmentatives make the speech more colourful and add various connotations to the basic meanings of the words from which they are derived. One whose native tongue is not Spanish has to be careful in the use of these forms because he may use a diminutive or augmentative formed with a certain suffix which has a basic connotation but which in certain forms may have additional connotations. The words in which they occur may have meanings other than those given in the list below as the meanings of these suffixes.

The most common diminutive suffixes are -ito, -cito, or -ecito; -ico or -cico (sometimes used with an ironical connotation); -illo, -cillo, or -ecillo; -uelo, -zuelo, or -ezuelo. (To form the feminine form of any of these diminutives, change the -o to -a). All these diminutives generally imply smallness, affection or admiration, but sometimes also ridicule or contempt. The suffixes -ito, -cito and -ecito generally express affection, while illo, -cillo, -ecillo and -uelo, -zuelo, -ezuelo often indicate contempt or pity. Examples:

libro	book	**librito**	booklet
hermano	brother	**hermanito**	dear little brother
caja	box	**cajita**	small box
hermana	sister	**hermanita**	dear little sister
amigo	friend	**amiguito**	dear little friend
chica	little girl	**chiquita**	nice little girl
hombre	man	**hombrecito**	dear little man
mujer	woman	**mujercita**	dear little woman
pie	foot	**piececito**	pretty little foot
mano	hand	**manecita**	pretty little hand
pan	bread	**panecito**	roll
flor	flower	**florecita**	beautiful little flower
cordero	lamb	**corderillo**	little lamb
cordera	ewe	**corderilla**	little ewe lamb
pueblo	town	**pueblecillo**	tiny town
flor	flower	**florecilla**	little flower
escritor	writer	**escritorzuelo**	wretched writer
puerta	door	**portezuela**	door (of a vehicle)

The first names may also be used with the diminutive suffix -ito (-ita) which denotes endearment:

Juan	John	**Juanito**	Johnny
Pepe	Joe	**Pepito**	Joey
Ana	Anna	**Anita**	Annie

The augmentative suffixes generally serve to intensify the meaning of the word to which they are attached, but often they have a depreciatory implication.

The most common augmentative endings are -ón, -azo (which usually indicate large size or awkwardness); -acho and -ucho (which generally express scorn); and -ote (which is usually depreciative).

The feminine is formed by adding -a to those ending in a consonant, and by changing -o or -e to -a in those that end in -o or -e. Examples:

hombrón	solterón	hombrazo	picarazo
big man	old bachelor	large man	big scoundrel
vinacho	animalucho	librote	palabrota
poor wine	ugly animal	large old book	swear word

§10. Cognate Suffixes

There is a number of suffixes in Spanish which are commonly used for the formation of nouns. Some of these suffixes have cognate forms in English as *carpintería* (carpentry) from *carpintero* (carpenter) but occasionally with a different meaning from the one they have in English: *librería* (book shop; *not* library) from *libro* (book). The most common of these suffixes which have cognates in English are:

-ada	(*brigada*)	corresponding to the English	-ade	(*brigade*)
-ador	(*orador*)	,, ,, ,, ,,	-ator	(*orator*)
-aje	(*personaje*)	,, ,, ,, ,,	-age	(*personage*)
-al	(*metal*)	,, ,, ,, ,,	-al	(*metal*)
-alto	(*asfalto*)	,, ,, ,, ,,	-alt	(*asphalt*)
-ano	(*veterano*)	,, ,, ,, ,,	-an	(*veteran*)
-ante	(*instante*)	,, ,, ,, ,,	-ant	(*instant*)
-ato	(*carbonato*)	,, ,, ,, ,,	-ate	(*carbonate*)
-cio	(*comercio*)	,, ,, ,, ,,	-ce	(*commerce*)
-culo	(*círculo*)	,, ,, ,, ,,	-cle	(*circle*)
-cto	(*producto*)	,, ,, ,, ,,	-ct	(*product*)
-cia	(*democracia*)	,, ,, ,, ,,	-cy	(*democracy*)
-ción	(*nación*)	,, ,, ,, ,,	-tion	(*nation*)
-ente	(*agente*)	,, ,, ,, ,,	-ent	(*agent*)
-gio	(*privilegio*)	,, ,, ,, ,,	-ge	(*privilege*)
-geno	(*oxígeno*)	,, ,, ,, ,,	-gen	(*oxygen*)
-grafo	(*autógrafo*)	,, ,, ,, ,,	-graph	(*autograph*)
-ia	(*energía*)	,, ,, ,, ,,	-y	(*energy*)
-ica	(*música*)	,, ,, ,, ,,	-ic	(*music*)
-ina	(*doctrina*)	,, ,, ,, ,,	-ine	(*doctrine*)
-isco	(*asterisco*)	,, ,, ,, ,,	-isk	(*asterisk*)
-ismo	(*turismo*)	,, ,, ,, ,,	-ism	(*tourism*)
-ista	(*turista*)	,, ,, ,, ,,	-ist	(*tourist*)
-ito	(*granito*)	,, ,, ,, ,,	-ite	(*granite*)
-mento	(*fragmento*)	,, ,, ,, ,,	-ment	(*fragment*)
-ncia	(*violencia*)	,, ,, ,, ,,	-nce	(*violence*)
-oide	(*celuloide*)	,, ,, ,, ,,	-oid	(*celluloid*)
-o	(*museo*)	,, ,, ,, ,,	-um	(*museum*)
-o	(*aparato*)	,, ,, ,, ,,	-us	(*apparatus*)
-or	(*actor*)	,, ,, ,, ,,	-or	(*actor*)
-ota	(*patriota*)	,, ,, ,, ,,	-ot	(*patriot*)
-rio	(*misterio*)	,, ,, ,, ,,	-ry	(*mystery*)
-scopio	(*microscopio*)	,, ,, ,, ,,	-scope	(*microscope*)
-sis	(*tesis*)	,, ,, ,, ,,	-sis	(*thesis*)
-tud	(*solitud*)	,, ,, ,, ,,	-tude	(*solitude*)
-ulo	(*capsulo*)	,, ,, ,, ,,	-ule	(*capsule*)
-ura	(*figura*)	,, ,, ,, ,,	-ure	(*figure*)

CHAPTER 3

THE ADJECTIVE

§11. Classes and Forms of the Adjective

1. There are two classes of adjectives in Spanish:

a) Those which end in *-o* in the masculine singular and have four forms (one for the masculine singular in *-o*, one for the feminine singular in *-a*, one for the masculine plural in *-os*, and one for the feminine plural in *-as*):

el cuarto pequeño	the small room	**las casa pequeña**	the small house
los cuartos pequeños	the small rooms	**las casas pequeñas**	the small houses

b) Those which end in *-e* or any vowel other than *-o*, or in a consonant have only two forms, one for the singular and one for the plural of both genders, the masculine and feminine forms being identical for each number:

el espejo grande	the large mirror	**la silla grande**	the large chair
los espejos grandes	the large mirrors	**las sillas grandes**	the large chairs
el examen fácil	the easy examination	**la lección fácil**	the easy lesson
os exámenes fáciles	the easy examinations	**las lecciones fáciles**	the easy lessons

2. The adjectives follow the same rules as the nouns for the formation of the plural.

a) The plural of adjectives ending in a vowel is formed by adding *-s*:

los perros blancos	the white dogs	**las paredes blancas**	the white walls

b) The plural of adjectives ending in a consonant is formed by adding *-es*:

los ensayos fáciles	the easy essays	**las lecciones fáciles**	the easy lessons

Note. If the adjective ends with *-z*, this is changed to *c* before adding *-es*:

> **los niños felices**   the happy children

3. The adjectives take their feminine form according to the following general rules:

a) Adjectives which end in *-o* form the feminine by changing the *o* to *a*.

b) Adjectives which denote nationality and end in -*es*, as well as all adjectives ending in -*an*, -*on*, and -*or*, add an *a* to form the feminine:

francés (*masc.*), **francesa** (*fem.*)   French
roncador (*masc.*), **roncadora** (*fem.*) snoring

Note. The following adjectives are exceptions and do not change for the feminine:

| **mayor** | greater | **anterior** | anterior |
| **menor** | less | **posterior** | posterior |

c) Adjectives ending in other consonants do not change in the feminine:

el ensayo fácil the easy essay   **la lección fácil** the easy lesson

4. The adjective agrees in gender and number with the noun it modifies:

el caballo blanco the white horse   **la casa blanca** the white house
los caballos blancos the white horses **las casas blancas** the white houses

5. An adjective which modifies two or more nouns is always used in its masculine plural form if at least one noun is masculine:

El hijo y la hija son buenos   The son and the daughter are good

Las paredes, las puertas, las ventanas, los pupitres y las sillas están limpios
The walls, the doors, the windows, the desks and the chairs are clean

§12. Position of Adjectives

1. In Spanish the normal position of the adjective is after the noun it modifies. This is the general rule for descriptive adjectives like those denoting colour, shape, size, degree, nationality or religion, as well as for all adjectival participles. These adjectives are used to distinguish a noun from other nouns of the same class:

el libro castaño   the brown book
el libro grande   the large book
el libro español   the Spanish book

2. Limiting adjectives, such as demonstrative, interrogative, possessive and indefinite pronominal adjectives and numerals, precede the noun they modify:

este libro	this book	otro libro	another book
¿qué libro?	which book?	cualquier libro	any book (at all)
mi libro	my book	el primer libro	the first book

3. Adjectives which express an inherent or characteristic quality of the modified noun, or which are used with a figurative meaning, generally precede the noun they modify:

la blanca nieve	the white snow
la verde hierba	the green grass
las olorosas gardenias	the fragrant gardenias
la dura necesidad	the hard necessity

4. Some adjectives change their meaning according to their position before or after the noun:

mi caro amigo	my dear friend	un nuevo coche	a new (another) car
el abrigo caro	the expensive overcoat	un coche nuevo	a brand-new car
cierta cosa	a certain thing	una pobre mujer	a poor (unfortunate) woman
una cosa cierta	a sure thing	una mujer pobre	a poor (poverty-stricken) woman
un gran hombre	a great man	su única idea	his only idea
un hombre grande	a big man	su idea única	his unique idea
media clase	half a class	varios libros	several books
la clase media	the middle class	libros varios	miscellaneous books
la misma niña	the same girl		
la niña misma	the girl herself		

Note. Descriptive adjectives, which normally follow the noun they modify, when the quality described by them is general or implicit and there is no need to single it out, precede it:

los grandiosos edificios de Londres
the great (magnificent) buildings of London

5. A few adjectives, such as *bueno* (good), *malo* (bad), *pequeño* (small), as well as the ordinal numerals, may appear before or after the noun they modify without any basic change in their meaning except that when they follow the noun they are more emphatic than when they precede it:

la parte segunda (segunda parte)	the second part
muchachos buenos (buenos muchachos)	good boys

§13. Substantivised Adjectives

The adjectives in Spanish, as in English, may be used as nouns:

el ciego	the blind man
la pobre	the poor woman
los pobres y los ricos	the poor and the rich
el inglés	(the) English (language)

§14. Comparison of Adjectives

1. The comparative is formed by placing *más* (more) before the adjective:

más hermoso	more beautiful

2. The superlative is formed by placing the article before the comparative:

el (la) más hermoso (-a)	the most beautiful

3. The following four adjectives have irregular comparative forms; two of them, *grande* and *pequeño*, have both the regular and irregular forms:

Positive		*Comparative*	
bueno	good	**mejor**	better
malo	bad	**peor**	worse
grande	big	**mayor** or **más grande**	larger
pequeño	little	**menor** or **más pequeño**	smaller

Note. In the case of *grande* and *pequeño*, the regular comparative is generally used to convey physical size, while the irregular forms are more often used figuratively:

Esta casa es más grande	This house is larger
Tiene mayor importancia	It has greater importance

§15. The Absolute Superlative

1. The absolute superlative is used to express a very high degree of a trait or characteristic of a person or thing, without any relation to other persons or things. It has no corresponding form in English, and can be translated only by using such words as "very," "extremely," "highly," etc. It is formed by adding -*isimo* to adjectives ending in a consonant, or, when the adjectives end with a vowel, by replacing the vowel with -*ísimo*:

fácil	easy	**hermoso**	beautiful
facilísimo	extremely easy	**hermosísimo**	very beautiful

2. Note the following orthographic changes in certain adjectives:
a) If the adjective ends in *-co* or *-go*, the absolute superlative ending is *-quísimo* or *-guísimo*:

rico	rich	**amargo**	bitter
riquísimo	very rich	**amarguísimo**	very bitter

b) Adjectives ending in *-z* change the *z* to *c* before adding the endings:

feliz	happy	**felicísimo**	very happy

c) Adjectives ending in *-io* drop the *i* as well as the *o*, to avoid repetition of the *i*:

limpio	clean	**limpísimo**	very clean

Note. If the *i* is stressed in the basic adjective form, it is retained, as in *frío, fríísimo.*

d) Adjectives ending in *-ble* have the special ending *-bilísimo*:

amable	amiable	**amabilísimo**	most amiable

e) If the stressed syllable of the adjective contains *ie*, this changes to *e* in the absolute superlative:

cierto	certain	**certísimo**	very certain

Note. In addition to the comparative of superiority, the formation of which was described above, there are comparatives of equality and of inferiority.

The comparative of equality with adjectives is formed with *tan . . . como* (as, so . . . as):

Ella es tan feliz como él	She is as happy as he
Ella no es tan rica como él	She is not so rich as he

The comparative of inferiority is formed with *menos . . . que* (less . . . than):

Las toronjas son menos dulces que las naranjas
Grapefruits are less sweet than oranges

§16. Pronominal Adjectives

Most of the limiting adjectives, the function of which as their name implies, is to limit the noun phrases (that is, phrases made up of nouns and their modifiers), are pronominal adjectives. They are primarily of four kinds: demonstrative, indefinite, interrogative, and possessive.

§17 Demonstrative Adjectives

These pronominal adjectives are used as their name indicates to point out the thing or person referred to. In Spanish a threefold distinction is made instead of the twofold distinction we have in English:

1. The demonstrative adjective *este* (this) is used to indicate an object which is near the person who speaks. Its forms are *este* for the masculine singular, *esta* for the feminine singular, *estos* for the masculine plural and *estas* for the feminine plural.

2. The demonstrative adjective *ese* (that) is used to indicate an object near the person addressed. Its forms are *ese* for the masculine singular, *esa* for the feminine singular, *esos* for the masculine plural and *esas* for the feminine plural.

3. The demonstrative adjective *aquel* (that) is used to indicate an object which is removed from both the person speaking and the person addressed. Its forms are *aquel* for the masculine singular, *aquella* for the feminine singular, *aquellos* for the masculine plural and *aquellas* for the feminine plural. They refer to persons as well as things, and stress the concepts of "far away" or long ago.

Examples:

esta casa	this house	**este hombre**	this man (*near me*)
esa casa	that house	**ese hombre**	that man (*near you*)
aquella casa	that house (in the distance	**aquel hombre**	that man (*near him*)

Note. The forms of demonstrative adjectives are used unchanged as demonstrative pronouns, the only difference between the two groups being that the pronouns are written with an accent mark on the stressed syllable:

éste, ésta	this one	} *near me* or *near us*
éstos, éstas	these (ones)	
ése, ésa	that one	} *near you*
ésos, ésas	those (ones)	
aquél, aquélla	that one	} *near him* (*her*) or *them*
aquéllos, aquéllas	those (ones)	

§18. Indefinite Adjectives

The following is a list of the more common indefinite adjectives:
1. Those that have four forms:

alguno, -a, -os, -as	some, any, a few
(**alguno, -a que otro, -a**	some . . . or other)
mucho, -a, -os, -as	much, many

ninguno, -a, -os, -as	not any, no
otro, -a, -os, -as	another, other
poco, -a, -os, -as	little, few
tanto, -a, -os, -as	as much, as many, so much, so many
todo, -a, -os, -as	all, every

Note. The difference in meaning between *algunos* and *unos* is that *unos* is used in a less restrictive sense.

2. Those that are invariable and have only one form:

cada	each	**los (las) demás**	the rest (of)

3. Those that have two forms, either one for the masculine and one for the feminine:

ambos, ambas   both

or one for the singular and one for the plural:

cualquiera (sing.), **cualesquiera** (pl.)   any (one) at all

§19. Interrogative Adjectives

The Spanish interrogative adjectives are:

1. *Qué* (what, which):

¿Qué libros usa Vd.? Los libros de Cervantes para estudiar el español
What books are you using? The books of Cervantes to study Spanish.

2. *Cuál*, pl. *cuáles* (which, what), very seldom used as an adjective:

¿Cuál lección aprendió Vd.?   Which lesson did you learn?[1]

3. *Cuánto, -a, -os, -as* (how much, how many):

¿Cuántas maletas tiene Vd.?   How many suitcases do you have?

§20. Possessive Adjectives

The following is a list of the more common possessive adjectives. They have two forms: a full form which is used after a noun or takes its place, and a short (unstressed) form which is used before a noun. The short forms are used more frequently. They are repeated before each noun unless the nouns all refer to the same person or thing:

[1] This expression is somewhat archaic. *¿Qué lección aprendió Vd.?* is more commonly used.

| SHORT FORMS | | LONG FORMS | | |
Singular	Plural	Singular	Plural	English
mi	mis	mío, -a	míos, -as	my
tu	tus	tuyo, -a	tuyos, -as	your
su	sus	suyo, -a	suyos, -as	his, her, its, your, their
nuestro, -a	nuestros, -as	nuestro, -a	nuestros, -as	our
vuestro, -a	vuestros, -as	vuestro, -a	vuestros, -as	your

Note. The possessive adjectives agree in gender and number with the thing possessed rather than with the possessor.

§21. The Numerals

The cardinal, ordinal and fractional numerals are listed in the Vocabulary of Lesson 5.

Cardinal Numbers

1. The cardinal numbers are all invariable except *uno* (-*a*) and the compounds of *ciento*, as *doscientos*, -*as*, etc.

2. *Uno* drops the -*o* and *ciento* its final syllable -*to* when they immediately precede a noun.

3. The numbers *diez y seis, diez y siete, veinte y uno, veinte y dos*, etc., may also be written as one word *dieciséis, diecisiete, veintiuno, veintidós*, etc., up to *veintinueve*.

4. Counting by hundreds in Spanish is limited to nine hundred; beyond that it is by thousands, with the numbers of hundreds following.

Ordinal Numbers

1. The ordinal numbers are inflected exactly as adjectives.

2. *Primero* and *tercero* drop the final *o* when they precede a noun:

El primer tomo   The first volume

3. In the names of kings the ordinals are used only up to *décimo* (tenth).

Mathematical Operations

1. *Addition:* $3+4=7$ **tres y cuatro (son) siete.**
2. *Subtraction:* $7-2=5$ **siete menos dos (son) cinco.**
3. *Multiplication:* $4\times2=8$ **cuatro por dos (son) ocho.**
4. *Division:* $9\div3=3$ **neuve dividido por tres (son) tres.**

CHAPTER 4

THE PRONOUNS

§22. Subject Pronouns

1. The personal pronouns used as *subjects* of verbs are:

Singular		*Plural*	
yo	I	**nosotros, -as**	we
tú	you	**vosotros, -as**	you
él	he, it	**ellos**	they
ella	she, it	**ellas**	they
usted (Vd.)	you	**ustedes (Vds.)**	you

Yo (I), *nosotros* (masc.) and *nosotras* (fem.) (we) are the pronouns of the first person singular and plural, respectively. *Nos.*, the abbreviation for *nosotros* or *nosotras*, must always be pronounced in full. *Tú* (you, sg. [thou]), *vosotros* (masc.) and *vosotras* (fem.) (you, pl.) are the pronouns of the second person. They imply intimacy and affection, and are used in addressing God, relations, intimate friends and children. *Vos.* is the abbreviation for *vosotros* or *vosotras*, and, like *nos.*, must always be pronounced in full.

Él (he), *ella* (she), *ellos* (masc.) and *ellas* (fem.) (they) are the singular and plural pronouns of the third person.

Usted is used in the usual style of conversation, when speaking to one person, and *ustedes* when speaking to more than one. These words are contractions for *vuestra merced* (your grace, your honour, your worship) and *vuestras mercedes* (your graces, your honours, your worships). With *usted* the verb must be in the third person singular, and with *ustedes* in the third person plural, because *¿desea usted?* means literally "does your grace wish?" and *¿desean ustedes?* "do your graces wish?" although both are translated by "you." The word *usted* is usually abbreviated to *Vd.*, *V.* or *Ud.*, and *ustedes* to *Vds.* or *Uds.*, but these abbreviations are always pronounced *usted* and *ustedes*, respectively.

2. The subject pronouns *yo*, *tú*, *él*, *ella*, etc., with the exception of *usted* and *ustedes*, are generally left out, except in case of questions, or ambiguity and when emphasising the meaning of the phrase:

¿Lo hago yo o lo hace él?	Do I do it, or does he?
Mientras ella estudia, él lee	While she studies, he reads
¿Qué he de hacer yo?	What can I do?

The English expressions *it is I, it is he, it was we*, etc., are translated into Spanish by *soy yo, es él, éramos nosotros*, etc.

§23. Object Pronouns

1. *Personal object pronouns.*

The direct personal pronouns in Spanish are:

	Singular			*Plural*
me	me		**nos**	us
te	you		**os**	you
le, lo	you (m.)	} (familiar form)	**{los, les**	you (m.)
la	you (f.)	} (polite form)	**{las**	you (f.)
le, lo	him, it		**los, les**	them
la	her, it			
		las them		
lo	it			

The forms for the first and second persons singular and plural of the indirect object personal pronouns are identical with those used for the direct object. The personal pronouns of the indirect object for the polite form of the second person singular and plural are *le* (to you) and *les* (to you), respectively. Those for the third person singular are *le* (*m.*, to him, to it) and *le* (*f.*, to her, to it) and *les* (to them) for both the masculine and feminine of the third person plural.

The forms *me, te, le, la, lo, se* and their plurals *nos, os, les, las, los, se* are placed before the verb, except in the case of an infinitive, an imperative or present participle in which cases they are placed after the verb and attached to it:

El me lo ha dicho	He has told me so
Nos han dado la noticia	They have given us the news
Necesito hablarle	I must speak to him
¿Quiere Vd. verle?	Do you want to see him?
Páguenos Vd. la cuenta	Pay us the bill
Págguesela Vd. (a él)	Pay it to him
Enséñeme Vd. el libro	Show me the book

2. *Prepositional pronouns.*

a) The forms of the personal pronouns used as objects of prepositions are:

Singular		*Plural*	
mí	me	**nostoros, -as**	us
ti	you	**vosotros, -as**	you
usted	you	**ustedes**	you
él	him, it	**ellos**	them (m.)
ella	her, it	**ellas**	them (f.)

b) For emphasis and to avoid ambiguity, the prepositional pronouns —usually preceded by the preposition *a*—are used after the verb, in addition to the object pronoun, which is placed before the verb:

Le hablo a él y no a ella
I speak to him and not to her

Les he dado la noticia a ellos
I have given the news to them (masc.)

Note 1. Another arrangement, less frequently used, has the prepositional pronoun at the beginning of the sentence, followed by the object pronoun and the verb:

A él le pago
I pay him

¿A mí qué me importa?
What do I care?

Note 2. A preposition can never be followed by *lo;* in such cases *lo* is replaced by *ello*.

Note 3. In the case of *usted*, both forms of that pronoun (*le* and *a Vd.*) are generally used:

Le digo a Vd. eso
I tell you that

¿Qué le ha dicho a Vd.?
What has he told you?

c) The pronouns *mí*, *ti* and *sí*, when governed by *con*, form one word consisting of that preposition, the pronoun and the particle *go*:

conmigo	**contigo**	**consigo**
with me	with you	with him, her, it, them

§24. Two-object Pronouns

1. When a verb governs two object pronouns, the indirect object must precede the direct object. *Se* always precedes all other pronouns, whether before or after the verb. Examples:

¿Me lo dirá Vd.?
Will you tell it to me?
Se lo daré a Vd. mañana
I'll give it to you to-morrow
Enséñeselos Vd. a él (ella)
Show them to him (her)
No quiero decírselo
I don't want to tell him so (it to him)

Ellos nos lo han dicho
They told us so (it to us)
Dígaselo ahora
Tell him so (it to him) now
No se los enseñaré a ellos
I won't show them to them

2. When *le* and *les* precede another object pronoun, they change to *se* for reasons of euphony, as follows:

Le le and **les le** change to	**se le**	**Le les** and **les les** change to	**se les**
Le la and **les la** „	**se la**	**Le las** and **les las** „	**se las**
Le lo and **les lo** „	**se lo**	**Le los** and **les los** „	**se los**

§25. Reflexive Pronouns

1. The pronouns of the first, second and third persons have a reflexive meaning when they refer to the same person as the subject:

Yo me equivoco	I am mistaken
Tú te equivocas	You are mistaken
El se equivoca	He is mistaken
Nosotros nos equivocamos	We are mistaken
Vosotros os equivocáis	You are mistaken
Ellos se equivocan	They are mistaken

Usted and *ustedes* are also replaced by *se* in the reflexive form:

(Usted) se engaña	You deceive yourself
(Ustedes) se engañan	You (pl.) deceive yourselves

2. The pronouns of the third person, including *usted*, can also refer to persons or things different from the subject:

El le equivoca	He gives him wrong information
El se equivoca	He makes a mistake
Vd. la engaña	You deceive her
Vd. se engaña	You are deceived

Vd. la cierra	You close it
Se cierra	It closes (itself)
El lo rompe	He breaks it
Se rompe	It breaks (itself)

Note. The translation of *se* is sometimes omitted as superfluous in English:

Se marchan en seguida	They depart at once
Se rompe, se abre, se cierra	It breaks, it opens, it shuts

§26. Additional Uses of se

The object pronoun *se* is used:

1. To make a verb impersonal:

Se habla español	Spanish is spoken
Se dice	It is said
Se cree	It is believed

2. In a reflexive meaning as a direct object:

Pedro se lava	Peter washes himself
El se calienta	He warms himself

3. In a reflexive meaning as an indirect object:

Juan se peina el cabello	John combs his hair
Pablo se lava las manos	Paul washes his hands
El se calienta las manos	He warms his hands

4. As an object pronoun in place of *le* or *les:*

Le doy el libro	I give him the book
Se lo doy	I give it to him

In this case it is plainly shown that *se* takes the place of *le*, while *lo* takes the place of "the book." As has been stated above, this is done solely to avoid the sounds of *le-lo, les-los,* etc.

§27. Interrogative Pronouns

The interrogative pronoun *¿quién?* (who? whom?) is of both genders, but refers to persons only.

¿Qué? (what) is used with things and in all other cases except in certain idioms. It is also not used before forms of the verb *ser* (to be) when no definition is asked.

¿Cuál? (which, which one) refers to persons or things, and is used to select or choose one or more than one from a larger group; *¿cuál?* meaning "what?" is used before forms of the verb *ser* (to be) when no definition is asked.

Only *quién* and *cuál* of the interrogative pronouns have plural forms. They are *quiénes* and *cuáles.*

¿Quién tiene mis cuadernos?	Who has my notebooks?
¿Con quién hablaba Vd.?	With whom were you talking?
¿Quiénes son aquellos hombres?	Who are those men?
¿Quiénes son aquellas muchachas?	Who are those girls?
¿Qué dijo ella?	What did she say?
¿Qué es poesía?	What is poetry?
¿Cuál es su ocupación?	What is your occupation?
¿Cuál de los libros le gusta más?	Which one of the books do you like best?

§28. Demonstrative Pronouns

There is no difference in form between the demonstrative pronouns *éste, ésta* (this one); *éstos, éstas* (these); *ése, ésa* (that one); *ésos, ésas* (those); *aquél, aquélla* (that one); and *aquéllos, aquéllas* (those) and the corresponding demonstrative adjectives discussed in §17). The only difference between the two groups is that the pronouns have a written accent on the stressed syllable while the adjectives are written without any accent. The demonstrative pronouns stand by themselves, but the demonstrative adjectives precede the nouns which they limit and modify.

Adjective: **Esta maleta es de Juan**   *Pronoun*: **Esta es mi maleta**
    This suitcase is John's   This is my suitcase

In addition to the demonstrative pronouns, which have corresponding forms used as demonstrative adjectives, there are the neuter pronouns *esto, eso,* and *aquello* which have no written accent and are used when the thing for which they stand is a statement, idea or something indefinite or unknown:

Esto es muy bueno   **¡Eso es!**
This is very good   That's it!

§29 Relative Pronouns

Que (who, whom, that, which) is the most common of the relative pronouns. It is used both as the subject or the direct object of a verb:

El hombre que habla es mi tío   **Me gusta el libro que me dió Vd.**
The man who is talking is my uncle   I like the book you gave me

Note in the above sentence that the word "that" (*que*), which may be and often is omitted in English, may never be omitted in Spanish.

Quien (who, whom) is used instead of *que* to introduce a nonrestrictive clause (that is, a clause which is not necessary to complete a sentence):

Ella dió la carta que recibió hoy a su madre, quien la leyó inmediatamente
She gave the letter she received to-day to her mother, who read it at once

Quien often includes its antecedent:

Quien trabaja mucho prospera por lo general
He who works hard, usually prospers

Quienes estudian el español diligentemente pueden gozar mejor sus viajes en España
Those who study Spanish diligently are better able to enjoy their travels in Spain

Quien is also used instead of *que* after a preposition when the antecedent refers to a person:

La mujer con quien hablaba es mi tía
The woman to whom I was speaking is my aunt

El que, la que, los que, las que, el cual, la cual, los cuales, las cuales may be used instead of *que* or *quien* to avoid ambiguity.

Lo que (that which, what, which) is used as a relative pronoun which refers to a fact, an event, or an idea rather than to a person or a thing:

Lo que hizo Vd. es muy difícil de comprender
What you did is very difficult to understand

Other relative pronouns are *cuyo, cuya, cuyos, cuyas* (whose):

El muchacho cuya madre fué mi maestra vive aquí
The boy whose mother was my teacher lives here

La muchacha cuyo padre es el gerente de esta compañía es mi amiga
The girl whose father is the manager of this company is my girl friend

§30. Possessive Pronouns

1. The forms of possessive pronouns in Spanish are identical with the long forms of the possessive adjectives but they are preceded by the definite article. They agree in gender and number with the noun for which they stand. Their forms are the following:

Masculine		*Feminine*		
Singular	*Plural*	*Singular*	*Plural*	
el mío	los míos	la mía	las mías	mine
el tuyo	los tuyos	la tuya	las tuyas	yours (lit., thine)
el suyo	los suyos	la suya	las suyas	his, hers, its, yours
el nuestro	los nuestros	la nuestra	las nuestras	ours
el vuestro	los vuestros	la vuestra	las vuestras	yours
el suyo	los suyos	la suya	las suyas	theirs, yours

2. The neuter form of the possessive pronouns *lo mío, lo tuyo, lo suyo, lo nuestro, lo vuestro, lo suyo* means "what is mine," "what is yours," "what is his," "what is hers," "what is yours," "what is ours," "what is yours," "what is theirs," respectively.

3. The interrogative possessive pronoun is *de quién*:

¿De quién es este libro?   Whose book is this?

4. The interrogative, demonstrative, and relative pronouns present a correlation regarding the concepts they express:

CLASSES OF PRONOUNS	CONCEPTS				
	Persons	*Things*	*Possession*	*Quantity*	*Quality*
Interrogatives	¿Quién?	¿Qué?	¿De quién?	¿Cuánto?	¿Cuál?
Demonstratives	Este, ése, a quél	Esto, eso, aquello	Mío, tuyo, suyo	Tanto	Tal
Relatives	Que, quien	Que	Cuyo	Cuanto	Cual

§31. Indefinite Pronouns

The most common indefinite pronouns in Spanish are:

1. *Alguien* (someone, somebody, anyone, anybody), which refers to persons only:

¿Ha venido alguien?	Has anybody come?

2. *Alguno -a, -os, -as* (somebody, someone, anybody, anyone) which refers to one of a group of persons or things (understood or already mentioned):

Alguno ha estado aquí   Somebody has been here
"¿Ha recibido Vd. algunos libros?" "Sí, he recibido algunos."
"Have you received any books?" "Yes, I received some."

In the last example *algunos* (masc. pl.) is used as an indefinite adjective before *libros* in the question, and as a pronoun in the answer

3. *Cualquiera* is a compound word of *cual* (which) and *quiera* (may wish), "the one you may wish." It may be rendered by the equivalent expressions *el que (la que) Vd. quiera* (or *guste*), *los que (las que) Vd. quiera* (or *guste*), that is, "any one you please." *Ser uno un cualquiera* is a Spanish idiom meaning "to be a person of no account."

4. *Nadie* (no one, nobody, none, no), which refers to persons only:

Nadie ha venido   Nobody has come

5. *Ninguno, -a, -os, -as* (no one, nobody, none, no) which refer to persons or things:

¿Ha recibido usted algunas cartas?   Have you received any letters?
No, no he recibido ninguna   No, I have not received any

6. *Otro, -a* (another, other), *otros, -as* (others), which refer to persons or things:

el otro día	the other day	**otro día**	another day
otra vez	another time, again	**el otro hombre**	the other man

It should be noted that *un otro* is never used for "another," which is always translated simply by *otro*, as in *Eso no lo hubiera dicho otro* ("Another would not have said so"), but requires the definite article *el* or *la* whenever a distinct person or thing is to be specified:

No me dé Vd. ése, déme el otro   Don't give me that, give me the other

7. Other indefinite pronouns are:

ambos, -as	both
cada uno	each one
uno u[1] otro	one or the other

and the relative indefinite

quienquiera (sing.), **quienesquiera** (pl.) whoever

[1] See §42. Note I.

CHAPTER 5

THE PREPOSITION

§32. The prepositions are used to indicate the relationship of the noun or pronoun they precede to the other elements of the sentence. Their use is one of the most difficult things to master in learning a foreign language because prepositional usage is largely idiomatic. Therefore, only a few generalisations about the use of the most common prepositions will be made here. The student should form the habit of observing and learning, through repetition and practice, the prepositional usages which differ from English as he encounters them.

Note, for example, that a sentence as *¿En qué consiste generalmente su desayuno?* is translated by "Of what does your breakfast usually consist?"

§33. The most common simple prepositions in Spanish are:

a	at, to	**durante**	during	**menos**	except
ante	before	**en**	in, on, at	**para**	for, to
bajo	under	**entre**	between, among	**por**	by, for, through
con	with	**excepto**	except	**según**	according to
contra	against	**hacia**	toward	**sin**	without
de	of, from	**hasta**	until	**sobre**	on, upon
desde	since	**mediante**	by means of	**tras**	behind

§34. The Preposition *a* (as well as its contracted form with the definite article *al*) is used:

1. Before indirect object nouns:
Ella le dió el libro a Pablo   She gave Paul the book

Note. The preposition can be omitted in English, but it cannot be omitted in Spanish.

2. Before nouns or pronouns which are used as direct objects and refer to definite persons, personified ideas and things, and sometimes to animals (see §8.3):

Amo a Juana
I love Joan

Tomás vió a Dolores, pero no a su perro
Thomas saw Dolores, but not her dog

3. Generally before geographical names which are direct objects of verbs:

Visitará a Mallorca
He will visit Majorca

Ella fué a Madrid
She went to Madrid

4. Before common nouns used as direct objects to avoid confusing them with the subjects:

¿Vió el perro al gato?   Did the dog see the cat?

5. Before adverbial phrases referring to time, price or rate:

Vendrá a la noche   **A dos pesos el tomo**
He will come at night   Two pesos a volume

6. Before an infinitive after a verb of motion:

Voy a escribir   I am going to write

7. Between two infinitives in order to indicate the difference of purpose between them:

Va mucho de decir a hacer   There is a great difference between saying and doing

§35. The Preposition *de* (as well as its contracted form with the definite article, *del*) is used:

1. To indicate possession:

Los libros de Juan están aquí   John's books are here

In Spanish this is the only way of indicating possession.

2. To express the adjectival relation of a noun to a preceding noun:

Un buzón de correos   A letter-box
Ella compró calcetines de lana para su esposo
She bought woollen socks for her husband

In Spanish, nouns can never be used as adjectives modifying other nouns by changing their position as they do in English, as is seen in the example above where "woollen socks" is used for "socks (made) of wool."

3. To indicate movement from a place:

El vino de Buenos Aires   He came from Buenos Aires

4. To indicate a person, place or object from which something comes or originates:

Recibí una carta de Pepe   **Lo tomé del armario**
I received a letter from Joe   I took it from the cupboard

5. To indicate cause or reason:

Tiembla de miedo
He trembles with (lit. of) fear

Está ciego de furor
He is blind with (lit. of) anger

6. After verbs of emotion or a form of the verb *ser* followed by a past participle:

La alumna es estimada de sus profesores
The girl student is regarded highly by her professors

7. In exclamations:

¡Infeliz de mí!
Unhappy me!

¡Pobre de mi padre!
My poor father!

8. After superlatives:

Este libro es el mejor de su clase   This book is the best of its kind

9. Before numerals and numerical expressions:

Ella me dío más de doscientas pesetas
She gave me more than two hundred pesetas

(See also §60.7).

§36. The Preposition *para*, which conveys the general idea of effect, is used:

1. Before infinitives translating the English phrase "in order to":

Comemos para vivir y no vivimos para comer
We eat in order to live and we don't live to eat

2. Before infinitives, after forms of the verb *estar*, translating the English phrase "about to":

Alma está para salir   Alma is about to leave

3. Before infinitives to express the purpose for which the object was made or intended:

Para subir a la oficina de mi padre usamos el ascensor
We use the lift to go up to my father's office

4. Before nouns, especially geographical names, indicating destination:

Alicia saldrá para Italia mañana   Alice will leave for Italy to-morrow

5. In expressions indicating some future time:

Estará lista para el lunes	This will be ready on Monday

6. Before a noun or pronoun to indicate that the quality described by the adjective is contrary to the expectation evoked by the word following *para:*

El tiempo es muy frío para julio	**Carlitos es muy alto para su edad**
The weather is very cold for July	Charlie is very tall for his age

§37. The Preposition *por*, which generally conveys the idea of cause, is used:

1. To indicate the agent after a verb in the passive voice:

El discurso será pronunciado por un gran orador
The speech will be made by a great orator

El poema "El Dos de Mayo" fué escrito por el poeta español Nicasio Gallego
The poem "The Second of May" was written by the Spanish poet Nicasio Gallego

2. In expressions of price, exchange, equivalent and percentage, as well as origin, direction and duration of time:

Quiere cinco chelines por eso	**Su dinero produce el cuatro por ciento**
He wants five shillings for that	Your money brings four per cent
Estuvo en España por dos meses	**Fuí a Ibiza por Mallorca**
He was in Spain for two months	I went to Ibiza by way of Majorca

3. In certain idiomatic expressions after the verbs *pasar, enviar, pedir, venir, ir* and some others:

Felipe pasa por hombre instruido
Philip passes for a learned man

Envíe por el médico	**Vinieron por tí**
Send for the doctor	They came for you

4. To indicate the cause:

Por usted, no visité a mi prima
On account of you, I did not visit my cousin

5. As an equivalent of *en vez de* (instead of) or *en lugar de* (in place of):

Lo compré por mi hermano	I bought it as my brother's agent

6. After forms of the verb *estar* and before an infinitive:

Ella está por esperarle   She is inclined to wait for him

7. After adverbs or adjectives and before *que* rendering the English expression "no matter how":

Por poco que estudie, siempre aprende
No matter how little he studies, he always learns

§38. Compound Prepositions

In Spanish in addition to the simple prepositions there is a relatively large number of compound prepositions which are formed by adverbs or adverbial expressions followed by the prepositions *de* or *a*.

The most important of these compound prepositions are:

1. Compound prepositions which require *de:*

acerca de	concerning, about	**dentro de**	within
además de	beside	**después de**	after
antes de	before	**detrás de**	behind
cerca de	near	**encima de**	above
debajo de	under	**fuera de**	outside
delante de	before	**lejos de**	far from

2. Compound prepositions which require *a:*

conforme a	according to	**frente a**	opposite
con respecto a	regarding	**junto a**	near, close by
contrario a	contrary to	**tocante a**	touching

CHAPTER 6

THE ADVERB

The adverbs are primarily used to indicate the manner, time, or place in which the action of the verb takes place. They are also used, in Spanish just as in English, to modify adjectives, other adverbs, adjectival and adverbial phrases.

§39. Formation of Adverbs

Most of the adverbs, especially those of manner, are formed by adding the suffix -*mente* to the singular feminine forms of adjectives:

completo, -a	complete	**completamente**	completely
hondo, -a	deep	**hondamente**	deeply
rápido, -a	quick	**rápidamente**	quickly
fácil	easy	**fácilmente**	easily
natural	natural	**naturalmente**	naturally

Note. In a series of adverbs in -*mente*, the suffix -*mente* is omitted from all except the last:

Mis amigos viven sabia, feliz y fácilmente[1]
My friends live wisely, happily and easily

Many adverbs are single words which have their own individual form. Such are most of the adverbs of place and time and all of the interrogative adverbs. (See §41.)

§40. Comparison of Adverbs

The comparative of adverbs is formed by placing *más* before the adverb; to form the superlative, *lo más* is placed before it:

francamente	**más francamente**	**lo más francamente**
frankly	more frankly	the most frankly

Four very common adverbs have irregular comparatives:

bien	well	**mejor**	better
mal	badly	**peor**	worse
mucho	much	**más**	more
poco	little	**menos**	less

[1] To say *Viven sabiamente, felizmente y fácilmente* would be wrong.

§41. Classes of Adverbs

The most common adverbs in Spanish presented according to their classes are:

1. *Adverbs of time:*

¿cuándo?	when?	de repente	suddenly
¿desde cuándo?	since when?	de prisa	in a hurry
¿hasta cuándo?	til when? how long?	siempre	always
hoy	to-day	ya	already
ayer	yesterday	todavía	yet
mañana	to-morrow	nunca, jamás	never
pasado mañana	day after to-morrow	entonces	then
anoche	last night	antes	before
ahora	now	después	afterwards
luego	afterwards	al fin, en fin	at last, finally
inmediatamente	immediately, at once	a menudo	often

2. *Adverbs of place:*

¿dónde?, ¿en dónde?	where?	delante	before
¿de dónde?	whence?	detrás	behind
¿para dónde?	which way?	dentro	inside
¿a dónde?	where to?	fuera	outside
aquí	here	lejos	far, afar
allí, ahí	there	cerca	near
acá	this way	adelante	forward, ahead
allá	that way	atrás	back, behind, backward
arriba	above	debajo	beneath
abajo	below		

3. *Adverbs of manner:*

¿cómo?	how?	así	so, thus
bien	well	claro	clearly
mal	badly	alto	aloud, loudly
despacio	slowly	bajo	soft, softly

4. *Adverbs of quantity:*

¿cuánto?, ¿cuánta?	how much?	bastante	enough
¿cuántos?, ¿cuántas?	how many?	algo	something
mucho	much	casi	almost
poco	little	apenas	scarcely
demasiado	too much	basta	that is enough

5. *Affirmative and negative adverbs:*

sí	yes	quizá (s)	
ciertamente	certainly	tal vez	perhaps
no	no	absolutamente	absolutely

Note. After verbs denoting question, answer, belief, declaration, doubt or suspicion, the English particles "yes" and "no" ("not") are translated by *que sí* and *que no* respectively, e.g.:

Yo digo que sí, y él dice que no	I say yes and he says no
Yo creo que sí, y él cree que no	I think so and he does not

CHAPTER 7

THE CONJUNCTION

Conjunctions are words used to connect sentences, clauses, phrases and words. There are two types of conjunctions: co-ordinating and subordinating.

§42. Co-ordinating Conjunctions join sentences, clauses, phrases and words of equal rank. The most common ones in Spanish are:

y and **o** or   **pero, mas,** but

and the correlatives

o . . . o, either . . . or	**ni . . . ni,** neither . . . nor
El hombre estudia y aprende	The man studies and learns
Carlos ni estudia ni aprende	Charles neither studies nor learns

Note. Before a word beginning with *i* or *hi* (but not *hi* in a diphthong, as in *hielo* [ice]) *y* changes to *e:*

Pedro e Isabel fueron al cine ayer
Peter and Elizabeth went to the cinema yesterday

When *o* occurs before a word beginning with *o* or *ho*, it changes to *u:*

Hace siete u ocho años que está en Gibraltar
He has been in Gibraltar for seven or eight years

2. *Pero* and *mas* are placed at the beginning of clauses and phrases expressing contrast or opposition, while *sino* (but) is used only when the preceding clause is negative:

No es blanco sino negro	*But:*	**Me dijo eso pero no es así**
It is not white but black		He told me that, but it is not so

§43. Subordinating Conjunctions introduce subordinate clauses and establish dependence between the verb of the main clause and that of the subordinate. The most common ones are:

a fin de que	in order to	**mientras que**	while
aunque	although	**para (que)**	in order to
como	as	**porque**	because
conque	so that, so then	**puesto que**	since

con tal que	provided that	**que**	that
cuando	when	**si**	if

After the conjunctions *cuando* (when), *que* (that), *aunque* (although, though) and the compound conjunctions *aun cuando* (even) *con tal que* (provided that) and *siempre que* (whenever), the subjunctive is used in the subordinate clause instead of the indicative when uncertainty, doubt, possibility or indefinite future time are expressed:

Aunque me lo haya dicho, no me acuerdo
Although he may have told me so, I do not remember it
Le doy el libro para que lo lea
I gave him the book to read

The relative pronoun *que*, corresponding to the English "that" is never omitted in Spanish.

CHAPTER 8

THE INTERJECTION

§44. Interjections are short, invariable words which are used to express such basic feelings as joy, pleasure, astonishment, grief, disgust, etc. Here are some of the most common interjections in Spanish and their approximate English meanings:

¡ay!	ouch!, ah!, alas!	¡hola!	hello!
¡ah!	ah!	¡viva!	hurrah!
¡bah!	pshaw!	¡caramba!	confound it!

Exclamative phrases can be considered a type of interjection:

¡Qué bonita!	How pretty!	¡Qué lástima!	What a pity!
¡Qué hermosa!	How beautiful!	¡Qué importa!	Never mind!

CHAPTER 9

THE VERB

§45. The Nature of the Spanish Verb

In English the form of the verb changes according to the subject. We say: I am, you are, he is, etc. In most cases, however, the English verb changes only in the third person singular in the present. For example, we say: *I study, you study, we study, they study*, but *he studies* or *she studies*. Since five of the six possible forms are identical, we are not especially conscious of the problem of verb endings. On the other hand the Spanish verb has a large number of endings which differ according to subject, tense and mood. The best way to learn the verb forms properly is to learn them in the frame of the context in which they are used. Memorising the endings without learning the patterns of speech in which they occur may help you recognise them but not actually to use them. The presentation of the uses of each tense following its models of conjugation, as it is arranged in this grammar, will help you to associate the forms with their uses.

§46. General Remarks about the Conjugations

All verbs in Spanish end in *-ar*, *-er* or *-ir*. These are called the endings of the infinitive.

The infinitive of the English verb is expressed by means of *to*, as *to speak, to eat, to leave*, i.e. in two words. One word only is needed in Spanish as *hablar, comer, partir*, etc.

The stem of a verb is what is left after striking off the ending of the infinitive; thus, *habl-, com-, part-* are the stems of *hablar, comer, partir*, respectively.

To these stems we must add the endings of the different moods, tenses and persons.

The regular verbs in Spanish preserve intact throughout their conjugation the *sound* that the stem has in the infinitive. It is only the *endings*, which are the same for verbs of one conjugation, that vary according to the inflection of *person, number, tense* and *mood*.

THE INDICATIVE MOOD

Simple Tenses

§47. The Present (Indicative)

The present indicative indicates an action going on at the present time. If we take the verb *to speak*, we find that in English there are three ways to indicate an action going on in the present: *I speak, I am speaking, I do speak*. Speakers of Spanish, however, say only *hablo* (I speak). In other words, the present tense of a Spanish verb is always expressed in one word. The present indicative of regular verbs is formed by taking the stem of the verb and adding to it the endings:

FIRST CONJUGATION (Verbs in -*ar*)

	Singular		*Plural*	
1*st person*	**yo habl-o**	I speak, etc.	**nos. habl-amos**	we speak
2*nd person*	**tú habl-as**		**vos. habl-áis**	etc.
3*rd person* (*m.*)	**él habl-a** ⎱		**ellos habl-an**⎱	
3*rd person* (*f.*)	**ella habl-a** ⎬		**ellas habl-an** ⎬	
Polite form of address	**Vd. habl-a** ⎰		**Vds. habl-an**⎰	

SECOND CONJUGATION (Verbs in -*er*)

yo com-o	I eat, etc.		**nos. com-emos**	we eat, etc.
tú com-es			**vos. com-éis**	
él com-e ⎱			**ellos com-en** ⎱	
ella com-e ⎬			**ellas com-en** ⎬	
Vd. com-e ⎰			**Vds. com-en** ⎰	

THIRD CONJUGATION (Verbs in -*ir*)

yo part-o	I leave, etc.		**nos. part-imos**	we leave, etc.
tú part-es			**vos. part-ís**	
él part-e ⎱			**ellos part-en** ⎱	
ella part-e ⎬			**ellas part-en** ⎬	
Vd. part-e ⎰			**Vds. part-en** ⎰	

As may be seen by comparing the endings of the present indicative in the three conjugations, the first person singular ends in -*o* in all verbs, although the following are exceptions: *he* (I have [auxiliary]), *doy* (I give), *soy* and *estoy* (I am), *sé* (I know), and *voy* (I go, I am going). The second and third persons singular of the first conjugation are characterised by -*a*, and of the second and third conjugation by -*e*. The plural endings in all three conjugations are identical as to their last part which is -*mos* for the first person, -*is* for the second, and -*n* for the third. The initial part of these endings is the characteristic vowel of each conjugation, which is found in the infinitive immediately before *r*.

Uses of the Present

1. The present tense represents an action as happening, or a fact as existing at the moment we are speaking:

Mientras yo dicto ella escribe   **Yo madrugo**
While I *dictate* she *writes*   I *get up* early

America es una nación que progresa sin cesar
America *is* a country which continually *progresses*

2. This tense is used sometimes instead of the preterite especially in *narration*, to add interest and emphasis to the conversation:

Apenas dió la hora, cuando llegan los invitados, se sientan a la mesa, y comienza la comida
The clock had just struck when the guests *arrived*, sat at the table and dinner *began*

3. Sometimes the present is used instead of the future, especially in conditions after the conjuction *si* (if), when the future is never used:

Si viene Vd. a mi casa saldremos a dar un paseo
If you *will come* to my house, we will go for a walk
¿Tiene Vd. la bondad?   **¿Me hace Vd. el favor?**
Will you *have* the kindness? *Will* you *do* me the favour?

4. The verb *hacer* is used idiomatically in the present to indicate an action or state *begun* in the past and *continuing* up to the present:

Hace tres años que no nos hablamos
It *has been* three years since we *spoke* to each other
Hace dos semanas que llueve
It *has been raining* for two weeks
¿Cuánto tiempo hace que está Vd. en este país?
How long *have* you *been* in this country?
Hace cinco años que estoy aquí
I *have been* here five years

§48. The Imperfect (Indicative)

The imperfect indicative of the three model regular verbs is as follows:

FIRST CONJUGATION

yo habl-aba	I was speaking	**nos. habl-ábamos**	we were speaking
tú habl-abas	or used to speak,	**vos. habl-abais**	or used to speak,
él habl-aba	etc.	**ellos habl-aban**	etc.
ella habl-aba		**ellas habl-aban**	
Vd. habl-aba		**Vds. habl-aban**	

SECOND AND THIRD CONJUGATIONS

yo com-ía	I was eating or	**yo part-ía**	I was leaving or
tú com-ías	used to eat etc.	**tú part-ías**	used to leave, etc.
él com-ía		**él part-ía**	
ella com-ía		**ella part-ía**	
Vd. com-ía		**Vd. part-ía**	

nos. com-íamos	nos. part-íamos
vos. com-íais	vos. part-íais
ellos com-ían ⎫	ellos part-ían ⎫
ellas com-ían ⎬	ellas part-ían ⎬
Vds. com-ían ⎭	Vds. part-ían ⎭

The basic ending of the imperfect of the first conjugation is -*aba* and of the second and third -*ía*, which is also the ending for both the first and third persons singular; to this the general endings -*s*, -*mos*, -*is* and -*n* must be added to form the remaining persons.

Uses of the Imperfect

1. The imperfect expresses a continuity of action in the past; it tells *what was going on* during an indefinite period of time or when another action took place:

Estaba en mi cuarto cuando Vd. tocó la campanilla
I *was* in my room when you rang the bell
Estaba en el parque cuando el hombre se pegó el tiro
I *was* in the park when the man shot himself

Note. Pegarse un tiro is used idiomatically to express the act of committing suicide with a firearm.

Hablábamos de Don Juan cuando vino a vernos
We *were speaking* of Mr. John when he came to see us
Llovía mucho ayer cuando yo salí
It *rained* hard yesterday when I went out

Note. In the above example we may also say *cuando yo salía.*

2. The imperfect is also used to express what was *customary* or *habitual*:

Antes me levantaba a las ocho
Formerly I *used to get up* at eight o'clock
Me gustaba bailar cuando era más joven
I *used to like* dancing when I *was* younger
El Capitán Scott era un gran explorador
Captain Scott *was* a great explorer
Los romanos eran grandes conquistadores
The Romans *were* great conquerors

3. The imperfect is often called a *descriptive* tense, because it is used to *describe* qualities of persons or things, and the *state, place* or *disposition* in which such persons or things were in the past.

Él era joven entonces
He *was* young then

El reloj era muy pequeño
The watch *was* very small

La mesa era de mármol y estaba colocada en el centro del cuarto
The table *was* of marble and *stood* (*was* placed) in the centre of the room

§49 The Future (Indicative)

FIRST CONJUGATION

yo habl-ar-é	I shall speak, etc.	nos habl-ar-emos	we shall
tú habl-ar-ás		vos. habl-ar-éis	speak, etc.
él habl-ar-á ⎫		ellos habl-ar-án ⎫	
ella habl-ar-á ⎬		ellas habl-ar-án ⎬	
Vds. habl-ar-á ⎭		Vds. habl-ar-án ⎭	

SECOND AND THIRD CONJUGATIONS

yo com-er-é	I shall eat, etc.	yo part-ir-é	I shall
tú com-er-ás		tú part-ir-ás	leave, etc.
él com-er-á ⎫		él part-ir-á ⎫	
ella com-er-á ⎬		ella part-ir-á ⎬	
Vd. com-er-á ⎭		Vd. part-ir-á ⎭	
nos. com-er-emos		nos. part-ir-emos	
vos. com-er-éis		vos. part-ir-éis	
ellos com-er-án ⎫		ellos part-ir-án ⎫	
ellas com-er-án ⎬		ellas part-ir-án ⎬	
Vds. com-er-án ⎭		Vds. part-ir-án ⎭	

This shows that the future is formed by adding to the *entire infinitive* of a verb the general endings of the future of all three conjugations: *-é, -ás, -á* for the singular, and *-emos, -éis, -án* for the plural.

Uses of the Future

1. The future represents an action that *will* occur or a condition that *will* exist at some future time:

Escribiré a mi amigo mañana	I *will write* to my friend to-morrow
No se sabe a quién elegirán presidente	It is not known who *will be elected* president
Consideraré lo que Vd. me propone, y le comunicaré mi decisión	I *will consider* what you propose, and I *will communicate* to you my decision

2. It is frequently used in *questions* and *answers,* when the speaker is convinced that his assertion cannot be denied:

¿Será cierto lo que he visto?	Is it true what I have seen?
¿Habrá felicidad semejante?	Is there such happiness?
No habrá desgracia como la mía	There is no misfortune like mine

3. It is also used to express probability or conjecture:

¿Qué será esto?	What *can* this be?
Habrá habido un accidente	There *must have been* an accident

§50. The Preterite (Indicative)

FIRST CONJUGATION

yo habl-é	I spoke, etc.	nos. habl-amos	we spoke, etc.
tú habl-aste		vos. habl-asteis	
él habl-ó		ellos habl-aron	
ella habl-ó		ellas habl-aron	
Vd. habl-ó		Vds. habl-aron	

SECOND AND THIRD CONJUGATIONS

yo	com-í	I ate, etc.	yo	part-í	I left, etc.
tú	com-iste		tú	part-iste	
él	com-ió		él	part-ió	
ella	„		ella	„	
Vd.	„		Vd.	„	
nos.	com-imos		nos.	part-imos	
vos.	com-isteis		vos.	part-isteis	
ellos	com-ieron		ellos	part-ieron	
ellas	„		ellas	„	
Vds.	„		Vds.	„	

Uses of the Preterite

1. The preterite denotes that the action or fact to which it refers took place and was *completed* in the past, whether an hour, months, years or ages ago:

Anoche estuve en el teatro	I *was* at the theatre last night
Le vi hace dos años	I *saw* him two years ago
César murió en Roma	Caesar *died* in Rome

2. It is therefore used in historical narrations, and for this reason it is also called a "historical tense":

Los franceses dieron muchas batallas en tiempo de Napoleón I	The French *fought* many battles in the time of Napoleon I
Los reyes católicos entraron en Granada el año 1492	The Catholic kings *entered* Granada in 1492

3. It is also used to express an action that takes place and is completed while another action (expressed by the imperfect) is in progress with no indication about its possible completion:

Mientras hablabamos Jorge entró en la oficina	While we spoke, George entered the office

(See also the examples in §48 1 on the use of the imperfect)

§51. The Conditional

FIRST CONJUGATION

yo habl-aría	I should or	nos. habl-aríamos	we should or
tú habl-arías	would speak,	vos. habl-aríais	would speak,
él habl-aría	etc.	ellos habl-arían	etc.
ella habl-aría		ellas habl-arían	
Vd. habl-aría		Vds. habl-arían	

SECOND AND THIRD CONJUGATIONS

yo	com-ería	I should or	yo	part-iría	I should or
tú	com-erías	would eat etc.	tú	part-irías	would leave, etc.
él	com-ería		él	part-iría	
ella	„		ella	„	
Vd.	„		Vd.	„	
nos.	com-eríamos		nos.	part-iríamos	
vos.	com-eríais		vos.	part-iríais	
ellos	com-erían		ellos	part-irían	
ellas	„		ellas	„	
Vds.	„		Vds.	„	

This shows that the conditional of all three conjugations is formed by adding to the *entire infinitive* of a verb the endings of the imperfect of the second and third conjugations.

Uses of the Conditional

1. The conditional is used mostly in conditional clauses in which the forms *-ra* or *-se* (see §56) with the conjunction *si* ("if" clause) establish the condition:

Yo iría a España si supiera (or supiese) español	I *would go* to Spain if I knew Spanish
Se consideraría dichoso si tuviera (or tuviese) la mitad de lo que Vd. dice	He *would consider* himself happy if he had half of what you say
Si tuviera un caballo lo montaría	If I had a horse I *would ride* it

2. It is used in place of the future or present to convey *doubt*, *possibility* or *convenience*:

¿Sería verdad lo que oí?	*Is it* true what I heard?
¿Podría venir ese hombre?	*Can* that man come?
Deberían salir Vds. en seguida	You *ought* to leave at once

3. It is also used to express *desire* or *request*:

Desearía ir a Málaga el verano próximo	I *should like* to go to Málaga next summer
Me alegraría que viniera Vd. a verme a menudo	I *should be glad* if you would come to see me often

4. Idiomatically, this tense denotes *proximity* of an act or *uncertainty* when speaking of such act:

Serían las dos de la mañana cuando me despertó el ruído	It *must have been* two o'clock in the morning when the noise awakened me.
No tendría tantos amigos cuando no le socorrieron	He could *not have had* so many friends when they did not help him.

COMPOUND TENSES

All compound tenses of both the indicative and the subjunctive are formed by the proper tense of the auxiliary verb *haber* plus the past participle.

§52. Perfect or Present Perfect (Indicative)

FIRST CONJUGATION

yo he hablado	I have spoken,	**nos. hemos hablado**	we have
tú has hablado	etc.	**vos. habéis hablado**	spoken, etc.
él ha hablado		**ellos han hablado**	
ella ha hablado		**ellas han hablado**	
Vd. ha hablado		**Vds. han hablado**	

SECOND AND THIRD CONJUGATIONS

yo he comido	I have eaten,	**yo he partido**	I have left,
tú has comido	etc.	**tú has partido**	etc.
él ha comido		**él ha partido**	
ella ha comido		**ella ha partido**	
Vd. ha comido		**Vd. ha partido**	
nos. hemos comido		**nos. hemos partido**	
vos. habéis comido		**vos. habéis partido**	
ellos han comido		**ellos han partido**	
ellas han comido		**ellas han partido**	
Vds. han comido		**Vds. han partido**	

The perfect is formed by the present of the auxiliary verb *haber* (see §65) plus the past participle of the verb.

Uses of the Perfect

1. By this tense we indicate that the time at which the action *has taken place* has not been definitely established:

He vendido los efectos	I *have sold* the goods
Italia ha producido grandes músicos	Italy *has produced* great musicians
He sabido la noticia hace un momento	I *learned* the news a moment ago

2. It also expresses a fact in *the past* related to a period of time *not yet completely elapsed*:

He estado en casa todo el día	I *have been* at home all day
El siglo veinte ha sido prodigioso en inventos	The twentieth century *has been* marvellous for inventions
He estado en Londres desde el año 1941	I *have been* in London since the year 1941
He trabajado mucho este año	I *have worked* hard this year

§53. The Pluperfect (Indicative)

FIRST CONJUGATION

yo	había	hablado	I had	nos.	habíamos	hablado	we had
tú	habías	„	spoken, etc.	vos.	habíais	„	spoken, etc.
él	había	„		ellos	habían	„	
ella	„	„		ellas	„	„	
Vd.	„	„		Vds.	„	„	

SECOND AND THIRD CONJUGATIONS

yo	había	comido	I had	yo	había	partido	I had
tú	habías	„	eaten,	tú	habías	„	left
él	había	„	etc.	él	había	„	
ella	„	„		ella	„	„	
Vd.	„	„		Vd.	„	„	
nos.	habíamos	„		nos.	habíamos	„	
vos.	habíais	„		vos.	habíais	„	
ellos	habían	„		ellos	habían	„	
ellas	„	„		ellas	„	„	
Vds.	„	„		Vds.	„	„	

Uses of the Pluperfect

This tense designates a fact passed previous to another fact that is also past:

Le había escrito a Vd. cuando recibí su carta	I *had written* you when I *received* your letter
Había visto en Nueva York al pianista antes de venir él aquí	I *had seen* the pianist in New York *before* he came here
Había leído el libro cuando lo devolví	I *had read* the book when I *returned* it

Note. In Spanish there are two past perfect tenses:

1. The *pluperfect* (formed by the imperfect of the auxiliary verb *haber* placed before the past participle of the verb).

2. The *preterite perfect* (formed by the preterite of *haber* [see §65] and the past participle of the verb).

The latter is very seldom used. It is a tense used in writing after adverbial expressions of time in situations where English and conversational Spanish would use a pluperfect.

§54 The Future Perfect and the Conditional Perfect

The future perfect is formed by the future of the verb *haber* and the past participle of the verb. The conditional perfect is formed by the conditional of *haber* (see §65) and the past participle of the verb.

FUTURE PERFECT

yo habré		
tú habrás		
él habrá		
ella		
Vd. „	hablado	I shall have spoken, etc.
nos. habremos	comido	I shall have eaten, etc.
vos. habréis	partido	I shall have left, etc.
ellos habrán		
ellas „		
Vds. „		

Uses of the Future Perfect

This tense is used in the same cases as its corresponding tense in English:

Mañana a estas horas habremos llegado
We shall have arrived to-morrow at this time
Habré acabado el libro en el mes de septiembre
I shall have finished the book in the month of September

CONDITIONAL PERFECT

yo habría		
tú habrías		
él habría		
ella „		
Vd. „	hablado	I should have spoken, etc.
nos. habríamos	comido	I should have eaten, etc.
vos. habríais	partido	I should have left, etc.
ellos habrían		
ellas „		
Vds. „		

Uses of the Conditional Perfect

The conditional perfect represents an action as having already occurred if the condition had been fulfilled. It is used in conditional clauses, while the forms -RA or -SE (see §56), with the conjuction *si,* establish the condition:

Habría ido a España si hubiese (or **hubiera**) **tenido dinero**
I would have gone to Spain *if I had had* the money
Si hubiera sabido que había hecho eso, le habría reñido
If I had known that he had done that, *I would have scolded* him

THE SUBJUNCTIVE MOOD

The subjunctive mood in Spanish is used in subordinate clauses in which action is presented as a possibility and not as a fact. The tenses of the subjunctive are the present, the imperfect, the future (very seldom used), the perfect, and the pluperfect.

§55. The Present Subjunctive

FIRST CONJUGATION

yo	habl-e	I may wish, etc.	nos.	habl-emos	we may wish, etc.
tú	habl-es		vos.	habl-éis	
él	habl-e		ellos	habl-en	
ella	„		ellas	„	
Vd.	„		Vds.	„	

SECOND AND THIRD CONJUGATIONS

yo	com-a	I may eat, etc.	yo	part-a	I may leave, etc.
tú	com-as		tú	part-as	
él	com-a		él	part-a	
ella	„		ella	„	
Vd.	„		Vd.	„	
nos.	com-amos		nos.	part-amos	
vos.	com-áis		vos.	part-áis	
ellos	com-an		ellos	part-an	
ellas	„		ellas	„	
Vds.	„		Vds.	„	

The subjunctive of the first conjugation is characterised by *e,* and the subjunctive of the second and third conjugations by *a.* Note that the endings of the present subjunctive of the verbs of the first conjugation (except for the first person) are identical to those of the present indicative of the verbs of the second conjugation. The endings of the present subjunctive of the verbs of the second and third conjugations (except for the first person) are identical to those of the present indicative of the verbs of the first conjugation.

§56. The Imperfect Subjunctive

The imperfect subjunctive has two forms, the first or RA form and the second or SE form. The two forms have the same meaning. A distinction between them is made only for the purpose of euphony when this part of the verb is used twice in the same sentence. In any other instance they may be used indiscriminately. However, in Spanish America the RA form is used almost exclusively in conversational Spanish.

The RA-Subjunctive

FIRST CONJUGATION

yo	habl-ara	I might speak	nos.	habl-áramos	we might speak,
tú	habl-aras	etc.	vos.	habl-arais	etc.
él	habl-ara		ellos	habl-aran	
ella	„		ellas	„	
Vd.	„		Vds.	„	

SECOND AND THIRD CONJUGATIONS

yo	com-iera	I might eat,	yo	part-iera	I might leave,
tú	com-ieras	etc.	tú	part-ieras	etc.
él	com-iera		él	part-iera	
ella	„		ella	„	
Vd.	„		Vd.	„	
nos.	com-iéramos		nos.	part-iéramos	
vos.	com-ierais		vos.	part-ierais	
ellos	com-ieran		ellos	part-ieran	
ellas	„		ellas	„	
Vds.	„		Vds.	„	

The SE-Subjunctive

FIRST CONJUGATION

yo	habl-ase	I might speak,	nos.	habl-ásemos	we might speak,
tú	habl-ases	etc.	vos.	habl-aseis	etc.
él	habl-ase		ellos	habl-aen	
ella	„		ellas	„	
Vd.	„		Vds.	„	

SECOND AND THIRD CONJUGATIONS

yo	com-iese	I might eat,	yo	part-iese	I might leave,
tú	com-ieses	etc.	tú	part-ieses	etc.
él	com-iese		él	part-iese	
ella	„		ella	„	
Vd.	„		Vd.	„	
nos.	com-iésemos		nos.	part-iésemos	
vos.	com-ieseis		vos.	part-ieseis	
ellos	com-iesen		ellos	part-iesen	
ellas	„		ellas	„	
Vds.	„		Vds.	„	

Note that for the first or RA form of the imperfect subjunctive the endings of the indicative present of the -*ar* verbs, with the exception of that of the first person singular, are added to the infinitive of the verbs of the first conjugation or to the stem plus the general ending -*ier* in the 2nd and 3rd conjugations. Care should be taken to stress the stem of the verb, to distinguish it from the future, with which it might easily be confused.

For the second or SE form of the imperfect subjunctive the partial general ending is -*ase* for the first conjugation and -*iese* for the second and third conjugations.

The future subjunctive *habl-are, habl-ares, habl-are, habl-áremos, habl-arais, habl-aren, com-iere, part-iere,* etc. is very seldom used to-day.

The perfect and pluperfect subjunctives are formed by the present and imperfect subjunctives of *haber* (see §65) respectively, plus the past participle of the verb.

§57. Uses of the Subjunctive

The uses of the subjunctive can be better understood when they are seen in comparison with the uses of the indicative.

1. While the indicative merely states or denies a fact, the subjunctive presents it under a certain condition or supposition:

INDICATIVE

Compraré el caballo que más me gusta	I shall buy the horse I *like* best

SUBJUNCTIVE

Compraré el caballo que más me guste	I shall buy the horse I *may* like best

Note. In the above example, the indicative is used when the speaker has already made up his mind as to which horse to buy. When, however, he has not yet selected or seen the horse, the subjunctive is required.

2. The subjunctive is always subordinated to a principal verb also called *antecedent,* and both are usually linked by the conjunction *que,* or by a *relative pronoun*:

Busco quien sepa hacer esto	I *am looking* for somebody *who may know* how to do this
No encuentro la persona que lo haga	I cannot *find* the person *who may* do it

3. The following compound conjunctions require the subjunctive: *a fin de que* or *para que* (in order that), *con tal que* or *con tal de que* (provided

that), *a menos que* or *a no ser que* (unless), *en caso de que* (in case that, if), *hasta que* (until), and a few others:

En caso de que venga, dígale Vd. que se vaya	In case that he should come, tell him *to go away*
No le pague Vd., a no ser que quiera hacerlo	Don't pay him *unless* he *wants* to do it
Con tal de que hiciera eso, se lo daría	Provided that he would do that, I should give it to him

4. A few conjunctions like *aunque* (although), *cuando* (when), *aun cuando* (even though), *siempre que* (whenever), etc., call for the indicative if a definite statement is expressed, and the subjunctive when a supposition or opinion is involved:

INDICATIVE

Aun cuando trabaja todo el día no se cansa	Even though he *works* the whole day, he does not get tired

The indicative is used here because it is a known fact that he works.

SUBJUNCTIVE

Aun cuando trabaje todo el día no se cansa	He does not get tired *though* he *may work* the whole day

The subjunctive in this sentence indicates possibility.

5. When the antecedent verb expresses desire, command, permission, doubt, fear, joy, regret, surprise, request, hope, disappointment, etc., the dependent verb must be in the subjunctive:

Deseo que vengan	I *wish* them *to come*
Quiero que lo haga Vd. así	I *want* you *to do* it so
¿Me permite Vd. que salga?	Will you *allow* me *to go out?*
Espero que no falte	I *hope* he will not *fail*
Temo que llueva hoy	I *am afraid* it *will rain* to-day
Desearía que hubiesen podido venir	I *would like* them *to have* been able to come

6. The subjunctive is likewise employed after impersonal expressions:

Es lástima que no venga	It is too bad that he *will* not *come*
Convendría que hubiese hecho lo que nos dijo	It *would be convenient* if he *had done* what he told us
Es muy extraño que hayan obrado así	It is *very strange* that they *should have* acted thus
Importa que le vea Vd.	It is *important* that you *see* him

Basta que lo diga Vd.	It *is sufficient* that you *say* so
Es necesario que lo haga Vd.	It *is necessary* that you *do* so
Seria preciso que viniera	It *would be necessary* for him *to come*
Será menester que estudie	It *will be necessary* for him *to study*

7. The same mood is also used in relative clauses, when the relation refers to persons, objects or thoughts pronounced in a doubtful or indefinite sense:

Sea lo que sea	*Be* it what *may*
"Cuando a Roma fueres, haz lo que vieres."	"When in Rome do as the Romans do."
Venga lo que viniera	*Come* what *will*

8. Also after verbs like *creer* (to believe), *decir* (to say), *pensar* (to think), etc., in interrogative and negative sentences:

¿Cree Vd. que él venga?	*Do* you *think* he *will* come?
¿No piensa Vd. que ella salga mañana?	Don't you *think* she *will leave* to-morrow?
¿Me diría Vd. que no lo hiciera?	*Would* you *tell* me not to *do* it?

§58. The Subjunctive—Sequence of Tenses

PRESENT

It is not possible to give an exact equivalent in English of the Spanish present subjunctive. It can be expressed by *may, let, will, could, should,* and even by the present infinitive, according to the meaning of the phrase.

The present subjunctive is used:

1. To make the negative form of the imperative, and also the third persons of the affirmative form when a command or proposition is voiced:

Que no escriba ella	**Que haga él eso**
Don't let her *write*	*Let* him *do* that
No trabajemos hoy	**No se lo dé Vd.**
Let us *not work* to-day	*Don't* you *give* it to him
No se vaya Vd.	**Que hable él**
Don't you *go away*	*Let* him *speak*

2. When the principal verb or antecedent is in the present, future or imperative:

Deseo que acabe Vd. para hablarle	**Me alegaré que no haga frío antes del primero de noviembre**
I *wish* you to *finish* so that I may speak to you	I *shall be glad* if *it* does not get cold before the first of November
Dígaselo cuando le vea	*Tell* him so when you *see* him

3. When expressing future design, possible or casual:

Hablaré a ese señor cuando le vea I *will speak* to that gentleman when I (*may*) *see* him **Es una casualidad que él la encuentre**	**Si ve Vd. a nuestro amigo dígale que venga a verme** *If* you *see* our friend, tell him to *come* to see me It is by *accident* if he *meets* her

4. After impersonal phrases in the present, such as: *puede ser que* (it may be that), *es menester que, es preciso que* (it is necessary that), *es imposible* and *es posible que* (it is impossible and it is possible that), *es natural que* (it is natural that), *es tiempo de que* (it is time that), etc., etc.:

Puede ser que venga *It may be* that he is *coming* **Es natural que él lo haga así**	**Es tiempo de que Vd. trabaje** *It is time that* you *should work* *It is natural that* he *do* it so

Note. The conjunction *si* (if) can never govern the present subjunctive:

Si viene dígale que se vaya	*If* he *comes*, tell him *to go away*

IMPERFECT

Both forms of this tense are used after the verbs in past tenses of the indicative, and after the future conditional:

Le suplicaron que fuera (*or* **fuese**) **a su casa** They *begged* him *to go* to his house **Creímos que estuviese en casa** We *thought* he *would be* at home	**Fué preciso que lo hiciera** (*or* **hiciese**) It *was necessary* for him *to do it* **Desearía que Vd. me hiciera ese favor** I *should wish* (that) you *would do* me that favour

PERFECT

This tense is used after verbs in the future, as well as in the present indicative and preterite when expressing an action that is past:

Dudo de que me haya visto I *doubt* whether *he may have seen* me **No volveré hasta que me haya restablecido**	**Espero que haya llegado** I *hope* he *has arrived* I *shall* not *return* till *I have recovered*

PLUPERFECT

The two forms of this tense are employed after verbs in any past tense indicative, as well as after the conjunctions *si* or *que* in sentences referring to the past:

Creía que hubiera (*or*) **hubiese llegado** I *thought* he *had* arrived	**Si hubieran** (*or* **hubiesen**) **tenido dinero habrían ido a París** *If* they *had* money they would have gone to Paris
El nos lo habría dicho si hubiese (*or* **hubiera**) **estado aquí más tiempo**	He would have told us so *if* he *had been here* longer

§59. The Imperative Mood

The true imperative is used only as a familiar form of the imperative in affirmative commands. This imperative has two forms, a singular and a plural. The singular form is identical with the third person singular of the present indicative, e.g. *habla* (speak), *come* (eat). The plural form is obtained by dropping the final *r* of the infinitive and adding a *d* in its place, e.g. *hablad* (speak), *comed* (eat).

The third person of the present subjunctive is used for the polite imperative, e.g. *hable* (speak), *coma* (eat). This is the form of the imperative used under normal cirumstances and corresponds to the *usted* form of the indicative and the subjunctive.

The imperative proper cannot be used negatively. For both the familiar and the polite forms of the negative imperative, the corresponding form of the present subjunctive must be used instead:

Que no hable Don't let him speak	**No escriba usted** Do not write	**No lo hagamos** Let's not do it	**No hables tanto** Don't talk so much

§60. The Infinitive

The infinitive is the basic form of the verb from which all other forms are derived in the case of all regular verbs. In English the infinitive is generally preceded by *to*.

In Spanish there are three main types of infinitives by which we distinguish the three regular conjugations: those ending in *-ar*, as *habl-ar* (first conjugation), those ending in *-er*, as *com-er* (second conjugation), and those ending in *-ir*, as *part-ir* (third conjugation).

Uses of the Infinitive

PRESENT

1. This tense is used preceded by *a* or *al*, when the corresponding English translation begins with an adverb of time or a conjunction:

Al entrar en casa me encontré con mi amigo *On entering* the house I met my friend	**A no haber estado yo aquí habría ocurido mayor desgracia** *If* I *had* not *been* here, it would have been a greater misfortune

A haber yo sabido que él estaba aquí no hubiese venido
If I *had known* he was here, I would not have come

Al salir del teatro me resfrié
When leaving the theatre I caught a cold

2. It must be used after any preposition and after impersonal phrases such as: *es necesario, es menester, es posible,* etc. (without *que*):

Es menester juzgar, después de oír
After hearing, one must judge

Para levantarse temprano, es necesario acostarse temprano
In order to get up early, *it is necessary to go to bed* early

Es menester estudiar para aprender una lengua
It is necessary to study in order to learn a language

Sin preguntar no se puede saber
One cannot know *without asking*

3. The infinitive is used as a noun when in English we would use the gerund:

El pasear es bueno para la salud
Walking is good for the health
El comer, beber y dormir son necesarios para vivir

El tener una buena voz es un don
Having a good voice is a gift
Eating, drinking and *sleeping* are necessary for living

Note. When there is more than one infinitive used as a noun, the definite article is used with the *first one only.*

4. When the infinitive is used after verbs expressing wish, doubt, fear, necessity, obligation, duty, etc., and both verbs have the same subject, no preposition is used:

Deseo hacer eso
I *wish to do* that
El necesita trabajar

Temo salir de casa
I *fear to leave* the house
He *needs* to *work*

Note. Decir must never be followed by an infinitive. Verbs of this class do not require a preposition before the infinitive e.g.:

aconsejar	to advise	**necesitar**	to want to
acostumbrar	to accustom	**negar**	to deny
afirmar	to affirm	**oír**	to hear
agradar	to be agreeable	**osar**	to dare
concebir	to conceive	**parecer**	to appear
confesar	to confess	**pensar**	to think
contar	to relate	**poder**	to be able
convenir	to be convenient	**preferir**	to prefer
creer	to believe	**presumir**	to presume
deber	to owe	**pretender**	to pretend

declarar	to declare	procurar	to try to
dejar	to leave	prohibir	to forbid
desear	to wish	prometer	to promise
determinar	to resolve to	proponer	to propose
esperar	to hope, to expect to	protestar	to protest
gustar	to like to	querer	to wish
hacer	to make	saber	to know
imaginar	to imagine	sentir	to feel
impedir	to prevent	soler	to be accustomed to
intentar	to intend	temer	to fear
mandar	to order	valer	to be worth
manifestar	to manifest	ver	to see

5. Verbs denoting movement, destination, inclination, habit and encouragement, as well as reflexive verbs expressing a moral decision or effort, require the preposition *a* before the infinitive they govern. Such verbs are the following:

animar a	to encourage to	enviar a	to send to
aprender a	to learn to	habituar a	to accustom to
aspirar a	to aspire to	inclinar a	to incline to
autorizar a	to authorise to	invitar a	to invite to
atreverse a	to dare to	ir a	to go to
ayudar a	to help to	negarse a	to refuse to
comenzar a	to commence to	obligar a	to oblige to
condenar a	to condemn to	pasar a	to come to
convidar a	to invite to	ponerse a	to begin to
dar a	to give to	resistirse a	to resist to
decidirse a	to resolve to	salir a	to go to
echar a	to begin to	tender a	to aim at
empezar a	to begin to	venir a	to come to
enseñar a	to teach to	volver a	to return to

6. The preposition *a* is used sometimes before the infinitive in idiomatic or elliptic phrases, like:

a ver	let us see	a saber	namely
a ser cierto	to be certain	a decir verdad	to speak truly

7. The preposition *de* is used before the infinitive when the infinitive depends on a preceding noun, and after certain adjectives like *fácil, difícil, posible, imposible, agradable,* etc.

Hágame Vd. el favor de venir conmigo
Do me the *favour* of coming with me

Tiene vergüenza de pedirlo
He *is ashamed to ask* for it

No tengo el gusto de conocer a esa señora
I have not the *pleasure of knowing* that lady

Los verbos son difíciles de aprender
Verbs are *difficult to learn*

The following verbs require the preposition *de* after the infinitive.

acabar de	to have just	**disuadir de**	to dissuade from
acordarse de	to remember	**encargar de**	to commission to
alegrarse de	to be glad to	**excusar de**	to excuse from
arrepentirse de	to repent of	**haber de**	to have to
cesar de	to cease to	**ocuparse de**	to be busy with
dejar de	to fail to	**olvidarse de**	to forget to
desistir de	to desist from	**tratar de**	to try to

8. The prepositions *de* or *para* must be used after the verb *ser* (to be) and before an infinitive, when the latter is employed as an impersonal:

Es de esperarse
It is to be hoped

Es para alegrarse de lo ocurrido
One ought to be glad of what has happened

9. The preposition *en* is necessary before an infinitive after verbs denoting occupation or persistence:

El se ocupa en enseñar
He *occupies* himself *in teaching*

Me empeño en leer ese libro
I *persist in reading* that book

10. The preposition *con* is used sometimes before an infinitive after verbs implying diversion or amusement:

Me divierto con leer Don Quijote   I *amuse* myself *by reading* Don Quixote

Note. The gerund may also be used in these cases, and so we may say (without preposition): *Me divierto leyendo Don Quijote* (*I amuse myself [by] reading Don Quixote*).

11. The preposition *para* is used to express intention or purpose:

Estudio para aprender
I *study in order to learn*

Le convida para complacerle
He *invites* him *to please him*

12. The infinitive is governed by the preposition *por* when expressing reason, motive, result, desire and anticipation:

Me respondió que sí por no disgustarme   **Habla por hablar**
He answered (me) yes, *in order* not *to vex me*   He talks *for the sake of talking*
Hago eso por tener que hacerlo   I do that *because I have to*

13. *Mandar* (to command) and *hacer* (to do or make), followed by the infinitive, have the meaning of to order or to ask for:

Se hizo traer un sombrero
He *had* a hat *brought*

El manda lavar su ropa
He *sends* his clothes *to be washed*

14. The verbs *oír* and *ver*, used as transitives, must be followed by the infinitive instead of the present participle as would be the case in English:

Le veo venir
I *see* him *coming*

Le oí llegar
I *heard* him *arriving*

§61. The Present Participle or Gerund

1. The gerund is invariable in gender and number. It is used most frequently in connection with the verb *estar* to form the progressive tenses, and it expresses an action that continues or is unfinished:

Estoy hablando
I am speaking

Estaremos comiendo
We shall be eating

¿Está lloviendo?
Is it raining?

Note. Ser connot be used with the gerund of *estar*, and rarely with the verbs *venir* and *ir*.

2. The gerund is used to denote the state or condition of the subject:

Canta bailando
He sings while *dancing*

Los dejé durmiendo
I left them *sleeping*

El lo dijo riendo
He said so *laughing*

3. It is also frequently used instead of the following words: *mientras* (while), *cuando* (when), *desde* (since), *si* (if) and *aunque* (although):

Estando escribiéndole (*or* mientras le escribía) a Vd. vino él a verme
While I was writing to you, he came to see me

Habiendo concluído (*or* cuando concluí) mi trabajo fuí a dar un paseo
Having finished my work, I went to take a walk

Enseñando (*or* mientras se enseña) se aprende
One learns by *teaching*

4. It is likewise used sometimes with the preposition *en*. Notice that the gerund with or without *en*, may receive an indefinite personal subject:

En llegando a España escribiré
I shall write *on my arrival* in Spain

Y en diciendo esto, picó a su caballo Rocinante
And *as he spoke* he put spurs to his horse Rosinante

§62. The Past Participle

The past participle is formed by adding -*ado* to the stem of the verbs of the first conjugation and -*ido* to those of the second and third conjugations:

| habl-ar | to speak | com-er | to eat | part-ir | to leave |
| habl-ado | spoken | com-ido | eaten | part-ido | left |

There is a small number of verbs which have irregular past participles:

abrir	abierto	to open	morir	muerto	to die
cubrir	cubierto	to cover	poner	puesto	to put
decir	dicho	to say	resolver	resuelto	to solve
escribir	escrito	to write	romper	roto	to break
freír	frito	to fry	ver	visto	to see
hacer	hecho	to do, to make	volver	vuelto	to turn
imprimir	impreso	to print			

The past participles of all verbs derived from these are of course irregular also, e.g. *descubrir* (to discover), *descubierto*.

Uses of the Past Participle

1. The past participle is used after forms of the auxiliary verb *haber* (to have) to form the compound tenses.

2. When *tener* or *llevar* are used as substitutes of *haber*, the past participle must agree in gender and number with the attribute:

Tengo hecha la traducción
I have made the translation

Llevo escrita la mitad de la obra
I have written half of the work

3. When the past participle is used after forms of the verb *ser* to form the passive voice, it must agree in gender and number with the subject. The same applies for the auxiliary *estar:*

Mi amiga está cansada
My friend is tired

4. When the past participle is not used with the form of an auxiliary verb, it is declined like an adjective, always agreeing in gender and number with the noun it modifies:

Un cuarto amueblado
A furnished room

Una mujer cansada
A tired woman

§63. Government of Verbs

Government in grammatical terminology means the influence of a word on the form of other words with which it forms a phrase or a sentence.

1. The object of a transitive verb is used *without* a preposition when it refers to *things;* but it is necessary to use the preposition *a* before the object when designating *animated beings* (see also §8):

Busco un pañuelo	**Busco a mi hermano**
I am looking for a handkerchief	I am looking for my brother
¿Qué lee Vd.?	**Leo un libro**
What are you reading?	I am reading a book
¿A quién lee Vd.?	**Leo a Baroja**
Whom are you reading?	I am reading Baroja

Note 1. The preposition *a* is omitted when the object is unknown or is not identified:

Espero algunos amigos	**Busco un sirviente**
I expect some friends	I am looking for a servant

Note 2. The preposition is not used either after the verb *tener*, when the latter expresses possession:

Tengo un buen amigo	I have a good friend

But it is not omitted if *tener* is used with the meaning of *estar*:

Tiene a su hijo enfermo (*or* su hijo está enfermo)	**Tengo a mi hermano en España** (*or* mi hermano está en España)
His son is sick	My brother is in Spain

2. The preposition *a* is necessary after the verb *querer* when the latter is used in place of *amar*:

Quiero a mi novia	**Quiso mucho a sus padres**
I love my sweetheart	*He loved* his parents very much

Querer, when not followed by a preposition, is synonymous with *desear*: *Quiero un buen tenedor de libros* (I want a good book-keeper).

3. Many verbs require different prepositions from those used in English, such as *de, con, por, para, sobre*, etc. Often these prepositions cannot be translated literally, and some of these verbs may govern different prepositions without changing their meaning (see §32 and following).

4. Nearly all the reflexive verbs, as well as verbs expressing a *state of mind, abundance, desire, separation* and *reproach*, are generally followed by the preposition *de*. Such are the following:

abusar de	to abuse	**lamentarse de**	to lament
acordarse de	to remember	**mofarse de**	to scoff at
admirarse de	to wonder at	**necisitar de**	to be in want of
alegrarse de	to rejoice at	**olividarse de**	to forget
aprovecharse de	to take advantage of	**prescindir de**	to do without

avergonzarse de	to be ashamed of	**privarse de**	to deprive	
burlarse de	to laugh at	**reírse de**	to laugh at	
carecer de	to lack	**renegar de**	to abominate	
compadecerse de	to pity	**servirse de**	to make use of	
desconfiar de	to distrust	**tener lástima de**	to pity	[of
dudar de	to doubt	**tener verguenza de**	to be ashamed	
fiarse de	to trust	**usar de**	to use	
gozar de	to enjoy	**valerse de**	to avail of	
jactarse de	to boast	**zafarse de**	to get rid of	

General Characteristics of the Regular Verbs

We say that a verb is regular when throughout its entire conjugation it retains the letters (or in some cases the *invariable sound*) of the stem and takes the inflectional endings of the tenses and persons in accordance with its model conjugation.

The fact that some regular verbs receive alterations in the letters of the stem for orthographic reasons, such as the changing of *c* into *z* or *qu-*, and similar other changes which have already been explained, must not be considered as an irregularity, since this is done to retain the uniformity of sound.

THE FOLLOWING RULES SHOW WHEN A VERB IS REGULAR

A verb is regular:

1. If it begins with the letter *ch*.
2. If it ends in one of this group of letters: *-ear, -iar, -oar, -oer* and *-uar*.
3. If while ending in *-ar* it has, in the syllable preceding such ending, the vowels *i, a,* or *u*, like *derribar, aplacar, mudar,* etc., except *andar, jugar* and their derivatives.
4. If it ends in *-bar* or *-brir*, except *herbar, probar* and their derivatives.
5. If it ends in *-car*, with the exception of *trocar, clocar, volcar* and their derivatives, and also *desflocar* and *emporcar*.
6. If it has an *f* in the last syllable.
7. If it ends in *-ger, -grar, -char* and *-jar*.
8. If it ends in *-lar*, except *helar* and *melar* and their derivatives.
9. If it ends in *-llar*, but not *-ollar*.
10. If it ends in either *-mar, -mer* or *-mir*, except *dormir* and *gemir*.
11. If it ends in *-nar*, except *sonar, tornar, invernar, infernar,* their derivatives and *descornar*.
12. If it ends in *-ñar*, except *soñar*.
13. If it ends in *-par, -per* and *-pir*.
14. If it ends in *-rar*, except *agorar*.
15. If it ends in *-sar*, but not *atravesar, confesar, pensar, engrosar* and their derivatives.
16. If it ends in *-rer*, except *querer* and its derivatives.

17. If it ends in -*atar*, -*etar*, -*itar*, -*otar*, -*utar* and their derivatives.
18. If it ends in -*var*, except *renovar* and *nevar*.
19. If it ends in -*yar*.
20. If it ends in -*azar*, -*ezar*, -*izar*, -*ozar* or -*uzar*, except *empezar* and *tropezar*.
21. If it ends in -*ir*, with an *i* in the preceding syllable, excluding *adquirir, inquirir, retiñir* and *restriñir*.

§64. Orthographic Changes in the Stems of Regular Verbs

Verbs ending in -*car*, -*gar*, -*zar*, -*cer*, -*ger*, -*cir*, -*gir*, -*guir* (*u* silent) and -*quir* (*u* silent) require in some persons and tenses a slight orthographic change in the stem, so as to enable them to preserve the original sound.

First Conjugation

VERBS ENDING IN -*car*, -*gar* AND -*zar*

The *c* of -*car* changes into *qu* before *e*, as in *tocar* (to play):

Pres. Subj.: **toque, toques, toque, toquemos, toquéis, toquen**
Imperative: **—, toca, toque, toquemos, tocad, toquen**
Preterite: **toqué, tocaste, tocó, tocamos, tocasteis, tocaron**

The *g* of -*gar* changes into *gu* before *e*, as in *pagar* (to pay):

Pres. Subj.: **pague, pagues, pague, paguemos, paguéis, paguen**
Imperative: **—, paga, pague, paguemos, pagad, paguen**
Preterite: **pagué, pagaste, pagó, pagamos, pagasteis, pagaron**

The *z* of -*zar* changes into *c* before *e*, as in *rezar* (to pray):

Pres. Subj.: **rece, reces, rece, recemos, recéis, recen**
Imperative: **—, reza, rece, recemos, rezad, recen**
Preterite: **recé, rezaste, rezó, rezamos, rezasteis, rezaron**

Second Conjugation

VERBS ENDING IN -*cer* AND -*ger*

The *c* of -*cer* changes into *z* before *o* and *a*, as in *vencer* (to vanquish):

Pres. Ind.: **venzo, vences, vence, vencemos, vencéis, vencen**
Pres. Subj.: **venza, venzas, venza, venzamos, venzáis, venzan**
Imperative: **—, vence, venza, venzamos, venced, venzan**

The *g* of -*ger* changes into *j* before *o* and *a*, as in *coger* (to catch):

Pres. Ind.: **cojo, coges, coge, cogemos, cogéis, cogen**
Pres. Subj.: **coja, cojas, coja, cojamos, cojáis, cojan**
Imperative: **—, coge, coja, cojamos, coged, cojan**

Third Conjugation

VERBS ENDING IN -*cir*, -*gir*, -*guir* (*u* silent) AND -*quir* (*u* silent)

The *c* of -*cir* changes into *z* before the endings *o* and *a*, as in *zurcir* (to darn):

Pres. Ind.: zurzo, zurces, zurce, zurcimos, zurcís, zurcen
Pres. Subj.: zurza, zurzas, zurza, zurzamos, zurzáis, zurzan
Imperative: —, zurce, zurza, zurzamos, zurcid, zurzan

The *g* of -*gir* changes into *j* before the endings *o* and *a*, as in *dirigir* (to address, to direct):

Pres. Ind.: dirijo, diriges, dirige, dirigimos, dirigís, dirigen
Pres. Subj.: dirija, dirijas, dirija, dirijamos, dirijáis, dirijan
Imperative: —, dirige, dirija, dirijamos, dirigid, dirijan

The *gu* of -*guir* (*u* silent) changes into *g*, i.e. the *u* is dropped whenever the endings are *o* or *a*, as in *distinguir* (to distinguish):

Pres. Ind.: distingo, distingues, distingue, distinguimos, distinguís, distinguen
Pres. Subj.: distinga, distingas, distinga, distingamos, distingáis, distingan
Imperative: —, distingue, distinga, distingamos, distinguid, distingan

The *qu* of -*quir* (*u* silent) changes into *c* whenever the endings are *o* or *a*, as in *delinquir* (to transgress the law):

Pres. Ind.: delinco, delinques, delinque, delinquimos, delinquís, delinquen
Pres. Subj.: delinca, delincas, delinca, delincamos, delincáis, delincan
Imperative: —, delinque, delinca, delincamos, delinquid, delincan

CHAPTER 10

AUXILIARY VERBS

§65. Conjugation of the Auxiliary Verb *haber*

Infinitive

hab-er to have

Gerund	*Past Participle*
hab-iendo having	**hab-ido** had

Indicative

PRESENT

yo	he	I have, etc.	nos.	hemos	we have, etc.
tú	has		vos.	hab-éis	
él	ha		ellos	han	
ella	„		ellas	„	
Vd.	„		Vds.	„	

IMPERFECT

yo	hab-ía	I had or used to	nos.	hab-íamos	we had or used
tú	hab-ías	have, etc.	vos.	hab-íais	to have, etc.
él	hab-ía		ellos	hab-ían	
ella	„		ellas	„	
Vd.	„		Vds.	„	

PRETERITE

yo	hube	I had, etc.	nos.	hubimos	we had, etc.
tú	hubiste		vos.	hubisteis	
él	hubo		ellos	hubieron	
ella	„		ellas	„	
Vd.	„		Vds.	„	

FUTURE

yo	habré	I shall have,	nos.	habremos	we shall have,
tú	habrás	etc.	vos.	habréis	etc.
él	habrá		ellos	habrán	
ella	„		ellas	„	
Vd.	„		Vds.	„	

CONDITIONAL

yo habría	I should or	nos. habríamos	We should or
tú habrías	would have,	vos. habrías	would have,
él habría	etc.	ellos habrían	etc.
ella „		ellas „	
Vd. „		Vds. „	

Subjunctive

PRESENT

yo haya	I may have,	nos. hayamos	we may have,
tú hayas	etc.	vos. hayáis	etc.
él haya		ellos hayan	
ella „		ellas „	
Vd. „		Vds. „	

IMPERFECT, 1ST FORM

yo hubiera	I might have,	nos. hubiéramos	we might have,
tú hubieras	etc.	vos. hubierais	etc.
él hubiera		ellos hubieran	
ella „		ellas „	
Vd. „		Vds. „	

IMPERFECT, 2ND FORM

yo hubiese	I might have,	nos. hubiésemos	we might have,
tú hubieses	etc.	vos. hubieseis	etc.
él hubiese		ellos hubiesen	
ella „		ellas „	
Vd. „		Vds. „	

Note 1. From the imperative of *haber* the only person in use is *he*, in the sense of "to behold," "to see," and "to be," as *he aquí a su amigo—* here is your friend (lit., here you have your friend); *he allí su libro* (there is your book), *he allí sus libros* (there are your books), *heme aquí* (here I am), *helos allí* (there they are), *hela allí* (there she is), etc.

Note 2. When *haber* is used as a transitive verb, the compound tenses are formed with its own past participle, e.g. *he habido* I have had), etc.

§66. Uses of the Auxiliary Verb *haber*

There are two verbs in Spanish, *haber* and *tener* which correspond to the English verb "to have." *Haber* is used only as an auxiliary, while *tener* is a principal verb denoting possession.

1. *Haber* is used, therefore, in forming the compound tenses, and always precedes the past participle of the principal verb. Examples:

Hemos hablado español
We *have spoken* Spanish

Habré escrito una carta
I *shall have written* a letter

In interrogative sentences the auxiliary *haber* is generally placed immediately before the principal verb, which is followed by the personal pronoun, as in:

¿Con quién ha hablado Vd.?   **¿Cuándo habra escrito Vd. la carta?**
With whom *have you spoken?*   When *will you have written* the letter?

Often the same construction is used as in English, i.e. the pronoun is placed between the auxiliary and principal verbs; this, however, never happens when the past indefinite is used. For instance, it would NOT be correct to say:

¿Ha Vd. hablado?   But: **¿Ha hablado Vd.?**
Have *you spoken?*   "Have *spoken you?*"

NEITHER can we say:

¿Hemos nosotros comprado?   But: **¿Hemos comprado nosotros?**
Have *we bought?*   "Have *bought we?*"

Note. The form of the past participle in the compound tenses with *haber* remains invariable, as in English, i.e. *hemos comprado* and NEVER *hemos comprados*.

2. *Haber*, when followed by *de*, takes the infinitive present of the principal verb immediately after it, in which case it is synonymous with the English phrase *to have to*. Examples:

He de ir a mi oficina   **Habré de hablar español**
I *have to go* to my office   I *shall have to speak* Spanish

3. *Haber* is also used as an impersonal verb, corresponding to the English *there is*. Being impersonal, only the third person singular can be used in Spanish, and these forms are the same as those of the auxiliary verb as conjugated, except in the present tense, when *hay* is used instead of *ha*.

§67. Conjugation of the Impersonal Verb *haber*

INDICATIVE		SUBJUNCTIVE	
hay	there is, there are	**haya**	there may be
había	there was, there were	**hubiera**	there might be
hubo	there was, there were	**hubiese**	there might be
habrá	there will, shall be	**si hubiera** }	if there should be,
habría	there should, would be	**si hubiese** }	if there were

Examples

Hay un hombre en la calle   **Hay dos mil personas en el teatro**
There is a man in the street   *There are* two thousand persons in the theatre

Habría baile esta noche si hubiera (hubiese) dinero para la música
There would be a ball to-night if *there were* money for the music

The *compound tenses* are formed in the same way as their corresponding tenses adding the past participle. The present is *ha habido* instead of *hay habido*.

INDICATIVE		SUBJUNCTIVE	
ha habido	there has been	**haya habido**	there may have been
había habido	there had been	**hubiera habido**	there might have been
habrá habido	there will have been	**si hubiera habido** ⎫	if there had, should have been
habría habido	there should, would have been	**si hubiese habido** ⎭	

Examples

Hoy ha habido un accidente en la calle
There has been an accident in the street to-day

Habrá habido muchos cambios
There will have been many changes

Habría habido más gente si no hubiese llovido
There would have been more people if it had not rained

In the interrogative sentences the construction is the same as that of a simple statement, and the interrogation is expressed by the inflection of the voice. In writing, the double question mark indicates the interrogation.

Haber, followed by the conjunction *que*, is synonymous with *ser necesario* (to be necessary), and is impersonal like *haber* (there to be), in which case the verb following must be used in the infinitive.

The conjugation of this form is therefore the same as that of *haber* (there to be), with *que* added, thus:

Conjugation of HABER QUE (*to be necessary*)

INDICATIVE		SUBJUNCTIVE	
hay que	it is necessary	**haya que**	it may be necessary
había que	it was or used to be necessary	**hubiera que**	it might be necessary
hubo que	it was necessary	**hubiese que**	it might be necessary
habrá que	it will be necessary	**si hubiere que**	if it should have been necessary
habría que	it should, would be necessary		

Examples

Hay que ir al correo
It is necessary to go to the post office

Habrá que leer los libros
It will be necessary to read the books

Si hubiese cartas habría que contestarlas
If there were any letters *it would be necessary* to answer them

The *compound tenses* are formed the same as their corresponding tenses (there to be), adding *que*, thus:

INDICATIVE		SUBJUNCTIVE	
ha habido que	it has been	**haya habido que**	it may have
había habido que	necessary,	**hubiera habido que**	been necessary
habrá habido que	etc.	**si hubiera (hubiese)**	etc.
habría habido que		**habido que**	

Example

Ha habido que ir a la aduana
It has been necessary to go to the Customs House

This construction is used in interrogative sentences, like in the impersonal *haber* (to be there).

Haber (there to be) may also be used in translating the verb "to be," when implying distance, e.g.:

¿Qué distancia hay?
How far *is it*?

No, hay cuatro millas

¿Habrá tres millas de la calle mayor a al castillo?
Is it three miles from Main Street to the Castle?

No, *it is* four miles

§68. Conjugation of the Verb *tener*

Infinitive

ten-er to have

Gerund

ten-iendo having

Past Participle

ten-ido had

Indicative

PRESENT

yo	tengo	I have, etc.	nos.	ten-emos	we have, etc.
tú	tienes		vos.	ten-éis	
él	tiene		ellos	tienen	
ella	„		ellas	„	
Vd.	„		Vds.	„	

IMPERFECT

yo	ten-ía	I had or used	nos.	ten-íamos	we had or used
tú	ten-ías	to have, etc.	vos.	ten-íais	to have, etc.
él	ten-ía		ellos	ten-ían	
ella	„		ellas	„	
Vd.	„		Vds.	„	

PRETERITE

yo	tuve	I had, etc.	nos. tuvimos	we had, etc.
tú	tuviste		vos. tuvisteis	
él	tuvo		ellos tuvieron	
ella	„		ellas „	
Vd.	„		Vds. „	

FUTURE

yo	tendré	I shall have,	nos. tendremos	we shall have,
tú	tendrás	etc.	vos. tendréis	etc.
él	tendrá		ellos tendrán	
ella	„		ellas „	
Vd.	„		Vds. „	

CONDITIONAL

yo	tendría	I should or	nos. tendríamos	we should or
tú	tendrías	would have,	vos. tendríais	would have,
él	tendría	etc.	ellos tendrían	etc.
ella	„		ellas „.	
Vd.	„		Vds. „	

Subjunctive

PRESENT

yo	tenga	I may have,	nos. tengamos	we may have,
tú	tengas	etc.	vos. tengáis	etc.
él	tenga		ellos tengan	
ella	„		ellas „	
Vd.	„		Vds. „	

IMPERFECT, 1ST FORM

yo	tuviera	I might have,	nos. tuviéramos	we might have,
tú	tuvieras	etc.	vos. tuvierais	etc.
él	tuviera		ellos tuvieran	
ella	„		ellas „	
Vd.	„		Vds. „	

IMPERFECT, 2ND FORM

yo	tuviese	I might have,	nos. tuviésemos	we might have,
tú	tuvieses	etc.	vos. tuvieseis	etc.
él	tuviese		ellos tuviesen	
ella	„		ellas „	
Vd.	„		Vds. „	

Imperative

ten	tú	have	tengamos nos.	let us have
tenga	él	let him have	ten-ed vos.	have
			tengan	let them have
„	ella	let her have	„ ellas	let them have
„	Vd.	have	„ Vds.	have

COMPOUND TENSES

Indicative

Infinitive		*Gerund*
haber tenido to have had	**habiendo tenido**	having had

PERFECT

yo	**he tenido** I have had,	**nos. hemos tenido**	we have had
tú	**has tenido** etc.	**vos. habéis tenido**	etc.
él	**ha tenido**	**ellos han tenido**	
ella	„	**ellas** „	
Vd.	„	**Vds.** „	

PLUPERFECT

yo **había tenido,** etc. **nos. habíamos tenido,** etc.
I had had, etc. we had had, etc

PRETERITE PERFECT

yo **hube tenido,** etc. **nos. hubimos tenido,** etc.
I had had, etc. we had had, etc.

FUTURE PERFECT

yo **habré tenido,** etc. **nos. habremos tenido,** etc.
I shall have had, etc. we shall have had, etc.

CONDITIONAL PERFECT

yo **habría tenido,** etc. **nos. habríamos tenido,** etc.
I should or would have had, etc. we should or would have had, etc.

Subjunctive

PERFECT

yo **haya tenido,** etc. **nos. hayamos tenido,** etc.
I may have had, etc. we may have had, etc.

PLUPERFECT, 1ST FORM

yo **hubiera tenido,** etc. **nos. hubiéramos tenido,** etc.
I might have had, etc. we might have had, etc.

PLUPERFECT, 2ND FORM

yo **hubiese tenido,** etc. **nos. hubiésemos tenido,** etc.
I might have had, etc. we might have had, etc.

§69. Uses of the Verb *tener*

1. *To have,* used as a transitive verb, is translated by *tener,* to indicate possession:

Tengo una pluma	**¿Tiene Vd. ese papel?**
I have a pen	Do you have that paper?
No; pero la tendré pronto	**El señor fulano tuvo mucho dinero**
No; but I shall have it soon	Mr. So-and-So had much money
¿Tendría Vd. esto?	Would you have this?

2. *Tener* is used in conjunction with the words *hambre* (hunger), *sed* (thirst), *frío* (cold), *calor* (warmth), *sueño* (sleep), *vergüenza* (shame), *miedo* (fear), *razón* (right)[1] and *ganas de* (a desire to do something) and in a number of expressions in which the verb *to be* is used in English. Examples:

¿Tiene Vd. sueño?	**Tengo hambre y sed**
Are you sleepy?	I *am* hungry and thirsty
Tengo ganas de comer	**¿Qué tiene Vd.?**
I *have* a desire to eat	What *is the matter with* you?
Yo no tengo nada, pero Juan tiene dolor de cabeza	**¿Tiene Vd. razón en tener miedo?**
Nothing *is the matter with* me, but John *has* a headache	*Are* you right in *being* afraid?
No, no tengo razón	**¿Tiene Vd. alguna cosa?**
No, I *am* not right	*Is* anything *the matter with* you?
Sí tengo frío	**¿Tiene Vd. frío o calor?**
Yes, I *am* cold	*Are* you cold or warm?
No tengo ni frío ni calor	I *am* neither cold nor warm

3. It takes the place of the English verb *to be* when expressing age and dimensions:

¿Cuántos años tiene Vd.?	**¿Qué edad tiene Vd.?**
How old *are* you?	What *is* your age?
Tengo treinta años	**¿Qué dimensiones tiene este cuarto?**
I *am* thirty years old	What *are* the dimensions of this room?

Creo que tendrá unos veinticinco pies de largo, por quince de ancho
I think it *will be* about twenty-five feet long by fifteen feet wide

4. *Tener* followed by *que* indicates necessity or obligation to do something, and has the meaning of "to have to" or "must"; in this case the conjunction *que* must always precede the infinitive of the principal verb:

Tengo que estudiar mi lección de español	**¿Tiene Vd. que ir a su oficina?**
I *have to* study my Spanish lesson	Do you *have to* go to your office?
Sí, porque tengo mucho que hacer	Yes, because I *have* much *to* do

[1] *Razón* (lit., *reason*) is used in the same sense as *right*. *To be wrong* is usually expressed as *no tener razón* (lit., not to have reason), as *él no tiene razón* (lit., "he has no reason"; he is not right).

Note. As shown in the last example, adverbs may be either placed immediately after the verb, followed by the conjunction *que*, or at the end of the sentence: *tengo mucho que hacer* or *tengo que hacer mucho*.

§70. Conjugation of the Verb *ser*

Infinitive
s-er, to be

Gerund	*Past Participle*
s-iendo, being	**s-ido, been**

Indicative

PRESENT

yo	soy	I am etc.	nos.	somos	we are, etc.
tú	eres		vos.	sois	
él	es		ellos	son	
ella	„		ellas	„	
Vd.	„		Vds.	„	

IMPERFECT

yo	era	I was or used	nos.	éramos	we were or
tú	eras	to be, etc.	vos.	erais	used to be, etc.
él	era		ellos	eran	
ella	„		ellas	„	
Vd.	„		Vds.	„	

PRETERITE

yo	fuí	I was, etc.	nos.	fuimos	we were, etc.
tú	fuiste		vos.	fuisteis	
él	fué		ellos	fueron	
ella	„		ellas	„	
Vd.	„		Vds.	„	

FUTURE

yo	s-eré	I shall be,	nos.	s-eremos	we shall be, etc.
tú	s-erás	etc.	vos.	s-eréis	
él	s-erá		ellos	s-erán	
ella	„		ellas	„	
Vd.	„		Vds.	„	

CONDITIONAL

yo	s-ería	I should or	nos.	s-eríamos	we should or
tú	s-erías	would be	vos.	s-eríais	would be etc.
él	s-ería	etc.	ellos	s-erían	
ella	„		ellas	„	
Vd.	„		Vds.	„	

Subjunctive

PRESENT

yo	sea	I may be,	nos. seamos	we may be,
tú	seas	etc.	vos. seáis	etc.
él	sea		ellos sean	
ella	„		ellas „	
Vd.	„		Vds. „	

IMPERFECT, 1ST FORM

yo	fuera	I might be,	nos. fuéramos	we might be
tú	fueras	etc.	vos. fuerais	etc.
él	fuera		ellos fueran	
ella	„		ellas „	
Vd.	„		Vds. „	

IMPERFECT, 2ND FORM

yo	fuese	I might be,	nos. fuésemos	we might be,
tú	fueses	etc.	vos. fueseis	etc.
él	fuese		ellos fuesen	
ella	„		ellas „	
Vd.	„		Vds. „	

FUTURE IMPERFECT[1]

yo	fuere	I should be,	nos. fuéremos	we should be,
tú	fueres	etc.	vos. fuereis	etc.
él	fuere		ellos fueren	
ella	„		ellas „	
Vd.	„		Vds. „	

Imperative

			seamos nos.	let us be
sé	tú	be	s-ed vos.	be
sea	él	let him be	sean ellos	let them be
„	ella	let her be	„ ellas	let them be
„	Vd.	be	„ Vds.	be

COMPOUND TENSES

Infinitive   *Gerund*

Haber sido to have been   **Habiendo sido** having been

PERFECT

yo	he sido	I have been,	nos. hemos sido	We have been,
tú	has sido	etc.	vos. habéis sido	etc.
él	ha sido		ellos han sido	
ella	„		ellas „	
Vd.	„		Vds. „	

[1] It is used rarely even in writing and is generally referred to as future subjunctive. In its place the present subjunctive is used today.

PLUPERFECT

yo había sido, etc.
I had been, etc.

nos. habíamos sido, etc.
We had been, etc.

FUTURE PERFECT

yo habré sido, etc.
I shall have been, etc.

nos. habremos sido, etc.
We shall have been, etc.

CONDITIONAL PERFECT

yo habría sido, etc.
I should or would have been, etc.

nos. habríamos sido, etc.
We should or would have been, etc.

Subjunctive

PERFECT

yo haya sido etc.
I may have been, etc.

nos. hayamos sido, etc.
We may have been, etc.

PLUPERFECT, IST FORM

yo hubiera sido, etc.
I might have been, etc.

nos. hubiéramos sido, etc.
We might have been, etc.

PLUPERFECT, 2ND FORM

yo hubiese sido, etc.
I might have been, etc.

nos. hubiésemos sido, etc.
We might have been, etc.

§71. Uses of the Verb *ser*

There are two verbs in Spanish corresponding to the English *to be*, but their respective meanings differ widely. The verb *ser* is what may properly be termed a definite verb, i.e. it governs the *inherent* and *mental* state of persons, *their rank, profession, trade* and *nationality*, and of *things absolute*, i.e. things not likely to undergo change.

1. Examples where the attribute is essential or inherent:

Mi cuarto es grande
My room *is* large

El hombre es alto
The man *is* tall

El es joven, rico y sano, y por lo tanto es feliz
He is young, rich and healthy, and therefore is happy

Note. In the last example *es* is used to express the condition of the man under the given cirumstances.

2. Referring to quality, rank, profession, dignity, trade, nationality, etc.:

El señor Martín es banquero, y es español	El es un gran orador
	He *is* a great orator
Mr. Martin *is* a banker and a Spaniard	
¿Quién es ese hombre?	Es el tenedor de libros de mi casa
Who *is* that man?	He *is* the book-keeper for my firm

3. *Ser* is also used when referring to possession, origin, or materials, followed by the preposition *de*, except when in combination with the possessive pronouns *mío* (mine), *tuyo* (yours), *suyo* (his, hers, or yours), *nuestro* (our) and *vuestro* (yours), when the preposition is not used:

Este libro es de mi hermano	El vino es de España
This book *is* my brother's	The wine *is from* Spain
El reloj es de oro	¿De quién es este reloj?
The watch *is of* gold	*Whose* watch *is* this?
No es suyo, sino mío	It *is* not *his*, but *mine*

4. *Ser* is also used when speaking of time:

¿Qué hora es?	Es la una
What time *is it*?	*It is* one o'clock
Son las cuatro	Es la una y cuarto
It is four o'clock	*It is* a quarter-past one
Son las cinco y media	*It is* half-past five

5. It is also used in all *impersonal expressions* and adverbial expressions referring to time:

Fué necesario	Será posible	No es fácil	Sería difícil
It was necessary	*It will* be possible	*It is* not easy	*It would be* difficult
Es de día	Es de noche	Es tarde	Es temprano
It is daylight	*It is* night	*It is* late	*It is* early

6. As it always implies permancy or inherent condition, it is also used with all adjectives implying the same:

Esta naranja es agria	El niño es limpio	Juana es lista
This orange *is* sour	The child *is* clean (in its habits)	Jane *is* clever

7. Finally, *ser* forms the passive voice together with the past participle of the verb used:

El niño es castigado por sus maestros	Soy amado de mis padres
	I *am loved* by my parents
The child *is punished* by his teachers	
El general fué expulsado de su país	The general *was expelled* from his country

§72. Conjugation of the Verb *estar*

Infinitive
est-ar to be

Gerund		*Past Participle*	
Est-ando being		**est-ado** been	

Indicative

PRESENT

yo	estoy	I am, etc.	nos.	est-amos	we are, etc.
tú	estás		vos.	est-áis	
él	está		ellos están		
ella	„		ellas	„	
Vd.	„		Vds.	„	

IMPERFECT

yo	est-aba	I was or used	nos.	est-ábamos	we were or used
tú	est-abas	to be, etc.	vos.	est-abais	to be, etc.
él	est-aba		ellos est-aban		
ella	„		ellas	„	
Vd.	„		Vds.	„	

PRETERITE

yo	estuve	I was, etc.	nos.	estuvimos	we were, etc.
tú	estuviste		vos.	estuvisteis	
él	estuvo		ellos estuvieron		
ella	„		ellas	„	
Vd.	„		Vds.	„	

FUTURE

yo	est-aré	I shall be,	nos.	est-aremos	we shall be,
tú	est-arás	etc.	vos.	est-aréis	etc.
él	est-ará		ellos est-arán		
ella	„		ellas	„	
Vd.	„		Vds.	„	

CONDITIONAL

yo	est-aría	I should or	nos.	est-aríamos	we should or
tú	est-arías	would be,	vos.	est-aríais	would be,
él	est-aría	etc.	ellos est-arían		etc.
ella	„		ellas	„	
Vd.	„		Vds.	„	

Subjunctive

PRESENT

yo	esté	I may be etc.	nos.	est-emos	we may be, etc.
tú	estés		vos.	est-éis	
él	esté		ellos estén		
ella	„		ellas	„	
Vd.	„		Vds.	„	

IMPERFECT, 1ST FORM

yo	estuviera	I might be, etc.	nos.	estuviéramos	we might be etc.
tú	estuvieras		vos.	estuvierais	
él	estuviera		ellos estuvieran		
ella	„		ellas	„	
Vd.	„		Vds.	„	

IMPERFECT, 2ND FORM

yo	estuviese	I might be, etc.	nos.	estuviésemos	we might be, etc.
tú	estuvieses		vos.	estuvieseis	
él	estuviese		ellos estuviesen		
ella	„		ellas	„	
Vd.	„		Vds.	„	

Imperative

		est-emos	nos.	let us be
está tú	be	est-ad	vos.	be
esté él	let him be	estén	ellos.	let them be
„ ella	let her be	„	ellas	let them be
„ Vd.	be	„	Vds.	be

COMPOUND TENSES

Infinitive		Gerund	
haber estado	to have been	habiendo estado	having been

Indicative

PERFECT

yo	he estado	I have been,	nos.	hemos estado	we have been,
tú	has estado	etc.	vos.	habéis estado	etc.
él	ha estado		ellos han estado		
ella	„		ellas	„	
Vd.	„		Vds.	„	

PLUPERFECT

yo había estado, etc.　　　　　nos. habíamos estado, etc.
　I had been, etc.　　　　　　　　we had been, etc.

FUTURE PERFECT

yo habré estado, etc.	**nos. habremos estado, etc.**
I shall have been, etc.	we shall have been, etc.

CONDITIONAL PERFECT

yo habría estado, etc.	**nos. habríamos estado, etc.**
I should or would have been, etc.	we should or would have been, etc.

Subjunctive

PERFECT

que yo haya estado, etc.	**que nos. hayamos estado, etc.**
that I may have been, etc.	that we may have been, etc.

PLUPERFECT, 1ST FORM

yo hubiera estado, etc.	**nos. hubiéramos estado, etc.**
I might have been, etc.	we might have been, etc.

PLUPERFECT, 2ND FORM

yo hubiese estado, etc.	**nos. hubiésemos estado, etc.**
I might have been, etc.	we might have been, etc.

§73. Uses of the Verb *estar*

The forms of *estar* are used to express the condition of persons or things in a state which is *temporary* or *accidental*, i.e. when a change may occur at any time:

Este pan está caliente	**Luisa está contenta**
This bread *is* hot	Louisa *is* pleased
La silla está rota	**El cuarto está limpio**
The chair *is* broken	The room *is* clean
El niño está cansado	**El café está dulce**
The child *is* tired	The coffee *is* sweet
Los muchachos están en la calle	**¿Dónde está mi sombrero?**
The boys *are* in the street	Where *is* my hat?
Su sombrero está en la percha	Your hat *is* on the hat-rack

Estar is also used when speaking of *the existence of* or *locations in general:*

¿Dónde está su socio de Vd.?	**Está en París**
Where *is* your partner?	He *is* in Paris
Barcelona está en España	**Yo estaba en mi casa**
Barcelona *is* in Spain	I *was* at home
Mi casa está en la calle Alcalá	My house *is* in Alcala Street

The following rules and examples will further explain the various applications of *estar:*

1. It is used to denote a *state of health:*

¿Cómo está Vd.?	Estoy bien
How *are* you?	I *am* well
Ese joven está enfermo	¿No está mejor?
That young man *is* ill	*Is* he not better?

2. When combined with certain adjectives it expresses a *way of being*, or *feelings* and *emotions*:

| estar alegre | estar satisfecho | estar triste |
| to be merry | to be satisfied | to be sad |

3. It is used in some *adverbial expressions*, such as:

| Mi sombrero está de moda | Estoy de prisa |
| My hat *is* fashionable | I *am* in a hurry |

4. It forms the *progressive form* ending in *-ando* or *iendo* (corresponding to the English ending *-ing*):

Estoy escribiendo un libro	Juan está estudiando
I *am writing* a book	John *is studying*
Nosotros estábamos hablando	We *were speaking*

Note. Estar is seldom used with the present participle of *ir* (to go) and *venir* (to come) in the same sense as it is used in English. For instance, we say: *yo voy* (I go) and *yo vengo* (I come) instead of *estoy yendo* (I am going) and *estoy viniendo* (I am coming).

5. Followed by the preposition *de*, it expresses *occupation* or *disposition* of the *body* or *mind*:

Hoy estoy de servicio	Estábamos de discusión
I *am on* duty to-day	We *were* discussing
El estaba de riña	He *felt like* quarrelling

It may also be employed, followed by the preposition *de*, instead o *ser* when speaking of *dignities* and *offices temporarily held*:

El señor Concha está de alcalde de Málaga
Mr. Concha *is* (acting) mayor of Malaga

It would, however, be perfectly correct to say:

El señor Concha es alcalde de Málaga

6. Before the preposition *para*, followed by the *infinitive* of the verb, it expresses *intention* or *proximity*:

| Estaba para escribir cuando Vd. llegó | Estamos para acabar |
| I *had the intention of writing* when you arrived | We *are about to finish* |

7. *Por*, used in connection with *estar* instead of *para*, denotes *indecision*, or refers to *action not completed* or *neglected*:

Estaba por salir	**Estoy por leer Don Quijote**
I intended to go out	*I intend to read* "Don Quixote"
La casa está por barrer	**La carta está aún por escribir**
The house is unswept	*The letter is still unwritten*

§74. Comparison of the Verbs *ser* and *estar*

It has already been explained that both these verbs represent the meaning of the English "to be," but since *ser* is *absolute* whereas *estar* is *transitory*, great care should be exercised in their use, for a misapplication would be apt to cause confusion. The following pairs of sentences, apparently similar, show the difficulty which is likely to occur and will clarify the difference in use between the two verbs. See also §78.

Ser (absolute)	*Estar* (transitory)
Juan es vivo	**Juan está vivo**
John *is* lively	John *is* alive (or lives)
Pedro es listo	**Pedro está listo**
Peter *is* clever	Peter *is* ready
Este hombre es bueno	**Este hombre está bueno**
This man *is* good	This man *is* well
El muchacho es malo	**El muchacho está malo**
The boy *is* bad	The boy *is* ill
Este vino es agrio	**Este vino está agrio**
This wine is sour (by nature)	This wine *has become* sour
Ese joven es muy callado	**Ese joven está muy callado**
That young man *is* very taciturn	That young man *is* very quiet
El niño es limpio	**El niño está limpio**
The child *is* clean (in its habits)	The child *is* clean (has been washed)
Este cuarto es alto (de techo)	**Este cuarto está alto**
The room is lofty	This room is high (a long way upstairs)

CHAPTER 11

REFLEXIVE VERBS

§75. Reflexive Verbs are those in which the action is directed back upon the subject (i.e. the agent): *yo me lavo* (I wash myself), *él se casó con Alicia* (he married [himself with] Alice).

The reflexive verbs therefore are conjugated with *two* personal pronouns: the first is the subject, either expressed or understood, and the second is the object.

These pronouns precede all verbs except in the infinitive, gerund and positive imperative, when the pronoun is placed after the verb and is attached to it:

El se alaba	**Nosotros nos enfadamos**
He praises *himself*	We (*ourselves*) become angry
Ellos se acordarían	**Levántense Vds.**
They would remember (*themselves*)	Get (*yourselves*) up
Voy a lavarme	**Estoy vistiéndome**
I am going to wash *myself*	I am dressing *myself*
Les encontró lavandose	**Está divirtiéndose**
He found them washing *themselves*	He is amusing *himself*
Figurémonos	**Figuraraos**
Let us imagine (*ourselves*)	Imagine (*yourselves*)

Note. The *s* of the first person plural and the *d* of the second person plural are dropped in the imperative as shown in the last two examples.

§76. The Conjugation of Reflexive Verbs

1. Conjugation of a typical reflexive verb:

Infinitive

lavarse to wash oneself

Gerund

lavándose washing oneself

Indicative

PRESENT

yo	me lavo	I wash myself,	nos.	nos lavamos	we wash ourselves,
tú	te lavas	etc.	vos.	os laváis	etc.
él	se lava		ellos	se lavan	
ella	„		ellas	„	
Vd.	„		Vds.	„	

IMPERFECT

yo	me lavaba	I was washing	nos.	nos lavábamos	we were washing
tú	te lavabas	or used to	vos.	os lavabais	or used to wash
él	se lavaba	wash myself	ellos	se lavaban	ourselves, etc.
ella	„		ellas	„	
Vd.	„		Vds.	„	

PRETERITE

yo	me lavé	I washed or	nos.	nos lavamos	we washed or
tú	te lavaste	did wash	vos.	os lavasteis	did wash
él	se lavó	myself etc.	ellos	se lavaron	ourselves, etc.
ella	„		ellas	„	
Vd.	„		Vds.	„	

FUTURE

yo	me lavaré	I shall wash	nos.	nos lavaremos	we shall wash
tú	te lavarás	myself, etc.	vos.	os lavaréis	ourselves, etc.
él	se lavará		ellos	se lavarán	
ella	„		ellas	„	
Vd.	„		Vds.	„	

CONDITIONAL

yo	me lavaría	I should or	nos.	nos lavaríamos	we should or
tú	te lavarías	would wash	vos.	os lavaríais	would wash
él	se lavaría	myself, etc.	ellos	se lavarían	ourselves, etc.
ella	„		ellas	„	
Vd.	„		Vds.	„	

Subjunctive

PRESENT

yo	me lave	I may wash	nos.	nos lavemos	we may wash
tú	te laves	myself, etc.	vos.	os lavéis	ourselves, etc.
él	se lave		ellos	se laven	
ella	„		ellas	„	
Vd.	„		Vds.	„	

IMPERFECT, 1ST FORM

yo	me lavara	I might wash	nos.	nos laváramos	we might wash
tú	te lavaras	myself, etc.	vos.	os lavarais	ourselves, etc.
él	se lavara		ellos	se lavaran	
ella	„		ellas	„	
Vd.	„		Vds.	„	

IMPERFECT, 2ND FORM

yo	me lavase	I might wash	nos.	nos lavásemos	we might wash
tú	te lavases	myself, etc.	vos.	os lavaseis	ourselves, etc.
él	se lavase		ellos	se lavasen	
ella	„		ellas	„	
Vd.	„		Vds.	„	

CONDITIONAL

yo	me lavare	I should wash	nos.	nos laváremos	we should wash
tú	te lavares	myself, etc.	vos.	os lavareis	ourselves, etc.
él	se lavare		ellos	se lavaren	
ella	„		ellas	„	
usted	„		ustedes	„	

Imperative

			lavémonos nos.		let us wash ourselves
lávate tú		wash yourself	lavaos	vos.	wash yourselves
lávese él		let him wash himself	lávense	ellos	let them wash themselves
„	ella	let her wash herself	„	ellas	let them wash themselves
„	Vd.	wash yourself	„	Vds.	wash yourselves

COMPOUND TENSES

Infinitive

haberse lavado   to have washed oneself

Gerund

habiéndose lavado   having washed oneself

PERFECT

	Singular			Plural	
yo	me he lavado	I have	nos.	nos hemos lavado	we have
tú	te has lavado	washed	vos.	os habéis lavado	washed
él	se ha lavado	myself,	ellos	se han lavado	ourselves
ellas	„	etc.	ellas	„	etc.
Vd.	„		Vds.	„	

PLUPERFECT

yo me había lavado, etc.   **nos. nos habíamos lavado,** etc.
I had washed myself, etc.   we had washed ourselves, etc.

PAST ANTERIOR

yo me hube lavado, etc.   **nos. nos hubimos lavado,** etc.
I had washed myself, etc.   we had washed ourselves, etc.

FUTURE PERFECT

yo me habré lavado, etc.   **nos. nos habremos lavado,** etc.
I shall have washed myself, etc.   we shall have washed ourselves, etc.

CONDITIONAL PERFECT

yo me habría lavado, etc.
I should or would have washed
myself, etc.

nos. nos habríamos lavado, etc.
we should or would have washed
ourselves, etc.

Subjunctive

PERFECT

yo me haya lavado, etc.
I may have washed myself, etc.

nos. nos hayamos lavado, etc.
we may have washed ourselves, etc.

PLUPERFECT, 1ST FORM

yo me hubiera lavado, etc.
I might have washed myself, etc.

nos. nos hubiéramos lavado, etc.
we might have washed ourselves, etc.

PLUPERFECT, 2ND FORM

yo me hubiese lavado, etc.
I might have washed myself, etc.

nos. nos hubiésemos lavado, etc.
we might have washed ourselves. etc.

2. Model of a reflexive verb conjugated with another verb:

Infinitive

querer lavarse
quererse lavar
} to wish to wash oneself

Gerund

queriendo lavarse
queriéndose lavar
} wishing to wash oneself

Past Participle

querido lavarse   wished to wash oneself

Indicative

PRESENT

yo quiero lavarme, etc.
yo me quiero lavar, etc.
} I wish to wash myself, etc.

IMPERFECT

yo quería lavarme, etc.
yo me quería lavar, etc.
} I wished to wash myself, etc.

PRETERITE

yo quise lavarme, etc.
yo me quise lavar etc.
} I wished to wash myself, etc.

FUTURE

yo querré lavarme, etc.
yo me querré lavar, etc. } I shall wish to wash myself, etc.

CONDITIONAL

yo querría lavarme, etc.
yo me querría lavar, etc. } I should wish to wash myself, etc.

Subjunctive
PRESENT

yo quiera lavarme, etc.
yo me quiera lavar, etc. } I may wish to wash myself, etc.

IMPERFECT, 1ST FORM

yo quisiera lavarme, etc.
yo me quisiera lavar, etc. } I might wish to wash myself, etc.

IMPERFECT, 2ND FORM

yo quisiese lavarme, etc.
yo me quisiese lavar, etc. } I might wish to wash myself, etc.

§77. Types of Reflexive Verbs

The reflexive verbs are either *purely* reflexive, i.e. they can only be used in the reflexive sense, as *arrepentirse* (to repent) and *acordarse* (to remember), or they can be formed from transitive and intransitive verbs, as *quemarse* (to burn oneself) from *quemar* (to burn), *calentarse* (to warm oneself) from *calentar* (to warm), etc.

The number of purely reflexive verbs is limited, but almost any verb can be used in the reflexive form.

1. The reflexive form is used more frequently in Spanish than it is in English, as may be seen from the following common expressions:

Llamarse, *to be called (named)*

¿Cómo se llama Vd.?   What is your name?
Me llamo Jorge   My name is George

Equivocarse, *to be mistaken*

Vd. se equivoca   You are mistaken

Sentarse, *to be seated*

Siéntese Vd., señora   Sit down, madam

Levantarse, *to rise (get up)*

¿A qué hora se levanta Vd.?	(At) what time do you get up?
Me levanto a las seis	I get up at six o'clock

Acostarse, *to go to bed*

¿Está Vd. acostándose?	Are you going to bed?
No, no estoy acostándome todavía, pero me acostaré pronto	No, I am not going to bed yet, but I will be soon

Pasearse, *to go for a walk*

¿Quiere Vd. pasearse conmigo?	Will you walk with me?
No tengo tiempo de pasearme	I have no time to walk

Enfadarse, *to get angry*

No se enfade Vd.	Do not *get* angry

Vestirse, *to dress*

Nos vestiremos más tarde	We shall dress later

Enriquecerse, *to become rich*

Don Fulano se ha enriquecido en muy poco tiempo	Mr. So-and-So *has become* rich in a very short time

Arrepentirse, *to repent*

El se arrepintió antes de morir	He repented before dying

Dirigirse, *to apply*

¿A quién debo dirigirme?	To whom must I apply?
Vd. puede dirigirse a mí	You may apply to me

Enfermarse, *to become ill*

El se enfermó al salir del teatro	He became ill while leaving the theatre

Irse, *to go away*

Me voy I am going away	Váyase Vd. Go away

Quejarse, *to complain*

Me quejo de mi suerte	I complain of my fate

Acordarse, *to remember*

Me acordaré siempre de eso	I'll always remember that.

2. From the above examples, it is seen that almost all verbs in the passive voice in English are reflexive in Spanish, as well as those composed with *to get* and *to become*. Other examples:

asustarse	to be frightened	calentarse	to get warm
disgustarse	to be displeased	enfermarse	to take ill
equivocarse	to be mistaken	enriquecerse	to become rich

3. *To become* or *to get* is translated by:

a) *Ponerse* to express a change in health:

Se ha puesto enfermo
He has become ill

Se puso bueno al otro día
He got well the next day

b) *Volverse* or *hacerse* if a change in the physical, professional or moral condition is expressed:

Se ha vuelto loco
He has become insane

Se hizo médico el año pasado
He became a physician last year

Note. When the change of condition is not due to the direct action of the subject, but is the result of his effort, *llegar a ser*, *venir a ser* or *ser hecho* are used:

Por su habilidad llegó a ser (or **vino a ser** or **fué hecho**) **capataz del taller**
By his skill he became foreman of the shop

4. Verbs *accidentally* reflexive often have a meaning which is different from that of their active form:

acostar	to put (someone) to bed	acostarse	to go to bed
acordar	to agree	acordarse	to remember
levantar	to raise	levantarse	to get up
poner	to put	ponerse a	to begin to
ir	to go	irse	to go away

5. Some verbs, when used reflexively in the plural, express a mutual or reciprocal action:

Nos ayudaremos siempre
We'll always help *each other*

Se escriben a menudo
They often write to *each other*

6. There are many verbs in Spanish which can be used in a reflexive form without changing their meaning:

Fiarse or **fiar de alguno**
To trust somebody
El se ha muerto or **ha muerto**
He has died

Reirse or **reir de alguno**
To laugh at someone
He has died

7. When the object of the verb refers to parts of the human body or to articles of clothing, the reflexive form is used:

Quítese Vd. el sobretodo
Take off your overcoat
Me lavo las manos
I wash my hands

¿No se pone Vd. el sombrero?
Won't you put on your hat?
I wash my hands

8. Reflexive verbs can be conjugated in an impersonal way by adding the pronoun *se* (third person singular), in which case the pronoun identifies the person:

Personal Inflection		*Impersonal Inflection*	
Decirse	to say to oneself	**Decirse**	to be told
yo me digo	I say to myself, etc.	**se me dice (a mí)**	I am told, etc.
tú te dices		**se te dice (a tí)**	
él se dice (a sí)		**se le dice (a él)**	
ella se dice		**se le dice (a ella)**	
Vd. se dice		**se le dice (a Vd.)**	
nos. nos decimos		**se nos dice (a nos)**	
vos. os decís		**se os dice (a vos.)**	
ellos se dicen		**se les dice (a ellos)**	
ellas se dicen		**se les dice (a ellas)**	
Vds. se dicen		**se les dice (a Vds.)**	

The passive voice is not so widely used in Spanish as in English; the impersonal form with the reflexive pronoun *se* is used instead:

Los cuadros se han vendido
The pictures *have been* sold
La apuesta se ganó y el dinero se perdió
The bet *was won* and the money *was lost*

Aquí se habla español
Spanish *is spoken* here

CHAPTER 12

PASSIVE VOICE

§78 The Passive Voice

The passive voice is formed in Spanish with the corresponding tenses of the auxiliary *ser* and the past participle of the principal verb. The past participle must agree in gender and number with the subject. Examples:

Los niños son castigados	**La casa fué vendida**
The children *are punished*	The house *was sold*
Ella ha sido muy amada	**Nosotros somos engañados**
She *has been* very much *loved*	We are *deceived*

El pan fué partido y distribuído entre los pobres
The bread *was sliced* and *distributed* among the poor

Note 1. However, a similar construction is used with the verb *estar* when the past participle functions as an adjective, i.e. when the state or condition of the subject is described without reference to action:

La carta estaba mal escrita	**El libro está concluído**
The letter *was* badly *written*	The book *is concluded*
Las manzanas están podridas	The apples *are rotten*

Note 2. *Estar* is also used instead of *ser* when the state or condition of the subject refers to location or situation in general:

La casa está bien situada	**Los libros están colocados en la mesa**
The house *is* well *located*	The books *are placed* on the table
Mi quinta está edificada cerca del mar	
My cottage *is built* by the sea	

See§ §71-73 for additional information on the uses of *ser* and *estar*.

§79. Uses of the Passive Forms

1. When the passive verbs are used in the *present* or *imperfect indicative,* they generally express a sentiment or mental action:

Pablo es amado por Virginia   Paul *is loved* by Virginia

2. If the sentiment or mental action is not expressed and the passive verb is in the *imperfect* or *present indicative,* the verb *estar* is used instead of *ser:*

El libro está escrito por un español	**La casa está vendida**
The book *is written* by a Spaniard	The house *is* sold
El puente estaba ya construído	The bridge *was* already *built*

3. The passive verbs are generally used in the active form, in the third person, singular or plural, with the pronoun *se*:

El café se vendió bien	**Se ama al hombre de bien**
Coffee *sold* well	The honest man *is loved*
Se admira la sabiduría de Sócrates	
The *wisdom* of Socrates *is admired*	

This personal (third person) form is in frequent use in Spanish when the subject is not a person, and the agent from whom the action proceeds is not expressed, i.e. understood, as *Las manzanas se vendieron caras* (The apples were sold at a high price).

4. The preposition *por* takes the place of "by" in English, after a verb in the passive voice, unless the action of the verb refers to a mental act, in which case *de* can be used instead:

Don Quijote fué escrito por Cervantes	**El discurso será pronunciado por un gran orador**
"Don Quixote" *was written by* Cervantes	The speech *will be made by a great* orador
El autor es muy celebrado por (de) sus compatriotas	
The author *is* very much *praised by* his compatriots	

5. The verbs *quedar* and *ir* are used sometimes instead of *ser* in forming the passive voice, in order to give more emphasis to the phrase:

La cuestión de la exposición ha quedado decidida	**Va demostrado que la cosa pasó así**
The exhibition affair *has been* decided	It *is proved* that the thing happened so

CHAPTER 13

IMPERSONAL VERBS

§80. Impersonal Verbs are generally conjugated only in the third person singular of all the tenses, the past participle and the gerund. The most important are:

amanecer }	to dawn	**llover**	to rain
alborear }		**lloviznar**	to drizzle
anochecer }	to grow dark	**granizar**	to hail
oscurecer }		**nevar**	to snow
helar	to freeze	**tronar**	to thunder
deshelar	to thaw	**ventear**	to blow

Models for the Conjugations

1. **Amanecer,** to dawn:

Gerund	*Past Participle*
amaneciendo	**amanecido**

Indicative		*Subjunctive*	
amanece	it dawns	**amanezca**	that it may dawn
amanecia	it was dawning	**amaneciera**	it might dawn
amaneció	it dawned	**amaneciese**	it might dawn
amanecerá	it will dawn	**amaneciere**	it should dawn
amaneceriá	it would dawn		

Anochecer and *oscurecer* are conjugated as *amanecer*.

2. **Helar,** to freeze:

Gerund	*Past Participle*
helando	**helado**

Indicative		*Subjunctive*	
hiela	it freezes	**hiele**	it may freeze
helaba	it was freezing	**helara**	it might freeze
heló	it froze	**helase**	it might freeze
helará	it will freeze	**helare**	it should freeze
helaría	it would freeze		

Deshelar, nevar, alborear, lloviznar, granizar, ventear and *tronar* are conjugated as *helar*, except for the corresponding irregularities.

3. **Llover,** to rain:

Gerund		*Past Participle*	
lloviendo		**llovido**	

Indicative		*Subjunctive*	
llueve	it rains	**llueva**	it may rain
llovía	it was raining	**lloviera**	it might rain
llovió	it rained	**lloviese**	it might rain
lloverá	it will rain	**lloviere**	it should rain
llovería	it would rain		

There are other impersonal verbs which are used in the third person singular and plural, among which the most important are:

acaecer	⎫		**convenir**	to suit
acontecer	⎬	to happen	**importar**	to matter
suceder	⎭		**parecer**	to appear, to seem

Examples

Ayer sucedió (aconteció or acae-
 ció) una desgracia
 A misfortune *happened* yesterday
 El niño parece tímido
 The boy *seems* timid

Ayer sucedieron (acontecieron or
 acaecieron) varias desgracias
 Several misfortunes *happened* yesterday
 Los niños parecen tímidos
 The boys *seem* timid

§81. Verbs Functioning as Impersonal Verbs

1. There are some other verbs which, although not impersonal, may be used as such:

a) Ser, in the following phrases:

Es muy tarde
 It is very *late*
 Es ya de día
 It is now *daylight*

No es temprano
 It is not *early*
 No es de noche todavía
 It is not *night* yet

b) Hacer, when referring to the weather, or when translated by "ago" indicating time elapsed:

Hace sol	**Hace luna**	**Hizo buen tiempo**
The sun shines	The moon *is* shining	*It was* good weather
Hará mal tiempo	**Hace muchos años**	
It will be bad weather	Many years *ago*	

c) Haber, as in the following examples:

Hay mucha fruta	**Habrá muchos hombres**
There is much fruit	*There will be* many men
Hay lodo	**Hubo polvo**
It is muddy	*It was* dusty
Hay cuatro millas de la calle Mejor al Castillo	**¿Habría mucha gente en el teatro si no lloviera?**
The Castle *is* four miles from Main Street	*Would there be* many people at the theatre if it should not rain?
Habría más gente	*There would be* more people

Note. **Ha** is sometimes used instead of *hay* or *hace* when referring to time. Observe that *ha* always follows the time, while *hay* or *hace* precedes it. Examples:

Doce años ha	
Hay (hace) doce años }	Twelve years ago

2. Most verbs can be used impersonally in the third person plural:

Dicen que la cosecha es buena	**¿Qué dirán?**
They say the harvest is good	What will they say?
Allí riñen	**Aseguran que sucedió así**
They are fighting there	They declare that it happened thus

3. The following *defective verbs* are in the same class as those of impersonal meaning:

Valer, *to be worth, to be better*

Más vale tarde que nunca	*Better* late than never

Bastar, *to suffice, to be sufficient*

Basta que Vd. se empeñe	*It is sufficient* that you persist in it
Su palabra basta	Your word *is enough*

Gustar, *to please, to be pleasant*

Gusta cuando uno se acostumbra	*It pleases* when one gets accustomed to it
El estudio de idiomas gusta	The study of languages *is pleasant*

Disgustar, *to displease, to be unpleasant*

Disgusta oír tal cosa	*It is unpleasant* to hear such a thing
Su conversación disgusta	His conversation *is unpleasant*

Placer, *to please*

Me place oírlo	*It pleases* me to hear it
¡Plegue a Dios!	*May it please* God!

Fastidiar, *to annoy, to be tiresome*

Fastidia quedarse en casa	*It is tiresome* to remain at home
Tanta lluvia fastidia	So much rain *is annoying*

Acomodar, *to suit*

Me acomoda hacerlo así	*It suits* me to do it so

Pesar,[1] *to regret*

Me pesa haberlo hecho	*I regret* having done it
Nos pesó después que lo hicimos	We *regretted* it after we did it

Doler, *to ache, to pain*

Me duele el brazo	My arm *aches*
Me dolió la cabeza esta mañana	My head *ached* this morning

Soler, *to be accustomed to*

Suelo levantarme a las siete y desayunar a las ocho	*I am in the habit* of rising at seven and breakfasting at eight
Hace años solía dar un paseo antes de desayunar	Years ago *I used* to take a walk before breakfast

Yacer, *to lie (in epitaphs)*

Aquí yace . . .	Here *lies* . . .

Antojarse, *to take a fancy to*

Se me antojó ese sombrero	I *took a fancy* to that hat

---

[1] Used only in the *third* person *singular*.

CHAPTER 14

IRREGULAR VERBS

§82. The Nature of Irregular Verbs

All verbs not following the conjugation of the models *desear, comer* and *partir* are called irregular.

These irregularities of the Spanish verbs are very simple, consisting for the greatest part in a slight change in the stem. The endings, except in rare cases, are always regular. The irregular verbs are divided into eight classes, besides those of special irregularities which will be dealt with in the table of irregular verbs at the end of this chapter.

§83. Classes of Irregular Verbs

Class 1

Some verbs ending in -*ar* and in -*er* with the vowel *e* in the second last syllable of the infinitive, such as *comenzar* (to start) and *entender* (to understand), change the *e* into *ie* in the singular and the third person plural of the present indicative, subjunctive and imperative.

Class 2

Some verbs ending in -*ar* or in -*er* with the vowel *o* in the second last syllable of the infinitive, such as *rogar* (to pray) and *volver* (to return), change the *o* into *ue* in the same tenses and persons as those of Class 1: in the singular and third person plural of the present indicative, subjunctive and imperative.

Class 3

Verbs ending in -*acer*, -*ecer*, -*ocer* and -*ucir* take a *z* before the *c* of the stem if followed by *a* or *o*, i.e. when the letter *c* takes the sound of *k*. This occurs in the first person of the present indicative, all the persons of the present subjunctive and second person, sing. and pl., of the imperative. Examples of verbs in this class are *complacer* (to please), *pertenecer* (to belong), *conocer* (to know) and *lucir* (to shine).

Class 4

Verbs ending in -*eer*, like *creer* (to believe) and *leer* (to read), change for the sake of euphony the diphthongs *ie* and *io* into *ye* and *yo*.

Class 5

a) Some irregular verbs ending in -*ir*, as *pedir* (to ask for) and *seguir* (to follow), change the *e* of the second last syllable into *i* in the first, second and third persons singular and the third person plural of the present indicative, subjunctive and imperative as well as the preterite and imperfect (both forms) of the subjunctive. The gerund as a rule follows the same irregularity.

b) Verbs ending in -*eir*, such as *reír* (to laugh), *freír* (to fry) and some others, drop the *i* of the irregular stem when the endings also begin with *i*, which is for reasons of euphony.

c) Verbs ending in -*ñir*, as *reñir* (to scold, to quarrel), drop the *i* of the endings in the third persons of the singular and plural of the preterite and all the persons of the 1st and 2nd forms of the imperfect subjunctive.

Class 6

Verbs ending in -*entir*, -*erir* and -*ertir*, as *sentir* (to feel), *herir* (to wound) and *invertir* (to invest), are subject to the irregularities of verbs in Class 1 and 5.

Class 7

The verbs *dormir* (to sleep), *morir* (to die) and their derivatives change the *o* of the stem into *ue* in the same tenses as persons as those of Class 2; with the exception of the first and second persons plural of the present subjunctive and the first person plural of the imperative, which change the *o* of the stem into *u*. This changing of *o* into *u* takes place also in all the past tenses in which the endings begin with the diphthongs *ie* or *io*. Examples: *dormir-durmiendo-dormido; morir-muriendo-muerto*.

Class 8

All verbs ending in -*uir* and -*guir*, as *huir* (to flee) and *arguir* (to argue), belong to this class, and their irregularity consists in that they take *y* after *u* in the present (indicative and subjunctive), the preterite (indicative only), the imperfect subjunctive and the imperative.

§ 84

IRREGULAR VERBS

Infinitive & Participles	Present	Imperfect	INDICATIVE Preterite	Future	Conditional	Imperative	Present	SUBJUNCTIVE Imperfect[1]	Imperfect[2]
1. andar, to go	ando	andaba	anduve	andaré	andaría	anda	ande	anduviese	anduviera
andando pres. p.	andas	andabas	anduviste	andarás	andarías		andes	anduvieses	anduvieras
	anda	andaba	anduvo	andará	andaría		ande	anduviese	anduviera
andado p.p.	andamos	andábamos	anduvimos	andaremos	andaríamos		andemos	anduviésemos	anduviéramo
	andáis	andabais	anduvisteis	andaréis	andaríais		andéis	anduvieseis	anduvierais
	andan	andaban	anduvieron	andarán	andarían	andad	anden	anduviesen	anduvieran
2. caber, to be able, to be contained	quepo	cabía	cupe	cabré	cabría	cabe	quepa	cupiese	cupiera
	cabes	cabías	cupiste	cabrás	cabrías		quepas	cupieses	cupieras
cabiendo	cabe	cabía	cupo	cabrá	cabría	cabed	quepa	cupiese	cupiera
	cabemos	cabíamos	cupimos	cabremos	cabríamos		quepamos	cupiésemos	cupiéramos
cabido	cabéis	cabíais	cupisteis	cabréis	cabríais		quepáis	cupieseis	cupierais
	caben	cabían	cupieron	cabrán	cabrían		quepan	cupiesen	cupieran
3. caer, to fall	caigo	caía	caí	caeré	caería	cae	caiga	cayese	cayera
	caes	caías	caíste	caerás	caerías		caigas	cayeses	cayeras
cayendo	cae	caía	cayó	caerá	caería		caiga	cayese	cayera
	caemos	caíamos	caímos	caeremos	caeríamos	caed	caigamos	cayésemos	cayéramos
caído	caéis	caíais	caísteis	caeréis	caeríais		caigáis	cayeseis	cayerais
	caen	caían	cayeron	caerán	caerían		caigan	cayesen	cayeran
4. dar, to give	doy	daba	di	daré	daría	da	dé	diese	diera
	das	dabas	diste	darás	darías		des	dieses	dieras
dando	da	daba	dió	dará	daría		dé	diese	diera
	damos	dábamos	dimos	daremos	daríamos	dad	demos	diésemos	diéramos
dado	dais	dabais	disteis	daréis	daríais		deis	dieseis	dierais
	dan	daban	dieron	darán	darían		den	diesen	dieran
5. decir to say, to tell	digo	decía	dije	diré	diría	di	digá	dijese	dijera
	dices	decías	dijiste	dirás	dirías		digas	dijeses	dijeras
diciendo	dice	decía	dijo	dirá	diría		diga	dijese	dijera
	decimos	decíamos	dijimos	diremos	diríamos	decid	digamos	dijésemos	dijéramos
dicho	decís	decíais	dijisteis	diréis	diríais		digáis	dijeseis	dijerais
	dicen	decían	dijeron	dirán	dirían		digan	dijesen	dijeran
6. estar, to be (see § 72)									
7. haber, to have (see § 65)									

IRREGULAR VERBS [§298]

8. hacer, to make, to do	hago	hacía	hice	haré	haría	haz	haga	hiciese	hiciera
	haces	hacías	hiciste	harás	harías	haced	hagas	hicieses	hicieras
	hace	hacía	hizo	hará	haría		haga	hiciese	hiciera
	hacemos	hacíamos	hicimos	haremos	haríamos		hagamos	hiciésemos	hiciéramos
	hacéis	hacíais	hicisteis	haréis	haríais		hagáis	hicieseis	hicierais
	hacen	hacían	hicieron	harán	harían		hagan	hiciesen	hicieran
haciendo									
hecho									
9. ir, to go	voy	iba	fui	iré	iría		vaya	fuese	fuera
	vas	ibas	fuiste	irás	irías	ve	vayas	fueses	fueras
	va	iba	fué	irá	iría	id	vaya	fuese	fuera
	vamos	íbamos	fuimos	iremos	iríamos		vayamos	fuésemos	fuéramos
	vais	ibais	fuisteis	iréis	iríais		vayáis	fueseis	fuerais
	van	iban	fueron	irán	irían		vayan	fuesen	fueran
yendo									
ido									
10. oír, to hear	oigo	oía	oí	oiré	oiría		oiga	oyese	oyera
	oyes	oías	oíste	oirás	oirías	oye	oigas	oyeses	oyeras
	oye	oía	oyó	oirá	oiría	oíd	oiga	oyese	oyera
	oímos	oíamos	oímos	oiremos	oiríamos		oigamos	oyésemos	oyéramos
	oís	oíais	oísteis	oiréis	oiríais		oigáis	oyeseis	oyerais
	oyen	oían	oyeron	oirán	oirían		oigan	oyesen	oyeran
oyendo									
oído									
11. poder, to be able	puedo	podía	pude	podré	podría		pueda	pudiese	pudiera
	puedes	podías	pudiste	podrás	podrías		puedas	pudieses	pudieras
	puede	podía	pudo	podrá	podría		pueda	pudiese	pudiera
	podemos	podíamos	pudimos	podremos	podríamos		podamos	pudiésemos	pudiéramos
	podéis	podíais	pudisteis	podréis	podríais		podáis	pudieseis	pudierais
	pueden	podían	pudieron	podrán	podrían		puedan	pudiesen	pudieran
pudiendo									
podido									
12. poner, to put	pongo	ponía	puse	pondré	pondría	pon	ponga	pusiese	pusiera
	pones	ponías	pusiste	pondrás	pondrías	poned	pongas	pusieses	pusieras
	pone	ponía	puso	pondrá	pondría		ponga	pusiese	pusiera
	ponemos	poníamos	pusimos	pondremos	pondríamos		pongamos	pusiésemos	pusiéramos
	ponéis	poníais	pusisteis	pondréis	pondríais		pongáis	pusieseis	pusierais
	ponen	ponían	pusieron	pondrán	pondrían		pongan	pusiesen	pusieran
poniendo									
puesto									
13. querer, to want	quiero	quería	quise	querré	querría	quiere	quiera	quisiese	quisiera
	quieres	querías	quisiste	querrás	querrías	quered	quieras	quisieses	quisieras
	quiere	quería	quiso	querrá	querría		quiera	quisiese	quisiera
	queremos	queríamos	quisimos	querremos	querríamos		queramos	quisiésemos	quisiéramos
	queréis	queríais	quisisteis	querréis	querríais		queráis	quisieseis	quisierais
	quieren	querían	quisieron	querrán	querrían		quieran	quisiesen	quisieran
queriendo									
querido									
14. saber, to know	sé	sabía	supe	sabré	sabría		sepa	supiese	supiera
	sabes	sabías	supiste	sabrás	sabrías	sabe	sepas	supieses	supieras
	sabe	sabía	supo	sabrá	sabría	sabed	sepa	supiese	supiera
	sabemos	sabíamos	supimos	sabremos	sabríamos		sepamos	supiésemos	supiéramos
	sabéis	sabíais	supisteis	sabréis	sabríais		sepáis	supieseis	supierais
	saben	sabían	supieron	sabrán	sabrían		sepan	supiesen	supieran
sabiendo									
sabedo									

Infinitive / Participles	Present Indicative	Imperfect Indicative	Preterite	Future	Conditional	Imperative	Present Subjunctive	Imperfect Subj. (-se)	Imperfect Subj. (-ra)
25. salir, to go out	salgo	salía	salí	saldré	saldría		salga	saliese	saliera
saliendo	sales	salías	saliste	saldrás	saldrías	sal	salgas	salieses	salieras
salido	sale	salía	salió	saldrá	saldría		salga	saliese	saliera
	salimos	salíamos	salimos	saldremos	saldríamos		salgamos	saliésemos	saliéramos
	salís	salíais	salisteis	saldréis	saldríais	salid	salgáis	salieseis	salierais
	salen	salían	salieron	saldrán	saldrían		salgan	saliesen	salieran
16. ser, to be (see § 70)									
17. tener, to have (see § 68)									
18. traducir, to translate	traduzco	traducía	traduje	traduciré	traduciría		traduzca	tradujese	tradujera
traduciendo	traduces	traducías	tradujiste	traducirás	traducirías	tra-duce	traduzcas	tradujeses	tradujeras
traducido	traduce	traducía	tradujo	traducirá	traduciría	tradu-cid	traduzca	tradujese	tradujera
	traducimos	traducíamos	tradujimos	traduciremos	traduciríamos		traduzca-mos	tradujésemos	tradujéramos
	traducís	traducíais	tradujisteis	traduciréis	traduciríais		traduzcáis	tradujeseis	tradujerais
	traducen	traducían	tradujeron	traducirán	traducirían		traduzcan	tradujesen	tradujeran
19. traer, to bring	traigo	traía	traje	traeré	traería		traiga	trajese	trajera
trayendo	traes	traías	trajiste	traerás	traerías	trae	traigas	trajeses	trajeras
traído	trae	traía	trajo	traerá	traería	traed	traiga	trajese	trajera
	traemos	traíamos	trajimos	traeremos	traeríamos		traigamos	trajésemos	trajéramos
	traéis	traíais	trajisteis	traeréis	traeríais		traigáis	trajeseis	trajerais
	traen	traían	trajeron	traerán	traerían		traigan	trajesen	trajeran
20. valer, to be worth	valgo	valía	valí	valdré	valdría	val(e)	valga	valiese	valiera
valiendo	vales	valías	valiste	valdrás	valdrías	valed	valgas	valieses	valieras
valido	vale	valía	valió	valdrá	valdría		valga	valiese	valiera
	valemos	valíamos	valimos	valdremos	valdríamos		valgamos	valiésemos	valiéramos
	valéis	valíais	valisteis	valdréis	valdríais		valgáis	valieseis	valierais
	valen	valían	valieron	valdrán	valdrían		valgan	valiesen	valieran
21. venir, to come	vengo	venía	vine	vendré	vendría		venga	viniese	viniera
viniendo	vienes	venías	viniste	vendrás	vendrías	ven	vengas	vinieses	vinieras
venido	viene	venía	vino	vendrá	vendría	venid	venga	viniese	viniera
	venimos	veníamos	vinimos	vendremos	vendríamos		vengamos	viniésemos	viniéramos
	venís	veníais	vinisteis	vendréis	vendríais		vengáis	vinieseis	vinierais
	vienen	venían	vinieron	vendrán	vendrían		vengan	viniesen	vinieran
22. ver, to see	veo	veía	vi	veré	vería	ve	vea	viese	viera
viendo	ves	veías	viste	verás	verías	ved	veas	vieses	vieras
visto	ve	veía	vio	verá	vería		vea	viese	viera
	vemos	veíamos	vimos	veremos	veríamos		veamos	viésemos	viéramos
	veis	veíais	visteis	veréis	veríais		veáis	vieseis	vierais
	ven	veían	vieron	verán	verían		vean	viesen	vieran

MODELOS PARA CORRESPONDENCIA

BEGINNINGS OF BUSINESS LETTERS

LIMA, Julio 15, 1942[1]

1

Sr. Don Juan Castaño,
                    Nueva York
    Muy señor mío:[2]

2

BARCELONA, 15 de Julio de 1942[1]

Sres. Don Juan Castaño y Cía.,
                            Londres
    Muy señores míos:[2]

3

NUEVA YORK, Junio 15, 1942

Sr. Don Juan Castaño,
                    Madrid
    Muy señor nuestro:

4

CARACAS, Mayo15, 1942

Sres. Don Juan Castaño y Cía.,
                            Madrid
    Muy señores nuestros:

5

SEVILLA, Agosto 30, 1942

Sra. Doña María Godínez,
                    Madrid
    Muy señora mía:

1 Las cartas pueden ser fechadas como en el primero o segundo ejemplo.
2 *Mío* es singular, y por lo tanto el que firma es una sola persona. También se puede decir, "*Mi estimado señor.*" Si ya ha mediado alguna correspondencia, o se conoce personalmente al sujeto, puede decirse: "*Muy señor mío amigo,*" o *Estimado señor y amigo,* etc. Lo mismo en plural.

ENDINGS OF BUSINESS LETTERS

1

Quedo[3] (*or* soy) de Vd. (*or* Vds.) atto.[4] (*or* attos.[4]) y S.S.[5] Q.B.S.M.[6]

3 *Quedo,* I remain.
4 *Atto,* es la abreviatura de *atento,* y *attos,* la de *atentos* (pl.).
5 S. S., son abreviaturas de *seguro servidor* (*sure servant*), o equivalente en inglés a *humble servant* o *yours truly.*
6 Q. (que), B. (besa), S. (su). M. (mano), es una fórmula de respeto que puede suprimirse si se quiere, aunque es bastante usada. Dirigiéndose a una señora o señorita se dice: Q. (que), B. (besa), S. (sus), P. (pies).

2
Me repito de Vd. atto, S.S.

José Morales

3
Nos. repetimos de Vds. attos. S. S.

José Morales e hijos

4
Aprovechamos esta oportunidad para ofrecernos de Vds. attos, S. S.

José Morales y hermanos

EXAMPLE OF A BUSINESS LETTER

LONDON, 10 de Mayo de 1942

Sres. Don Rafael Careaga y Cía.,

Madrid, España

Muy Sres. nuestros:

Confirmamos[7] ntra.[8] anterior última 2 del corriente, según la inclusa copia de prensa, y ha llegado a´ntro. poder su grata[9] de Vds., fha. 29 del ppdo., cuyo contenido hemos anotado de conformidad.

Les agradecemos el nuevo pedido que, por varios artículos, se sirven Vds. confiarnos, los cuales embarcaremos a la primera oportunidad, de acuerdo con sus instrucciones.

Sin otro particular, esperamos sus nuevas órdenes y quedamos, como siempre, de Vds., attos. y S. S.

Antonio Vargas y Cía.

SOCIAL LETTERS

(A GENTLEMAN TO A YOUNG LADY OR LADY)

1

CADIZ, Setiembre 3, 1942[10]

Srta. (or Sra.) Da. Carmen Molina.

Señorita (or Señora): (or Distinguida, or Estimada señorita or señora).

. . . .

Quedo a los pp. (pies) de Vd. atto. y

S. S.

7 *Confirmar*, to confirm. *Ultima*, last. *Corriente*, current. *Según*, as per. *Inclusa*, inclosed. *Copia*, copy. *Prensa*, press. *Poder*, power. *Grata*, favour. *Contenido*, contents. *Anotar*, to make a note of, to note.

De conformidad, in conformity. *El pedido*, the order. *El artículo*, the article. *Confiar*, to confide. *Embarcar*, to ship. *De acuerdo con*, in accordance with.

8 Las siguientes abreviaturas son muy usuales: nuestro, etc., *ntro.*, *ntra.*, *ntros.*, *ntras.*; fecha, *fha.*; próximo pasado, *ppdo.*; corriente, *cte.*; primera, 1ª; siempre, *spre.*, etc.

9 *Grata*, *gta.*, sinónimo de estimada, apreciable, *apble.*

10 La Fecha se puede colocar al principio y a la derecha de la primera página de una carta, o al fin y a la izquierda.

or,
Quedo de Vd. atto. y S. S.

Q. B. S. P.

2

Sra. Da. Isabel Serrano.
Muy señora mía: (*or* Distinguida, etc., señora).

3
(FROM ONE LADY TO ANOTHER)
Mi apreciable (querida, estimada, etc.) señora (*or* señorita).

Soy de Vd. (*or* tuya) afma. (afectísima), *or* atta. S. S.

4
(A YOUNG LADY TO A YOUNG MAN)
Señor Don José M. Martínez.
Muy Sr. mío: (*or* estimado, apreciable, etc., señor).

Quedo de Vd. atta. S. S.

Q. B. S. M.

SEVILLA, Abril 3, 1942
or,
Soy de Vd. respetuosamente (*or* sinceramente, *or* afma).

5
(BETWEEN FRIENDS)
Querido amigo:[11] (*or* amigo Ramírez).

Quedo suyo (*or* de Vd., *or* tuyo) afmo. (afectísimo).

---

11 Cuando se escribe a los padres o hermanos, el final de la carta debe estar de acuerdo con el principio; así se dirá. *Mi querido padre,* etc., o *querido papá,* etc. *Tu amante hijo,* etc. *Tu afmo. hermano,* etc.

APPENDIX

LA FAMILIA

El abuelo, the grandfather	**La abuela,** the grandmother
El bisabuelo, the great-grand-father	**La bisabuela,** the great-grandmother
El nieto, the grandson	**La nieta,** the granddaughter
El biznieto, the great-grandson	**La biznieta,** the great-granddaughter
El padrastro, the step-father	**La madrastra,** the step-mother
El hijastro, the step-son	**La hijastra,** the step-daughter
El tío, the uncle	**La tía** the aunt
El sobrino, the nephew	**La sobrina,** the niece
Los primos, the cousins (male)	**Las primas,** the cousins (females)
Primo hermano, first cousin	**Prima hermana,** first cousin
El cuñado, the brother-in-law	**La cuñada,** the sister-in-law
El yerno, the son-in-law	**La nuera,** the daughter-in-law
El padrino, the godfather	**La madrina,** the godmother
El ahijado, the godson	**La ahijada,** the goddaughter
El suegro, the father-in-law	**La suegra,** the mother-in-law

FESTIVIDADES DEL AÑO[1]

Noche Buena[2] (*noh'chay bway'nah*)	Christmas Eve
Navidad[3] or **Natividad** (*nah-vee-dahd'*)	Christmas
Víspera de Año Nuevo (*vees'pay-rah*)	New Year's Eve
El día de Año Nuevo (*ah'nioh nway'voh*)	New Year's Day
Día de Fiesta (. . . *fee-ays'tah*)	Holiday
Día de Ayuno (. . . *ah-yoo'noh*)	Fast day
Miércoles de Ceniza (*mee-ayrr'koh-lays*)	Ash Wednesday
Carnaval (*kahrr-nah-vahl'*)	Carnival
Cuaresma[4] (*kwah-rays'mah*)	Lent
Semana Santa (. . . *sahn'tah*)	Holy Week
Viernes Santo (*vee-ayrr'nays* . . .)	Good Friday
Sábado de Gloria (. . . *gloh'ree-ah*)	Holy Saturday
Pascua de Resurrección (*pahs'kwah* . . .)	Easter Sunday

1 *Festivities of the year.*
2 *Noche Buena,* lit., night good.
3 *Navidad* is a contraction of *Natividad,* the former is more often used than the latter.
4 *Cuaresma,* from Lat. *quadragesima* (fortieth), *the forty days of Lent.*

COUNTRIES OF THE WORLD

País	*Country*	*Nationality*
Europa	Europe	*El europeo*
Alemania	Germany	„ *alemán*
Bélgica	Belgium	„ *belga*
Bulgaria	Bulgaria	„ *búlgaro*
Dinamarca	Denmark	„ *dinamarqués*
España	Spain	„ *español*
Finlandia	Finland	„ *finlandés*
Francia	France	„ *francés*
Grecia	Greece	„ *griego*
Holanda	Holland	„ *holandés*
Hungría	Hungary	„ *húngaro*
Inglaterra	England	„ *inglés*
Escocia	Scotland	„ *escocés*
Gales	Wales	„ *galés*
Irlanda	Ireland	„ *irlandés*
Italia	Italy	„ *italiano*
Noruega	Norway	„ *noruego*
Portugal	Portugal	„ *portugués*
Rumanía	Rumania	„ *rumano*
Rusia	Russia	„ *ruso*
Suiza	Switzerland	„ *suizo*
Suecia	Sweden	„ *sueco*
Turquía	Turkey	„ *turco*
Yugoeslavia	Yugoslavia	„ *yugoeslavo*
Norte América	North America	„ *norteamericano*
Canadá	Canada	„ *canadiense*
Estados Unidas	United States	„ *estadounidense*
Méjico	Mexico	„ *mejicano*
América del Sur	South America	*el sudamericano*
La Argentina	Argentina	„ *argentino*
Bolivia	Bolivia	„ *boliviano*
El Brasil	Brazil	„ *brasileno*
Colombia	Columbia	„ *colombiano*
Chile	Chile	„ *chileno*
El Ecuador	Ecuador	„ *ecuatoriano*
El Paraguay	Paraguay	„ *paraguayo*
El Perú	Peru	„ *peruano*
Uruguay	Uruguay	„ *uruguayo*
Venezuela	Venezuela	„ *venezolano*
Centro América	Central America	*el centroamericano*
Costa Rica	Costa Rica	„ *costarricense*

Guatemala	Guatemala	„ guatemalteco
Honduras	Honduras	„ hondureño
Nicaragua	Nicaragua	„ nicaraguense
Panamá	Panama	„ panameño
El Salvador	El Salvador	„ salvadoreño

Antillas	West Indies	„ antillano
Cuba	Cuba	„ cubano
Haití	Haiti	„ haitiano
Jamaica	Jamaica	„ jamaicano
Puerto Rico	Puerto Rico	„ puertorriqueño
Rep. Dominicana	Dominican Rep.	„ dominicano

Asia	Asia	„ asiático
Arabia	Arabia	„ árabe
China	China	„ chino
Japón	Japan	„ japonés
India	India	„ hindú, indio

LOS COLORES

Amarillo	Yellow	Bermellón	Vermilion
Naranja	Orange	Carmín	Carmine
Azul	Blue	Rosado o rosa	Pink
Azul claro	Pale Blue	Encarnado	Flesh-colour
Azul oscuro	Dark Blue	Morado	Purple
Ultramarino	Ultramarine	Lila	Lilac
Blanco	White	Negro	Black
Castaño	Brown	Verde	Green
Gris	Grey	Verde esmeralda	Emerald green
Colorado o rojo	Red	Verde olivo	Olive green

EL HOGAR Y SUS ACCESORIOS[1]

La chimenea, el fogón.................the chimney, the fireplace
Un fósforo, una cerilla.................a match
La lumbre (*loom'bray*) .... }
El fuego (*fway'goh*) .... } the fire
El carbón[2] (*kahrr-bohn'*).............................. }
El carbón de piedra .... } coal
La leña[3] (*lay'nyah*).....................................fire-wood
La ceniza (*thay-nee'thah*) ....ashes
La llama (*lliah'mah*) ....flame

1 *The fireplace and its appurtenances.*
2 *Carbón* refers generally to *charcoal*, while *carbón de piedra* (lit., *coal of stone*) is rendered by *coal*.
3 There are two different names for *wood* in Spanish: *leña* means *firewood*, while *madera* signifies all kinds of wood for manufacturing purposes. *Board* is rendered by *tabla.*

Las ascuas (*ahs'kwahs*) .... live coals
Las tenazas .... tongs
El humo⁴ (*oo'moh*) .... smoke
El gas⁵ (*gahs*) .... gas

EL CAMPO Y EL MAR

Un bosque, un desierto .... a forest, a desert
Una zanja, un prado .... a ditch, a meadow
Una colina, una montaña .... a hill, a mountain
Un valle, una llanura .... a valley, a plain
El tronco de un árbol. .... the trunk of a tree
Una rama, las hojas .... a branch, the leaves
Una raíz, la simiente .... a root, the seed
Hierba or yerba, un campo .... grass, a field
Un manantial, un arroyo .... a spring, a brook
Un río, un lago, un estanque .... a river, a lake, a pond
Una laguna, un pantano .... a swamp, a marsh
Un golfo, un estrecho, un canal .... a gulf, a straight, a canal
El mar, la orilla, la bahía. .... the sea, the shore, the bay
La playa, el balneario .... the beach, bathing resort
La calma, la tormenta. .... the calm, the storm
Un buque mercante, de guerra.. ...... a merchant ship, a man-of-war
Las anclas, los palos .... the anchors, the masts
Las velas, las banderas .... the sails, the flags
El piloto, el práctico. .... the helmsman, the pilot
Los oficiales, los marineros .... the officers, the sailors
El camarote, el puente .... the cabin, the bridge
La cubierta, proa, popa. .... the deck, bow, stern
Babor, estribor .... port, starboard
La bodega .... the hold

EL CUERPO HUMANO

El cuerpo, la cabeza .... the body, the head
Los miembros .... the limbs, the members
Las piernas, los brazos .... the legs, the arms
El codo, el puño .... the elbow, the fist
La mano, los dedos .... the hand, the fingers
El dedo pulgar, el índice .... the thumb, the index
El medio, el anular .... the middle, the ring
El meñique (or pequeño). .... the little finger

4. Though *humo* stands for *smoke*, the verb *to smoke* is *fumar*, regular verb of the first conjugation.

5 Nouns ending in *s* are masculine, with the exceptions of *la tos*, the cough; *la bilis*, the bile; *la tisis*, the phthisis, consumption; and all such nouns derived from the Greek. *Cutis* (skin), of human beings, and *análisis* (analysis) are either masculine or feminine.

Los dedos del pie .... the toes
La mano derecha (izquierda) .... the right (left) hand
Las uñas, el cabello or el pelo .... the nails, the hair
La frente, las sienes .... the forehead, the temples
La cara, las facciones .... the face, the features
Los ojos, los párpados................. the eyes, the eyelids
Las cejas, las orejas .... the eyebrows, the ears
La nariz, las mejillas .... the nose, the cheeks
La boca, los labios .... the mouth, the lips
Los dientes, las muelas................ the teeth, the molar teeth
La lengua, el paladar .... the tongue, the palate
La barba, las pestañas .... the chin (the beard), eyelashes
El bigote, las patillas .... the moustache, the whiskers
La garganta, el cuello .... the throat, the neck
La espalda, los hombros .... the back, the shoulders
El pecho, el seno .... the chest, the bosom
Las costillas, el costado .... the ribs, the side
Los pulmones, los nervios .... the lungs, the nerves
El estómago, los intestinos .... the stomach, the bowels
El hígado, el corazón .... the liver, the heart
El pellejo, la piel, el cutis .... the skin
Los huesos, un tendón .... the bones, a sinew
Las venas, la sangre.................. the veins, the blood
El pulso, el sudor .... the pulse, the perspiration
El aliento, la voz .... the breath, the voice
Las rodillas, el talón .... the knees, the heel

LOS SENTIDOS Y LAS SENSACIONES CORPORALES

La vista, el oído .... the sight, the hearing
El olfato, el gusto, el tacto .... the smell, the taste, the touch
El juicio, la razón[1] .... the judgment, the reason
La imaginación,[1] el pensamiento....... the imagination, the thought
La voluntad, el deseo .... the will, the desire
La esperanza .... the hope
La memoria, la idea.................. the memory, the idea
El gozo, el placer .... the joy, the pleasure
El amor, el odio .... the love, the hatred
Los celos, el genio .... the jealousy, the temper or genius
El carácter, la digestion[1] .... the character, the digestion
Un suspiro, un quejido .... a sigh, a groan
Un grito, un estornudo .... a scream, a sneeze
Un bostezo, hipo .... a yawn, hiccough
Los sollozos, una lágrima .... the sobs, a tear
El ronquido, roncar .... the snoring, to snore
La risa, una carcajada................ the laughter, a bust of laughter

[1] The greater part of English nouns ending in *tion* are rendered in Spanish by changing the letter *t* to *c*; as, *station, approbation, education*, etc., which become *estación, aprobación, educación*, etc. Nouns ending in *n* are masculine, but those in *ión* are feminine and all abstract nouns in *on*; as, *la razón* (the reason), etc., besides *la clin* or *crin* (the horse-hair).

La enfermedad,[2] la debilidad ....the sickness, the weakness
Las arrugas, la robustez[3] ....the wrinkles, the robustness
La salud, la vejez,[3] la juventud........the health, the old age, the youth
La adolescencia, la niñez ....the adolescence, the childhood
La hermosura, la fealdad ....the beauty, the ugliness
El hambre,[4] la sed ....the hunger, the thirst

LA AGRICULTURA

Un hortelano, un trabajador ....a farmer, a workman
El jornal ....the wages (for farmers)
La hoz, una pala ....the sickle, a shovel
El arado, un adazón, el látigo ....the plough, a hoe, the whip
El carretero, un carro ....the cart-driver, the cart
La cosecha, el grano..................the harvest, the grain
Una espiga de trigo ....an ear of wheat
El heno, la paja ....the hay, the straw
Centeno, avena, cebada ....rye, oats, barley
Una mazorca de maíz ....a corn-cob
Algodón en rama.....................raw cotton

LA GRANJA

La huerta ....the orchard
Un jardín, una planta ....a garden, a plant
Sembrar, la siembra ....to sow, the sowing

LOS ARBOLES

Un limonero, naranjo ....a lemon-tree, orange-tree
Un moral, cerezo....................a mulberry-tree, cherry-tree
Un ciruelo, melocotonero ....a plum-tree, peach-tree
Un manzano, peral ....an apple-tree, pear-tree
Una higuera, una palma ....a fig-tree, a palm-tree
Un nogal, un castaño ....a walnut-tree, chestnut-tree
Un olivo, un almendro ....an olive-tree, almond-tree
Un roble, un fresno ....an oak-tree, an ash-tree
Un olmo, un laurel ....an elm-tree, a laurel-tree
Un cedro, un pino ....a cedar-tree, a pine-tree

LAS FRUTAS

Limón, naranja, mora, cereza ....lemon, orange, mulberry, cherry
Ciruela, melocotón, manzana ....plum, peach, apple

2 Nouns ending in d are feminine with the exceptions of el huésped, el laúd, etc.
3 To form the plural of words ending in z, change z to c and add es as, for instance,
    The plural of pez, fish, is peces;
    The plural of juez, judge, is jueces;
    The plural of vez, time, is veces.
4 Hambre, hunger, is feminine. All feminine nouns beginning with a long a or ha take the masculine article el instead of the feminine la for the sake of euphony; as, el agua, el hambre.

Higo, dátil, pera	fig, date, pear
Nuez, castaña, almendra	nut, chestnut, almond
Albaricoque.........................	apricot
Grosella, plátano, aceituna	currant, banana, olive
Uva, uva espina, pasa	grape, gooseberry, raisin
Frambuesa, fresa	raspberry, strawberry
Melón, sandía	melon, water-melon
Piña, avellana	pineapple, hazelnut

LAS LEGUMBRES

La patata or **papa, batata**	the potato, sweet potato
Col, lechuga, cebollas	cabbage, lettuce, onions
Alcachofa or **alcaucil**	artichoke
Rábanos, nabos, pepino	radishes, turnips, cucumber
La zanahoria........................	carrot
Espinaca, coliflor	spinach, cauliflower
Espárragos, apio, calabaza	asparagus, celery, pumpkin
Setas, remolachas	mushrooms, beets
Guisantes, lentejas	peas, lentils
Habichuelas or **frijoles**	beans

LAS FLORES

La rosa	Rose	**El jazmín**	Jasmine
El capullo	Rosebud	**La camelia**	Camellia
La violeta	Violet	**La magnolia**	Magnolia
El mirto	Myrtle	**La pasionaria**	Passion flower
La azucena	White lily	**La madreselva**	Honeysuckle
El lirio de mayo	Lily-of-the-valley	**La margarita**	Daisy
El nomeolvides	Forget-me-not	**La dalia**	Dahlia
El pensamiento	Pansy	**El jacinto**	Hyacinth
La amapola	Poppy	**El tulipán**	Tulip
El clavel	Carnation	**El azahar**	Orange blossom
La orquídea	Orchid	**El heliotropo**	Heliotrope

LOS CUADRUPEDOS

El caballo, la yegua	the horse, the mare
El burro, el cerdo	the donkey, the pig
La vaca, la ternera	the cow, the calf
El buey, el toro	the ox, the bull
El becerro, el carnero	the calf, the ram
La oveja, el cordero	the sheep, the lamb
El perro, el gato......................	the dog, the cat
El ciervo, la cabra	the deer, the goat
La llama, la vicuña....................	the llama, the vicuña
La mula, la ardilla	the mule, the squirrel
La liebre, el conejo	the hare, the rabbit
La rata, el ratón	the rat, the mouse
El león, el tigre	the lion, the tiger

El elefante, la hiena .... the elephant, the hyena
El leopardo, la pantera .... the leopard, the panther
La jirafa, el camello .... the giraffe, the camel
El hipopótamo, el lobo .... the hippopotamus, the wolf
El rinoceronte, la zorra............... the rhinoceros, the fox
El cocodrilo, la serpiente .... the crocodile, the serpent
El oso, el jabalí[1]..................... the bear, the boar
La foca, el mono .... the seal, the monkey
El gorila, el orangután .... gorilla, the orang-outang
La víbora, el alacrán .... the viper, the scorpion
El topo, la onza .... the mole, the snow leopard

LAS AVES

El gallo, la gallina .... the cock, the hen
El pato, el ganso .... the duck, the goose
El pavo, la paloma .... the turkey, the dove
El pavo real, el loro .... the peacock, the parrot
El cuervo, la alondra .... the raven, the lark
La gaviota, el gorrión .... the sea-gull, the sparrow
El águila, el avestruz .... the eagle, the ostrich
El canario, la golondrina .... the canary, the swallow
La tórtola, la perdíz .... the turtle-dove, the partridge

AJETIVOS NUMERALES
NUMEROS CARDINALES

0	cero	300	trescientos, etc.
1	uno	500	quinientos
10	diez	600	seiscientos
20	veinte	700	setecientos
21	veintiuno	750	setecientos
22	veintidós		cincuenta, etc.
23	veintitrés	800	ochocientos
24	veinticuatro	831	ochocientos treinta
25	veinticinco		y uno
26	veintiséis	900	novecientos
27	veintisiete	915	novecientos quince
28	veintiocho	925	novecientos
29	veintinueve		veinticinco
30	treinta	930	novecientos treinta
31	treinta y uno	931	novecientos treinta
32	treinta y dos, etc.		y uno
40	cuarenta	999	novecientos noventa
41	cuarenta y uno		y nueve
42	cuarenta y dos, etc.	1,000	mil
50	cincuenta	1,200	mil doscientos
51	cincuenta y uno, etc.	2,000	dos mil

1 Nouns ending in *i* are masculine, with the exception of all those derived from the Greek, such as *la diócesi* (the diocese); *la metrópoli* (the metropolis), etc.

60	sesenta		2,001	dos mil uno
61	sesenta y uno, etc.		3,000	tres mil
70	setenta		4,500	cuatro mil
71	setenta y uno, etc.			quinientos
80	ochenta		5,000	cinco mil
81	ochenta y uno, etc.		5,130	cinco mil ciento
90	noventa			treinta
91	noventa y uno, etc.		10,000	diez mil
100	ciento		40,000	cuarenta mil
101	ciento uno, etc.		90,000	noventa mil
120	ciento veinte		100,000	cien mil
121	ciento veintiuno, etc.		200,000	doscientos mil
130	ciento treinta, etc.		500,000	quinientos mil
141	ciento cuarenta y		500,001	quinientos mil uno,
	uno, etc.			etc.
200	doscientos		1,000,000	un millón

NUMEROS ORDINALES[1]

1o[2]	1a[2]	Primero,[3] -ra[3] (pree-may'roh, -rah)	1st
2o	2a	Segundo, -da (say-goon'doh, -dah)	2nd
3o	3a	Tercero,[3] -ra (tair-thay'roh, -rah)	3rd
4o	4a	Cuarto, -ta (kwahr'toh, -tah)	4th
5o	5a	Quinto, -ta (keen'toh, -tah)	5th
6o	6a	Sexto, -ta (sayks'toh, -tah)	6th
7o	7a	Séptimo, -ma (sayp'tee-moh, -mah)	7th
8o	8a	Octavo, -va (ohk-tah'voh, -vah)	8th
9o	9a	Noveno, -na or nono, -na (no-vay'noh, -nah)	9th
10o	10a	Décimo, -ma (day'thee-moh, -mah)	10th
11o	11a	Undécimo, -ma (oon-day'thee-moh, -mah)	11th
12o	12a	Duodécimo, -ma (dwoh-day'thee-moh, -mah)	12th
13o	13a	Decimotercio, -cia (day'moh-tair'thee-oh, -ah)	13th
14o	14a	Decimocuarto, -ta (day'thee-moh-kwahr'toh, -tah)	14th
15o	13a	Decimoquinto, -ta (day'thee-moh-keen'toh, -tah)	15th
16o	16a	Decimosexto, -ta (day'thee-moh-seks'toh, -tah)	16th
17o	17a	Decimoséptimo, -ma (day'thee-moh-sayp'tee-moh)	17th
18o	18a	Decimoctavo, -va (day'thee-mohk-tah'voh, -vah)	18th
19o	19a	Decimonono, -na or décimonoveno, -na	19th
20o	20a	Vigésimo, -ma (vee-hay'see-moh, -mah)	20th
21o	21a	Vigésimo primero, -ra, etc.	21st
30o	30a	Trigésimo, -ma, etc. (tree-hay'see-moh, -mah)	30th
40o	40a	Cuadragésimo, -ma, etc. (kwah-drah-hay'see-moh)	40th
50o	50a	Quincuagésimo, -ma, etc. (keen-kwah-hay'see-moh)	50th
60o	60a	Sexagésimo, -ma, etc. (sayk-sah-hay'see-moh, -mah)	60th
70o	71a	Septuagésimo, -ma, etc. (sayp-twah-hay'see-moh, -mah)	70th
80o	80a	Octogésimo, -ma, etc. (ohk-toh-hay'see-moh, -mah)	80th

1 Los números ordinales no se usan en español tanto como en inglés, empleándose los cardinales en su lugar a partir del *duodécimo*. Para los días del mes se usan siempre los números cardinales, a excepción del *primero*.

2 En estas dos columnas se ponen las abreviaturas masculina y femenina.

3 El cambio de *o* en *a*, en la desinencia, forma el femenino, como: *primera* casa. *Primero, tercero* y *postrero* pierden la *o* final delante de un nombre masculino singular.

900	90ª	Nonagésimo, -ma, etc. (*noh'nah-hay'see-moh, -mah*)	90th
1000	100ª	Centésimo, -ma, etc. (*thain-tay'see-moh, -mah*)	100th
2000	200ª	Ducentésimo, -ma, etc. (*doo-thain-tay'see-moh, -ma*)	200th
3000	300ª	Tricentésimo, -ma, etc. (*tree-thain-tay'see-moh, -ma*)	300th
4000	400ª	Cuadragentésimo, -ma, etc. (*kwah-drah-hain . . .*)	400th
5000	500ª	Quingentésimo, -ma, etc. (*keen-hain . . .*)	500th
6000	600ª	Sexcentésimo, -ma, etc. (*sayks-thain-tay'see-moh, -mah*)	600th
7000	700ª	Septegentésimo, -ma, etc. (*sayp-tay-hain-tay'see-moh*)	700th
8000	800ª	Octogentésimo, -ma, etc. (*ohk-toh-hain-tay'see-moh*)	800th
9000	900ª	Nonagentésimo, -ma, etc. (*no-nah-hain-tay'see-moh*)	900th
1,0000	1,000ª	Milésimo, -ma, etc. (*mee-lay'see-moh, -mah*)	1,000th
10,0000	10,000ª	Diezmilésimo, -ma, etc.	10,000th
1,000,0000	1,000,000ª	Millonésimo, -ma, etc.	1,000,000th

Ultimo, -ma, or postero, -ra (*pohs-tray'roh, -rah*)   last

NUMEROS FRACCIONARIOS

La mitad[4] (*mee-tahd'*) ....the half
Un medio (*may'dee-oh*) ....one half
Un tercio (*tair'thee-oh*)............................one third
Dos tercios ....two thirds
Un cuarto..one quarter
Tres cuartos ....three quarters
Un quinto (*keen'toh*) ....one fifth
Un décimo (*day'thee-moh*) ....one tenth
Un undécimo (*oon-day'thee-moh*) ....one eleventh
Un dozavo[5] (*doh-thah'voh*) ....one twelfth
Un trezavo (*tray-thah'voh*).......................one thirteenth
Un catorzavo (*kah-tohrr-tha'voh*) ....one fourteenth
Un quinzavo (*keen-thah'voh*) ....one fifteenth
Un dieciseisavo (*deeay'thie-sayee-sah'voh*) ....one sixteenth
Un dieciochavo (*deeay'thie-oh-chah'voh*) ....one eighteenth
Un veintavo (*vay'een-tah'voh*) ....one twentieth
Un treintavo (*tray'een-tah'voh*) ....one thirtieth
Un centavo (*thayn-tah'voh*) ....one hundredth, one cent
Un milavo ....one thousandth

NUMEROS COLECTIVOS

Un par (*parr*) ....a pair, couple
Una decena (*day-thay'nah*) ....a number of ten
Una docena (*doh-thay'nah*) ....a dozen
Una quincena (*keem-thay'nah*) ....a number of fifteen
Una veintena.................................a score
Una centena ....a number of hundred
Un millar (*mee-lliahrr'*) ....a number of thousand

4 *Mitad* es sinónimo de *medio*, pero aquél es un nombre y éste un adjetivo. *Medio* y las otras fracciones toman la forma femenina refiriéndose a medidas, como: *media libra; una cuarta* (de vara) de paño.

5 En los números fraccionarios, la partícula *avo* corresponde a la *th* de los fraccionarios ingleses, y es declinable: *avo* (masc.), *ava* (fem.); *avos* (masc. pl.), y *avas* (fem, pl.).

ADJETIVOS MULTIPLES Y DE REPETICION

Simple (*seem'play*)	single
Doble (*doh'blay*)	double
Triple (*tree'play*)	treble
Cuádruplo or **cuádruple**	quadruple
Quíntuplo or **quíntuple**	quintuple
Séxtuplo or **séxtuple**	sextuple
Séptuplo or **séptuple**	septuple
Octuplo or **óctuple**	octuple
Nónuplo or **nónuple**	nonuple
Décuplo or **décuple**	decuple
Céntuplo	centuple
Una vez (*vayth'*)	once
Dos veces (*vay'thays*)	twice
Tres veces, etc.	three times, etc.
Cien veces	one hundred times
Un millón de veces	one million times
Esta vez	this time
Otra vez	another time
Cada vez	each time
Aquella vez	that time
Esta, aquella y la otra vez	this, that, and the other time
Rara vez	seldom
La primera vez	the first time
La última vez **La postera vez**	} the last time
La próxima vez	the next time
Algunas veces	sometimes
Varias veces	several times
Muchas veces	many times
Pocas veces	few times
Todas las veces	all times
A menudo	often

ADVERBIOS DE TIEMPO[1]

¿Cuándo? ¿desde cuándo?	when? since when?
¿Hasta cuándo?	till when? how long?
Hoy, ayer	today, yesterday
Anteayer or **antes de ayer**	day before yesterday
Mañana pasado mañana	to-morrow, day after to-morrow
Al amanecer, de madrugada	at daybreak
Anoche	last night
Al anochecer	at nightfall
Ahora, luego	now, afterward
Al instante, inmediatamente	instantly, immediately

[1] *Adverbs of time.*

S.C.

21

De repente, de pronto	suddenly
De prisa	in a hurry (hurriedly)
Siempre	always
Ya, todavía	already, yet
Nunca, jamás	never
Entonces	then
Antes, después	before, afterward
Al fin, en fin	at last, finally
A menudo	often

ADVERBIOS DE DUDA[2]

Quizá ⎫		**Acaso** ⎫	
Quizás ⎬ Perhaps		**Por ventura** ⎬ Perhaps	
Tal vez ⎭		**¿No es verdad?** ⎫ Is it not so?	
¿Es verdad?	Is it true?	**¿No es así?** ⎭	
¿Es así?	Is it so?	**Si acaso**	If by chance
En caso	In case		

ADVERBIOS DE ORDEN[3]

Primeramente	Firstly	**Sucesivamente**	Successively
Ultimamente	Lastly	**Antes (de)**	Before
Finalmente	Finally	**Después (de)**	After

ADVERBIOS DE COMPARACION[4]

Más	More	**Tanto**	So, so much
Menos	Less	**Tan**	As, as much
Mejor	Better	**Tanto** or **tanta como**	So much as
Peor	Worse	**Tan como**	As much as
		Igual a	equal to, like

ADVERBIOS DE LUGAR[5]

¿Dónde? ⎫ Where?		**Delante**	Before
¿En dónde? ⎭		**Detrás**	Behind
¿De dónde?	Whence?	**Dentro**	Within
¿Para dónde?	Which way?	**Fuera**	Without
¿A dónde?	Where to?	**Lejos**	Far, afar
Aquí	Here	**Cerca**	Near
Allí, ahí	There	**Adelante**	Forward
Acá	This way	**Atrás**	Backward
Allá	That way	**Debajo**	Beneath
Arriba	Above	**A la derecha**	To the right
Abajo	Below	**A la izquierda**	To the left

2 *Adverbs of uncertainty.*
3 *Adverbs of order.*
4 *Adverbs of comparison.*
5 *Adverbs of place.*

ADVERBIOS DE CANTIDAD[6]

¿Cuánto? ¿Cuánta?	How much?	Bastante	Enough
¿Cuántos? ¿Cuántas?	How many?	Algo	Something
Mucho	Much	Casi	Almost
Poco	Little	Apenas	Scarcely
Demasiado	Too much	Basta	That is enough

ADVERBIOS DE MODO[7]

¿Como?	How?	Claro	Clearly
Bien, mal	Well, ill	Alto	Aloud, loudly
Despacio	Slowly	Bajo (quedo)	Soft, softly
Así así	So so	Así	So, thus
De veras	Truly	De balde	} Gratis
De burla	For fun	Gratis	

ADVERBIOS DE AFIRMACION[8]

Es verdad	It is so	Sí[8]; sí, señor	Yes; yes, sir
Es cierto	It is certain	Ciertamente	Certainly

ADVERBIOS DE NEGACION

No[8]; no señor	No; no, sir	De ningún modo	In no way
No es verdad	It is not so	Nada de eso	} Not at all
		Absolutamente	Absolutely

CONJUNCIONES

Que	That	Conque	} So that
También	Also	De modo que	So then
Además de	Moreover	Pues, puesto que	Since
Y, e	And	Por	By, for
Ni—ni	Neither—nor	Por lo tanto	Therefore
O, u—o	{ Or (either)—or Whether—or	Para que[10]	} In order that
Sea que	Whether	A fin de que[10]	So that
Tampoco	Neither	Si	If
Mas, pero, sino[9]	But	A menos que[10]	Unless

6 *Adverbs of quantity.*

7 *Adverbs of manner.*

8 Después de verbos que denotan *pregunta, respuesta, creencia, declaración, duda* o *sospecha,* las partículas inglesas *yes* y *no* (*not*) se traducen por *que sí* y *que no,* por ejemplo: *Yo digo que sí,* y *él dice que no,* I say *yes* and he says *no; Yo creo que sí, y él cree que no,* I think *so* and he does *not.*

9 *Pero* y *mas* se colocan al *principio de frases adversativas,* mientras que (*while*) *sino,* puede únicamente ser empleado *precedido por una cláusula negativa;* v. gr.: *no* es blanco *sino* negro, it is not white *but* black; me dijo eso *pero* (*mas*) no es así, he told me that, but it is not so.

10 Después de estas *conjunciones* es necesario usar el modo subjuntivo, cuando se expresa *incertidumbre, duda, posibilidad* o *tiempo futuro indefinido;* v. gr.: *aun cuando* (*aunque*) me lo *haya* dicho, no me acuerdo (*although he may have told me so, I do not remember it*); *con tal* que lo *haga,* no me importa (*provided that he may do it, it does not matter*). Le doy el libro *para que* lo *lea.*

Mientras que[10]	While	Con tal que[10]	Provided that
Aun cuando[10]	Even	Como, así como	As
Aunque[10]	Although, though	Así	So, thus
Porque	Because	Siempre que[10]	Whenever
¿Por qué?	Why?	Ya	Already

INTERJECCIONES

¡Ay! ¡Ah!	Alas! Ah!	¡Qué hermosa!	How beautiful
¡Ay de mí!	Woe is me!	¡Qué feo!	How ugly!
¡He! ¡Ea!	Lo! Well!	¡Por Dios!	For God's sake!
¡Hola! ¡Viva!	Hallo! Hurrah!	¡Vamos, pronto!	Come, be quick!
¡Cuidado!	Be careful	¡Silencio!	Silence!
¡Ojalá!	God grant!	¡Caramba!	Hah, strange!
¡Qué lástima!	What a pity!	¡De veras!	Indeed!

PREPOSICIONES

1. LAS *PREPOSICIONES SIMPLES* SON:

A[11]	At, to	Hasta	Until
Ante[12]	Before	Mediante	By means of
Bajo	Under	Menos	But, except
Con	With	No obstante	Notwithstand-
Contra	Against		ing
De[13]	Of, from	Para	For, to
Desde	From	Por	By, for, through
Durante	During	Según	According to
En	In, on, at	Sin	Without
Entre	Between, among	Sobre	On, upon
Excepto	Except	Tras	Behind
Hacia	Toward		

2. *PREPOSICIONES* QUE REQUIEREN *DE* DESPUES, SON

Acerca de	Concerning, about	Dentro de	Within
		Después de	After
Además de	Beside	Detrás de	Behind
Antes de[13]	Before	Encima de	On, over

11 Se usa después de verbos transitivos para designar *el objeto directo*, como: amo *a* Juana, él estima *a* su mujer. Precede a las formas adverbiales referentes a *tiempo, precio* o *tipo* (rate): vendrá *a* la noche; *a* dos pesos el tomo; ¿*a* cuánto?—*a* tanto. Después de ciertos verbos para expresar *propósito*: voy *a* escribir. Entre *dos infinitivos, a* indica la diferencia del resultado de ambos, v. gr.: va mucho de decir *a* hacer (*there is a great difference between saying and doing*).

12 *Ante* significa *en presencia de : ante* el juez. Refiérese a *orden* o *preferencia: ante ayer;* pasó *ante* mí; *ante* todo. En lugar de *ante* es muy general usar *antes de,* v. gr.: *antes de* la comida.

13 *De* se usa en conexión con palabras que en inglés son expresiones compuestas: un buzón *de* correos (*a letter-box*), un talón *de* equipaje, etc. *De* denota *causa :* tiembla *de* miedo, no puedo moverme *de* frío. Expresa peculiaridad *física* o *moral, vestido, abundancia* y *escasez :* ciego *de* furor; vestido *de* luto (mourning dress); pobre *de* agua; etc. Se usa en *exalmaciones :* ¡infeliz *de* mí!; ¡pobre *de* mi padre!

Cerca de	Near	Fuera de	Outside
Debajó de	Under	Lejos de	far from
Delante de	Before		

3. *PREPOSICIONES* QUE REQUIEREN *A* DESPUES, SON:

Conforme a	According to	Junto a	Near, close by
Contrario a	Contrary to	Con respecto a	With respect to
Frente a	Opposite	Tocante a	Touching

PRONOMBRES INDEFINIDOS

Alguien,[1] nadie ....somebody, nobody
Alguno, ninguno ....someone, no one
Cualquiera[2] ....any, any one, whatever
Cualesquiera.................................whoever, whatever
Quienquiera ....whoever
Quienesquiera ....whoever
Cada uno ....each one
Ambos ....both
Uno u[3] otro[4] ....one or the other

1 *Alguien, some one, somebody, any one, anybody,* and *nadie, no one, nobody,* refer to persons only; as, *¿ha venido alguien?* has anybody come? *nadie ha venido,* nobody has come. *Alguno, alguna* (somebody, some one, anybody, any one); *algunos, algunas* (some, any, a few); and *ninguno, ninguna, ningunos, ningunas* (no one, nobody, none, no), refer to persons and things; as, *alguno* (or *alguien*) *ha estado aquí; ninguno* (or *nadie*) *ha llegado todavía. ¿Ha recibido Vd. algunos libros?* have you received *any* books? *no, Sr., no he recibido ninguno,* no sir, I have not received *any; he recibido algunos,* I have received *some; no tengo ninguno,* I have *not* any (*none*).

2 *Cualquiera* (sing.), *cualesquiera* (pl.), *any whatever, any one,* lose the final *a* before a noun, remaining *ualquier* and *cualesquier,* and refer to persons and things; as, *deme Vd. cualquiera,* give me *any one* you please. *Qualquiera* is a compound word of *cual* (which) and *quiera* (may wish), *the one you may wish.* It may be rendered by *el que* (*la que*) *Vd. quiera* (or *guste*), *los que* (*las que*) *Vd. quiera* (or *guste*), i.e., *any one you please. Ser uno un cualquiera,* Spanish idiom, meaning a person of *no account.*

3 *O* (or) becomes *u* (or) before words beginning with *o* or *ho;* as, *uno u otro* (one or another); *mujer u hombre* (woman or man). This change is made for the same euphonic reasons that necessitate the substitution of *e* for *y* (and) in all words commencing with *i* or *h.*

4 *Otro, otra* (another, other), *otros, otras* (others), refer to persons and things; as, *el otro día* (the *other* day); *otro día* (*another* day); *otra vez* (*another* time, again); *el otro hombre* (the *other* man). It must be noticed that we never say in Spanish *un otro* for *another,* but simply *otro;* as, *eso no lo hubiera dicho otro, another* would not have said so; but requires the definite article *el, la,* whenever a distinct person or thing is to be specified as, *no me dé Vd. ése, deme el otro,* don't give me that, give me *the other.*

FRASES USUALES

PARA OFRECER
Permítame Vd. que le ofrezca esto
Sírvase Vd. aceptar esta friolera
Tómelo Vd. por complacerme

TO OFFER
Allow me to offer you this
Please accept this trifle
Take it to please me

DUDA, SORPRESA, ADMIRACION
¡Cómo! ¿De veras?
Vd. me sorprende
Dudo que eso sea verdad
¿Quién lo hubiera creído?
No lo hubiera creído nunca
¡Es increíble!
¡Es admirable!
¡Es verdaderamente magnífico!
*¡Qué maravilla! Estoy completamente
  encantado*

DOUBT, SURPRISE, ADMIRATION
What! Really?
You astonish me
I doubt that this is true
Who would have believed it?
I would never have believed it
It is incredible!
It is admirable!
It is really magnificent!
What a wonder! I am quite
charmed

SIMPATIA Y ANTIPATIA
Es mi mejor amigo
Es mi amigo íntimo
Haría cuanto pudiese por él
Ese hombre no me gusta
Su cara no le recomienda
Le detesto (odie)
Todo el mundo le aborrece
Me alegraría que se fuera
Por fin se fué

SYMPATHY AND ANTIPATHY
He is my best friend
He is my intimate friend
I would do anything for him
I do not like that man
His looks are not in his favour
I detest (hate) him.
He is hated by everybody
I wish he would go
At last he is gone

PARA SUPLICAR
¿Quiere Vd. hacerme un favor?
¿Tendría Vd. la bondad de . . .?

Me haría Vd. un servicio
Cuento con Vd., ¿no es verdad?

TO REQUEST
Will you do me a favour?
Would you have the kindness to
. . .?
You would do me a favour
I may count upon you, may I not?

PARA DAR GRACIAS
Gracias. Muchas gracias
Le estoy a Vd. muy agradecido
Vd. es muy amble }
Vd. es muy bondadoso

TO THANK
Thanks. Many thanks
I am much obliged to you

You are very kind

PARA MANIFESTAR CONTENTO
Me alegro mucho de ello
Me causa gran satisfacción
¡Qué feliz soy!
Le felicito a Vd.
Le doy a Vd. la enhorabuena }

TO EXPRESS JOY
I am very glad of it
It gives me great joy
How happy I am!

I congratulate you

PARA EXPRESAR DOLOR

Lo siento mucho
Es una lástima
¡Qué lástima!
Es una pérdida irreparable

TO EXPRESS SORROW

I am very sorry
It is too bad
What a pity
It is an irreparable loss

EXPRESIONES DE COLERA

Estoy muy enfadado
No puedo contenerme de cólera
Estoy fuera de mí
El no está de buen humor
El lo quiere así
Lo quiere absolutamente
Atienda Vd. a lo que le digo
¡No conteste Vd.! ¡Silencio!
¡Cállese Vd.!

EXPRESSIONS OF ANGER

I am very angry
I cannot contain my anger
I am beside myself
He is not in a good humour
He will have it so
He insists upon it
Mind what I tell you
Do not answer! Silence!
Be quiet!

INFORMACION DEL CAMINO

¿Es éste el camino para . . .?
¿Se va por aquí a . . .? }
¿Cuál es el camino más corto?
¿Por dónde se va al paseo?
¿Por dónde es preciso que vaya?
Vaya Vd. derecho
Tome Vd. a la derecha (izquierda)
No puede Vd. equivocarse
¿Está lejos de aqu.?
No; no está lejos
¿Quiere Vd. que le acompañe?
Me hará Vd. un gran favor

INQUIRING THE WAY

Is this the way to . . .?

What is the shortest way?
Which is the way to the promenade?
Which way must I go?
Go straight ahead
Turn to your right (left)
You cannot miss your way
Is it far from here?
No; it is not far
Shall I accompany you?
You will do me a great favour

PROVERBIOS Y DICHOS ESPANOLES

CON VERBOS[1]

"Quien mucho **abarca** poco aprieta."

Grasp all, lose all.

Acostarse con las gallinas.

To go to bed very early.

Adelantar como el cangrejo.

To advance like a crab.

"Bienes mal **adquiridos** a nadie han enriquecido."

Ill-gotten gains never prosper.

"Quien bien **ama** tarde olvida."

He who loves truly is slow to forget.

"Quien lo feo **ama** hermoso le parece."

Love is blind to defects or imperfections.

"Quien **ama** el peligro, perece en él."

He who loves danger will perish by it.

"Cuando Dios **amanece** para todos aparece."

The sun shines on the just and on the unjust.

No se **ande** Vd. en cumplimientos.

No ceremony, pray!

Andando el tiempo.

In the course of time.

Andar de Zeca en Meca.

To rove about from Dan to Beersheba.

"**Ande** yo caliente y ríase la gente."

If I am comfortable, I care little for ridicule.

"Quien mal **anda,** mal acaba."

Bad habits lead to worse ends.

"Quien **anda** al revés **anda** el camino dos veces."

He who takes the wrong road makes the journey twice.

Andar en mangas de camisa.

To be in one's shirt-sleeves.

"El mentir y el compadrar, ambos **andan** a la par."

Beware of false friends.

"Lo que se **aprende** en la cuna, siempre dura."

What is learned in childhood is never forgotten.

Aprovechar la ocasión.

To take the opportunity.

Apurar la copa del dolor hasta las heces.

To drain the cup of misery to the dregs.

---

[1] La siguiente es una lista de *proverbios* o *refranes*, y *dichos*; los que tienen verbos están impresos primero, y en ellos seguimos alfabéticamente las primeras letras de *éstos*, y a continuación los que no los tienen, formando con ellos una serie aparte, por el orden alfabético de sus primeras palabras. Los *proverbios* están marcados con comillas (" ") para diferenciarlos de los *dichos*.

"Quien no se **arriesga** no pasa la mar." — Nothing ventured, nothing won.

"Quien a buen árbol se **arrima**, buena sombra le cobija." — Old oak gives good shade.

"Quien bien **ata** bien desata." — He who hides knows where to find.

"Quien tiene tienda que la **atienda**." — Let the shopkeeper mind his shop.

"A quien madruga, Dios le **ayuda**." — The early bird catches the worm.

"Al hierro caliente **batir de** repente." — Strike while the iron is hot.

Beber como una cuba. — To drink like a fish.

Buscar a tientas. — To grope.

Buscar cinco pies al gato teniendo cuatro. — To seek a quarrel.

"El pez que **busca** el anzuelo, busca su duelo." — He who plays with fire will burn his fingers.

"Honra y provecho no **caben** en un lecho." — Honour and riches are seldom found united.

Caer simpático. — To become a favourite.

Caérsele a uno la cara de vergüenza. — To blush with shame.

Caer en gracia. — To please.

"Más vale **caer** en gracia que ser gracioso." — Charm is more appreciated than wit.

Caer en el chiste. — To see the point (of a joke).

"Del árbol **caído** todos hacen leña." — From the fallen tree everybody makes firewood.

"Quien **calla** otorga." — Silence gives consent.

"Quien **canta, su mal** espanta." — A cheerful spirit lessens many troubles.

"Al gallo que **canta**, le aprietan la garganta." — Mum's the word, or else.

Como el gallo de Morón, sin pluma y **cacareando**. — The defeated cock loses feathers, but not conceit.

"Antes que te **cases** mira lo que haces." — Look before you leap.

"Para mal **casar**, más vale nunca maridar." — Better never marry than marry unwisely.

"Gato con guante no **caza** ratones." — A cat in mittens seldom catches mice.

"En boca **cerrada** no entran moscas." — A wise head keeps a close mouth.

A ojos **cerrados**.	Blindly.
"Lo que no has de **comer**, déjalo cocer."	Do not meddle in other people's business.
Coger a uno la palabra.	To take one at his word.
"**Comer** y rascar basta empezar."	Appetite comes with eating.
Costar un ojo.	To be very dear.
Creer a ojos cerrados.	To believe without proof.
"Dios los **cría** y ellos se juntan."	Birds of a feather flock together.
Chuparse los dedos.	To feel great delight.
Darse la mano.	To shake hands.
Dar de sí.	To stretch.
Me **doy** por vencido.	I give up.
"Quien **da** primero, da dos veces."	He who hits promptly, hits twice.
No **dársele** a uno un pito (un bledo).	Not to care a straw.
"Donde las **dan** las toman."	As a man sows so he must reap.
Dar una bofetada.	To give a slap on the face.
Dar los días.	To congratulate on one's birthday.
"Al necio y al aire, **darle** calle."	Never contradict a fool.
Dar las espaldas.	To turn one's back.
"**Dime** con quien andas y te diré quien eres."	Tell me your friends and I will tell you what you are.
No **decir** esta boca es mía.	To keep a profound silence.
Dicho y hecho.	No sooner said than done.
"Los niños y los tontos **dicen** la verdad."	Children and fools speak the truth.
Disparar a quema ropa.	To fire point-blank.
Disparar a boca de jarro.	To fire point-blank.
Dormir como un lirón.	To sleep like a top.
Echar un trago.	To take a dram.
Echarse a reir.	To begin to laugh.
Echar los bofes.	To pant.
"Cobra buena fama, y **échate** a dormir."	Get the name of early rising, and you may lie abed all day.
"La caridad bien entendida **empieza** por sí mismo."	Charity begins at home.

Sin **encomendarse** a Dios ni al diablo.	To do something recklessly
Enfadarse por nada.	To make a mountain out of a mole-hill.
"Quien te **engañó**, te **engañará**; y si repite, bien te **estará**."	If a man deceives you once, shame on him; if twice, shame on you.
"El ojo del amo **engorda** el caballo."	The eye of the master fattens the horse.
Entrarse como Pedro por su casa.	To be too familiar in a neighbour's house.
Quien **espera** desespera.	He who hopes also fears.
Estar empeñado hasta los ojos.	To be deeply in debt.
Estar en babia.	To be wool-gathering.
Quien **evita** la ocasión **evita** el ladrón.	He who avoids temptation avoids sin.
Faltar a la palabra.	To break one's promise.
"Quien **fía** o **promete** en deuda se mete."	A promise is made to be kept.
"No se **ganó** Zamora en una hora."	Rome was not built in a day.
"Quien se **guarda**, Dios le guarda."	God helps him who helps himself.
El hábito no **hace** al monje.	Beware of the wolf in sheep's clothing.
"No **hay** mal que por bien no venga."	Every cloud has a silver lining.
"No **hay** más bronce que años once."	True metal is youth.
"No **hay** atajo sin trabajo."	No gains without pains.
"No **hay** rosas sin espinas."	There is no rose without a thorn.
"A buena hambre no **hay** pan duro."	A hungry man does not find fault with his food.
"No **hay** peor cuña que la del mismo palo."	The worst enemy is he who was once a friend.
"Casa donde no **hay** harina, todo se vuelve tremolina."	When poverty comes in, love flies out.
"Debajo de una mala capa suele **haber** un buen bebedor."	Appearances are often deceptive.
Aun no **ha** salido del cascarón y ya tiene presunción."	Scarcely hatched, yet thinks himself cock of the walk.
"A pobreza no **hay** vergüenza."	Poverty is no shame.
No **hay** regla sin excepción.	The exception proves the rule.
"A caballo regalado no **hay que** mirarle el diente."	Never look a gift horse in the mouth.

Sobre gustos no **hay** nada escrito.	There is no accounting for taste.
No **hay** quince años feos.	Youth is never ugly.
"A mucho **hablar,** mucho errar."	Much talking, much erring.
"La ocasión **hace** al ladrón."	Opportunity makes the thief.
"Necios y porfiados **hacen** ricos a los letrados."	Fools and obstinate people make the lawyers rich.
"De escarmentados se **hacen** los avisados."	Experience teaches wisdom.
"A donde fueres, **haz** lo que vieres."	When in Rome, do as the Romans do.
Hacer una de las suyas.	To play one of his tricks (pranks).
"Un loco **hace** ciento."	One fool makes many.
"**Hágase** el milagro y **hágalo** el diablo."	Handsome is as handsome does.
"Quien **hace** un cesto, hace ciento."	He who steals a penny will steal a pound.
"Más **hace** el que quiere que el que puede."	Where there's a will there's a way.
"No se **hizo** la miel para la boca del asno."	Do not cast your pearls before swine.
"Del dicho al **hecho** hay gran trecho."	Saying is one thing, doing another.
Cada uno **hace** de su capa un sayo.	Every one may do as he likes with his own.
"Costumbres y dineros **hacen** a los hijos caballeros."	Wealth and manners soon make a gentleman.
Poco a poco **hila** la vieja el copo.	Drops make up the ocean.
"Quien a su mujer no **honra,** a sí mismo se **deshonra.**"	He who does not honour his wife, dishonours himself.
Gato escaldado del agua fría **huye.**	Once bitten twice shy.
Irsele a uno la cabeza.	To lose one's presence of mind.
Eso ni me **va,** ni me **viene.**	That does not concern me.
Ir al grano.	To get to the point.
"**Ir** a la guerra, ni casar no se debe aconsejar."	In war and love beware of interference.
"**Vanse** los amores y quedan los dolores."	When love is gone sorrow remains.
"Perro que **ladra,** no muerde."	His bark is worse than his bite.
"Quien se **levanta** tarde, ni oye misa ni come carne."	Indolence stands in the way of many blessings.

"El buey suelto bien se **lame**." — Liberty is a blessing.

"Sol que mucho **madruga**, poco dura." — Premature things have little endurance.

La cosa **marcha**. — The affair is making progress.

"Quien a hierro **mata**, a hierro muere." — Who lives by the sword dies by the sword.

"Entre padres y hermanos no **metas** tus manos." — Avoid meddling in family quarrels.

Nombrando al ruín de Roma al punto asoma. — Talk of the devil and he will appear.

Oir campanas y no saber dónde. — To hear without understanding.

"Amor con amor se **paga**." — Love repays love.

Pasar los ojos, o la vista. — To glance over.

"**Piensa** el ladrón que todos son de su condición." — The thief judges others by himself.

Mal que le **pese**. — In spite of him.

"Sarna con gusto, no **pica**, pero mortifica." — Some will have their pleasure, even though it is painful.

Poner manos a la obra. — To set oneself to work.

"Quien **presta** al amigo, a menudo cobra un enemigo." — He who lends to a friend often makes an enemy.

"El hombre **propone** y Dios dispone." — Man proposes and God disposes.

"Quien **quiere** a Beltrán, quiere a su can." — Love me, love my dog.

Para las cuestas arriba te **quiero** mulo, que las cuestas abajo yo me las subo. — I wish assistance in difficult matters; in easy ones I can help myself.

"Quien bien te **quiere** te hará llorar." — He who loves you will chasten you.

"De lo ajeno, lo que **quiera** su dueño." — Take from no man that which he does not wish you to have.

"El que **quiera** azul celeste que le cueste." — Obtain good things by paying their worth.

La codicia **rompe** el saco. — Catch not the shadow and lose the substance.

La cuerda se **rompe** por lo más delgado. — A chain is as strong as its weakest link.

Saber algo de buena tinta. — To know a thing on good authority.

Cada uno **sabe** donde le aprieta el zapato.	Every one knows where his own shoe pinches.
"Más **sabe** el loco en su casa que el cuerdo en la ajena."	A fool knows more of his own business than a wise man can tell him.
Salirse con la suya.	To have one's own way.
Salvarse en una tabla.	To escape miraculously.
No **es** oro todo lo que reluce.	All is not gold that glitters.
"Hombre prevenido nunca **fué** vencido."	Forewarned is forearmed.
"Mientras que en mi casa estoy rey **soy**."	A man's house is his castle.
Ciertos **son** los toros.	As sure as fate.
"Donde fuiste caballero, no **seas** escudero."	Where you have been a gentleman do not stoop to being a servant.
De noche todos los gatos **son** pardos.	Darkness covers a multitude of sins.
"En tierra de ciegos el tuerto **es** rey."	In the country of the blind the one-eyed man is king.
"En la boca del discreto lo público **es** secreto."	Do not be a scandalmonger.
"Amigo en la adversidad **es** amigo de verdad."	A friend in need is a friend indeed.
Primero **es** la obligación **que** la devoción.	Business before pleasure.
Mañana **será** otro día.	Tomorrow is another day.
"La pobreza no **es** vileza, mas **es** ramo de pereza."	Poverty is no crime, but sometimes implies a want of energy.
Los duelos con pan **son** menos.	Money cannot bring happiness but can make unhappiness bearable.
"Para el mal que hoy se acaba, no **es** remedio el de mañana."	Two wrongs do not make a right.
Es grano de anís.	It is nothing (ironical).
Cuando el río **suena** agua lleva.	Where there is smoke there is fire.
Tener malas pulgas.	To be ill-tempered.
"Muertos e idos no **tienen** amigos."	The absent must always bear the blame.
Tomar el rábano por las hojas.	To put the cart before the horse.
"Más **vale** maña que fuerza."	The pen is mightier than the sword.

Más valè que sobre que no que falte.	It is better to have too much than to be in want.
Más vale doblarse que quebrarse.	Better to bend than to break.
"Más vale pájaro en mano que ciento volando."	A bird in the hand is worth two in the bush.
Vender hasta la camisa.	To sell everything.
Venga lo que viniere.	Come what may.
Meterse en lo que no va ni viene.	To meddle in what does not concern one.
Verse entre la espada y la pared.	Between the devil and the deep blue sea.
Si te vi no me acuerdo.	Out of sight, out of mind.
Hacer ver a uno las estrellas.	To see stars in the daytime.
"El que de ajeno se viste en la calle lo desnudan."	He who wears borrowed plumes risks exposure.
"Aunque la mona se vista de seda mona se queda."	You can't make a silk purse out of a sow's ear.
Volver patas arriba una cosa.	To turn a thing upside down.
"Al cabo de años mil, vuelve el agua por do solía ir."	Time brings old customs round again.

PROVERBIOS Y DICHOS SIN VERBOS

A lo hecho pecho.	What is done must be endured.
A otro perro con ese hueso.	Tell that to the marines.
A porfía.	With intent; with obstinacy.
A propósito.	Apropos (by the way).
A solas.	Alone.
A tiro.	Within reach.
A la vuelta.	On the next page (P.T.O.).
Aprendiz de todo, oficial de nada.	Jack of all trades, master of none.
Al asno muerto la cebada al rabo.	Lock the stable-door after the horse has bolted.
"Antes cabeza de ratón que cola de león."	Better be the head of a mouse than the tail of a lion.
Bienes raíces.	Real estate.
Cada loco con su tema.	Everyone has his hobby.
Cada oveja con su pareja.	Like seeks like.

Con todo eso.	Notwithstanding.
De buenas a primeras.	Without being expected, suddenly.
"De dinero y calidad la mitad de la mitad."	Take everything with a pinch of salt.
De oídas.	By hearsay.
De tal palo tal astilla.	A chip off the old block.
De tal padre tal hijo.	Like father, like son.
De par en par.	Wide open.
De sobra.	Over and above.
De cuando en cuando.	Now and then.
De un tirón.	At one stroke.
En resumidas cuentas.	In short.
El gozo en un pozo.	It has all gone up in smoke.
En un santiamén.	In an instant.
Gente de medio pelo.	People of little account.
Gente de poco más o menos.	People of little account.
"Genio y figura hasta la sepultura."	What is bred in the bone will stay in the flesh.
Juego de palabras.	A pun.
"La cruz en los pechos y el diablo en los hechos."	The cross on one's breast and the devil in one's deeds.
Lo dicho dicho.	What I have said I abide by.
Mal que le pese.	In spite of him.
Por término medio.	On an average.
Sendos golpes.	Heavy blows.
Sin más acá ni más allá.	Without further ado.
Sin qué ni para qué.	Without cause or motive.
Tal para cual.	Tit for tat.
"Vida sin amigos muerte sin testigos."	Friendless in life, friendless in death.
¡Voto a tal!	By Jove!

English-Spanish Dictionary

A

a, an un, una
able, to be poder
above encima, arriba
absolutely absolutamente
accelerator acelerador *m.*
accident accidente *m.*
accidental accidental
accompany, to acompañar
according to según, conforme a
ache dolor *m.*
action acción *f.*
actor actor *m.*
actress actriz *f.*
address dirección *f.*
adjust, to ajustar
admirable admirable
adolescence adolescencia *f.*
advanced adelantado, -a
advertise, to anunciar
advertisement anuncio *m.*
aeronautic aeronáutico, -a
aeroplane aeroplano *m.* avion *m.*
after después
against contra
age, old vejez *f.*
agency agencia *f.*
agent agente *m.*
agreeable agradable
agriculture agricultura *f.*
air aire *m.*
airmail correo aéreo
airport aeropuerto *m.* puerto aéreo *m.*
alas! ¡ay!
alcohol alcohol *m.*
alike conforme

all todo, -a; todos, -as
allow me permítame
allow, to permitir, dejar
almond almendra *f.*
almost casi
alone solo, -a
already ya
also también
although aunque
always siempre
ambulance ambulancia *f.*
American americano, -a
among entre
amount importe *m.*
amusing gracioso
and y
angry enojado, -a
animal animal *m.*
ankle tobillo *m.*
announce, to anunciar
annual anual
answer, to contestar
answered contestado, -a
antenna antena *f.*
antiseptic antiséptico, -a
any cualquier
anyone cualquiera
apartment apartamento *m.*
aperitif aperitivo *m.*
appear, to parecer
appetite apetito *m.*
applaud aplaudir
apple manzana *f.*
appointment cita *f.*; compromiso *m.*
appreciate, to apreciar
appreciation apreciación *f.*
approve, to aprobar, celebrar

apricot albaricoque *m.*
April abril *m.*
aquatic acuático, -a
archæology arqueología *f.*
architect arquitecto *m.*
architecture arquitectura *f.*
argue, to discutir
arm brazo *m.*
armchair sillón *m.*
aromatic aromático, -a
arrival llegada *f.*
arrive to llegar
art arte *m.*
artichoke alcachofa *f.*
article artículo *m.*
artificial artificial
artist artista *m.*, *f.*
artistic artístico, -a
as como
ash ceniza *f.*
ask, to preguntar, pedir
asparagus espárrago *m.*
aspirin aspirina *f.*
assistance asistencia *f.*
astringent astringente *m.*
at a, en
at once ahora
atomic atómico, -a
attend, to asistir, atender
attendance asistencia *f.*
attractive atractivo -a
August agosto *m.*
aunt tía
authority autoridad *f.*
automobile automóvil, auto *m.*
autumn otoño *m.*
avenue avenida *f.*
aviation aviación *f.*
avoid, to evadir
away, to go irse

B

back espalda *f.*
backward atrasado, -a; atrás
bacon tocino *m.*
bad malo, -a
badly mal
baggage equipaje *m.*
balcony balcón *m.*
banana plátano *m.*

band banda *f.*
bank banco *m.*
bar bar *m.*
barley cebada *f.*
barometer barómetro *m.*
baseball beisbol *m.*
basket canasta *f.*
bath baño *m.*
bathe (yourself), to bañarse
bathroom cuarto de baño *m.*
bathtub bañera *f.*
battery acumulador *m.*
be, to ser, estar, haber
be careful! ¡cuidado!
beach playa *f.*
beans fríjoles *m.*
bear oso *m.*
beautiful hermoso, -a
beauty hermosura *f.*
beauty parlour salón de belleza
become, to volverse
bed cama *f.*
bedroom dormitorio, *m.* alcoba *f.*
bedspread colcha *f.*
beef carne de res *f.*
beefsteak biftec *m.*
been estado
beer cerveza *f.*
beet remolacha *f.*
before delante, ante, antes de
beg, to rogar
begin, to comenzar
begun comenzado, -a
behind detrás, atrás
believe, I yo creo
believe, to creer
bell (electric) timbre *m.*
below abajo, debajo
belt cinturón *m.*
beneath debajo
bet apuesta *f.*
bet, to apostar
better mejor
better, to get mejorarse
between entre
bicycle bicicleta *f.*
big grande
bill cuenta *f.*
bird pájaro *m.*
birth nacimiento *m.*
biscuit galleta *f.*

bite, to morder
bitter amargo, -a
black negro, -a
blizzard ventisca
block cuadra *f.*
blond rubio, -a
blouse blusa *f.*
blue azul *m.*
blush, to ruborizarse
boarding house casa de huéspedes, pensión *f.*
boat barco *m.*
boil, to hervir
book libro *m.*
bookshop librería *f.*
boot bota *f.*
born, to be nacer
boss jefe, patrón *m.*
both ambos
bother, to molestar
bottle botella *f.*
bought comprado, -a
box caja *f.*
box office taquilla *f.*
boy niño, muchacho *m.*
bracelet pulsera *f.*
brakes (car) frenos *m.*
brandy aguardiente *m.*
bravery valor *m.*
bread pan *m.*
break, to romper, quebrar
breakfast desayuno *m.*
breeze brisa *f.*
bridge puente *m.*
bring, to traer
broad ancho, -a
broiled asado, -a
brother hermano
brother-in-law cuñado *m.*
brown pardo
brunette moreno, -a
brush cepillo *m.*
brush, to cepillar
bucket balde *m.*
bud capullo *m.*
build, to construir
building edificio *m.*
bull toro *m.*
bullfight corrida *f.*
bullfighter torero *m.*
bullring plaza de toros *f.*

burn, to encender
bus autobús *m.*; camión *m.* (Mex.); guagua *f.* (Cub.)
business negocio *m.*
busy ocupado, -a
but pero, sino
butchers' shop carnicería
butter mantequilla *f.*
button botón *m.*
buy, to comprar
   where can I ...? ¿dónde puedo comprar?
by por
by means of mediante

C

cabbage col *f.*; repollo *m.*
cabin camarote *m.*
cabin, aeroplane cabina *f.*
cablegram cablegrama *m.*
cake pastel *m.*
calendar calendario *m.*
calf becerro *m.*
call, to llamar
called, to be (name) llamarse
camera cámara *f.*
canary canario *m.*
cap gorra *f.*
car carro *m.*; coche *m.*
carbon carbón *m.*
card tarjeta *f.*
cardinal cardinal
care, to take cuidar
carnation clavel *m.*
carnival carnaval *m.*
carrot zanahoria *f.*
carry, to llevar
cart driver carretero *m.*
cashier cajero, -a *m.,f.*
cat gato, -a
catch, to coger
cathedral catedral *f.*
Catholic católico, -a
cattle ganado *m.*
cauliflower coliflor *f.*
caution cuidado *m.*
celebrate, to celebrar
celebrity celebridad *f.*
celery apio *m.*

cent céntimo *m.*
centigrade centígrado
central central
centuple céntuplo
century siglo *m.*
cereal cereal *m.*
certain cierto, -a
chair silla *f.*
chance, by por ventura
change cambio *m.*
change, to cambiar
character carácter *m.*
charm gracia *f.*
charming simpático, -a
cheap barato, -a
check (restaurant) cuenta *f.*
check, to facturar
cheese queso *m.*
chemist's shop botica, farmacia *f*
cheque cheque *m.*
cherry cereza *f.*
chest of drawers cómoda *f.*
chestnut castaña *f.*
chewing-gum chicle *m.*
chicken pollo *m.*
child niño, -a
childhood niñez *f.*
Chinese chino, -a
chocolate chocolate *m.*
choose, to seleccionar
chops chuletas *f. pl.*
Christmas Navidad *f.*
Christmas Eve Noche Buena *f.*
church iglesia *f.*
cigar cigarro puro *m.*
cigarette cigarrillo *m.*
cinema película *f.*
cinema screen pantalla *f.*
circular circular
city ciudad *f.*
class clase *f.*
clean limpio, -a
clean, to limpiar
cleaner's shop tintorería *f.*
clearly claro
climate clima *m.*
climb, to ascender
clinic clínica *f.*
close junto
close, to cerrar
closed cerrado, -a

cloth paño *m.*
clothes ropa *f.*
cloudy nublado, -a
club casino, club *m.*
clutch embrague *m.*
coal carbón *m.*
coast costa *f.*
coat chaqueta *f.*; saco *m.*
cock gallo *m.*
cock fights pelea de gallos *f.*
cock pit gallera *f.*
cockroach cucaracha *f.*
cocktail coctel *m.*
cocoa cacao *m.*
coconut coco *m.*
coffee café *m.*
coffee, with milk café con leche
coffee pot cafetera *f.*
cold frío, -a
cold (illness) resfrío, resfriado
cold, I am tengo frío
cold, to catch resfriarse
cold, to get enfriarse
collar cuello *m.*
colony colonia *f.*
colour color *m.*
comb peine *m.*
come, to venir
come down, to bajar
come in, to entrar
comfortable cómodo, -a
commercial comercial
company compañía *f.*
comparison comparación *f.*
complain, to reclamar
complaint reclamación *f.*
concern firma *f.*
concerning acerca de, tocante a
concert concierto *m.*
conductor conductor *m.*
confetti confeti *m.*
congratulate, to congratular
consist, to consistir
construct, to construir
consultation consulta *f.*
contract, to contraer
contrary contrario, -a
convenient conveniente
conversation conversación *f.*
convince, to convencer
cook cocinero, -a

cook, to cocinar
cool fresco, -a
copper cobre *m.*
copy copia *f.*
cordial cordial
corkscrew sacacorchos *m.*
corn, sweet maíz *m.*
corn, ear of mazorca *f.*
corner esquina *f.*
correct correcto, -a
correction corrección *f.*
correspondence correspondencia *f.*
corridor corredor *m.*
cosmetic cosmético *m.*
cost, to costar
cotton algodón *m.*
cough tos *f.*
count, to contar
country campo, pais *m.*
couple par *m.*
course, of por supuesto
courteous cortés
courtesy cortesía *f.*
cousin primo, -a
cover, to cubrir
crazy loco, -a
cream crema *f.*
credential credencial *f.*
credit crédito *m.*
criminal criminal
cry, to llorar
crystal cristal *m.*
Cuban cubano, -a
cucumber pepino *m.*
cuff puño *m.*
cup taza *f.*
cupboard armario *m.*
curtain cortina *f.*
custard natilla *f.*
custom's aduana *f.*
cut, to cortar
cutlet filete *m.*

D

daily diario *m.*
dance baile *m.*
dance, to bailar
danger peligro
dangerous peligroso, -a
dark oscuro, -a

dark, to become anochecer
darkness oscuridad *f.*
date (appointment) cita *f.*; compromiso *m.*
date (fruit) dátil *m.*
date (of calendar) fecha *f.*
daughter hija
day día *m.*
day after tomorrow pasado mañana
day before yesterday anteayer
daybreak amanecer *m.*
December diciembre *m.*
decide, to decidir
decision decisión *f.*
declaration declaración *f.*
decorate, to decorar
deduction deducción *f.*
deer ciervo *m.*
defect defecto *m*
defective defectivo, -a
defend, to defender
degree grado *m.*
delicious delicioso, -a
deliver, to entregar
delivery entrega *f.*
demand, to exigir
dentist dentista *m., f.*
departure salida *f.*
deposit, to depositar
descend, to descender
describe, to describir
description descripción *f.*
desire deseo *m.*; gana *f.*
desk escritorio *m.*
dessert postre *m.*
detain, to detener
detest, to detestar
detour desvío *m.*
diamond diamante *m.*
dictionary diccionario *m.*
difference diferencia *f.*
different diferente
difficult difícil
difficulty dificultad *f.*
digestible digestible
digestion digestión *f.*
dine, to cenar
dining-room comedor *m.*
direct directo, -a
direction dirección *f.*

director director, -a
directory directorio *m.*
dirty sucio, -a
disagreeable desagradable
disappear, to desaparecer
disastrous desastroso, -a
discount descuento *m.*
discover, to descubrir
discuss, to discutir
discussion discusión *f.*
dish plato *m.*
disobey, to desobedecer
distance distancia *f.*
distribute, to distribuír
divide, to dividir
dizziness mareo *m.*
doctor doctor, -a; médico, -a
dog perro *m.*
dollar dólar *m.*
donkey burro, -a
door puerta *f.*
door (car) portezuela *f.*
dot punto *m.*
double doble
doubt duda *f.*
doubt, to dudar
dove paloma *f.*
dozen docena *f.*
draft giro *m.*; letra *f.*
draught corriente *f.*
dream sueño *m.*
dream, to soñar
dress vestido *m.*
dress, to vestir
dress (yourself), to vestirse
dressing (sauce) salsa *f.*
dressmaker modista *f.*
drink, to beber, tomar
drive, to manejar
driver conductor *m.*
drunk, to get emborracharse
dry, to (yourself) secarse
duck pato *m.*
dump, to echar
durable durable, duradero, -a
during durante
duty deber *m.*
duty (tax) impuesto *m.*

E

each cada
eagle águila *f.*
ear oreja *f.*
ear (of wheat) espiga *f.*
earlier más temprano
early temprano
earth tierra *f.*
ease facilidad *f.*
east oriente *m.*
Easter Pascua *f.*
easy fácil
eat, to comer
effective efectivo, -a
egg huevo *m.*
egg, fried huevo frito
egg, hard boiled huevo duro
egg, soft boiled huevo pasado por agua
eight ocho
eighteen dieciocho
eighty ochenta
elbow codo *m.*
electric eléctrico, -a
electricity electricidad *f.*
elegant elegante
elephant elefante *m.*
elevator elevador, ascensor *m.*
eleven once
embark, to embarcar
embroidery bordado *m.*
emergency emergencia *f.*
encounter encuentro *m.*
encounter, to encontrar
end fin *m.*
engineer ingeniero *m.*
enough bastante, suficiente
enough, that is basta
enter, to entrar
entertain, to entretener
entertainment diversión *f.*
enthusiasm entusiasmo *m.*
enthusiastic entusiástico
envelope cubierta *f.*; sobre *m.*
equal igual
equivalent equivalente
errand mandado *m.*
error error *m.*
essential esencial

establish, to establecer
evade, to evadir
eve víspera *f.*
evening noche *f.*
everything todo
exact exacto, -a
exactly exactamente, en punto
exaggerate, to exagerar
exaggeration exageración *f.*
examine, to examinar
excavation excavación *f.*
except excepto, menos
excessive excesivo, -a
exchange cambio *m.*
excuse, to dispensar
excuse me excúseme, dispénseme
exhibition exhibición *f.*
existence existencia *f.*
exit salida *f.*
expect, to esperar
expected esperado
expensive caro, -a
experience experiencia *f.*
explain, to explicar
export, to exportar
express, to expresar
exterior exterior

F

fabric tela *f.*
face cara *f.*
facial facial
factory fábrica *f.*
fail, to fracasar
failure fracaso *m.*
fair justo, -a
fall, to caer
family familia *f.*
famous famoso, -a
fan aficionado, -a
far lejos
farm granja *f.*
farmer agricultor
fashion moda *f.*
fast pronto
fat gordo, -a
father padre *m.*
favour favor *m.*
favourite predilecto, -a
fear miedo *m.*

fear, to temer
feast festividad, fiesta *f.*
February, febero *m.*
feel, to sentir
felt fieltro *m.*
fervour fervor *m.*
festival festival *m.*
fever fiebre *f.*
fifteen quince
fifty cincuenta *m.*
fig higo *m.*
film película *f.*
film roll rollo *m.*
finally finalmente, en fin
find, to encontrar
find out, to enterarse
finger dedo *m.*
finish, to terminar
finished terminado, -a
firm firma *f.*
first primero, -a
first class primera clase
fish pescado *m.*
fish, to pescar
fit, to ajustar
five cinco *m.*
flame llama *f.*
flannel franela *f.*
flight vuelo *m.*
float, to flotar
floor piso *m.*
flower flor *f.*
fly mosco *m.*
fly, to volar
food alimento *m.*
foot pie *m.*
for para, por
foreign extranjero, -a
foreigner extranjero, -a
forget, to olvidar
fork tenedor *m.*
form, to formar
formal formal
fort fuerte *m.*
fortune fortuna *f.*
forty cuarenta
forward adelante
fountain fuente *f.*
four cuatro
fourteen catorce
fox zorro *m.*

France Francia *f.*
free de balde, gratis
freeze, to helar
French francés, -sa
French bean ejote *m.*
frequently frecuentemente
fresh fresco
Friday viernes *m.*
fried frito, -a
friend amigo, -a
frightened, to get asustarse
from desde, de
front, in al frente
frost helada *f.*
frozen congelado, -a
fruit fruta *f.*
fry, to freír
funeral funeral *m.*
funny chistoso, -a
fur piel *f.*
furnished amueblado, -a
furniture muebles *m. pl.*

G

gamble, to jugar
game juego *m.*
garage garage *m.*
garden jardín *m.*
gardener hortelano, -a
garlic ajo *m.*
general general *m.*
generator generador *m.*
gentleman señor, caballero
get off or down, to bajar
get rid of, to deshacerse
gin ginebra *f.*
girl niña, muchacha
give, to dar
give, to dar, de (imp.)
give it to me démelo
glad, to be alagrarse
glove guante *m.*
go, to ir
go in, to entrar
go to bed, to acostarse
go down, to descender
go, let's vámonos
goat cabra *f.*
God Dios
gold oro *m.*

golf golf *m.*
good bueno, -a; buen
good afternoon buenas tardes
good luck buena suerte
good morning buenos días
good night buenas noches
goods artículos *m. pl.*
goose ganso *m.*
government gobierno *m.*
graceful gracioso, -a
gracious! ¡caramba!
grain grano *m.*
gramophone fonógrafo *m.*
gramophone record disco *m.*
granddaughter nieta *f.*
grandfather abuelo *m.*
grandmother abuela *f.*
grandson nieto *n.*
grape uva *f.*
green verde
greet, to saludar
greeting saludo *m.*
grey gris *m.*
groan quejido *m.*
gross gruesa *f.*
ground suelo *m.*
ground floor piso bajo
grow, to crecer
growth crecimiento *m.*
guest invitado, -a
guitar guitarra *f.*

H

hair pelo *m.*
half medio-a, mitad
hall corredor *m.*
ham jamón *m.*
hand mano *f.*
hand (of a watch) manecilla *f.*
handbag cartera *f.*
handkerchief pañuelo *m.*
handsome guapo, -a
happiness felicidad, ventura *f.*
happy contento, -a
hard duro, -a
hare liebre *f.*
harvest cosecha *f.*
haste prisa *f.*
hat sombrero *m.*
hat shop sombrerería *f.*

hate, to odiar
hatred odio *m.*
have, to tener
hay heno *m.*
hazelnut avellana *f.*
he él
head cabeza *f.*
health salud *f.*
hear, to oír
hearing oído *m.*
heat calor *m.*
heating calefacción *f.*
heel talón *m.*
hen gallina *f.*
here aquí
hiccough hipo *m.*
high alto, -a: elevado, -a
highway carretera *f.*
hire, to alquilar
history historia *f.*
holiday fiesta *f.*
home hogar *m.*
honey miel de abejas *f.*
honeymoon luna de miel *f.*
honour honor *m.*
hope esperanza *f.*
hope, to esperar
horse caballo *m.*
horse race carrera de caballos
hospital hospital *m.*
hospitality hospitalidad *f.*
hot caliente
hot, I am tengo calor
hour hora *f.*
house casa *f.*
how? ¿cómo?
how are you? ¿cómo está usted?
how far is it? ¿qué tan lejos es?
how many? ¿cuántos?
how much? ¿cuánto?
humidity humedad *f.*
humour humor *m.*
hundred ciento
hunger hambre *f.*
hungry, I am tengo hambre
hurry, to apurarse, darse prisa
hurry up! ¡apúrese! dése prisa
hurt, to doler
hurt yourself, to lastimarse
husband esposo, marido *m.*

I

I yo
ice hielo *m.*
ice cream helado *m.*
idea idea *f.*
if si
ignorance ignorancia *f.*
ignorant ignorante
ill mal
ill, to become enfermarse
ill, very grave
illegal ilegal
illustration ilustración *f.*
imagination imaginación *f.*
imitation imitación *f.*
immense inmenso, -a
impatience impaciencia *f.*
import, to importar
important importante
impossibility imposibilidad *f.*
impossible imposible
in en
incidentally por cierto
include, to incluír
income renta *f.*
incompetent incompetente
incorrect incorrecto, -a
indeed en verdad
independence independencia *f.*
indigestion indigestión *f.*
indisposed indispuesto, -a
industrial industrial
infection infección *f.*
influence influencia *f.*
inform, to informar
inhabitant habitante
initial inicial
ink tinta *f.*
inoculate, to inocular
insect insecto *m.*
inside adentro, dentro
install, to instalar
instant instante *m.*
insult insulto *m.*
insurance seguro *m.*
intelligent inteligente
interior interior
international internacional
interrupt, to interrumpir

intimate íntimo, -a
introduce, to presentar
introduction introducción
invitation invitación f.
invite, to invitar
invoice factura f.
iron, to planchar
is es
it is es
itinerary itinerario m.

J

jacket chaqueta f.
jail cárcel f.
jam (tight spot) aprieto m.
January enero m.
jealousy celos m.
jest burla f.
jewel joya f.
jewellery shop joyería f.
Jewish judío
joke chiste m.
journal diario m.
journey viaje m.
joy gozo m.
judgment juicio m.
juice jugo m.
July julio m.
jump, to saltar
June junio m.
just justo, -a
justice justicia f.

K

keep out! ¡prohibida la entrada!
key llave f.
kilogram kilo m.
kind clase f.
kitchen cocina f.
knife cuchillo m.
knock on the door, to llamar a
la puerta
know, to saber
know, to (people, places) conocer

L

laborious laborioso, -a
lace encaje m.

lack, to faltar
ladder escalera f.
lake lago m.
lamb cordero m.
lamp lámpara f.
lamp shade pantalla f.
language idioma m.
large grande
lark alondra f.
last último, -a; postrero, -a
last night anoche
last, at al fin, por fin
last, to durar
lately últimamente
later más tarde, luego
laugh, to reír
laughter risa f.
laughter, burst of carcajada
laundry lavandería f.
lavatory baño m.
lawyer abogado m.
lazy perezoso, -a
leaf hoja f.
learn, to aprender
lease, to arrendar
leather piel f.
leave, to dejar; salir
left izquierda f.
leg pierna f.
legal legal
lemon limón m.
lemonade limonada f.
lend, to prestar
lentil lenteja f.
less menos
lesson lección f.
let, to dejar
letter carta, letra f.
letter-box buzón m.
lettuce lechuga f.
library biblioteca f.
lie mentira f.
lie, to mentir
lie down, to acostarse
life vida f.
lift ascensor m.
lift, to levantar
light luz f.
light, to encender
lightning relámpago m.
like, to gustar

lily lirio *m.*
lime lima *f.*
linen lino *m.*
lion león *m.*
list lista *f.*
listen! ¡oíga!
little poco, -a; menudo, -a; chiquito, -a
live, to vivir
living-room sala *f.*
lobby vestíbulo *m.*
local local
location sitio *m.*
lock in, to encerrar
long largo, -a
long, too muy largo, -a
look! ¡míre!
lorry camión *m.*
lose, to perder
lottery lotería *f.*
loud alto, -a
love amor *m.*
love, to querer
low bajo, -a
lubricant lubricación *f.*
lubricate, to lubricar
lubrication lubricante *m.*
luck suerte *f.*
luggage equipaje *m.*
luggage receipt talón *m.*
lunch almuerzo *m.*
lunch (to have) almorzar
luxury lujo *m.*

M

machine máquina *f.*
machinery maquinaria *f.*
maid criada *f.*
maid, chamber camarera *f.*
mail correo *m.*
major mayor
make, to hacer, realizar
man hombre
manage, to manejar
manner modo *m.*
mansion mansión *f.*
many muchos, -as
many, as, so tantos, as
map mapa *m.*
March marzo *m.*

market plaza *f.*
market place mercado *m.*
marmalade mermelada *f.*
match fósforo *m.*
mattress colchón *m.*
May mayo *m.*
maybe tal vez
mayor alcalde *m.*
me mí
measure, to medir
meat carne *f.*
mechanic mecánico, -a
medicine medicina *f.*
meet, to encontrar
melon melón *m.*
melt, to derretir
memory memoria *f.*
mend, to remendar
menu menú *m.*
merchandise mercancía *f.*
merchant comerciante *m.*
metal metal *m.*
Mexican mexicano, -a
midday mediodía *m.*
middle medio *m.*
midnight medianoche *f.*
milk leche *f.*
mine mío, -a
mine mina *f.*
mineral mineral *m.*
minute minuto *m.*
mistake, to make a equivocarse
mix, to revolver, mezclar
modern moderno, -a
moment momento *m.*
Monday lunes *m.*
money dinero *m.*
money, paper billete
monkey mono *m.*
month mes *m.*
moon luna *f.*
more más
moreover además
morning mañana *f.*
mother madre
motor motor *m.*
motorist motorista *m.*, *f.*
mouse ratón *m.*
move, to mudar, mover
moving moviendo
much mucho, -a

much, as, so tanto, -a
much, too demasiado
mud lodo, fango *m.*
mule mula *f.*
municipal municipal
mural mural
museum museo *m.*
mushroom seta *f.*
music música *f.*
mustard mostaza *f.*
mutton carnero *m.*
my mi, mis
myself mí

N

name nombre *m.*
napkin servilleta *f.*
narrow estrecho, angosto, -a
nation nación *f.*
national nacional
nationality nacionalidad *f.*
native nativo, -a
natural natural
naturally naturalmente
navy marina *f.*
near cerca, junto
near to cerca de
necessary necesario, -a
necessity necesidad *f.*
neck cuello *m.*
need, to necesitar
needle aguja *f.*
needlework costura *f.*
negative negativo
negligent negligente
neighbour vecino, -a
neither ningún, ninguno, -a, tampoco ni
nephew sobrino *m.*
nervous nervioso, -a
never nunca, jamás
new nuevo, -a
New Year Año Nuevo
news noticias *f. pl.*
newspaper periódico *m.*
newsreel noticiario *m.*
next próximo, -a
niece sobrina *f.*
night noche *f.*
nine nueve *m.*

nineteen diecinueve
ninety noventa
no no
no one ninguno, -a
noble noble
nobody nadie
noon mediodía *m.*
nor ni
north norte *m.*
North America Norte América *f.*
North American norteamericano, -a
note nota *f.*
note, to notar
notebook cuaderno *m.*
nothing nada
notice, to notar
November noviembre *m.*
now ahora
now, right ahora
number número *m.*
numerous numeroso, -a
nut nuez *f.*

O

oat avena *f.*
obtain, to obtener
occasion ocasión *f.*
occupation ocupación *f.*
occupy, to ocupar
occur, to ocurrir
October octubre *m.*
oculist oculista *m.*
odd raro, -a
of de
offend, to ofender
offended ofendido, -a
offensive ofensivo, -a
offer, to ofrecer
office oficina *f.*
official oficial
often a menudo
oil aceite *m.* ·
old viejo, -a
olive aceituna *f.*
omelette tortilla *f.*
on en, sobre
once una vez
one uno, -a
one way una vía
onion cebolla *f.*

open abierto, -a
open, to abrir
opera ópera *f.*
operation operación *f.*
operator operadora *m., f.*
opinion opinión *f.*
opposite al frente
or o
orange naranja *f.*
orange juice jugo de naranja *f.*
orchard huerto *m.*
orchestra orquesta *f.*
orchid orquídea *f.*
order orden *f.*
order, to pedir
ordinarily generalmente
ordinary ordinario, -a
original original
ornament adorno *m.*
other otro, -a
ounce onza *f.*
our, ours nuestro, -a
ourselves nosotros, -as
out of order descompuesto, -a
outside exterior, fuera, afuera
oven horno *m.*
overcoat abrigo *m.*
overturn, to volcar
own propio, -a
owner dueño, -a
ox buey *m.*
oyster ostra *f.*

P

package paquete *m.*
paint, to pintar
painting pintura *f.*
pair par *m.*
palace palacio *m.*
palm tree palma, palmera *f.*
paper papel *m.*
park parque *m.*
park, to estacionar
parking parqueadero *m.*
parrot loro *m.*
pass, to pasar
past pasado, -a
paste pasta *f.*
patience paciencia *f.*
patient paciente

patriotic patriótico, -a
pattern patrón *m.*
pavement acera *f.*
pay, to pagar
payment pago *m.*
peaceful tranquilo, -a
peach melocotón *m.*
pear pera *f.*
peas guisantes *m.*
peasant peón; campesino *m.*
pen pluma *f.*
pencil lápiz *m.*
penicillin penicilina *f.*
pension pensión *f.*
people gente *f.*
pepper pimienta *f.*
per cent por ciento
percentage tanto por ciento
perfect perfecto, -a
perform, to realizar
perfume perfume *m.*
perhaps quizá, quizás, acaso
permanent permanente
permanent wave permanente *f.*
permitted permitido, -a
person, in personalmente
personal personal
personally personalmente
perspire, to sudar
persuade, to persuadir
peso peso *m.*
petrol gasolina *f.*
petrol station estación de gasolina *f.*
petroleum petróleo *m.*
photograph fotografía *f.*
photograph, to fotografiar
pick up, to levantar
picture pintura *f.*; cuadro *m.*; retrato
  (portrait) *m.*
pie pastel *m.*
pier muelle *m.*
pig cerdo *m.*
pill píldora *f.*
pillow almohada *f.*
pilot piloto *m.*
pine tree pino, *m.*
pineapple piña *f.*
pipe pipa *f.*
pitcher jarra *f.*
place sitio, lugar *m.*
plan plan *m.*

plant planta *f.*
plate plato *m.*
platter fuente *f.*
play, to jugar
play, to (instrument) tocar
pleasant agradable
pleasure gusto, placer, *m.*
plum ciruela *f.*
pocket bolsillo *m.*
point punto *m.*
point, to señalar
policeman policía *m.*
politics política *f.*
poor pobre
poppy amapola *f.*
popular popular
pork, pig puerco, cerdo *m.*
pork chop chuleta de cerdo
port puerto *m.*
position posición *f.*
positive positivo, -a
possible posible
possibly posiblemente
postal postal
potato papa *f.* patata *f.*
pour, to echar
powder polvo *m.*, polvos **(cosmetic)**
  m. pl.
practical práctico, -a
practise, to practicar
precious precioso, -a
prefer, to preferir
preferred predilecto, -a
prepare, to preparar
prescription receta *f.*
present presente, regalo **(gift)** *m.*
present, to presentar
pretty bonito, -a
price precio *m.*
principal principal
print, to imprimir
prize premio *m.*
probably probablemente
proceed, to proceder
produce, to producir
product producto *m.*
profession profesión *f.*
profit ganancia *f.*
programme programa *m.*
progress progreso *m.*
progress, to progresar

prohibit, to prohibir
promise, to prometer
pronounce, to pronunciar
pronunciation pronunciación *f.*
proof prueba *f.*
propeller hélice *f.*
proper propio, -a
protection protección *f.*
protest, to protestar
Protestant protestante
prove, to probar
province provincia *f.*
public público, -a
pulse pulso *m.*
pumpkin calabaza *f.*
punctual puntual
purchase compra *f.*
purse bolso, -a
put, to poner
put on, to ponerse
put out, to apagar, echar
put to bed, to acostar

Q

quantity cantidad *f.*
quarter cuarto *m.*
quarterly trimestre
question pregunta *f.*
quickly aprisa
quotation cotización *f.*

R

rabbit conejo *m.*
racial racial
radiator radiador *m.*
radio radio *f.*
radish rábano *m.*
railway ferrocarril *m.*
railway carriage coche *m.*
rain lluvia *f.*
rain, to llover
raincoat impermeable *m.*;
  gabardina *f.*
raise, to levantar, alzar
raisin pasa *f.*
ranch rancho *m.*
rapid rápido, -a
rapidly rápidamente
rare raro, -a

raspberry frambuesa *f.*
rat rata *f.*
raw crudo, -a
rayon rayón *m.*
razor navaja de afeitar *f.*
razor blade hoja de afeitar *f.*
read, to leer
ready listo, -a
realise, to realizar
reality realidad, verdad *f.*
really? ¿de veras?
reason razón *f.*
receipt recibo *m.*
receive, to recibir
recent reciente
recognise, to reconocer
recommend, to recomendar
recommendation recomendación *f.*
recreation recreación *f.*
red colorado, rojo, -a
red snapper pargo *m.*, huachinango *m.* (Mex.)
reduce, to reducir
refresh, to refrescar
refrigeration refrigeración *f.*
refrigerator refrigeradora, nevera *f.*
region región *f.*
register, to registrar, matricular
registration registración, matriculación *f.*
regularity regularidad *f.*
relation relación *f.*
relative pariente *m.*
remain, to quedarse
remember, to recordar, acordarse de
remind, to recordar, avisar
rent renta *f.*
rent, to arrendar
repair, to componer, reparar
repeat, to repetir
require, to requerir
resemble, to parecerse
residential residencial
respectable respetable
responsible responsable
rest, to descansar
restaurant restaurante *m.*
restriction restricción *f.*
return, to regresar, devolver, volver

reunion reunión *f.*
rib costilla *f.*
ribbon cinta *f.*
rice arroz *m.*
ride, to montar
ride, to take a pasear
ridiculous ridículo, -a
right (direction) derecha *f.*; correcto
rise, to ascender, subir
river río *m.*
road camino *m.*
road map guía del viajero
roast, to asar
roast beef rosbif *m.*
roasted asado, -a
rob, to robar
robbery robo *m.*
romantic romántico, -a
room pieza, habitación *f.*, cuarto *m.*
roomy espacioso, -a
rosary rosario *m.*
rose rosa *f.*
route ruta *f.*
rubber goma *f.*; caucho *m.*
rug alfombra *f.*
rum ron *m.*
rumba rumba *f.*
rumour rumor *m.*
rural rural
Russian ruso, -a
rye centeno *m.*

S

safe seguro, -a
sail, to embarcar
salad ensalada *f.*
salary salario *m.*
salt sal *f.*
salty salado, -a
same mismo, -a
sample muestra *f.*
sandwich sandwich *m.*
sardine sardina *f.*
satisfy, to satisfacer
Saturday sábado *m.*
sauce salsa *f.*
save, to salvar
say, to decir
scarcely apenas
school colegio *m.*; escuela *f.*

scissors tijeras *f. pl.*
scorpion alacrán *m.*
Scotland Escocia *f.*
Scottish escocés, -a
scrape lío *m.*
scratch, to rascar
scream grito *m.*
scream, to gritar
sculpture escultura *f.*
seal sello *m.*
seasick, to get marearse
season estación *f.*
seat asiento *m.*
second segundo, -a
second class segunda clase
secretary secretario, -a
section sección *f.*
sedative sedativo *m.*
see, to ver
seem, to parecer
seldom rara vez
select, to seleccionar
selection selección *f.*
self starter arranque automático *m.*
sell, to vender
send, to mandar
sensation sensación *f.*
September septiembre *m.*
serve, to servir
service servicio *m.*
seven siete
seventeen diecisiete
seventy setenta
several varios, -as
sew, to coser
shade sombra *f.*
shave, to afeitar
she ella
sheep oveja *f.*
sheet sábana, hoja *f.*
shepherd pastor *m.*
shipment despacho, envío *m.*
shirt camisa *f.*
shoe zapato *m.*
shoe shop zapatería *f.*
shop almacén *m.*, tienda *f.*
short corto, -a
short, too muy corto, -a
shoulder hombro *m.*
shout, to gritar
shovel pala *f.*

show, to enseñar, mostrar, señalar
shrimp camarón *m.*
shut, to cerrar
sick enfermo, -a
sick, I am estoy enfermo
sickness enfermedad *f.*
sigh suspiro *m.*
sight vista *f.*
sign letrero *m.*
sign, to firmar
silence silencio *m.*
silk seda *f.*
simple simple
simplicity simplicidad *f.*
since desde, pues
sincerity sinceridad *f.*
sing, to cantar
single solo, simple, único
sink fregadero *m.*
sister hermana *f.*
sister-in-law cuñada *f.*
sit, to sentar
sit down, to sentarse
situate, to situar
situation situación *f.*
six seis
sixteen dieciséis *m.*
sixty sesenta
size talla *f.*
sky cielo *m.*
sleep, to dormir
sleep, to go to dormirse
sleeve manga *f.*
slip, to resbalar
slipper zapatilla *f.*
slow despacio, lento
small pequeño, chiquito, -a
small, too muy pequeño, -a; muy
  chiquito, -a
smell, to oler
smile, to sonreír
smoke, to fumar
sneeze estornudo *m.*
snore, to roncar
snow nieve *f.*
snow, to nevar
so (thus) así
so long hasta luego
so that conque
soap jabón *m.*
soap dish jabonera *f.*

sob sollozo *m.*
sociable sociable
social social
society sociedad *f.*
sock calcetín *m.*
sofa sofá *m.*
soft suave, blando, -a
soft drink bebida gaseosa *f.*
sole suela *f.*
solution solución *f.*
some unos, -as
somebody alguien
someone alguno, -a
something algo
son hijo
song canto *m.*, canción *f.*
soon pronto
sorry, I am lo siento
sorry, to be sentir
soup sopa *f.*
south sur *m.*
South America Sud América *f.*
souvenir recuerdo *m.*
sow, to sembrar
sowing siembra *f.*
space espacio *m.*
spacious espacioso, -a
Spain España *f.*
Spaniard español, -a
Spanish español, -a
spark plug bujía *f.*
sparrow gorrión *m.*
speak, to hablar
special especial
specially especialmente
speech discurso *m.*
speed velocidad *f.*
spicy picante
spinach espinaca *f.*
sponge esponja *f.*
spoon cuchara *f.*
spoonful cucharada *f.*
spring primavera *f.*
square plaza *f.*; cuadrado, -a
squirrel ardilla *f.*
stadium estadio *m.*
staircase escalera *f.*
stairs escalones *m.*
stamp sello *m.*; estampilla *f.*
stand up, to pararse
state estado *m.*

station estación *f.*
station wagon camioneta *f.*
stationery shop papelería *f.*
statue estatua *f.*
stay, to quedarse
steak bisté *m.*
steal, to robar
steam vapor *m.*
steamship vapor *m.*
steps escalones *m.*
stew guisado *m.*
stockings medias *f. pl.*
stomach estómago *m.*
stone piedra *f.*
stop! ¡pare!, ¡alto!
stop, to parar
storm tormenta *f.*
story cuento *m.*
stove estufa *f.*
straight, straight ahead derecho, -a
strange extraño, -a
straw paja *f.*
strawberry fresa *f.*
street calle *f.*
student estudiante
stupid estúpido, -a
style moda *f.*; estilo *m.*
suburb suburbio *m.*
success éxito *m.*
successively sucesivamente
suddenly de pronto, de repente
sufficient suficiente, bastante
sugar azúcar *m.*
sugar bowl azucarero *m.*
suit traje *m.*
suitcase maleta *f.*
summer verano *m.*
sun sol *m.*
Sunday domingo *m.*
supper cena *f.*
supper, to have cenar
supposed supuesto
sure cierto, -a
surprise, to sorprender
swallow golondrina *f.*
sweater suéter *m.*
sweep, to barrer
sweet dulce
sweet potato batata *f.*
swim, to nadar

S.C.

23

swimming pool piscina *f.*
system sistema *m.*

T

table mesa *f.*
tablecloth mantel *m.*
tailor sastre *m.*
tailor's shop sastrería *f.*
take, to llevar, tomar
take leave, to despedirse
tall alto, -a
tango tango *m.*
tank tanque *m.*
taste gusto *m.*
taste, to probar, gustar
tasteless desabrido, -a
tea té *m.*
teach, to enseñar
teacher maestro, -a
tear (weeping) lágrima *f.*
tear, to romper
teaspoon cucharita *f.*
telegram telegrama *m.*
telegraph operator telegrafista
telephone teléfono *m.*
television televisión *f.*
tell, to decir
tell me dígame
temper genio *m.*
temperature fiebre, temperatura *f.*
ten diez *m.*
tender tierno, -a
tenth décimo, -a
terrace terraza *f.*
terrible terrible
test, to probar
thank you gracias
that ese, eso, -a, aquel, -la, que, quien, cual
that way por allá
the el, la, los, las
the, about del
the, at al
the, from del
the, of del
the, to al
theft robo *m.*
then entonces, luego
there ahí, allí, allá
there, is, are hay

these estos, estas
thin delgado, -a
thing cosa *f.*
think, I yo creo, yo pienso
think, to creer, pensar
third, one tercio
thirsty, I am tengo sed
thirteen trece
thirty treinta
this este, esta
this one éste, ésta
this way por aquí
thought pensamiento *m.*
thousand mil
thread hilo *m.*
three tres
throw, to echar
thunder trueno *m.*
Thursday jueves *m.*
ticket boleto, billete, pasaje *m.*
tidy aseado, -a
tie corbata *f.*
tiger tigre *m.*
tight apretado estrecho, -a
tile mosaico *m.*
till (money) gaveta *f.*
time tiempo *m.*; vez *f.*
time, in, on a tiempo
time, to have a good divertirse
times veces *f. pl.*
timetable itinerario, horario *m.*
tin estaño *m.*
tip propina *f.*
tired cansado, -a
tired, to get cansarse
to para, a
toast tostada *f.*
toast, to tostar
tobacco tabaco *m.*
today hoy
together juntos, -as
tomato tomate *m.*
tomorrow mañana *f.*
tongue lengua *f.*
to-night esta noche
tooth diente *m.*
toothbrush cepillo de dientes *m.*
torrent torrente *m.*
toss, to echar
total total *m.*
touch, to tocar

tourist turista, viajero
toward hacia
towel toalla *f.*
town pueblo *m.*
town hall ayuntamiento *m.*
toy juguete *m.*
traffic tráfico *m.*
train tren *m.*
transaction transacción *f.*
translate, to traducir
transparent transparente
transport, to transportar
travel, to viajar
traveller viajero, -a
traveller's cheque cheque de viajero
tray bandeja *f.*
tree árbol *m.*
trimming adorno *m.*
trip viaje *m.*
trivial trivial
tropical tropical
tropics trópico *m.*
trouble dificultad *f.*; lío *m.*
trousers pantalones *m. pl.*
trout trucha *f.*
truck camión *m.*
trunk baúl *m.*
truth veras, verdad *f.*
try it on mídaselo
try to, to tratar de
Tuesday martes *n.*
turkey pavo *m.*
turn off the light, to apagar
turn over, to volcar
turnip nabo *m.*
twelve doce
twenty veinte
twenty-five veinticinco
two dos
type tipo *m.*
typewriter máquina de escribir *f.*
typical típico, -a
tyre llanta *f.*

U

ugliness fealdad *f.*
ugly feo, -a
ultramarine ultramarino, -a
umbrella paraguas *m.*

uncertainty duda *f.*
uncle tío *m.*
under debajo, bajo
understand, to comprender, entender
underwear ropa interior
undress, to desvestirse
until hasta
until we meet again hasta la vista
unwrap, to desenvolver
up to hasta
up, to go subir
upon sobre
urgent urgente
us nos, nosotros, -as
used to be era
utility utilidad *f.*

V

vain, in en balde
value valor, importe *m.*
vaseline vaselina *f.*
veal ternera *f.*
vegetable legumbre *f.*
vehicle vehículo *m.*
velvet terciopelo *m.*
ventilate, to ventilar
ventilator ventilador *m.*
vertical vertical
very muy
very well muy bien
vest camiseta *f.*
Viennese vienés, -a
view vista *f.*
vinegar vinagre *m.*
violet violeta *f.*
visit visita *f.*
visit, to visitar
vitamin vitamina *f.*
vocabulary vocabulario *m.*

W

wage pago, sueldo, jornal *m.*
waist cintura *f.*; talle *m.*
waistcoat chaleco *m.*
waistline cintura *f.*
wait, to esperar
waited esperado
waiter camarero, -a

waitress camarera
wake up, to despertar
walk, to take a pasear, caminar
wall pared *f.*
wallet cartera *f.*
waltz vals *m.*
want, to querer
warm caloroso, caliente
was era
was, there había, hubo
wash basin lávabo *m.*
wash, to lavar
wash (yourself), to bañarse
watch reloj *m.*
watchmaker relojero *m.*
watchmaker's shop relojería *f.*
water agua *f.*
watermelon sandia *f.*
waterproof impermeable *m.*
wave ola *f.*
we nosotros, -as
weakness debilidad *f.*
wear, to llevar
Wednesday miércoles *m.*
week semana *f.*
week, by the por semana
weigh, to pesar
weigh (yourself), to pesarse
weight peso *m.*
well bien
well done bien asado
were era
were, there había, hubo
west occidente *m.*
West Indies Antillas
what? ¿qué?
whatever cualquiera
wheat trigo *m.*
wheel rueda *f.*
when cuando
whenever siempre que
where donde
which que; cual, -es
whip látigo *m.*
white blanco, -a
who? ¿quién?
whoever quienquiera
wide amplio, ancho, -a
wife esposa *f.*

will voluntad *f.*
wind viento *m.*
window ventana *f.*
windscreen parabrisa *m.*
windscreen wiper limpiavidrios *m.*
wine vino *m.*
winter invierno *m.*
wish, to desear
with con
with me conmigo
within dentro de
without sin, fuera
witness testigo *m.*
wolf lobo *m.*
woman mujer
wonderful admirable
wood madera *f.*
woods bosque *m.*
wool lana *f.*
word palabra *f.*
work trabajo *m.*
work, to trabajar
workman trabajor
world mundo *m.*
worried preocupado, -a
worry, to preocupar
worse peor
wrap, to envolver
wrapped envuelto, -a
wrinkle arruga *f.*
write, to escribir
writing escribiendo
written escrito

Y

yawn bostezo *m.*
year año *m.*
yellow amarillo, -a
yes sí
yesterday ayer
yet todavía, aún
young joven
youth juventud *f.*

Z

zero cero *m.*

Spanish-English Dictionary

A

a at, to
abajo below
abierto, -a open
abogado m. lawyer
abrigo m. overcoat
abril m. April
abrir to open
absolutamente absolutely
abuela f. grandmother
abuelo m. grandfather
acabar de to have just
academia f. academy
acaso perhaps
acaso si if, by chance
acceso m. access
accidental accidental
accidente m. accident
acción f. action
aceite m. oil
aceituna f. olive
acelerador m. accelerator
aceptar to accept
acera f. pavement
acerca de concerning, with regard to
acercamiento m. approach
acercarse to approach
acertar to ascertain, to make sure
acompañar to accompany
acordar to remind
acordarse to remember
acostar to lay down, to put to bed
acostarse to go to bed, to lie down
actividad f. activity
actor m. actor
actriz f. actress

acuático, -a aquatic
acueducto m. aqueduct
acuerdo m. agreement
de . . . con in agreement with
acumulador m. battery
adaptar to adapt
adelantado, -a advanced, fast
adelante forward
adelanto m. advancement
además moreover
además de besides
adentro inside
admirable wonderful, admirable
adoración f. worship, adoration
adorno m. ornament, trimming
adquirir to acquire, to gain
aduana f. custom's
adverbio m. adverb
advertir to warn, to advise
aeródromo m. airport
aeronáutico, -a aeronautic
aeroplano m. aeroplane
aeropuerto m. airport
afeitarse to shave
aficionado m. fan (of a sport)
agencia f. agency
agente m. agent
agosto m. August
agradable agreeable, pleasant
agradecer to thank for
agrado m. pleasure
agregar to add
agricol, -a agricultural
agricultor m. farmer
agricultura f. agriculture
agua f. water
agua caliente hot water

agua fría cold water
agua helada iced water
aguardiente *m.* brandy
águila *f.* eagle
aguja *f.* needle
ahijado, -a godson, goddaughter
ahora now
ahora mismo right now, at once
aire *m.* air
ajo *m.* garlic
ajustar to adjust, to fit
al to the, at the, on the
alargado, -a lengthened, elongated
alargar to lengthen
albaricoque *m.* apricot
alcachofa *f.* artichoke
alcalde *m.* mayor
alcance *m.* pursuit, reach
alcanzar to reach, to be enough
alcoba *f.* bedroom
alcohol *m.* alcohol
alegarse to be glad
alegre glad, happy, cheerful
alemán, -a German
Alemania *f.* Germany
alfombra *f.* rug
algo something, some
algodón *m.* cotton
alguien somebody
alguno, -a someone
alimento *m.* food
allá there, in that place
allá por that way
allí there
almacén *m.* shop
almendra *f.* almond
almendro *m.* almond tree
almohada *f.* pillow
almorzar to have lunch
almuerzo *m.* lunch
aló hello
alojar to lodge
alondra *f.* lark
alquilar to hire
alrededor about, around
alrededores *m.* outskirts
alto loud, high, tall
alto stop (imp.)
altura *f.* height
amanecer *m.* daybreak
amapola *f.* poppy

amargo, -a bitter
amarillo, -a yellow
ambos, -as both
ambulancia *f.* ambulance
América Central *f.* Central America
América del Sur *f.* South America
americano, -a American
amiga *f.* friend
amigo *m.* friend
amistad *f.* friendship
amor *m.* love
ampliar to enlarge, to extend
amplio, -a wide
amueblado, -a furnished
ancho, -a broad, wide
andar to walk
angosto, -a narrow
animal *m.* animal
anoche last night
anochecer to become dark
anotar to write down
ansiosamente anxiously
ante, antes de before
anteayer day before yesterday
anticipado, -a anticipated, in advance
antiguo, -a ancient, old
Antillas *f.* West Indies, Antilles
antiséptico, -a antiseptic
anual annual
anunciar to advertise, to announce
anuncio *m.* advertisement
año *m.* year
Año Nuevo *m.* New Year
apagar to put out, turn off
apenas scarcely
aperitivo *m.* apéritif
apetito *m.* appetite
apio *m.* celery
aplaudir to applaud
aplauso *m.* applause
apostar to bet
apreciación *f.* appreciation
apreciar to appreciate
aprender to learn
apretado, -a tight
aprieto *m.* jam, tight spot
aprisa quickly
aprovechar to make use of
aprovechar de to profit

apuesta *f.* bet
apurarse to hurry
apúrese hurry up (imp.)
aquel, aquella that (pron.)
aquí here
aquí por this way
árabe *m.* Arab
árbol *m.* tree
ardilla *f.* squirrel
ardo *m.* plough
argentino, -a Argentinian
armario *m.* cupboard, wardrobe
aromático, -a aromatic
arqueología *f.* archæology
arquitecto *m.* architect
arquitectónico, -a architecctural
arquitectura *f.* architecture
arrancar to pull out
arranque automático self-starter
arreglar to arrange
arrendamiento *m.* lease, renting
arrendar to rent, to lease
arriba above
arriendo *m.* lease, rental
arroz *m.* rice
arte *m.* art
artículos *m.* goods, articles
artificial artificial
artista *m.,f.* artist
artístico, -a artistic
asado, -a roasted, broiled
asado bien well done
asar to roast
ascender to rise, to climb
ascensor *m.* elevator, lift
aseado, -a tidy
asegurar to secure
así so, thus
asiento *m.* seat
asimismo likewise
asistencia *f.* assistance, attendance
asistir to attend
aspecto *m.* aspect, appearance
aspirina *f.* aspirin
astringente *m.* astringent
asuntos *m.* affairs
asustarse to get frightened
atención *f.* courtesy, care, attention
atender to attend
atento, -a polite
aterrizar to land

atómico, -a atomic
atractivo, -a attractive
atraer to attract
atrás backward, behind
atrasado, -a slow, backward
atravesar to cross
atroz terrible, awful, atrocious
auge *f.* boom (in the market)
aun still, yet
aunque although
aurora *f.* dawn
auto *m.* car
autobús *m.* bus
automóvil *m.* motor-car
autopista *f.* highway
autor *m.* author
autoridad *f.* authority
avellana *f.* hazelnut
avena *f.* oats
avenida *f.* avenue
avestruz *m.* ostrich
aviación *f.* aviation
aviador *m.* aviator, flyer
avión *m.* aeroplane, airliner
¡ay! alas!
ayudar to aid, to help
ayuno *m.* fast
ayuntamiento *m.* town hall
ayer yesterday
azadón *m.* hoe
azúcar *m.* sugar
azucarero *m.* sugar bowl
azucena *f.* white lily
azul *m.* blue

B

bacalao *m.* codfish
bahía *f.* bay, harbour
bailar to dance
baile *m.* dance
baile, pista de dance floor
bajar to go or come down, to get off,
    to get down
bajo, -a a low, soft, under
balcón *m.* balcony
balde *m.* bucket
balde, de free
balde, en in vain
balneario *m.* bathing resort
banco *m.* bank

banda *f.* band
bañarse to bathe oneself
bañera *f.* bath
baño *m.* bath
baño, cuarto de bathroom
bar *m.* bar
barato, -a cheap
barco *m.* ship
barómetro *m.* barometer
barrer to sweep
barrio *m.* district
base *f.* district
basta that is enough
bastante enough, quite, sufficiently
batata *f.* sweet potato
baúl *m.* trunk
beber to drink
bebida *f.* drink
bebida gaseosa soft drink
becerro *m.* calf
beisbol *m.* baseball
Bélgica *f.* Belgium
belleza *f.* beauty
bello, -a beautiful
bermellón *m.* vermilion
biblioteca *f.* library
bicicleta *f.* bicycle
bien well
bien, yo estoy I am well
bienvenida *f.* welcome
bienvenido, -a welcome
biftec *m.* beefsteak
billete *m.* ticket, paper money
bisabuelo, -a great-grandfather, great-grandmother
bisté *m.* steak
biznieto, -a great-grandson, great-granddaughter
blanco, -a white
blando, -a soft
blusa *f.* blouse
boca *f.* mouth
bocina *f.* car horn
boda *f.* wedding
boleto *m.* ticket
bollo *m.* rolls (bread)
bolsa *f.* bag, purse, pocket, stock exchange
bolsillo *m.* pocket
bonito, -a pretty
bordado *m.* embroidery

bordo *m.* board
bordo, a on board
borracho drunkard, drunk
bosque *m.* woods
bostezo *m.* yawn
botas *f.pl.* boots
botella *f.* bottle
botica *f.* chemist's shop
botón *m.* button
Brasil *m.* Brazil
brazo *m.* arm
brillante brilliant, bright
brindar to drink a person's health
brisa *f.* breeze
buen good
bueno, -a good
buena suerte good luck
buenas noches good night
buenas tardes good afternoon
buenos días good morning
buey *m.* ox
bujía *f.* spark plug
burla *f.* mockery, jest
burla, de for fun
burro *m.* donkey
buscar to seek, to look for
buzón *m.* letter-box

C

caballero *m.* gentleman
caballo *m.* horse
cabaret *m.* cabaret, night club
cabeza *f.* head
cabina *f.* aeroplane cabin
cable *m.* cable
cablegrama *m.* cablegram
cabra *f.* goat
cacao *m.* cocoa
cada each
cadena *f.* chain
caer to fall
caerse to fall down
café *m.* coffee
café con leche coffee with milk
cafetera *f.* coffee-pot
caja *f.* box
cajero, -a cashier
calabaza *f.* pumpkin
calamar *m.* squid
calcetines *m.pl.* socks

calefacción *f.* heating
calendario *m.* calendar
cálido, -a warm
caliente hot
calle *f.* street
calma *f.* calm
calor *m.* warmth, heat
calor, tengo I am hot
calzado *m.* footwear
cama *f.* bed
cámara *f.* camera
camarera *f.* chamber-maid
camarero, -a waiter, waitress
camarón *m.* shrimp
camarote *m.* cabin
cambiar to change
cambiarse to change (clothes)
cambio *m.* change, exchange
camello *m.* camel
caminar to walk
camino *m.* road
camión *m.* lorry; bus (Mex.)
camioneta *f.* station wagon
camisa *f.* shirt
camiseta *f.* vest
campana *f.* bell
campeador surpassing in bravery
campesino *m.* peasant, farmer
campo *m.* country, field
canal *m.* canal
canario *m.* canary
canasta *f.* basket
canción *f.* song
cansado, -a tired
cansarse to get tired
cantar to sing
cantera *f.* quarry
cantidad *f.* quantity
canto *m.* song
caña *f.* cane, reed
caña de azúcar sugar cane
cáñamo *m.* hemp
cañería *f.* water pipe
capacidad *f.* capacity
capullo *m.* bud, cocoon
cara *f.* face
carácter *m.* character
¡caramba! *inter.* gracious! strange!
carbón *m.* carbon, coal
carcajada *f.* burst of laughter
cárcel *f.* jail

cargador *m.* porter
cariñoso, -a affectionate, loving
carnaval *m.* carnival
carne *f.* meat
carne de res *f.* beef
carnero *m.* sheep, mutton
carnicería *f.* butcher's shop
caro, -a expensive
carreras de caballos horse races
carretera *f.* highway
carretero *m.* cart-driver
carro *m.* cart
carta *f.* letter
carta, papel de writing paper
cartera *f.* handbag, wallet
casa *f.* home, house
casa de huéspedes boarding house
casi *adv.* almost
casino *m.* club
castaña *f.* chestnut
castaño *m.* chestnut tree, brown
catarro *m.* cold (illness)
catedral *f.* cathedral
católico, -a catholic
catorce fourteen
caucho *m.* rubber
cebada *f.* barley
cebolla *f.* onion
celebración *f.* celebration
celebrar to celebrate, to approve
celebridad *f.* celebrity
celos *m.pl.* jealousy
cena *f.* supper
cenar to dine, to have supper
ceniza *f.* ash
centavo *m.* cent
centeno *m.* rve
centígrado centigrade
central central
céntrico, -a central
centro *m.* centre, middle
Centro América *f.* Central America
centroamericano, -a Central Am-
merican
cepillarse to brush (oneself)
cepillo *m.* brush
cepillo de dientes toothbrush
cerca near
cercano, -a near, neighbouring
cerdo *m.* pig
cereal *m.* cereal

cereza *f.* cherry
cerezo *m.* cherry-tree
cerilla *f.* match
cero *m.* zero
cerquito, -a quite near
cerrado, -a closed
cerrar to close, shut
cerro *m.* hill
cerveza *f.* beer
cielo *m.* sky
ciento hundred
ciento, por per cent
cierto, -a certain, sure
cierto, por incidentally
ciervo *m.* deer
cigarrillo *m.* cigarette
cigarro *m.* cigar
cinco *m.* five
cincuenta *m.* fifty
cine *m.* cinema
cinta *f.* ribbon
cintura *f.* waist, waistline
cinturón *m.* belt
circo de toros *m.* bullring
ciruela *f.* plum
cita *f.* appointment, date
ciudad *f.* city
ciudadela *f.* citadel
civilización *f.* civilisation
claro clearly, pale, light
clase *f.* class, kind
clase, primera first class
clase, segunda second class
clásico, -a classic
clavel *m.* carnation
clima *m.* climate
clínica *f.* clinic, surgery
club *m.* club
cobre *m.* copper
coche *m.* car
cocina *f.* kitchen
cocinar to cook
cocinera *f.* cook
coco *m.* coconut
cocodrilo *m.* crocodile
coctel *m.* cocktail
codo *m.* elbow
coger to catch
coincidencia *f.* coincidence
col *f.* cabbage
colcha *f.* bedspread

colchón *m.* mattress
colectivo, -a collective, co-operative
colegio *m.* school
coliflor *f.* cauliflower
colombiano, -a Columbian
colonia *f.* colony
colonial colonial
color *m.* colour
colorado, -a red
colorido *m.* colouring, pretext
columna *f.* column
comedor *m.* dining-room
comenzar to begin
comer to eat
comercial commercial
comerciante *m.* merchant
comercio *m.* commerce, trade
comida *f.* dinner, food
como as
¿cómo? how?
cómoda *f.* chest of drawers
cómodamente comfortably
cómodo, -a comfortable
compañero *m.* companion
compañía *f.* company
comparación *f.* comparison
comparar to compare
compartir to share
completar to complete, to finish
componer to compose, to repair
compostura *f.* repair
compra *f.* purchase
comprar to buy
¿comprar, dónde puedo? ... where can I buy?
comprender to understand
comprendido, -a understood
comprensión *f.* comprehension
comprobar to prove
compromiso *m.* appointment, date
común common, mutual
comunicación *f.* communication
comunicar to communicate, to connect
comúnmente commonly
con with
concierto *m.* concert
conducir to conduct, to lead
conductor *m.* driver, conductor
conejo *m.* rabbit
confeti *m.* confetti

confianza f. confidence
confirmación f. confirmation
confirmar to confirm
conforme alike, suitable
conforme a according to
congelado, -a frozen
conmigo with me
conocer to know (people, places), to be introduced to
conocimiento m. knowledge; bill of lading
conque so then, so that
conseguir to get, to attain
conservar to keep, to preserve
consistir to consist
consocio m. associate, colleague, partner
constar to consist
constituir to constitute, to form
construcción f. construction
constructor m. builder
construir to build, to construct
consulta f. visit (doctor's); consultation
contacto m. contact
contado, -a rare
contado -a, al (for) cash
contar to count
contemplar to contemplate
contemporáneo, -a contemporary
contener to contain
contento, -a happy
contestar to answer
continuar to continue
contra against
contraer to contract
contrario, -a contrary
contrario, -a, al on the contrary
contraste m. contrast
contrato m. contract
convencer to convince
conveniente convenient
conversación f. conversation
conversar to talk, to converse
cooperación f. co-operation
copia f. copy
corbata f. tie
cordero m. lamb
cordial cordial
corrección f. correction
correcto, -a correct

corredor m. corridor, hall
correo m. mail
correo aéro airmail
correspondencia f. correspondence
corresponder to correspond
correspondiente corresponding
corrida de toros bullfight
corriente f. current, draught
cortar to cut
corte m. cut
corte f. royal court
cortés courteous
cortesía f. courtesy
cortina f. curtain
corto, -a short
corta, -a, muy too short
cosa f. thing
cosecha f. harvest
coser to sew
cosmético m. cosmetic
costa f. coast
costar to cost
costillas f. ribs
costumbre f. custom, habit
costura f. seam, sewing
cotización f. quotation
crecer to grow
crecido, -a grown
crecimiento m. growth
credencial f. credential
crédito m. credit
crédito, a on credit
creer to believe, to think (opinion)
crema f. cream
crepé m. crêpe
criada f. maid
criminal m. criminal
cristal m. crystal
Cristo m. Christ
crudo, -a raw
cruz f. cross
cruzar to cross
cuaderno m. notebook
cuadra f. block, stable
cuadrado m. square
cuadro m. picture
cual which
cuales which
cualesquiera whoever
cualquier any
cualquiera anyone, whatever

cuando when
¿cuánto? how much, how many?
cuarenta forty
cuaresma *f.* lent
cuarto *m.* quarter, fourth, room
cuatro four
cubano, -a Cuban
cubierta *f.* envelope, cover
cubierto *m.* silverware
cubrir to cover
cucaracha *f.* cockroach
cuchara *f.* spoon
cucharada *f.* spoonful
cucharita *f.* teaspoon
cuchilla *f.* razor blade
cuchillo *m.* knife
cuello *m.* collar, neck
cuenta *f.* bill, restaurant check, account
cuento *m.* story
cuervo *m.* raven
cuidado caution
¡cuidado! be careful!
cuidar to take care of
culminar to culminate, to come to a climax
culto, -a cultured
cultura *f.* culture
cumbre *m.* peak, summit
cumpleaños *m.* birthday
cumplir to fulfill
cuñada *m.* brother-in-law
cuñado *f.* sister-in-law
curiosidad *f.* curiosity
curva *f.* curve

CH

chaleco *m.* waistcoat
chanclos *m.* galoshes
chaqueta *f.* coat, jacket
chelín *m.* shilling
cheque *m.* cheque
cheque viajero traveller's cheque
chicle *m.* chewing-gum
chimenea *f.* chimney
chino, -a Chinese
chiquito, -a small, little
chiste *m.* joke
chistoso, -a funny
chocolate *m.* chocolate

chófer *m.* driver
chuleta *f.* chop
chuleta de puerco pork chop

D

dama *f.* lady
danza *f.* dance
dar to give
darse cuenta to realise
datil *m.* date
de from, of
dé give (imp.)
debajo beneath, under
deber ought, should, must
debilidad *f.* weakness
decidir to decide
decimo -a tenth
decir to say, to tell
decisión *f.* decision
declaración *f.* declaration
declarar to declare
decorar to decorate
dedicar to devote
dedo *m.* finger
deducción *f.* deduction
defectivo, -a defective
defecto *m.* defect
defender to defend
definitivamente definitively
dejar to leave, to allow, to let
del of the, from the, about the
delante before
deleitar to delight
delgado thin
delicioso, -a delicious
demás the rest, the others
demasiado too much
démelo give it to me
demorar to delay
dentista *m., f.* dentist
dentro inside
dentro de within
departamento *m.* department
depositado deposited
depositar to deposit
derecha *f.* right
derecho straight, straight ahead
derretir to melt
derrotar to defeat
desabrido, -a tasteless

desagradable disagreeable
desalquilado, -a free, unhired, unrented
desamueblado, -a unfurnished
desaparecer to disappear
desarrollo *m.* development
desastroso, -a disastrous
desayuno *m.* breakfast
descansar to rest
descender to descend, to go down
decompuesto, -a out of order
descontar to discount
describer to describe
describiendo describing
descubridor *m.* discoverer
descubrimiento *m.* discovery
descripción *f.* description
descriptivo, -a descriptive
descubrir to discover
descuento *m.* discount
desde from
desear to wish
desenvolver to unwrap
deseo *m.* desire
deshacerse to get rid of
desinfectante *m.* disinfectant
desnudarse to undress
desnudo, -a nude, naked
desobedecer to disobey
despacho *m.* office, despatch, shipment
despacio slowly
despedida *f.* departure
despedirse to take leave of
despertar to wake up
después after
destacado, -a distinguished
destruir to destruct
desvío *m.* detour
detalle *m.* detail
detener to detain
detestar to detest
detrás behind
devolver to return (a thing)
día *m.* day
diagnóstico *m.* diagnosis
diamante *m.* diamond
diario *m.* daily, journal
diccionario *m.* dictionary
diciembre *m.* December
dictar to dictate

diecinueve nineteen
dieciocho eighteen
dieciséis sixteen
diecisiete seventeen
diente *m.* tooth
diez ten
diferente different
difernencia *f.* difference
difícil difficult
dificultades *f.* troubles, difficulties
dígame tell me
digestible digestible
digestión *f.* digestion
digo I say, tell
dije I said, told
dinero *m.* money
Dios God
diplomacia *f.* diplomacy
diplomático, -a diplomat
dirección *f.* address, direction
directamente directly
directo, -a direct
directorio *m.* directory
dirigir to direct, to address
disco *m.* gramophone record
discurso *m.* speech
discusión *f.* discussion
discutir to discuss, to argue
dispensar to excuse
dispénseme excuse me
disponer to dispose
disposición *f.* disposal
distancia *f.* distance
distinto, -a different
distribución *f.* distribution
distribuir to distribute
diversión *f.* entertainment
divertirse to have a good time
dividido divided
dividir to divide
doble double
doce twelve
docena *f.* dozen
doctor, -a doctor
documento *m.* document
dólar *m.* dollar
doler to hurt
dolor *m.* ache
dominación *f.* rule
dominar to dominate, to rule
domingo *m.* Sunday

donde where
dormir to sleep
dormirse to go to sleep
dormitorio *m.* bedroom, dormitory
dos two
doy I give
drama *m.* drama
duda *f.* doubt, uncertainty
dudar to doubt
dueño, -a owner
dulce sweet
durable durable
duradero, -a durable, lasting
durante during
durar to last
duro, -a tough, hard

E

¡Ea! Well!
economía *f.* economy
ecuestre equestrian
echar to pour, to thow, to dump, to put out
edificio *m.* building
educar to educate, to bring up
efectivo, -a effective
efectivo, -a, hacer to cash
efecto *m.* effect
efectos *m.pl.*, goods
ejotes *m.* French beans
el the
él he
electricidad *f.* electricity
eléctrico, -a electric
elefante *m.* elephant
elegante elegant
elegir to choose, to select, to elect
elevado, -a high
elevador *m.* elevator, lift
ella she
ello it, that
embarcar to sail embark
emborracharse to get drunk
embrague *m.* clutch
emergencia *f.* emergency
emoción *f.* emotion
emperador *m.* emperor
empleado *m.* servant, employee
empresa *f.* enterprise
en in, on, at

enano *m.* dwarf
encaje *m.* lace
encantar to enchant
encanto *m.* enchantment, charm
encargar to put in charge
encargarse de to take charge of
encender to light, to burn
encender la luz to put on the light
encerrar to lock in
encima above, overhead
encima de on, upon
encontrar to meet, to find, to encounter
encontrarse con to meet with
encuentro *m.* encounter
enero *m.* January
enfermarse to become ill
enfermedad *f.* illness
enfermo, -a sick, ill
enfermo, estoy I am sick, ill
enfriarse to get cold
enojado, -a angry
enorme enormous
ensalada *f.* salad
enseñar to teach, to show
entender to understand
entendido understood
enterarse to find out
entiendo, yo I understand
entonces then
entrada *f.* entrance
entrar to enter, to go in, to come in
entre between, among
entrega *f.* delivery
entregar to deliver
entretención *f.* amusement
entretener to entertain
entretenido, -a amusing, diverting
entrevista *f.* interview, appointment
entusiasmarse to get enthusiastic
entusiasmo *m.* enthusiasm
enviar to send
envidiar to envy
envío *m.* shipment
envolver to wrap
envuelto, -a wrapped
epico, -a epic
episodio *m.* episode
época *f.* epoch, period
equipaje *m.* luggage
equivalente equivalent

equivaler to be equal, to be equivalent
equivocarse to make a mistake
era *f.* era
era was, were, used to be, it was, it used to be
error *m.* error
es is, are, it is
escalera *f.* staircase, ladder
escalones *m.* stairs, steps
escapar(se) to escape
esclusa *f.* lock
escocés Scottish
Escocia *f.* Scotland
escribiendo writing
escribir to write
escritor, -a writer
escritorio *m.* desk
escuchar to listen to
escuela *f.* school
escultórico, -a sculptural
escultura *f.* sculpture
esencial essential
eso, -a that
espacioso, -a spacious, roomy
espalda *f.* back
España *f.* Spain
español, -a Spaniard, Spanish
espárragos *m.* asparagus
especial special
especialmente specially
espectáculo *m.* spectacle
esperado hoped, waited, expected
esperanza *f.* hope
esperar to hope, to wait, to expect
espiga *f.* ear (of wheat)
espinaca *f.* spinach
espiritual spiritual
espléndido, -a splendid
esponja *f.* sponge
esposa *f.* wife
esposo *m.* husband
esquina *f.* corner
esta *f.* this
ésta *f.* this one
está is (you), are
está, ¿cómo . . . usted? how are you?
establecer to establish
estación *f.* station, season
estación de gasolina petrol station

estacionar to park
estadio *m.* stadium
estado *m.* state
Estados Unidos *m.* United States
estamos we are
estampilla *f.* stamp
están they are, you are
estaño *m.* tin
estar to be
estatua *f.* statue
este, -a this
este *m.* east
éste this one
estilo *m.* style
estimar to value, to respect
estómago *m.* stomach
estornudo *m.* sneeze
estos *m.* these
estoy I am
estrecho, -a tight, narrow
estudiante student
estudio *m.* study
estúpido, -a stupid
estuve I was
etapa *f.* station, stage
Europa *f.* Europe
evadir to evade, avoid
evocador *m.* evocator
evolución *f.* evolution
exacto, -a exact
exageración *f.* exaggeration
exagerar to exaggerate
examinar to examine
excavación *f.* excavation
excelente excellent
excepto except
excesivo, -a excessive
excuséme excuse me
exhibición *f.* exhibition
exhibir to exhibit
exigir to demand
existencia *f.* existence
éxito *m.* success
experiencia *f.* experience
experimentar to test, to experience
explicación *f.* explanation
explicar to explain
explicativo, -a explanatory
explotar to exploit
exportación *f.* export
exportar to export

expresar to express
expresión *f.* expression
exquisito, -a exquisite
extender to extend, to spread
exterior exterior, outside room
extraer to extract
extranjero, -a foreign, foreigner
extraño, -a strange, foreign
extraordinario, -a extraordinary
extremo, -a extreme, farthest
extremo *m.* extreme, end

F

fábrica *f.* factory
facial facial
fácil easy
facilidad *f.* facility, ease
facilitar to facilitate, to make easy
facturar to check, to invoice
facultad *f.* faculty
fachada *f.* front, facade
faja *f.* girdle
falda *f.* skirt
falta *f.* lack, want
faltar to lack, to miss
familia *f.* family
famoso, -a famous
fango *m.* mud
farmacia *f.* chemist's
favor *m.* favour
favorecer to favour
fealdad *f.* ugliness
febrero *m.* February
fecha *f.* date
felicidad *f.* happiness
felicitar to congratulate
feliz happy
feo, -a ugly
ferrocarril *m.* railway
fertilizante *m.* fertiliser
fervor *m.* fervour, enthusiasm
festival *f.* festival
festividad *f.* festivity, feast
fiebre *f.* fever, temperature
fieltro *m.* felt
fiesta *f.* feast
fiesta, día de holiday
fijar to fix, to establish
fijarse to imagine
fijarse en to pay attention to

filete *m.* cutlet
fin *m.* end, conclusion
fin, al at last
fin, por at last
fin en finally
finalmente finally
fino, -a fine
firma *f.* firm, concern
firmar to sign
flor *f.* flower
florista *m.,* *f.* florist
flotando floating
flotar to float
fluctuación fluctuation
foca *f.* seal
fogón *m.* fireplace, stove
fonógrafo *m.* gramophone
formal formal
formar to form
formar parte de to be a member of
formulario *m.* form (to fill in)
fortalesa *f.* fortress, courage
fortuna *f.* fortune
fósforo *m.* match
foto *f.* photograph
fotografía *f.* photograph
fotografiar to photograph
fracasar to fail
fracaso *m.* failure
fracción *f.* fraction
frambuesa *f.* raspberry
francés, -a French, Frenchman, Frenchwoman
Francia *f.* France
franela *f.* flannel
frecuentemente frequently
fregadero *m.* sink
freír to fry
frenos *m.* car brakes
frente in front, opposite
fresa *f.* strawberry
fresco *m.* cool, fresh
fríjoles *m.* beans
frío, -a cold
frío, tengo I am cold
frito, -a fried
fruta *f.* fruit
fuente *f.* platter, tray, fountain
fuera without, outside
fuerte *m.* fort
fuí I was, I went

fumar to smoke
función *f.* function, performance
funcionar to function
funcionario *m.* public official
fundador *m.* founder
fundar to establish
funeral *m.* funeral
fútbol *m.* football (soccer)

G

gabardina *f.* gabardine, raincoat
gala *f.* gala, elegance
galería *f.* gallery, corridor
gallego, -a Galician
gallera *f.* cock pit
galleta *f.* biscuit
gallina *f.* hen
gallo *m.* cock
gallos, pelea de cock fight
ganado *m.* cattle
ganancia *f.* profit
ganas *f.* desire, yen
ganso *m.* goose
garage *m.* garage
gas *m.* gas
gasolina *f.* petrol
gato *m.* cat
gaveta *f.* locker
gaviota *f.* sea-gull
generador *m.* generator
general *m.* general
generalmente generally, ordinarily
género *m.* material, gender
genio *m.* genius, temper
gente *f.* people
gentil graceful, courteous
gerencia *f.* management
gerente *m.* manager
Ginebra *f.* Geneva
ginebra *f.* gin
gira *f.* tour, excursion
giralda *f.* weather-cock, vane
girar to spin
giro *m.* draft
gloria *f.* glory
gobernar to rule, to govern
gobierno *m.* government
golf *m.* golf
golondrina *f.* swallow
goma *f.* rubber

gordo, -a fat
gorila *m.* gorilla
gorra *f.* cap
gorrión *m.* sparrow
gótico, -a Gothic
gozar (de) to enjoy
gozo *m.* joy
gracia *f.* grace, charm
gracias *f.* thank you, thanks
gracioso, -a graceful, amusing
grado *m.* degree
grande, gran large, big
grandioso, -a magnificent
granja *f.* farm
grano *m.* grain
gratis gratis, free
grato, -a pleasant
grave grave, very ill
Grecia *f.* Greece
griego, -a Greek
gris *m.* grey
gritar to shout, to scream
grito *m.* shout, scream
grosella *f.* currant
gruesa *f.* gross
grupo *m.* group
guagua *f.* bus (Cub.)
guantes *m.pl.* gloves
guapo, -a handsome
guía *m.* guide
guía *f.* time-table, guide book
guía del viajero road map
guisado *m.* stew
guisantes *m.* peas
guitarra *f.* guitar
gustar to like
   si gusta if you please
gusto *m.* taste, pleasure

H

ha you have (he, she, it) has
haber to be
había there was, there were, was
   there? were there? there used to
   be, did there used to be?
habichuelas *f.* beans
habitación *f.* room, chamber
habitantes *m.pl.* inhabitants
habla (he, she) speaks (you) speak
hablado talked

hablar to speak
hacer to do
hacia towards
hacienda *f.* ranch, large farm
haitiano, -a Haitian
hambre *f.* hunger
hambre, tengo I am hungry
harmonía *f.* harmony
hasta up to, until
hasta la vista; hasta luego until we meet again
hay there is, there are
hay que it is necessary
hazaña *f.* deed, exploit, feat
helada *f.* frost
helado *m.* ice-cream
helar to freeze
hélice *f.* propeller
heno *m.* hay
hermana *f.* sister
hermano *m.* brother
hermoso, -a beautiful
hermosura *f.* beauty
hervir to boil
hielo *m.* ice
hierro *m.* iron
higo *m.* fig
higuera *f.* fig-tree
hija *f.* daughter
hijastro, -a step-son, step-daughter
hijo *m.* son
hilandera *f.* spinner
hilo *m.* thread
hipo *m.* hiccough
historia *f.* history
historiador *m.* historian
histórico, -al historical
hogar *m.* home
hoja *f.* sheet, leaf
¡Hola! Hello!
holandés, -a Dutch
hombre *m.* man
hombro *m.* shoulder
honor *m.* honour
hora *f.* hour, time
horario *m.* hour hand, time-table
horno *m.* oven
hortelano *m.* farmer, gardener
hospital *m.* hospital
hospitalidad *f.* hospitality
hotel *m.* hotel

hoy today
hoz *f.* sickle
hubo there was, there were, was there? were there?
huerta *f.* vegetable garden
huésped *m.* guest, host
huerto *m.* orchard
huevo *m.* egg
huevo duro hard boiled egg
huevo frito fried egg
huevo pasado por agua soft boiled egg
humano, -a human
humedad *f.* humidity
humor *m.* humour
hundir to sink, to sag
húngaro, -a Hungarian

I

iba (he, she, it) went, used to go, was going
idea *f.* idea
idear to plan, to invent
idioma *m.* language
iglesia *f.* church
ignorancia *f.* ignorance
ignorante ignorant
igual equal
ilegal illegal
ilustración *f.* illustration
imagen *f.* image
imaginación *f.* imagination
imborrable indelible
imitación *f.* imitation
impaciencia *f.* impatience
imperio *m.* empire
impermeable *m.* raincoat, waterproof
importación *f.* import
importante important
importar to import
importe *m.* amount, value
imposibilidad *f.* impossibility
imposible impossible
impresión *f.* impression
imprimir to print
impuesto *m.* duty, tax
incluír to include
incompetente incompetent
incorrecto, -a incorrect

increíble incredible
independencia *f.* independence
indicación *f.* suggestion, hint
indigeno, -a indigenous
indigestión *f.* indigestion
indio, -a Indian
indispuesto, -a indisposed
individuo *m.* individual
indolente indolent
industria *f.* industry
industrial industrial
infección *f.* infection
influencia *f.* influence
información *f.* information
informar to inform
ingeniería *f.* engineering
ingeniero *m.* engineer
Inglaterra *f.* England
inglés -a English
inicial initial
iniciar to begin, to start
inmenso, -a immense
inmediatamente immediately
inmediato, -a immediate
inocular to inoculate
insecto *m.* insect
insignificante insignificant
instalación *f.* installation
instalar to install
instante *m.* instant
instructivo, -a instructive
insultar to insult
insulto *m.* insult
inteligente intelligent
intercambio *m.* exchange, interchange
interés *m.* interest
interesante interesting
interesar to interest
interior *m.* interior
internacional international
interrumpir to interrupt
íntimamente intimately
íntimo, -a intimate
intranquilidad *f.* uneasiness
introducción *f.* introduction
invadir to invade
invasor *m.* invader
invierno *m.* winter
invitación *f.* invitation
invitado, -a guest, visitor

invitar to invite
ir to go
irse to go away
isla *f.* island
isleño, -a islander
Italia *f.* Italy
italiano, -a Italian
itinerario *m.* timetable, itinerary
izquierda *f.* left

J

jabalí *m.* boar
jabón *m.* soap
jabonera *f.* soap-dish
jamás never
jamón *m.* ham
Japón *m.* Japan
jardín *m.* garden
jarra *f.* pitcher
jefe *m.* chief, boss
jira *f.* excursion, tour
jornales *m.* wages
joven young
joyería *f.* jewellery store
judío, -a Jewish
juego *m.* game
juego hacer to match
jueves *m.* Thursday
jugar to play (a game), to gamble
jugo *m.* juice
juguete *m.* toy
juicio *m.* judgment
julio *m.* July
junio *m.* June
junto near, close
juntos, -as together
justamente justly, exactly
justicia *f.* justice
justillo *m.* brassière
justo, -a just, fair
juventud *f.* youth

K

kilo *m.* kilo, kilogramme
kilómetro *m.* kilometre

L

la the
laborioso, -a laborious, assiduous

lado *m.* side
lado, al, de by the side of
lago *m.* lake
lágrima *f.* tear
laguna *f.* lagoon
lámpara *f.* lamp
lana *f.* wool
lancha *f.* launch, boat
lápiz *m.* pencil
largo, -a long
largo, -a, muy too long
lástima *f.* pity
lastimarse to hurt oneself
látigo *m.* whip
latín *m.* Latin
latinoamericano, -a Latin America
lavabo *m.* wash basin
lavandería *f.* laundry
lavar to wash
lavarse to wash (oneself)
leal loyal
lección *f.* lesson
leche *f.* milk
lechuga *f.* lettuce
leer to read
legal legal
legumbre *f.* vegetable
lejos far
lejos, ¿qué tan . . . es? how far
 is it?
lengua *f.* tongue
lentejas *f.* lentils
león *m.* lion
leopardo *m.* leopard
letra *f.* letter
letrero *m.* sign
levantar to raise, to lift, pick up
levantarse to get up
ley *f.* law
liar to tie
libertador *m.* liberator
libre free
librería *f.* bookshop
libreta *f.* booklet
libro *m.* book
liebre *f.* hare
lima *f.* lime
limón *m.* lemon
limonada *f.* lemonade
limonero *m.* lemon-tree
limpiar to clean

limpiavidrios *m.* windscreen wiper
limpio, -a clean
línea *f.* line
líneas aéreas *f.pl.* airlines
lino *m.* linen
lío *m.* a scrape, trouble
lirio *m.* lily
lista *f.* list
lista de platos bill of fare, menu
listo, -a ready
literario, -a literary
literatura *f.* literature
lo *m.* it, him
lobo *m.* wolf
local local
local *m.* premises, site
loco, -a crazy
lodo *m.* mud
lógicamente logically
lona *f.* canvas
Londres *m.* London
loro *m.* parrot
lotería *f.* lottery
lubricación *f.* lubrication
lubricante *m.* lubricant
lubricar to lubricate
luchar to fight
lucir to shine
luego later
luego, hasta so long
lugar *m.* place
lujo *m.* luxury
luna *f.* moon
lunes *m.* Monday
luz *f.* light

LL

llama *f.* flame
llamar to call
llamarse to be called (named)
llanta *f.* tyre
llave *f.* key
llegada *f.* arrival
llegada, al upon arrival
llegar to arrive
llegué I arrived, got here, got
 there
llevar to wear, to carry, to take
 (someone or something somewhere)
llorar to cry

llover to rain
lluvia *f.* rain

M

madera *f.* wood
madrastra *f.* stepmother
madre *f.* mother
madrina *f.* godmother
madrugada *f.* dawn
maestro, -a teacher
magnífico, -a magnificent, splendid
mago *m.* magician, wizard
Magos, los tres Reyes the three Wise Men
mal badly, ill
maleta *f.* suitcase
malo, -a bad
mamá *f.* mama
mandado *m.* errand
mandar to send
manecillas hands (of a watch)
manejar to drive, to manage
manga *f.* sleeve
manifestación *f.* manifestation, demonstration
mano *f.* hand
mansión *f.* mansion
mantel *m.* tablecloth
mantener to maintain
mantequilla *f.* butter
manzana *f.* apple
manzano *m.* apple-tree
mañana *f.* morning, tomorrow
mañana, por la, tomorrow morning
mapa *m.* map
máquina *f.* machine
máquina de escribir typewriter
maquinaria *f.* works, machinery
mar *m. f.* sea
maravilloso, -a wonderful
marcha *f.* march
marcha, en it is starting
marearse to get seasick, airsick
mareo *m.* dizziness
marido *m.* husband
marina *f.* navy
mármol *m.* marble
martes *m.* Tuesday
marzo *m.* March

más more
más que more than
masa *f.* bread, dough
material *m.* materials, stuff
matriculación *f.* registration
matricular to matriculate, to register
mayo *m.* May
mayor main, major, eldest
mazorca *f.* corn-cob
mecánico, -a mechanic
medianoche *f.* midnight
mediante by means of
medias *f.* stockings
medicina *f.* medicine
médico *m.* doctor
medio means, middle, half
medio, por . . . de by means of
mediodía *m.* midday, noon
medir to measure
mejicano, -a Mexican
mejor better
mejor, a lo probably, maybe, perhaps, unexpectedly
mejorarse to get better
melocotón *m.* peach
melón *m.* melon
memoria *f.* memory
menina *f.* young lady-in-waiting
menos but, except, less
menos, al at least
mentir to lie
mentira *f.* lie
menú *m.* menu
menudo, -a small. little, minute
menudo, -a, a often
mercadito *m.* small market place
mercado *m.* market
mercancía *f.* merchandise
mercurio *m.* mercury
mermelada *f.* marmalade
mes *m.* month
mes, por by the month
mesa *f.* table
metal *m.* metal
metro *m.* metre
mi my
mí me, myself
mídaselo try it on (imp.)
miedo *m.* fear
miel de abejas *f.* honey

miembro *m.* member
mientras while
miércoles *m.* Wednesday
mil thousand
militar military
militarmente militarily
millón *m.* million
mina *f.* mine
mineral *m.* mineral
ministerio *m.* ministry
minutero *m.* minute hand
minuto *m.* minute
minuto, espere un wait a minute
mío, -a mine
mirar to look at
mire look (imp.)
mirto *m.* myrtle
mis my
misa *f.* mass
mismo, -a same
mitad *f.* half
moda *f.* fashion, style
modernizar to modernise
moderno, -a modern
modista *f.* dressmaker
modo *m.* manner
molestar to bother
momento *m.* moment
moneda *f.* money, currency
monetario, -a monetary
mono *m.* monkey
montaña *f.* mountain
montañoso, -a mountainous
monumento *m.* monument
mora *f.* mulberry
moral *m.* mulberry-tree
morder to bite
moreno, -a brunette
morir to die
morisco, -a Moorish
moros *m.pl.* Moors
mosaico *m.* mosaic, tile
mosca *f.* fly
mostaza *f.* mustard
mostrar to show
motivar to cause
motivo *m.* motive, reason, theme
motor *m.* motor
motorista *m., f.* motorist
moviendo moving
mozo *m.* waiter, servant

muchacha *f.* girl
muchacho *m.* boy
mucho, -a much
muchos, -as many
mudar to move
mueble *m.* furniture
muelle *m.* pier
muestra *f.* sample
mujer *f.* woman
mula *f.* mule
mundo *m.* world
mural *m.* mural
museo *m.* museum
música *f.* music
mutuo, -a mutual
muy very
muy bien very well

N

nabo *m.* turnip
nacer to be born
nacimiento *m.* birth
nación *f.* nation
nacional national
nacionalidad *f.* nationality
nada nothing
nadar to swim
nadie nobody
naranja *f.* orange
naranja, jugo de *m.* orange juice
naranjada *f.* orangeade
narración *f.* narration
narrativo, -a narrative
natilla *f.* custard
nativo, -a native
natural natural
naturalmente naturally
navegable navigable
Navidad *f.* Christmas
necesario, -a necessary
necesidad *f.* necessity
necesitar to need
negativo negative
negligente negligen
negocio *m.* business
negro *m.* negro
negro, -a black
nena *f.* baby girl
nene *m.* baby boy
nervioso, -a nervous

nevar to snow
nevera *f.* refrigerato.
ni . . . ni neither . . . nor
nieta *f.* granddaughter
nieto *m.* grandson
nieve *f.* snow
ninguno no one
niña *f.* girl
niñez *f.* childhood
niño, -a child
nivel *m.* level
no no
no . . . ni not even
noble noble
noche *f.* evening, night
noche, esta to-night
Noche Buena *f.* Christmas Eve
nocturno, -a nocturnal
nogal *m.* walnut-tree
nombre *m.* name
nomeolvides *m.* forget-me-not
norte *m.* north
Norte América *f.* North America
norteamericano, -a North American
Noruega *f.* Norway
nos us, ourselves
nosotros, -as we, us
nota *f.* note
notar to note, to notice
notario *m.* notary-public
noticiario *m.* newsreel
noticias *f.* news
novela *f.* novel
noventa ninety
noviembre *m.* November
nube *f.* cloud
nublado, -a cloudy
nuera *f.* daughter-in-law
nuestro, -a our, ours
nueve nine
nuevo, -a new
nuez *f.* nut
número *m.* number
numeroso, -a numerous
nunca never

O

o either, or
obligar to oblige
obra *f.* work

obrero *m.* workman, labourer
observar to observe, to watch
obtener to obtain
ocasión *f.* occasion
occidente *m.* west, occident
océano *m.* ocean
ochenta eighty
ocho eight
octubre *m.* October
oculista *m., f.* oculist
ocupación *f.* occupation
ocupado, -a busy
ocupar to occupy
ocurrente witty
ocurrir to occur
odiar to hate
odio *m.* hatred
ofender to offend
ofendido, -a offended
ofensivo, -a offensive
oficial official
oficina *f.* office
ofrecer to offer
ofrecimiento *m.* offer, offering
oído *m.* hearing
oiga listen, hear (imp.)
oír to hear
ojalá I hope (or I wish) that
ola *f.* wave
oleo *m.* oil
olfato *m.* smell
olivo *m.* olive-tree
olmo *m.* elm-tree
olvidar to forget
once eleven
onza *f.* ounce
ópera *f.* opera
operación *f.* operation
operador *m.* operator
opinión *f.* opinion
oportunidad *f.* opportunity
oportuno, -a fitting, appropriate
orden *m.* order, series; *f.* order, command
órdenes orders
órdenes, a sus at your service
ordinario, -a ordinary
oreja *f.* ear
oriente east, orient
origen *m.* origin, source
original original

orilla *f.* shore, bank
orquesta *f.* orchestra
orquídea *f.* orchid
oro *m.* gold
oscuro, -a dark
oso *m.* bear
ostra *f.* oyster
otoño *m.* autumn
otorgar to give, to grant
otro, -a other
otro, uno u one or the other
otros, -as others, other
oveja *f.* sheep
oye hear, listen (imp.)

P

paciencia *f.* patience
paciente patient
pacífico *m.* Pacific Ocean
padrastro *m.* stepfather
padre *m.* father
padres *m.* parents
padrino *m.* godfather
pagar to pay
pago *m.* payment
pagué I paid
país *m.* country
paisaje *m.* landscape
paja *f.* straw
pájaro *m.* bird
pala *f.* shovel
palabra *f.* word
palacio *m.* palace
pálido, -a pallid, pale
palma *f.* palm-tree
palmeras *f.* palm-trees
paloma *f.* dove
pan *m.* bread
Panamá *m.* Panama
pantalones *m.* trousers
pantalla *f.* cinema screen, lamp shade
paño *m.* cloth
pañuelo *m.* handkerchief
papa *f.* potato
papel *m.* paper
papelería *f.* stationer's shop
paquete *m.* package
par *m.* pair, couple
para for, to

parabrisa *m.* windscreen
parada *f.* stop
parado, -a stopped
paraguas *m.* umbrella
pararse to stand up, to stop
parcial partial
parcialmente partially
pardo brown
pare stop (imp.)
parecer to appear, seem
parecerse to resemble
parecido *m.* similarity
pared *f.* wall
pareja *f.* couple, partner
pargo *m.* red snapper (braise)
parientes *m.* relatives
parque *m.* park
parqueadero *m.* parking
parilla *f.* grill
parte *f.* part
parte, de su on his behalf
partes, entodas everywhere
partida *f.* departure, game, item, war campaign
pasa *f.* raisin
pasado, -a past
pasado, -a mañana day after tomorrow
pasaje *m.* ticket, journey
pasajero *m.* passenger
pasaporte *m.* passport
pasar to pass
Pascua *f.* Easter
pasear to take a walk, a ride
paseo, dar un to go for a walk, ride
paso *m.* pace, passage
pasta *f.* paste
pastel *m.* pie, cake
pastelillo *m.* little pie
pastor *m.* shepherd
patio *m.* inner court
pato *m.* duck
patria *f.* country, fatherland
patriótico, -a patriotic
patrón *m.* boss, pattern
pavimento *m.* pavement
pavo *m.* turkey
pavo real *m.* peacock
pedir to order, to ask
peine *m.* comb
película *f.* film

peligro *m.* danger
peligroso, -a dangerous
pelo *m.* hair
penicilina *f.* penicillin
pensamiento *m.* thought, pansy
pensar to think
pensión *f.* pension, boarding house
peón *m.* peasant
peor worse
pepino *m.* cucumber
pequeño, -a small
pequeño, -a, muy too small
pera *f.* pear
peral *m.* pear-tree
perder to lose
perderse to get lost
perdiz *f.* partridge
perdonar to forgive, to pardon
perezoso, -a lazy
perfecto, -a perfect
perfume *m.* perfume
periódico *m.* newspaper
perla *f.* pearl
permanecer to remain, to stay
permanencia *f.* sojourn, stay
permanente permanent, permanent wave
permítame allow me
permitido, -a permitted
permitir to allow
pero but
perro *m.* dog
persistir to persist
personal personal
personalidad *f.* personality
personalmente personally, in person
persuadir to persuade
pesar to weigh
pesar, a . . . de in spite of
pesarse to weigh yourself
pescado *m.* fish
pescar to fish
peso *m.* weight, peso
petróleo *m.* petroleum, crude oil
picante hot, spicy, piquant
pie *m.* foot
piedra *f.* stone, jewel
piel *f.* leather, hide
pierna *f.* leg
pieza *f.* room, piece, part

píldora *f.* pill
piloto *m.* pilot
pimienta *f.* pepper
pintado, -a painted
pintar to paint
pintor *m.* painter
pintoresco, -a picturesque
pintura *f.* painting
piña *f.* pineapple
pipa *f.* pipe
pirata *m.* pirate
piscina *f.* swimming pool
piso *m.* floor
piso baja ground floor
placer *m.* pleasure
plan *m.* plan
planchar to iron
planeta *m.* planet
plano *m.* plan, drawing
planta *f.* plant
plantación *f.* plantation
plátano *m.* banana
plato *m.* dish, plate
playa *f.* beach
plaza *f.* square, market
plaza de toros *f.* bullring
pleno, -a full, complete
pluma *f.* pen
pobre poor
poco, -a little
poco a poco little by little
poder to be able
poema *m.* poem
poesía *f.* poetry, poem
poeta *m.* poet
policía *m.* policeman
política *f.* politics
pollo *m.* chicken
polvos *m.* powder
poner to put, to set
ponerse to put on, to become
popular popular
populoso, -a densely populated
por by, for, through
por qué why
porque because
portezuela *f.* car door
portugués, -a Portuguese
posible possible
posiblemente possibly
posición *f.* position

positivo, -a positive
postal *f.* postal
postre *m.* dessert
postrero, -a last
practicar to practise
práctico, -a practical
prado *m.* lawn, meadow
precio *m.* price
precioso, -a precious
precisión *f.* precision
predilecto, -a preferred, favourite
preferir to prefer
pregunta *f.* question
preguntar to ask
premio *m.* prize
preocupado, -a worried
preocupar to worry
preparación *f.* preparation
preparar to prepare
presencia *f.* presence
presentar to present, to introduce
presente *m.* present
presidencial presidential
presidente *m.* president
presidir to preside
prestar to lend
primavera *f.* Spring
primero, -a first
primitivo, -a primitive
primo, -a cousin
princesa *f.* princess
principal principal
príncipe *m.* prince
principio *m.* beginning
principios de, a at the beginning of
prisa *f.* haste
prisa, de quickly, fast
prisa, dése hurry (imp.)
privilegiado, -a privileged
probablemente probably
probar, to taste, to prove, to test
proceder to proceed
producción *f.* production
producir to produce
producto *m.* product
profesión *f.* profession
profundo, -a profound, deep
programa *m.* programme
progresar to progress
progreso *m.* progress
prohibir to prohibit

prohibida la entrada keep out
prometer to promise
pronto soon, fast
pronto de suddenly
pronunciación *f.* pronunciation
pronunciar to pronounce
propiedad *f.* property
propina *f.* tip
propio, -a proper, own
proponer to propose
proporcionar to furnish with, to supply
prosa *f.* prose
protección *f.* protection
protestante Protestant
protestar to protest
provechoso, -a useful
provincia *f.* province
provincial provincial
próximo, -a next
prueba *f.* proof
publicación *f.* publication
público, -a public
pueblo *m.* town, people
puente *m.* bridge
puerco *m.* pork, pig
puerta *f.* door
puerto *m.* port
pues since, for
pulsera *f.* bracelet
pulsera, reloj de wrist-watch
pulso *m.* pulse
punta *f.* point, tip
punto *m.* point, dot
punto, en exactly
puntual punctual
puño *m.* cuff, fist
pureza *f.* purity
puro *m.* cigar

Q

que that, which
¿qué? what, which?
¿qué es eso? what is that?
quebrar to break
quedar(se) to stay, to remain
quejido *m.* groan
quemar to burn
querer to want, to love
querido, -a dear, beloved

queso *m.* cheese
quien who (rel. pron.)
quién who (interr. pron.)
quienquiera whoever
quince fifteen
quizás perhaps

R

rábano *m.* radish
racial racial
radiador *m.* radiator
radio radio
raíz *f.* root
rancho *m.* ranch
rápidamente rapidly
rápido, -a rapid
rara vez seldom
raro, -a rare, odd
rascarse to scratch
rata *f.* rat
rato *m.* moment
ratón *m.* mouse
rayón *m.* rayon
raza *f.* race
razón *f.* reason
real royal
realidad *f.* reality
realidad, en in fact
realista realistic
realizar to make, perform, realise
recepción *f.* reception
receta *f.* prescription
reciber to receive
recibidor *m.* living-room
recibo *m.* receipt
reciente recent
reclamación *f.* complaint
reclamar to complain (against)
recomendación *f.* recommendation
recomendar to recommend
reconocer to recognise
reconocimiento *m.* recognition
recordar to remember
recorrer to go over, to travel
recreación *f.* recreation
recuerdo *m.* souvenir
recuerdos *m.pl.* regards
reducir to reduce
reemplazar to replace
refajo *m.* slip, underskirt

refrescar to refresh
refresco *m.* refreshment
refrigeración *f.* refrigeration
refrigeradora *f.* refrigerator
regadera *f.* shower
regalo *m.* present
región *f.* region
registración *f.* registration
registrar to register
regla *f.* ruler, rule
regresar to return
regreso *m.* return
regularidad *f.* regularity
reinar to reign
reírse to laugh
relación *f.* relation
relámpago *m.* lightning
relatar to relate, to tell
relativo, -a relative
relegar to relegate
reloj *m.* watch
relojería *f.* watchmaker's shop
relojero *m.* watchmaker
remendar to mend
remolacha *f.* beet
renacimiento *m.* renaissance
renombrado, -a renowned
renovar to renew, to replace
renta *f.* rent, income
reparar to repair
repartir to distribute
repente, de suddenly
repitir to repeat
repollo *m.* cabbage
representante representative
representar to represent
república *f.* republic
requerir to require
resbalarse to slip, to slide
reserva *f.* reserve, reservation
reservar to reserve
resfriado *m.* cold (illness)
resfriarse to catch cold
residencial residential
residir to reside
respectivamente respectively
respecto a with respect to
respetable respectable
respeto *m.* respect
responsable responsible
restaurante *m.* restaurant

resto *m.* rest
resto, el the rest
restricción *f.* restriction
resurrección *f.* resurrection
retiro *m.* retirement
reunión *f.* reunion
reunir to reunite
reunirse to meet, to assemble
revisar to examine, to revise
revolver to mix
revuelto scrambled
rey *m.* king
ridículo, -a ridiculous
río *m.* river
riqueza *f.* riches
risa *f.* laughter
rito *m.* rite
robar to steal, to rob
robo *m.* theft, robbery
robustez *m.* robustness
rogar to beg
rojo, -a red
rollo *m.* roll film
romano, -a Roman
romántico, -a romantic
romper to tear, to break
ron *m.* rum
roncar to snore
ronquido *m.* snoring
ropa *f.* clothes
ropa interior underwear
rosa *f.* rose
rosario *m.* rosary
rosbif *m.* roast beef
rubio, -a blond
ruborizarse to blush
rueda *f.* wheel
ruido *m.* noise
ruina *f.* ruin
rumba *f.* rumba
rumor *m.* rumour
rural *m.* rural
Rusia *f.* Russia
ruso Russian
ruta *f.* route

S

sábado *m.* Saturday
sábana *f.* sheet
saber to know

sabio, -a wise
sacacorchos *m.* corkscrew
saco *m.* coat
sal *f.* salt
sala *f.* parlour, large room, living-room
salado, -a salty
salario *m.* salary
salida *f.* departure, exit
salir to leave
salsa *f.* sauce, dressing
saltar to jump
salud *f.* health
saludar to greet
saludo *m.* greeting
salvar to save
sandía *f.* watermelon
sandwich *m.* sandwich
sangre *f.* blood
sarape *m.* Mexican blanket
sardina *f.* sardine
sastre *m.* tailor
sastrería *f.* tailor's shop
satisfacción *f.* satisfaction
satisfacer to satisfy
secante *m.* (blotting) paper
secarse to dry (yourself)
sección *f.* section
secretario, -a secretary
secreto *m.* secret
sector *m.* sector
sed *f.* thirst
sed, tengo I am thirsty
seda *f.* silk
sedativo *m.* sedative
seguir to follow, to proceed, to continue
según according to
segundo, -a second
seguridad *f.* security, certainty
seguro, -a safe, sure
seguro *m.* insurance
seis six
selección *f.* selection
seleccionar to select, choose
sello *m.* stamp, seal
semana *f.* week
semana, por by the week
semana santa Holy Week
semana, esta this week
sembrar to sow

semejante similar
semidestruido, -a half-destructed
sencillo, -a simple
sensación f. sensation
sentar to sit, to fit
sentarse to sit down
sentir to feel, to be sorry
señalar to show, point
señor m. Mr., sir, gentleman
señorita f. Miss, young girl
separar to separate
septiembre m September
séptimo, -a seventh
sepultado, -a buried
ser to be
serie f. series, suite
serpiente f. serpent
servicial servicable
servicio m. service
servilleta f. napkin
servir to serve
sesión f. session
seta f. mushroom
sevilliano, -a from Seville
sexto, -a sixth
si if
sí yes
siembra f. sowing
siempre always
siempre que whenever
siento I feel
siento, lo I am sorry
siete seven
siglo m. century
siguiente following
silencio m. silence
silla f. chair
sillón m. arm-chair
simbolizar to symbolise
simpático, -a charming, sympathetic
simple single, simple
simplicidad f. simplicity
sin without
sinceridad f. sincerity
sincero, -a sincere
sino but, except
síntomas m. symptoms
sistema m. system
sitio m. place, location
situación f. situation

situar to situate
soberbio, -a superb
sobre on, upon
sobre m. envelope
sobrecogedor, -a surprising
sobrecoger to surprise
sobremanera exceedingly, most
sobrina f. niece
sobrino m. nephew
sociable sociable
social social
sociedad f. society
sofá m. sofa
sofocante suffocating
sol m. sun
solamente only
soler to have the custom of
solicitar to request, to apply for
sollozo m. sob
sólo only
solo, -a alone
soltero, -a unmarried, single
solución f. solution
sombra f. shade
sombrerería f. hat shop
sombrero m. hat
soñar to dream
sonar to sound
sonreírse to smile
sopa f. soup
sorprender to surprise
sorprendente surprising
soso, -a insipid, tasteless
suave soft
subir to enter, to go up
suburbio m. suburb
sucesivamente successively
sucio, -a dirty
sucursal f. branch
sud m. south
Sud América f. South America
sudar to perspire
Suecia f. Sweden
suegra f. mother-in-law
suegro m. father-in-law
suela f. sole
suelo m. ground
sueño m. dream
suerte f. luck
suéter m. sweater
suficiente sufficient, enough

sugerencia *f.* suggestion
sugerir to suggest, to hint
Suiza *f.* Switzerland
superior, -a superior
suponer to suppose
supuesto assumed, supposed
supuesto, por of course
sur *m.* south
Sur América *f.* South America
suspiro *m.* sigh
suyo yours, his, hers

T

tabaco *m.* tobacco
tabla *f.* board
tacón *m.* heel
tacto *m.* touch
talón *m.* luggage ticket
tal vez maybe
talla *f.* size
tallar to carve, to cut (stone)
talle *m.* waist
también also
tambor *m.* drum
tampoco neither
tango *m.* tango
tanque *m.* tank
tanto, -a as much, so much
tanto . . . como as well as
tantos, -as as many, so many
taquilla *f.* box office
tarde *f.* afternoon, late
tarde, más later
tarea *f.* task
tarjeta *f.* card
taxi *m.* taxi-cab
taza *f.* cup
té *m.* tea
teatral theatrical
teatro *m.* theatre
tela *f.* fabric
telefonear to telephone
teléfono *m.* telephone
telegrafista *m., f.* telegraph operator
telegrama *m.* telegram
televisión *f.* television
tema *m.* subject, topic, theme
temer to fear
temperatura *f.* temperature
temporada *f.* season, time spent

temprano early
tenedor *m.* fork
tener to have
tener que to have to
tenis *m.* tennis
tercero, -a third
terciopelo *m.* velvet
terminado, -a finished
terminar to finish
termómetro *m.* thermometer
ternera *f.* veal, calf
terraza *f.* terrace, veranda
terremoto *m.* earthquake
terrible terrible
territorio *m.* territory
testigo *m.* witness
tía *f.* aunt
tiempo *m.* time
tiempo, a in time
tienda *f.* shop
tierno, -a tender
tierra *f.* earth
tigre *m.* tiger
tijeras *f.* scissors
timbre *m.* electric bell
tinta *f.* ink
tintero *m.* inkstand
tinto *m.* red (wine)
tintorería *f.* dyer's or cleaner's shop
tío *m.* uncle
típico, -a typical
tipo *m.* type
toalla *f.* towel
tobillo *m.* ankle
tocador *m.* dressing-table, boudoir
tocante a concerning
tocar to play (instrument), to ring, to knock on the door
tocino *m.* bacon
todavía yet
todo everything
todo el, (toda la) the whole
todos, -as all
tomar to take, to drink
tomate *m.* tomato
toreo *m.* bullfight
torero *m.* bullfighter
tormenta *f.* storm
toro *m.* bull
torre *f.* tower
torrente *m.* torrent

torrentes, a pouring
tortilla f. omelette
tórtola f. turtle-dove
tos f. cough
tostada f. toast
tostar to toast
total m. total
trabajador m. workman
trabajar to work
trabajo m. work
traducir to translate
traer to bring, to wear
tráfico m. traffic
tragedia f. tragedy
trago m. drink, swallow
traje m. suit
tranquilo, -a tranquil, peaceful
transacción f. transaction
tránsito m. transit, passage
transparente transparent
transportar to transport
tras behind
tratar (de) to try (to)
trece thirteen
treinta thirty
tren m. train
tres three
trigo m. wheat
trimestre m. quarterly
trimestre, por every three months
triste sad
trivial trivial
tropical tropical
trópico m. tropics
trucha f. trout
trueno m. thunder
tú you
tumba f. tomb
túnel m. tunnel
turista m. tourist
Turquía f. Turkey

U

últimamente lately
último, -a last
ultramarino, -a ultramarine
un m., una f. a, an
único, -a unique
universal universal
universidad f. university

uno, -a one
uno one
unos m., unas f. some
uranio m. uranium
urgente urgent
usar to use
usted (usually abbreviated V., Vd., U., Ud.) you
ustedes you (pl.)
útil useful
utilidad f. utility, profit
uva f. grape
uva espina f. gooseberry

V

vaca f. cow
vacación f. holiday
vacilar to hesitate
vainilla f. vanilla
vajilla crockery
valle m. valley, vale
valor m. value, bravery
vals m. waltz
vámonos let's go
vapor m. steamship, steam
varios, -as several
vaselina f. vaseline
vaso m. drinking-glass
veces f. occasions, times
vecino, -a neighbour
vehículo m. vehicle
veinte twenty
vejez f. old age
velocidad f. speed
vender to sell
venezolano, -a Venezuelan
venir to come
venta f. sale
ventana f. window
ventilador m. ventilator, electric fan
ventilar to ventilate
ventisca f. blizzard
ventura f. happiness, luck, chance
ventura, por by chance
ver to see
verano m. summer
veras f.pl. reality, truth
¿veras, de? really?
verdad f. truth
¿verdad, es? Is it so?

¿**verdad, no es?** Is it not so?
verdad, en indeed
verdaderamente truly
verde green
verse to appear, to look
verso *m.* verse
vertical vertical
vestíbulo *m.* lobby
vestido *m.* dress
vestido, -a dressed
vestir to dress
vestirse to dress (yourself)
vez *f.* time
vez, una once
vez, cada each time
vez, tal maybe
vía, una one way
viajar to travel
viaje *m.* trip
viajero, -a traveller
víbora *f.* viper
vida *f.* life
vidrio *m.* glass
viejo, -a old
vienés, -a Viennese
viento *m.* wind
viernes *m.* Friday
vinagre *m.* vinegar
vino *m.* wine
violeta *f.* violet
visita *f.* visit
visita facultativa doctor's visit
visitante visitor
visitar to visit
víspera *f.* eve, day before
vista *f.* view, sight

vista a, con overlooking
vistoso, -a showy, beautiful
vital vital
vitamina *f.* vitamin
¡**Viva!** Hurrah!
vitrina *f.* shop window
vivir to live
vivo, -a lively
vocabulario *m.* vocabulary
volar to fly
volcar to turn over, overturn
voluntad *f.* will
volver to return
volverse to become
vuelo *m.* flight
vulgar vulgar, common, coarse

Y

y and
ya already
yate *m.* yacht
yegua *f.* mare
yendo going
yerno *m.* son-in-law
yo I
yodo *m.* iodine

Z

zanahoria *f.* carrot
zapatería *f.* shoe shop
zapatilla *f.* slipper
zapato *m.* shoe
zona *f.* zone
zorro *m.* fox